IVERPOOL HOPE UNIVERSITY
THE SHEPPARD - WORLOCK LIBRAR

# OPEN PLAN SCHOOLS

*Open Plan Schools: Teaching, Curriculum, Design* is the report of the Schools Council Project 'Open Plan Schools: an Enquiry (5-11)', directed by Professor Neville Bennett, and based at the Department of Educational Research, University of Lancaster from 1975-8.

# *Open Plan Schools*

---

*Teaching • Curriculum • Design*

*Neville Bennett, Jenny Andreae,*
*Philip Hegarty, Barbara Wade*

*NFER Publishing Company for the Schools Council*

*Published by the NFER Publishing Company Ltd.,*
*Darville House, 2 Oxford Road East,*
*Windsor, Berks SL4 1DF*
*Registered Office: The Mere, Upton Park, Slough, Berks SL1 2DQ*
*First published 1980*
*ISBN 0 85633 188 0*

---

*Plans by Sue Ribbans*
*Typeset and Printed by King, Thorne & Stace Ltd., School Road, Hove, Sussex BN3 5JE*
*Distributed in the USA by Humanities Press Inc.,*
*Atlantic Highlands, New Jersey 07716 USA*

# *Contents*

APPENDIX E, *Instrumentation,* including the Questionnaires, the Interview Schedules, the Learning Experiences Schedule, the Pupil Behaviour Schedule and the Use of Space Schedule, is available as a separate publication from the Schools Council.

# *Acknowledgements*

This report could never have been produced without the active help and cooperation of a large number of people involved in the design, administration and running of open plan schools. It is not possible to mention all, but the following deserve special thanks.

Firstly the teachers, advisers and architects in the 27 local education authorities visited in the first months of the project, and the associated teacher groups. Without these visits and discussions it would not have been possible to conceptualize adequately the nature and variability of such schools. We would particularly like to express our gratitude to the teaching staff of the 23 schools who allowed us the freedom to observe and interview in their units; and to their headmasters and local education authorities for permission to include plans in the book. The information gained in these schools forms a central feature of the report. Thanks are also due to a number of architects who developed our knowledge and understanding of the factors in the design process, in particular Eric Pearson, David Medd, Henry Swain and Peter Page.

In turning to the report itself a special word of gratitude is due to Terry Hyland who wrote the excellent background to the development of open plan schools which appears as Chapter 1; to Judy Crompton who coped admirably with all the secretarial demands made on her; to Penny Hegarty who analysed the open-ended questionnaire items and drew the pupil process charts, and to the secretarial staff of the Department of Educational Research who rallied round to type the final draft.

Finally we would wish to take this opportunity to express our gratitude to our consultative committee whose support, discussion and evaluation made an invaluable contribution to this finished product.

# *Introduction*

Some ten per cent of all primary schools in England and Wales are now of open plan design and, given current cost limits, this proportion is likely to increase. Yet this development, like so many others in education, has progressed haphazardly and has attracted little research. Often, therefore, discourse on the topic has been based on stereotype rather than evidence.

The project on which this report is based was funded by the Schools Council in the period 1975–78 to provide a comprehensive picture of current practice, to highlight successful practice as perceived by teachers, and to identify problem areas so that suggestions for improvements could be made. This has been achieved by national questionnaire surveys, extensive periods of observation in schools, interviews with all interested parties and many informal visits to schools and discussions with teacher groups.

The report has been written for a number of different audiences, since one of the major problems which emerged is the lack of effective communication between the people involved in the design and those involved in the use of such schools. It is therefore hoped that readers will find the whole report of interest but for those who may be especially interested in certain parts of it, a brief resumé of the structure of the book follows.

Chapter 1 traces the development of the open plan concept and analyses the differing influences on the origin of changes in school design. It is argued that the early development was based on an educational rationale but that cost factors soon became pre-eminent, and further evidence about this is provided in Chapter 9.

Chapter 2 provides a comprehensive review of previous research in this area followed by details of the research design in Chapter 3.

Chapters 4 and 5 present the information gained from the national questionnaire survey to head and class teachers in England and Wales. Chapter 4 reports on teaching and curriculum organization and Chapter 5 on aims and attitudes, staffing and training. The broad, but relatively shallow, picture provided by the questionnaire data is a useful backcloth against which to view the information gained from observation and interview studies presented in Chapters 6 to 10.

Chapter 6 contains a descriptive account of the teaching organizations employed in the 23 schools observed. No two organizations were identical and neither were they static. Organizations evolve over time and to highlight some of the factors involved two case studies of organizational history are also presented.

Chapters 7 and 8 both concern curriculum allocation and pupil involvement, the former chapter concentrating on infants and the latter on juniors. Curriculum allocation is concerned with the amount of time devoted to differing curriculum areas and how that balance varies. Pupil involvement relates to the amount of time pupils are engaged on the tasks set. Both show tremendous variations. In Chapter 7, a contrast is also made between active and passive organizations and in Chapter 8 an analysis is provided comparing involvement levels in team teaching organizations.

Chapter 9 is concerned with the use teachers make of the available space in open plan units and demonstrates how the siting and visibility of spaces crucially affect usage. This is illustrated with case study material.

In order to consider teaching units as a whole, Chapter 10 comprises seven case studies. The first six are organized in three groups of two to allow comparisons of (a) differing approaches to the education of inner city children (b) to contrast two team teaching organizations and (c) to compare the different organizations set up in two identically designed units. The final case study highlights typical design problems in open plan schools.*

In the conclusion a summary of the findings is presented together with implications, not only for teachers, but for teacher trainers, advisers, architects and administrators. For only when these groups begin to work more closely together will the promise of open plan schooling be fully realized.

* All plans of schools included in this, and previous chapters, represent the layout of the school at the time of observation only.

*Chapter 1*

# *Philosophical and Historical Background**

---

## The Concept of Open Plan Schooling

The use of open plan design in primary school building originated in the period following the introduction of government cost and area per place limits in 1950, and the central ideas of open planning have been generalized and publicized in various MOE and DES Building Bulletins since 1949 (Seaborne and Lowe, 1977, p.170). But the ideas which provided the educational base and rationale of open planning go back much further than this, and are to be found in the progressive tradition of primary school theory and practice which has been evolving in this country since the beginning of the century. The main ideas of this tradition are contained in various government reports, including the Hadow Reports on primary and nursery and infant schools (1931, 1933) and the 1959 Ministry of Education Handbook on primary education (Great Britain, Ministry of Education, 1959), and receive their fullest and clearest expression in the Plowden Report of 1967.

This theoretical background is referred to by nearly all writers on open plan schools. Blishen (1969, p.515) and Collins (1973, p.150) cite the desire of educators to provide informal and flexible learning environments as one of the chief reasons for the introduction of open planning. Rintoul and Thorne (1975) state simply that open plan design is intended to 'help teachers plan their work in accordance with the modern trends in primary education', to allow them to 'experiment and innovate' with such practices as the integrated day, team teaching, and vertical grouping (p.5). Similarly, Sadler (1975) describes the establishment of open planning as part and parcel of the 'teaching revolution' (p.9) that has occurred in British primary schools in recent years.

In considering the development of open planning in the primary sector it is important to have in mind a concept of open plan schooling which incorporates this background of educational ideas. Such a concept is much wider than that of open plan design itself, for it includes both architectural or building elements *and* those ideas and practices which open plan environments are intended to accommodate. The notion of an open plan environment is, in fact,

---

* This chapter was written by Terry Hyland.

neither a wholly distinctive nor a definitive one. The DES investigators noted that the term 'open plan', though widely used, was 'imprecise', a view shared by the NUT document on open planning (1974).

That there are different types of school environments, with a corresponding variety of practices and forms of organization, included under the general label of 'open plan' is a point which will be touched upon later on in the study. In addition, it would be wrong to think that the procedures commonly associated with open planning cannot be implemented in schools of traditional design. However, this inquiry *is* primarily concerned with that combination of architectural and educational elements contained in the concept of open plan schooling outlined above, and the examination of varied physical settings in conjunction with the practices and teaching methods such settings are ideally designed to facilitate.

Moreover, some such general, if perhaps idealized, concept provides a useful background against which to set both historical and contemporary remarks about open plan schools. Without such a background it might be tempting to view anything which remotely resembles an open plan environment as an instance of open schooling. Particularly important here will be any consideration of criticisms and weaknesses of open planning, and of examples of clashes between school design and educational philosophy. Pluckrose (1975), for example, describes open plan schools 'where teachers are working in tight class units, their desks across the openings instead of doors', and Adelman and Walker (1974) comment about 'open space designs where uncommitted teachers are wrestling with problems arising from a clash between their own educational assumptions and those imposed upon them by their immediate environment'. These seem to be clear cases of open plan schools which are failing to live up to expectations, yet, viewed out of perspective, there might be a tendency to examine open plan schooling in the light of these cases in which schools are, so to speak, failing to live up to their image, rather than by looking at the actual image itself. This is something which critics like the one quoted in a recent Black Paper (1975) might remember. When problems and difficulties do arise in open plan schools (as they inevitably arise in *all* schools), it is as reasonable to regard them as instances of inferior or misguided open planning as it is to see them as part and parcel of an innovation which has proved to be a total disaster.

**Historical Background**

To learn more about the ideas and theories which go to make up the 'image' of open plan schooling, we can profitably look at the early development of state schooling in this country. But it is here that we have to take care to avoid hasty generalizations and over-simplifications. Seaborne (1971b) and Hamilton (1977), for instance, suggest that the post-1944 experiments in group and individual teaching are really a reversion to much older forms of teaching that were characteristic of the monitorial system operating in elementary schools in the first half of the nineteenth century. In the same vein, Gartner *et al.* (1971) have argued that cooperative learning, which is also closely associated with contemporary open planning, can be traced back to the same tradition. Before considering such comments in detail it would be useful to fill in the historical background.

After 1833, voluntary provision of schools was aided by a progressively increasing government grant, and the 1840s and 50s saw a considerable expansion in the building of elementary schools. Faced for the first time with the task of providing for mass education, administrators turned initially to the type of school which had been common in England since the Middle Ages (Seaborne, 1971b). This consisted of one very large schoolroom in which a number of forms were taught at the same time, usually by one master and several assistants known as ushers. The whole system turned on there being just one teacher responsible for the school, with only semi-trained help available.

Following the introduction of mass elementary education with the 1870 Education Act, the increase in the numbers of children in the schools meant that it was now no longer possible to run an elementary school with only one certificated teacher. Although the development of the 'class' as a unit of organization and teaching can be traced back to Wilderspin's school opened at Spitalfields in 1820 (Seaborne, 1971a), it was not until after the 1870 Act that this system became common. Changes in the staffing of elementary schools were largely responsible for this development. Previously, the existence of a large body of monitors or pupil–teachers meant that the master, who was usually also the head of the school, had to keep a close watch on proceedings, and this tended to perpetuate the one-schoolroom plan. But, although the number of certificated teachers did not increase dramatically until the beginning of the twentieth century, the replacement of pupil–teachers by student–teachers or unqualified assistants allowed the head to delegate responsibility and leave staff members to teach classes on their own. Most schools now came to be organized on a class basis with assistant teachers in charge of particular groups of children, and this development was clearly reflected in the architecture of the new schools with buildings being divided into separate classrooms.

The demand for mass education was met during the last quarter of the nineteenth century by the building of very large schools on the central-hall plan (Seaborne, 1971b). On this plan (also known as the 'Prussian system' after the influential Prussian elementary schools much admired at the time), the classrooms were situated on three or four sides of the main hall, separated from each other by partitions which were usually glazed, so that the head teacher was still able to keep an eye on the proceedings in the various classrooms. This was the model used for elementary school building up to the First World War, when the 'veranda' and 'quadrangle' types of schools, in which classrooms were grouped together but now with separate access away from the school hall, became the norm (Seaborne, 1971b). The new buildings reflected the then current concern for health and hygiene amongst education officials and the medical profession, and also the new approach to elementary education following the Hadow Report of 1926. The class remained as the basic teaching unit throughout the inter-war years and it is interesting to note that, in spite of a strand of thought running counter to this system in progressive circles, schools continued to be built with separate classrooms up to the present time when, in the last few decades, open planning began to have an impact on primary school building.

How far, then, can comparisons be made between the recent development of methods and practices associated with the evolution of open plan schools and the organization of schools before 1870? Since the evolution of open planning has gone hand in hand with the demise of separate classrooms in schools and with the demise of the class as a basic teaching unit (though *not*, as will be pointed out later, as a unit of school organization and pastoral care), it could be said that the one-room schoolhouses of the monitorial system which preceded the development of class teaching were very similar to schools built in response to contemporary educational trends. The most common architectural design for monitorial schools was the Lancaster model which consisted of a schoolroom to accommodate about 320 children. It measured 70 x 32 feet (21.34 x 9.75 m), (allowing 6 or 7 square feet (0.56 or 0.65 sq. m) per child), and the rows of desks were arranged to face the master's platform, spaced so as to allow the monitors to move freely between the rows (Seaborne, 1971a). The rival system devised by Andrew Bell involved the pairing of 'pupils' and 'tutors' so that help could be given to the less proficient in the preparation of lessons for recitation to the teacher or a monitor. The monitorial system also allowed room in the schoolhouse for children to assemble in small groups to practice reading and arithmetic under the supervision of monitors.

There do appear to be certain similarities between these practices and forms of organization and characteristics of modern open plan schools. For example, the architectural features are strikingly similar with an absence of separate classrooms in both cases. In addition, scope was allowed in the schools of Bell and Lancaster for some group work and for pupils to teach each other, and the same practices occur in many modern primary schools. But, if we dig a little deeper, it becomes immediately clear that this superficial similarity is all that can reasonably be claimed.

What has to be examined is the background to the practices under consideration – to look at the basis on which they are recommended and the arguments used to support them. Contemporary advocates of open planning value the child's individual and many-sided development, and hold the objective of fostering the capacity for autonomous reasoning and behaviour in children. The stress on individuality and autonomy informs both the process of learning, and also features in the determination of products, the fostering of certain moral and social ideals. But all these notions would have been totally alien to Bell and Lancaster. Curtis (1948) argues that Lancaster only introduced his system of pupil–teachers because he found it difficult to cope when the number of boys at his school in Borough Road increased dramatically in the 1780s. The procedures involved arose out of expediency and were justified in strict cost-efficiency terms without reference to any educational principle or theory. It was a 'factory system' whose sole objective was to 'instruct large masses of children by mechanical means' (Curtis, op.cit.). This illustrates the chasm that exists between these ideas and those which inform present-day practices in open plan primary schools. Such historical comparisons demonstrate the importance of keeping in mind a general concept of open plan schooling which involves elements of architectural openness in conjunction with certain principles of organization, teaching methods, and ideas about the learning process.

The genesis of open plan schooling (or, at least, the ideas on which it is based) is more profitably to be sought in the progressive tradition which has grown up in Britain in the present century. What writers pointing to the influence of the one-room schoolhouses are appealing to (in this country it is the village school, in America the prairie schoolhouse) is the general ethos of a school which is a single unit whose members are learning and living together. And, no doubt, it can be illuminating to draw parallels between the life of such schools and the principles underpinning open plan schools. But it is also necessary to take into account the intellectual and social climate against which educational practice is to be viewed.

The move towards the building of large 'veranda' and 'quadrangle' type schools and the organization of teaching on a class basis at the beginning of the twentieth century was only one of the developments resulting from the introduction of mass elementary education in this country. At the same time, the new educational climate was causing a number of educators to turn their attention to the nature and purpose of the whole enterprise. It would be difficult to place a date on the origins of progressive education for, clearly, many of the theories which influenced British educational debate owed their origins to writers such as Froebel, Pestalozzi and Rousseau who lived centuries before their ideas received any large scale publication and application. For the purposes of the present examination, however, it seems reasonable to agree with Selleck (1972) who suggests that the origins of a view of education which can legitimately be labelled 'progressive' are to be found in the period following the publication of Edmund Holmes's book *What Is and What Might Be* in 1911.

Any examination of the evolution of progressive theory and practice in Britain must take account of various spheres of influence and strands of development. The pioneering progressive schools, the work of individual educators and practitioners, the various official reports reflecting the new ideas, and the piecemeal application of progressive notions in state schools, are all factors which contributed to the development. This examination of the tradition will be necessarily selective, picking out the main trends which can be said to have contributed most to the evolution of those ideas which spawned the theory and practice which is now incorporated into the notion of open plan schooling. But it is as well to remember that this theory and practice was not worked out in any systematic or coherent way until after the Second World War, and did not have any really noticeable impact upon state schooling until well into the 1950s.

**Open Planning and the Progressive Tradition**

It was suggested earlier that the single most important factor in the evolution of those practices associated with open planning was the breakdown of the class as the basic unit of teaching. By the early 1920s progressive education had already advanced some way in this direction. In 1922, Sir John Adams published his book *Modern Developments in Educational Practice* in which he was able to write of the 'knell of class teaching'. He went on to suggest that it was the influence of the methods of Maria Montessori which was, more than anything else, responsible for the gradual erosion of the belief in the efficacy of the class as a teaching unit. The theory of Montessori warrants a special emphasis, for it is in her pedagogy that the origins of the theory of open planning are to be found.

Her book *The Montessori Method* appeared in 1912 and, by 1919, when she was invited to London to conduct a training course (which was heavily oversubscribed), her influence was widespread and her methods in use in quite a number of schools (Stewart, 1968). Sir Percy Nunn, whose own writings made a significant contribution to the evolution of progressivism, remarked that the introduction of Montessori methods in classrooms at this time brought about astonishing changes; there was a marked contrast between the bondage of the old methods and the calm, happy, absorbed atmosphere of the Montessori class (Nunn, 1920).

An essential aspect of the Montessori technique was the use of special apparatus which aimed at improving children's discrimination of length, size, weight, shape, colour and texture (the concrete experience later called for by the followers of Piagetian theory); and the apparatus was introduced in such a way as to confront rather than force children to experiment with it. The classroom thus becomes an environment rich in learning resources, an environment 'in which all the objects are attuned to the child's developmental needs' (Montessori, 1949). That this approach was designed to foster the sort of individual work favoured by many contemporary educators is brought out well in P.B. Ballard's remark that the chief advantage of Montessori methods was that they enabled children to work 'independently, in the same room at the same time' (Ballard, 1925).

The rather negative opposition to the elementary school tradition, which in this period was really all that advocates of the 'New Education' had in common, was now enriched by the positive alternatives provided by Montessori's techniques. It is her conception of the role of the teacher, and her recommendations about the organization of the learning environment that gives to her ideas an uncannily contemporary ring. In place of the authoritarian pedagogue, the Montessori teacher was to be a 'directress', a guide and organizer whose responsibility was to ensure that learning took place through interested activity rather than as the result of the false incentives of external rewards and punishments. This duty consisted essentially in 'securing for the child the opportunity of satisfying his spontaneous tendency towards well-ordered activities' (Culverwell, 1913).

This idea of the teacher as a 'directress' working within an environment rich in learning resources, and in which children are encouraged to select activities and experiences guided by the teacher, is at the heart of modern primary school practice and, perhaps especially, that associated with open planning in the primary sector. The central progressive ideas surrounding the notions of activity, direct experience, interests, and individual developments are all present in Montessori's pedagogy, as also is the special emphasis on the importance of the physical setting in which learning and teaching takes place. Consider, for example, this statement, from *The Secret of Childhood,* which attacks traditional conceptions of discipline in schools (Stewart, 1968)

> In fact in every educational ideal, in all pedagogy up to our own time, the word education has been almost synonymous with the word punishment. The end has always been to subject the child to the adult . . . The child's hands and feet are fastened to the desk by stern looks which hold them motionless as the nails of the cross in the feet of Christ . . .

This implied equation of movement and activity with genuine learning captures completely the spirit of present-day primary school methods. Montessori's contribution to the development of that tradition which spawned open planning is significant.

Also important during the inter-war years was the introduction of the Dalton Plan into schools. This system was originated at Dalton High School in Massachusetts in 1920 by Helen Parkhurst, a young teacher who had studied under Montessori. Calling for various changes in traditional classroom organization, the Plan had its basis in the assignment system which involved the replacement of the orthodox timetable by a series of 'contract jobs' consisting of pieces of work covering the various disciplines. Special emphasis was laid upon the 'child's living while he does his work, and the manner in which he acts as a member of society rather than upon the subjects of the curriculum' (Parkhurst, 1922). Not only are the origins of contemporary project and topic work in evidence in this approach, but also the essential features of 'child-centredness' which have influenced so many of the developments in primary education in recent years.

The Dalton Plan, after a number of articles publicizing it had appeared in *The Times Educational Supplement* during 1921, had an 'astonishing vogue' in English educational circles throughout the 1920s (Smith, 1957). In 1925, Ballard was claiming that 'Daltonism' had broken out in school after school (1925). Its popularity was due in no small part to a flexibility which allowed for liberal interpretations of its main recommendations. Catering for 'individual differences' is a process which allows for wide interpretation, and it was this aspect of Daltonism (fitting in so well with the philosophical assumptions of progressivism) which gave rise to the new practices in the schools of the time. Writing in 1924 after a year's trial of the Plan, Lynch (1924) claimed that the 'individual work' approach greatly improved class work and results in general. Teachers in state schools welcomed Parkhurst's insistence that her scheme did not legislate for any specific type of curriculum, and that it could be modified in 'accordance with the circumstances of any school' (1922). Selleck points out that, to a teacher worried about his everyday practice as a result of the spread of progressive ideas, the Dalton Plan had a particular attraction. It offered a specific methodology; a set of procedures and a system of organization which could accommodate new methods but which did not entail a total rejection of the old (Selleck, 1972). It is, perhaps, this factor which helps us to account for the first really noticeable manifestation of progressive ideas in state schools.

There were, of course, many other important aspects of the development of progressive ideas during this period. For instance, the various 'experimental' schools such as Macmunn's Tiptree Hall, opened in 1919, did much to pioneer and publicize the new teaching methods. Similarly, the work of Susan Isaacs at the Malting House Garden School in the 1920s, and the pioneering schools of Homer Lane and A.S. Neill also contributed to the development of the tradition. At the 1969 Dartington Hall Colloquium on progressive education, Schiller claimed that without the work of the progressive schools of this period 'what has happened in State Primary schools could not have happened'. But it was, perhaps, the ideas of Montessori and the introduction of programmes based on the Dalton Plan which had the most direct influence on state schooling at this time.

By 1939 the progressives had, according to Selleck, obtained a firm foothold in the teacher training institutions, and a substantial majority of educational opinion leaders were working within their intellectual orbit. And, although it would be wrong to suggest a wholesale conversion of teachers to progressive methods, it is fair to say that the main ideas of progressivism were now beginning to inform opinion at this level. Important in this respect were the official reports of the 1930s which reflected a new rationale of primary education consisting largely of the ideas and practices progressive educators had been advocating in the previous two decades. The 1931 Hadow Report on primary education, for example, urged that the curriculum should now be thought of in terms of 'activity and experience' rather than inert pieces of knowledge, and that there should be a 'new orientation of school instruction' bringing it 'into closer connection with the natural movement of children's minds'. In addition to the more formal elements, scope was to be allowed for children's 'interests' and for work on individual or group 'projects'. In the 1933 Report on infant and nursery schools, the origins of those practices characteristic of modern open plan schooling are clearly in evidence. The ideal infant school, according to the authors of the Report: 'Is not a classroom but a playground, that is to say, not a limited space enclosed by four walls and a ceiling, but an open area . . . where the interests natural to this historical stage of growth can be stimulated and pursued'.

Although it would be an exaggeration to say that Adams's 1922 prophecy about the knell of class teaching had been fulfilled by 1939, it is fair to say that this mode of teaching was receiving more adverse criticism by this time. By the 1930s, methods and practices based on individual and group work of various kinds were in operation in state schools in the infant and junior sector, and this trend was reflected in some of the new buildings of the period which provided for the use of flexible furniture which could be arranged in groups, and for larger working spaces in classrooms (Seaborne, 1971b). The appropriateness of class teaching, argued the 1933 Hadow Report, was now 'no longer accepted'. When teachers began to 'take account of the individuality of children', they began to 'question the efficacy of class instruction and to look for something better'. This search was to continue as the message was reaffirmed and intensified in the post-1944 period.

The building of schools before and immediately after the Second World War did not reflect any noticeable change in educational direction, but displayed the same pre-war concern with physical hygiene, providing for good lighting and ventilation, and making use of sites with spacious surroundings. Schools built during this early period made use of the corridor-plan or 'finger-plan' model, so called because of the resemblance of the plan to a hand, with the hall and administrative rooms forming the 'palm', and the rows of classrooms the 'fingers' (Seaborne, 1971b). By present-day standards, these schools were very spacious, but improvements tended to be channelled into non-teaching areas such as the provision of extra corridor and dining space. Ironically, it was to be the extravagance of this type of school building which, during a period of economic stringency and a rising school population in the post-war years, was to bring about the reappraisal of primary school design.

Annual school building programmes were introduced for the first time in 1949, and detailed cost controls in 1950, and it is from this time on that real changes in primary school buildings can be seen. The area of actual teaching space had not been increased in new buildings since 1936, and the new controls brought about an actual reduction in cost per place allowed in schools after 1950. In this climate a new approach to design was inevitable; the old 'finger-plan' type of school with its wide corridors and spacious surroundings was now out of the question. Architects, educators and officials had to build schools which could maintain or strengthen educational provisions but, now, within the new cost limits. It was this novel situation which provided the initial impetus for the fundamental reappraisal of building design in the primary sector; it entailed what Bower (1968) describes as a 'rationalizing of the design of the traditional school'.

**The Development of Open Plan Schools**

The rationalization of building design in the period after 1950 resulted in the reduction of area space per child (on average from about 6.50 sq.m. to 3.71 sq.m., i.e. 70 square feet per place to around 40), but this was achieved without a reduction in the actual teaching space. The Ministry of Education figures for the years between 1949 and 1956 indicate that, though the total area per place was cut by about 40 per cent during this period, the amount of teaching space was either maintained or, in certain cases, actually increased (Seaborne, 1971b). Typical innovations included such things as the reduction in the height of rooms (which also, happily, 'brought the buildings into scale with the children, and made them much more homelike' (Pearson, 1972)), the use of dual purpose areas such as a combined hall and dining space, and the reduction of total area by merging corridor space with classroom space. It was when these developments came together with both the new educational ideas and the new architectural trends (the replacement of monumental with functional design), that the open plan type of school building began to emerge.

In the government publication *The Story of Post-War School Building* issued in 1957 (Great Britain, Ministry of Education, 1957), the authors pointed to the close links between school architecture and the 'current ideas of the aims and methods of education', and referred to the greater emphasis now laid on practical activities in the schools and the tendency of teachers to 'break down the class or form unit into several working groups'. It was from this time on that educational considerations began to receive much more emphasis in the planning of primary schools, and many of the trends referred to above were now legitimized through this new approach and channelled into specifically educational directions.

A feature of many of the new schools being built in the 1950s, particularly the ones in Hertfordshire using what became known as the 'grid system', was the use of standardized materials and fittings (Seaborne, 1971b). The success of this system enabled the quicker completion of schools and aided the drive for compactness which was coupled with the demand for more flexible teaching arrangements. The activity spirit of the 1930s was reaffirmed, and schools were now asked to provide an environment rich in resources and materials for learning. In the 1959 Handbook of suggestions for primary school teachers, the Ministry of Education authors outlined the new principles on which schools were to operate, mentioning the use of projects in learning, of centres of interest, the importance of creative work, and of 'arranging the environment in the classroom and school so that children can learn for themselves, either individually or in small groups' (Great Britain, 1959).

Bower (1968) explains the links between this new methodology and the primary schools being built at the time. By the 1960s, he argues, primary schools had 'developed their teaching methods and extended their activities' to such a degree that 'even the best designed traditional building' was not able to accommodate them. It was in this climate that architects responded to the needs of children and teachers, and their brief was, in Baines's (1971) words

> to create a building allowing for as wide a range as possible of children's activities, based upon their needs and interests, to be available at one and the same time, and to do this whilst also creating a building that gave the possibility of the teachers having recourse to as many known teaching techniques and resources as possible.

The idea seemed to be that the newer teaching techniques demanded a much more flexible environment, and this could only be provided (or, at least, could ideally be provided) in buildings displaying the new architectural features. There was the suggestion also that open planning was simply a natural response to the way primary teachers were already organizing their classrooms. Such teachers had already moved some way towards breaking down the traditional classroom base in their attempts to create a certain type of learning environment. In American experiments with British progressive methods there is a great emphasis placed on the use of corridors as teaching space and of open-door classrooms. In Lilian Weber's project organized in Harlem schools in the late 1960s, for example, the concept of an 'open corridor' facilitating movement between classes was central to the learning environment the teachers were trying to create (Tobier, 1972). Similarly, Ridgway (1976) has referred to the beginning of open planning in schools with 'open doors in ordinary schools, with children spilling out of self-contained classrooms into corridors and circulating space'. It was not far from this to the removal of classroom divisions altogether, and the concept of the primary school as a single, though multi-dimensional, unit in which children and teachers made use of space and resources as these were required by the activities and experiences they wanted to engage in.

This is the picture which has informed school organization and design in the primary sector up to the present time. The sort of individual and group work typical of progressive practice is now linked with a particular teaching strategy and form of school organization, and all this is placed within a certain type of school building. A prototype of the 'semi-open plan' design which first incorporated features of this kind was built at Amersham in the 1950s (see Figure 1), and publicized in the Ministry of Education Building Bulletin No. 16 issued in 1958. The school had eight classes which were arranged in two groups of four in such a way as to allow access from one room to another without the use of corridors. Two of the classrooms also shared a practical working space, with two others having large bays used for practical work of all kinds by the whole school. Furniture and equipment at Amersham were designed specifically for the kinds of activities the school was built to accommodate, and 'flexibility' became the key word and cornerstone of the system (Seaborne and Lowe, 1977).

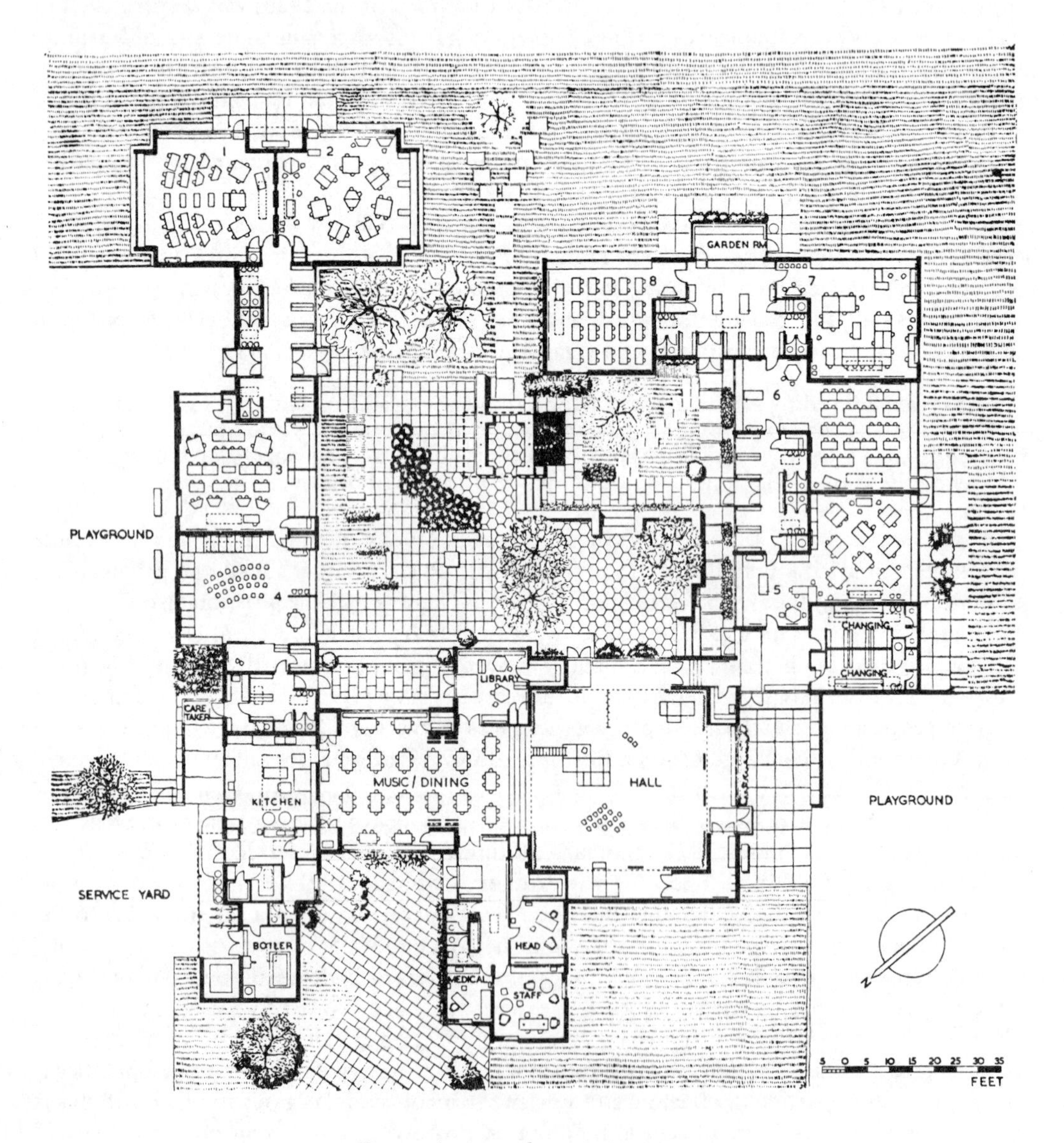


*Figure 1 Amersham School Plan*

Mention has already been made of the role of the village school in the development of progressive ideas, and it was this model applied to the building of the village school at Finmere in Oxfordshire in 1958–59 which was to 'set the course of primary school design for at least a decade' (Pearson, 1972). The school, providing for fifty children between the ages of five and

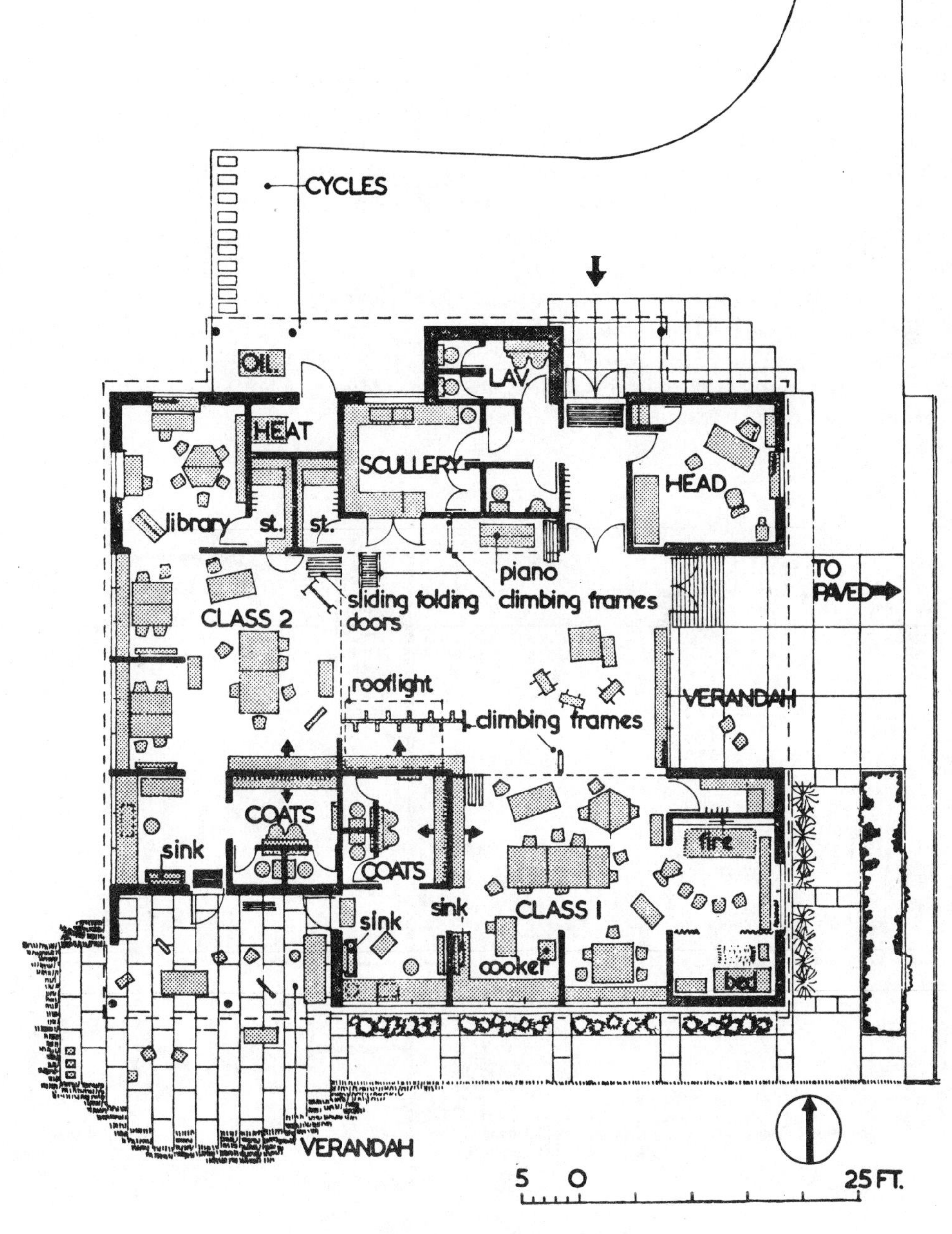


*Figure 2 Finmere Village School, 1959*

eleven, had just one assembly hall and two classrooms, and the whole of the floor space could be opened up by means of sliding doors, the class space being subdivided into alcoves and bays designed for particular activities. The guiding principle owed its meaning to the notion of the school as a 'series of linked working areas' (Seaborne and Lowe, op.cit.), and it was praised highly by the Plowden investigators who claimed that in the 'fluid arrangements' facilitated by the Finmere plan 'many observers see the solution to some of the most pressing design problems' (1967).

By the 1960s some of these ideas on school design began to attract wider attention, particularly amongst those responsible for the building of primary schools in urban areas. The various LEA Consortia (initiated with CLASP in 1957) were very interested indeed in designs which managed to accommodate facilities which were apparently in demand whilst, at the same time, keeping within building and place cost limits. Probably the most influential school based on the open plan model during this period was the Eveline Lowe Primary School opened in Southwark in 1966. This school, in which the Central Advisory Council took a hand in planning, was designed against the background of the development of new ideas on primary education at the time. The outstanding influences were the greatly increased range and variety of activities being offered in primary schools, the more personal and informal relationships between teachers and children in this sphere, and the greater scope being given for individual and group work (Great Britain, DES, 1972a).

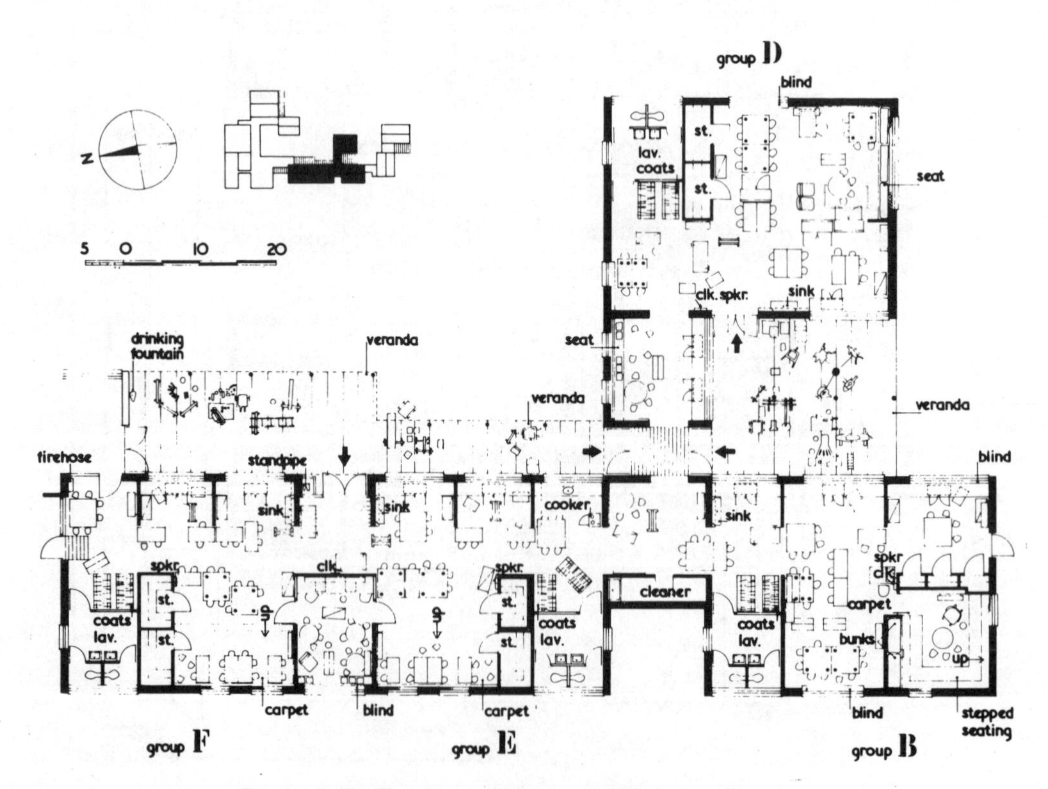


*Figure 3 Eveline Lowe Primary School, London, 1966*

The building project represented the first serious attempt to implement open plan principles of the kind that had proved successful at Finmere and other semi-rural areas in a predominantly urban area with larger numbers of children and the sort of environmental and social problems typical of such areas. Designed for 320 children aged between $3^1/_2$ and 9, Eveline

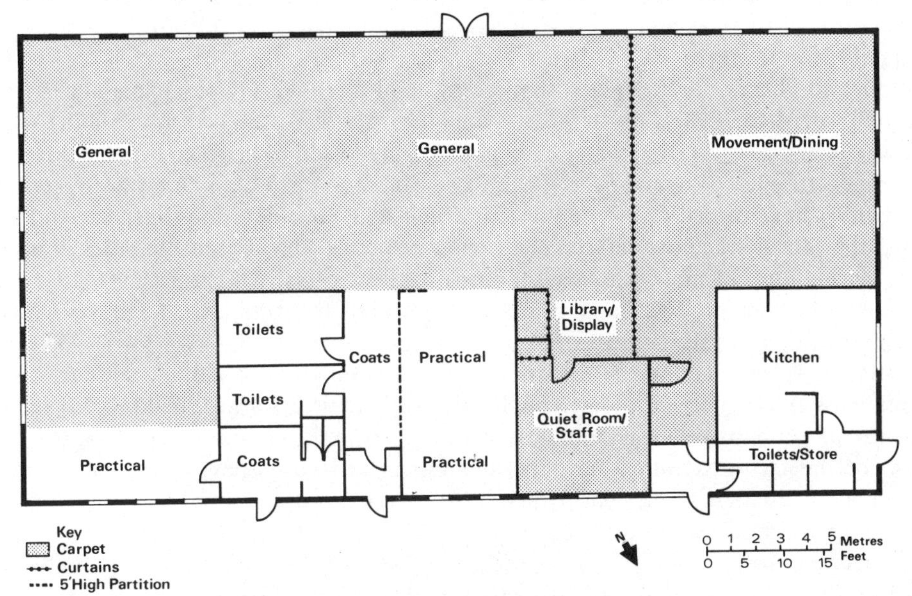


*Figure 4 Eastergate C. of E. Primary School*

Lowe school followed an L-shape plan and was arranged in four large areas (roughly differentiating between the infant, upper and lower junior, and the hall sections), each with plenty of open space. The teaching units contained learning bays, interest areas, workshop spaces of various kinds, and spaces for 'home bases' in which particular groups of children could meet with assigned teachers (Pearson, op.cit.). The school was publicized in a special Building Bulletin issued in 1967, and also in the Plowden Report which referred to its design as one which enabled teachers to 'co-operate more easily' and to provide for 'flexibility of organization and individual learning', thus allowing schools to take account of developing ideas about primary school practice.

The concept of open planning was developed and modified throughout the 1960s reaching its 'furthest possible extension' by the early 1970s (Seaborne and Lowe, op.cit.). Although the idea of further opening up buildings and abolishing partitions was attempted in a few places, most notably at Eastergate Primary School in West Sussex opened in 1970 (see Figure 4), the 'fully' open plan design did not win the same degree of support as the 'partially' open system typified at Eveline Lowe. It appears that teachers wanted new buildings in which the advantages of space could be combined with the provision of areas designed for specific purposes – interest and practical areas, quiet study areas, home bases where contact between teachers and particular groups of children could be established on a regular basis.

Indeed, as Palmer (1971) observes, it would hardly be true to say that in planning new primary schools Britain has adopted an 'open plan – full stop' policy. Educators and planners realized that the notion of 'open space' would be both literally and conceptually vacuous if it was not planned in accordance with the people whom the building was designed to serve. Thus, though separate classrooms disappeared along with the class as a basic unit of teaching, many open plan designs provided for the retention of 'home base' areas where 'classes' could meet for particular purposes. The retention of some such form of organization had been recommended in Plowden, and the message was re-emphasized in the later DES (1972b) and NUT (1974) investigations in this area.

Rintoul and Thorne (1975) suggest that recent building trends are best explained in terms of a continuing drive for 'flexibility' or 'maximum opportunity' in primary schools, and to achieve this it was realized that the notion of open planning had itself to be given rather more content than the general idea of open space. The most influential open plan designs of recent years, consequently, have turned out to be those in which such considerations have been taken into account; they are characteristic of the 'semi-open' principle which, according to Seaborne, has guided the building of most primary schools in recent years. St Thomas Primary School, opened in a Manchester educational priority area in 1970, for instance, is an illustration of the way scope for opportunity and flexibility in learning can be combined with a wide range of areas offering special facilities (Pearson, op.cit.). It is only by providing such facilities that planners can avoid the danger, pointed out by the DES architect, David Medd (1973), of merely replacing classroom boxes in schools with school boxes. And it has been the awareness of such a danger on the part of architects, teachers and planners that has been responsible for what has been called the 'greatest single achievement of post-war primary school architecture', namely the bringing of schools more into scale with their occupants (Seaborne and Lowe, op.cit.).

The introduction of open plan designs in schools made the period between 1945 and 1970 a distinct epoch in the history of primary school building in Britain, and the main factors contributing to this unique development have been identified and explained above. But there is a marked tendency for certain writers on the topic to concentrate on some aspects of this development to the exclusion of others. In conclusion, therefore, it would be useful to attempt to attain some overall perspective on the origins of open planning in this country.

**The Origins of Open Plan Schooling**

One common approach, found mainly in writings of open plan advocates and in DES reports and Building Bulletins, suggests that open plan design was simply a continuation of those ideas on primary education which had evolved with the progressive tradition in the 1930s and which received practical application in state schools in the 1950s and 60s. Rintoul and Thorne, for instance, talk about designers of the new schools responding to 'integrated ways of working', and Baines refers to the 'brief given to architects' by educators and teachers. Similarly, Pearson claims that the new architectural trends were based on 'the needs of children as perceived by discerning educators and architects'. Pluckrose simply asserts that the 'move away from the box-like classroom' was caused by 'pressure from teachers demanding better facilities for the children with and for whom they worked'.

Yet it would be a mistake to think that the educational base of open planning had been given the lion's share of the attention in this debate. On the contrary, it is probably fair to say that the idea that open planning was a simple and natural administrative response to the introduction of cost and place limits in the 1950s represents the most widespread and popular opinion of all on this matter. Thus when the leader of the Pilkington Research Unit on primary school design declared in the 1967 Report that changes in ideas about primary school design were 'clearly prompted by economic pressures and the average architect's knowledge of educational theory is rudimentary', this seemed to confirm what hard-headed realists had always been inclined to believe. The persuasiveness of this line of argument has helped to colour popular opinion on this issue, and the same basic ideas can be glimpsed, for instance, in the NUT investigation. Claiming to make no value-judgements, and insisting that there is no suggestion that open planning was taken up merely to provide cheaper alternatives to traditional schools, the authors of the Report, nevertheless, go on to speak of open planning as 'no more than the resultant of the usual combination of forces in the world of education', and these are 'necessity, expediency, financial pressure' and 'imaginative adaptation on the part of teachers'. These comments are equivocal and guarded, but it will be argued below that there is no need for equivocation here since the economic argument can be shown to present a picture of the origins of open plan schooling which is both distorted and historically inaccurate.

To illustrate this the attempt will be made, as it were, to 're-write' history in this sphere, leaving out one or more of the relevant contributory factors and observing the way this changes or influences our perspective on the evolution of open plan schooling. If we imagine a set of conditions obtaining in the 1950s in which cost limits and place reductions are not included, then it seems that we have to say that this does not significantly affect the possibility of open plan designs emerging in primary school building. New educational ideas had already found their way into a number of state schools with the project work and grouping practices of the 1930s. In addition, the movement away from whole class instruction was well underway by the 1950s with an increasing number of schools using 'activity' methods for at least part of the time. Whitbread (1972) notes that 'informal' or 'experimental' schools in the nursery-infant sector (which many writers believe opened up the way for changes in primary schools) were relatively common by the 1950s and widespread by the 60s, and Gardner's research (1966) was undertaken in the light of the growing number of 'experimental' schools in the junior sector.

Thus, those writers like Pluckrose and Ridgway who speak of open planning as being a natural consequence of the methods and forms of organization a number of teachers were actually tending to adopt in the 1950s and 60s have a case. It appears that the development of open plan schooling would not have been significantly interrupted if the economic conditions of the period had not obtained. Indeed, it is not unreasonable to suggest that, if more money had been available, open planning might have been developed on a much larger scale, rather than in the piecemeal manner that has characterized the development in a number of areas. Given greater resources, new building materials and architectural ideas, such a state of affairs might have resulted in open plan primary schools being far more numerous than in fact they are today.

If, on the other hand, we omit from our list of conditions the state of educational theory in the 1950s (that is, eradicate the progressive influence), then it seems that the economic conditions prevailing in the years after 1950 need not have given rise to the open plan model. The move towards compactness need not have entailed the move to open planning and, in addition, there are all sorts of other measures which could have been adopted. There could, for instance, have been reductions in staffing (as is the case in the present climate of economic stringency), or there might have been a return to the philosophy of the elementary schools with an attempt to make schooling a factory operation turning out children with the basic minimum of skills to fit them for society in the most cost-efficient manner. This latter policy might even have involved some aspects of architectural openness such as those characteristics of the Victorian one-room schoolhouses, but this would be introduced, not for the purposes of providing greater scope and flexibility for teachers and pupils, but to improve the school's efficiency in economic terms.

After all, the new building materials available at this time need not have been used to build schools offering a wide range of activities and facilities, but could conceivably have been used to build very large schools, perhaps on the 'Prussian system' referred to earlier, designed to instruct large numbers of children in the most economical way. Granted that there was a development within architectural circles which favoured social or functional design over the traditional monumental design, in this imaginary climate 'functional' might easily have been interpreted purely in this cost-efficient way. Educational theory in this climate might have consisted of a return to the mechanical notions of Joseph Lancaster, and planners might have taken as their model for new school building the Jews' Free School in Spitalfields rebuilt by the Victorian architect, Robson, in 1904–5. This school had four halls, seventy-six classrooms, catered for no less than 3,500 children, and was reputed to be the largest elementary school in the world (Robson, 1972). This system would have been more than adequate to accommodate the cost and place limits of the 1950s.

The reason why measures of this kind were not adopted is, of course, that they would have been quite unacceptable, and indeed, fantastic, in the educational climate of the 1950s. But, more importantly, there were more positive alternatives available in the shape of the new designs which could meet the cost requirements and, at the same time, allow teachers to plan and organize their work in accordance with the ideas then developing in this sphere. Faced with the problem of mass education for the first time, nineteenth-century school planners turned naturally to the form of organization that had been common in schools since the Middle Ages. However, though the one-room schoolhouses happened to be highly suited to the requirement of the period, it can hardly be said that there was much else on offer at the time. But, in the 1950s, school planners and architects were able to examine the economic aspects of their task against the background of a body of educational ideas and practices which had been developing in this country since the beginning of the century. The sort of procedures many educators and officials were recommending at the time were being employed in a growing number of state schools, and it was the realization that these could be catered for by the flexible new designs, within the cost limits and facilitated by the new building materials, that was to lead to the development of the open plan model.

However, it is unlikely that any single point of view on this topic can provide an adequate explanation of the recent building trends in the primary sector. The reappraisal of school design which took place in the period after 1950 simply cannot be divorced from either the educational or the economic climate of the time. All the relevant factors – the new architectural ideas, the cost limitations, the DES Building Bulletins, and the developing ideas on teaching and learning – must, therefore, be taken into account and given due consideration.

Yet for the reasons outlined above, it does seem reasonable to suggest a tentative rank order of priorities operating in this sphere in which the educational base of open planning has pride of place. The development of open planning and its relationship with the progressive tradition cannot be explained in terms of expediency or economic pressure. These links are not accidental but owe their meaning to the educational ideas and practices themselves. The physical setting of open plan primary schools is related both pragmatically and symbolically to the practices which go on inside them (Proshansky and Wolfe, 1974). The arrangement of space in particular ways does not simply accommodate various practices and procedures, but reflects and symbolizes a certain sort of learning atmosphere, a way of looking at primary education. It is this which suggests that the emergence of a particular philosophy of teaching in primary education, with its new procedures and practices, can be regarded as the *sine qua non* of the genesis of open planning.

On a final note, it might be worth remembering that, even if the idea of open planning had never been floated, those educational ideas which gave it meaning would probably still be found operating in quite a number of our primary schools today.

*Chapter 2*

# *A Review of Research on Open Plan Schools*

---

**Introduction**

The growth of open plan schools in the last decade is a worldwide phenomenon. In North America building began sporadically in the late 1950s and early 1960s but rapidly increased towards the end of that decade. Brunetti, writing in 1971, reported that 'within the last four years the majority of new schools around the country have been of open design'. Of over 2,500 schools built in the period 1967–69 in 43 states, 50 per cent had open designs, the influence being strongest at elementary level where only 9 per cent of designs were conventional. This pattern of growth is similar in Canada and in Britain, where, by 1975, approximately one school in ten was of open design (see Chapter 3) and where a conventionally designed primary school has rarely been built since 1971. Other countries entered the field later. In New Zealand for example the first open plan school was built in 1970, but by June 1975 16,000 children and 651 teachers were housed in 124 open plan schools, and by 1978 one child in twelve will be taught in such schools (New Zealand, 1977).

As so often happens in the field of education this innovation was accompanied not by evaluation but 'by a torrential increase in the number of educational articles praising the new style of building and the new style of teaching' (SEF, 1971). Gray (1976), writing in similar vein, asserted that the literature contains few cautions against jumping wildly on the bandwagon without fully understanding what the open plan concept entails in terms of teaching and learning. Instead the literature mainly presented an unquestioned plethora of philosophical beliefs, given as reasons, for building open plan schools. Initially few teaching programmes were described and even fewer research studies reported.

It was therefore the convention in early reviews to deplore the lack of studies, but this is no longer true. A computerized search via the ERIC system provided nearly 350 references and this was by no means exhaustive. Nevertheless the literature is of very variable quality and is widely scattered. Much of it derives from doctoral theses undertaken in American and Canadian universities, from journals with localized circulation and from North American boards of education where reports are often out of print. Therefore when primary material was unobtainable it has been necessary to rely on secondary sources.

This review of research comprises four sections. The first considers the theory–practice link by ascertaining whether open (informal) education practices obtain in open plan schools. The second concentrates on questionnaire and interview surveys of teacher opinions and attitudes to a number of issues including teaching organization, work load, noise and distraction, school design, staffing and training. The third section considers studies of the attitudes and personality characteristics of pupils, and the fourth reviews studies which have tested pupil achievement.

**Theory and Practice**

It was argued in the previous chapter that the development of open plan schools was based on a number of influences, but that the most important was changing teaching approaches. This is the theory, but does practice match the theory? Do open plan schools typically contain informal or open education practices?

On the basis of her personal observations Seefeldt (1973) wrote: 'Yet when one settles down carefully to observe and scrutinise the teaching–learning process that is taking place in many open plan schools, the observer leaves with a somewhat different and disquieting feeling. Open spaces . . . do not necessarily guarantee freedom in the classroom . . . it is clear that it is just as easy to restrict learning to rigid segments in open spaces as in closed classrooms. Perhaps educators need to examine and re-examine what does in fact occur within open space.' Adelman and Walker (1974) and Evans (1974) have commented similarly on the basis of their informal observations in British open plan schools. Evans commented on the fact that schools with open designs were sometimes run as closed schools. She was struck by the isolation of many teacher territories where linking doors between adjoining classrooms were bolted or plastered over with display materials so that opening them could have created a major disturbance. Low furniture arranged down the middle of shared practical areas sometimes indicated a boundary, and where it did not exist in physical reality there was often an imaginary line across which the children in a particular class were not encouraged to cross. Allen (1976) reports a similar situation among Canadian teachers. Observers noted that a variety of means were being used to establish and maintain territories. Most common were bookshelves and blackboards. Open space between clusters of desks was also used as a boundary-defining mechanism and the effect was often reinforced by varying the orientation and arrangement of desks and tables. It would seem from these observations that some teachers find it more difficult than others to take advantage of the opportunities for flexible use of space, and attempt to retain their 'own' territory. But open plan designs remove walls, and thereby remove fixed territories.

The role of the wall in defining areas to which people can relate and in which they have specific defined responsibilities is a somewhat neglected aspect of open plan (Drew, 1970). He argued that the 'territorial imperative' would seem to have relevance in terms of the design of open plan schools. The psychological implication of walls is one of protection, a defence against danger. Open space induces anxiety, whereas enclosure induces security and meditation.

The need of many teachers to retain their own personal space and then teach traditionally has been termed the regressive classroom by Cook (1973) 'because in spite of the open space (plan) setting there has been a retreat to the traditional classroom organisation. Not surprisingly teachers in these open rooms often feel an open space offers no advantages over the classroom at all. This phenomenon of the regressive classroom reminds us that space itself does not inevitably bring with it a certain organisation.'

The foregoing are impressionistic accounts, but they gain support from larger surveys of open plan schools. Four British studies bear directly on this aspect.

A questionnaire survey of 87 schools in the Strathclyde region of Scotland (1976) highlighted the prevalence of independent teaching. They found that 88 per cent of teachers wanted a closed classroom base, and concluded that 'it would appear that, regardless of type of building, there still exists a basic one-teacher–one-class organization with generally the basic skills being taught in the morning – with environmental studies, projects, centres of interest, choice activities etc. in the afternoons.'

This 'split day' organization was also prevalent in the Cumbria schools studied by Bennett *et al.* (1975). In this interview study of 74 teachers in eleven open plan schools many admitted that they were not operating as an open plan school. The majority were working independently. Less than one third taught in a team for more than half a day and this was usually in the context of project or topic work.

A survey by Derbyshire education advisers spelt out the same message (Arkwright *et al.* 1975). They commented on the poor use of space and found that teachers were still teaching inflexibly to whole class groups, particularly in junior schools. Most schools used other spaces as a class group base. This meant that open areas for maths, language, creative activities etc. tended to be used in rotation according to a timetable, providing, in the views of the advisory team, the worst of all educational worlds.

Finally Hurlyn (1975) visited and interviewed teachers in four schools to assess the extent to which they were centralized, i.e. to which pupils were dependent on teacher for materials, resources, ideas on subject matter, methods of procedure and initiation of tasks. He found all schools to be strongly centralized, none being involved in inquiry/discovery work. Two schools were very timetable conscious, changes being based on bells. He concluded that as far as the curriculum was concerned actual arrangements of teaching spaces and their relationship to each other had little effect. Architects and advisers may have a definite purpose in mind for these buildings but heads and teachers use them as they wish. It is not known whether these studies reflect practice nationally, but it is interesting to note that Jarman (1977), in commenting on the Oxfordshire experience, wrote 'to have an open plan school building, I have observed, means nothing in educational terms'.

In Britain at least the link between open plan architecture and open education practices would seem to be a tenuous one, whereas studies carried out on the North American continent present a mixed picture of practice. Traub *et al.* (1973) and Fisher (1974) used a teacher questionnaire (DISC) to assess programme openness or informality in schools in the Toronto area and found greater openness in open plan schools. However Traub *et al.* concluded that there were sufficient differences in their study to warrant considering them as separate factors.

In another Canadian study Allen *et al.* (1976) noted that in their samples there was very little difference between open plan and self contained classrooms in teaching approach, as did Nash and Christie (1972) in another Canadian study. They questioned principals, teachers and students in three open and three conventional* schools on open education assumptions. Many

* Throughout this review the term 'conventional' is used in relation to school design and the term 'traditional' to refer to teaching approach. The American term 'open education' is similar to the terms 'progressive' or 'informal' as used in Britain.

of these assumptions were not supported. In fact the greatest amount of agreement with the philosophy of the open school was expressed by the teachers in conventional schools. They concluded that the relative lack of difference between the two types of school may be indicative of a failure to use the full potential of the open plan buildings.

On the other hand O'Brien and Feeney (1973) questioned teachers in grades 4, 5 and 6 in 21 open and 18 conventional schools and reported that more teachers in open plan schools used team teaching organizations.

Questionnaire surveys have also been carried out to assess the organizational climate of open and conventional schools. Seidman (1975) sent the Halpin Organizational Climate Questionnaire to a random selection of 133 open plan elementary schools in the United States. From the responses of 1,763 teachers she found that the number of schools with closed climates was significantly higher than those with open climates. This pattern did not vary when the length of time the school had been open was taken into account. In a smaller study using the same questionnaire Jaworwicz (1972) reported that the interaction patterns between head and staff were not different in open and conventional schools and neither was the headteachers' perceived leadership behaviour. When these same schools were retested on a later occasion all of them had moved nearer to the closed end of the climate continuum. In a study of 12 schools containing both open plan and self-contained classrooms Holmquist (1972) found no difference in climate, as did Warner's (1970) study of one school.

Questionnaire studies can only present reported practices, which may or may not be valid. Observation studies on the other hand can give a more detailed picture of the reality of classroom practice. Three studies combined both questionnaire and observation. The Canadian SEF 5 (1971) investigation compared practices in 16 schools and found that open style teaching occurred in conventional schools but not as frequently as in open plan schools. In the latter there were more variable grouping patterns, pupils spent less time in their class base, moved around the school more often, talked to a larger number of teachers, used audio-visual (AV) equipment more, visited the library and went on field trips more often.

Nash and Christie (1972) found few differences between schools in the use of open education practices but noted from observation that pupils in open plan worked in groups more frequently and were involved in more group discussion. But pupils in conventional classes talked to each other more often. No differences in the amount of pupil–teacher talk were recorded. Unlike the SEF study there were no differences in the amount of use of audio-visual (AV) equipment, printed matter or learning material. In fact the use of learning materials by teachers was greater in conventional schools.

Allen (1972) combined questionnaire, interviews and half-day observations of 200 teachers in open plan schools together with 68 principals and superintendents. Formal instruction in large groups was not a popular practice but there was a strong emphasis on traditional subject areas and on ability grouping for maths and language arts.

Dilling and Tran (1973) focussed on teacher–pupil interaction in open and conventional classrooms. Teachers in 29 schools were first given the DISC questionnaire to assess the openness of their teaching and this was followed by observation using the Flanders Interaction Analysis schedule. They found that there was less teacher talk from teachers following an open teaching approach. They concluded that open plan and open education was not synonymous, a conclusion supported by Warner (1970) and Townsend (1971) on the basis of their observational studies.

In turning to studies which have been based entirely on observation Ellison *et al.* (1969) also used the Flanders schedule to try to determine whether there was a relationship between physical structure, school organization and verbal interaction. Grade 4 to 6 teachers in one open and one conventional school were observed for a minimum of 20 minutes per subject taught. Teachers in the open plan school spent 26 per cent of their time presenting information compared to 14 per cent by those in self contained classes. On a summed index of teacher talk, teachers in open plan talked 46 per cent of the time and in self contained classes 37 per cent. They concluded that teachers in open plan are more inclined to continuous verbal interaction and less inclined to supervise other activities than teachers in self contained classrooms.

This same study also ascertained how teachers utilized their time. They found that teachers in the conventional school spent more time in routine duties, whereas teachers in open plan spent more time observing other teachers, talking with other adults and in transition from one activity to another. On this evidence the research team concluded that the differences between the two schools did not appear to greatly affect practices within them.

This was also Kyzar's (1971) conclusion, although it is of interest to note that in one open plan school which had carefully oriented the teachers there were significant differences in favour of more open teaching approaches. It was also stated that classroom design did not appear to influence the utilization of floor and display area.

Gump (1974) was concerned to ascertain the relationship between design and teaching environment, and for this purpose decided to focus observation on target pupils. He found that pupils in open plan schools used a larger number of spaces and met a larger number of teachers than their counterparts in self-contained classes. However they also spent more time in 'non-substance' or transition periods: moving, waiting or getting organized. Gump uses this non-substance time as an index of operating efficiency. In his terms open plan teachers are less efficient, usually because a teacher is 'not ready to start an operation because she was busy closing out a previous one or dealing with a special problem'.

Pupil grouping practices varied little although small groups were less in evidence in open plan settings. The open plan environment was more active, however, and in this sense more stimulating, but pupils spent less time in activities where they were self-paced or were being individually guided. Open plan pupils were given little choice in activities and little opportunity for leadership behaviour.

Gump argued that although open plan pupils lost more time, the more stimulating environment might be expected to result in more on-task behaviour. The observations did not support this, however, since, overall, pupils in conventional schools spent more time on-task.

Angus *et al.* (1975) also observed differences in task-oriented behaviour. Overall, conventional classrooms were characterized by more individual pupil work, and open plan by more pupil and teacher interaction. The amount of pupil–pupil talk varied little in the two settings. Task involvement was higher in conventional classrooms and was higher among higher achieving pupils, the latter supported by both Bennett (1976) and Roecks (1978). In comparing practices in open plan and conventional schools the authors stated that 'on the whole instruction and learning experiences were being conducted along relatively traditional lines. However the results should discourage commentators from automatically associating a particular teaching style with a particular school design.'

The danger that pupils in open settings may, without adequate organization, display less work involvement can also be guaged from the DES survey of open plan schools (Great Britain,

1973). They commented on the waste of time in transitional activities, and specifically on the practice of bringing children together at the end of the morning or beginning of the afternoon. In large areas this took 15 to 20 minutes and carried with it the attendant risk of behaviour problems. They also commented that much very sound work was seen, but that some children were working at less than capacity. Examples of this were presented: a class in which never less than one third of the children idly queued, waiting for the teacher; a six-year old girl who neatly packed her books together and moved to another area whenever one of the teaching team approached – she did 15 minutes' work all morning; two boys who spent two hours writing out, first, every sixth, and then, every seventh number to 99. Further indication of the widely differing practices seen in British open plan schools can be gained from a comparison of the case studies by Alderson and Hird (1973) and Dennison (1976) (cf. Bennett, 1978).

**Summary**

A summary is hardly required for this section since the message is so uniform. An open plan school is no guarantee of open or informal education practices. For many the removal of walls is akin to the removal of trousers – privacy and security are lost and alternative cover is arranged — thus the prevalence of the so-called regressive classroom. Whether or not a regressive classroom is a regressive practice is of course open to debate. What must be of concern however is the evidence which points to the decline in pupil involvement, although this would appear to be a function of organization rather than design. Indeed, the message of this section would appear to be that architecture can modify the environment but not the activities that go on in the environment. As Drew notes 'ultimately no architectural solution, no matter how brilliant, can be successful educationally without intelligent, imaginative and committed teachers. If open space has done anything it has made us more aware of the crucial role of the teacher.'

**Teacher Opinions and Attitudes to Aspects of Open Plan Schools**

*Team/ Cooperative Teaching*

No distinction is made here between team and cooperative teaching. As yet there appear to be no agreed definitions and the terms are often used synonymously. Neither is it clear in many studies whether the teachers are commenting in the context of a formal team teaching structure or of informal cooperative efforts.

Brunetti *et al.* (1972) assert that the team organization is of critical significance to open plan schools. In their comparison of 110 teachers in open plan schools with team teaching organizations with 120 teachers in self-contained classrooms it was found that the former reported much more teacher interaction related to work, and that it occurred in different contexts. The open plan teachers talked more about curriculum planning, teaching and evaluation , whereas in self-contained situations talk was more often related to administration and routine (Meyer and Cohen, 1971). More communication between teachers is also reported by Kaelin (1970) and in the South Australian study (Australia, 1976), although in these studies it is not clear whether these were general comments about working in open plan schools, or specifically related to team teaching organizations.

One of the more interesting findings of the Brunetti *et al.* study was that teachers perceived they had greater influence in decision making in the team teaching open plan setting. The role of the teacher changes from an isolated position of authority to a highly involved person carrying joint authority and joint responsibility. However, a recent replication by Charters (1978) failed to find an increased feeling of autonomy among teachers. He argued that autonomy is not a function of team teaching but depends critically on the headteacher. Nevertheless he did support the findings on increased communication between teachers, as did Traub *et al.* (1973). Teachers in open plan schools in the latter study had more frequent interactions with other members of staff and had their work evaluated more frequently (cf. Marram, 1972). These teachers also acknowledged a larger number of sources of influence on their work than did those in conventional schools. They also tended to hold more positive attitudes to various aspects of their work and felt they had more influence in school affairs. This study extended that by Brunetti *et al.* by clarifying to some extent the effects of school design compared with the effects of teaching approach. In general, attitude differences appear to be related to design whereas improved influence patterns are more related to the openness of the teaching approach.

Team teaching appears not to be prevalent in open plan schools and the evidence from studies of teacher opinions would indicate a degree of ambivalence. Teachers are reported as arguing that cooperation must exist, and even be the cornerstone of organization (Mister and McCann, 1971; Fowler, 1970) but the difficulties experienced in cooperative efforts are more frequently mentioned (Halton Co., 1969; Murray, 1971; Pritchard and Moodie, 1971; New Zealand, 1977). This can be seen clearly in the responses of the Cumbrian teachers (Bennett *et al.*, 1975), who listed the advantages of team teaching as: the pooling of ideas, good for specialization, for probationary teachers and for improved discipline. But these were countered by the disadvantages of (in order of frequency): personality clashes, more preparation time needed. stress, not good for probationers or for discipline. The quality of interpersonal relationships between cooperating teachers appears to be of paramount importance and incompatibility appears not to be uncommon. Brunetti *et al.* were not unaware of this and of its effect on teacher performance: 'it is true that problems of interpersonal relations that hinder effective team developments is probably the most important problem that occurs in open space (plan)'.

In one of the very few studies to assess the determinants of teacher satisfaction in teams, Arikado (1973) questioned 529 teachers, in 134 teams, in 71 open plan schools. Thirty-eight of the teams had a formal leader, but teachers reported greater satisfaction in teams without a formal leader. Satisfaction in a formally lead team is not surprisingly related to the team's rating of the adequacy of the leader. Teachers who were given the choice to team teach and who had a say in the selection of fellow team members were also more satisfied. The balance of the team was also important. Satisfaction was higher in teams with a balanced status structure and in smaller teams (those of up to four teachers). The Halton Co. (1969) study also noted that balance was important, particularly the ratio of experienced teachers, and Salmon (1972), Brunetti (1971) and Pritchard and Moodie (1971) provide data to show that the size of the team is a mediating factor in satisfaction and compatibility. The Derbyshire study (Arkwright *et al.,* 1975) noticed that in several of the schools five or six teachers were housed with 200 or so pupils in the available space and that often this was broken down into sub-units by creating barriers with screens. In other words, teachers preferred to work in smaller teams. They thus recommended that the size of units be restricted to three teachers with 105 children. Seidman (1975) in her observations and interviews in open plan schools also demonstrated a link with staffing problems. In a number of schools excessive teacher turnover had caused frequent reorientation and integration of team members. This had led to loss of morale, as had the fact that too many experienced teachers were often assigned to the same team, and that teachers were not usually consulted about team assignments. Incompatible educational philosophies and discordant personalities were mentioned as causes of team dissension.

*Role of the Headteacher*

The role of the headteacher in this area is vital (Brunetti *et al.*, 1972; and Charters, 1978). Romans (1974) argues that the headteacher can play a crucial role by encouraging and taking part in discussion among teachers, without which the cooperative working of a group of teachers is not likely to succeed. The DES survey concurred, arguing that the head is the keystone of any school, but even more so in open plan, when teachers in unfamiliar settings look to him for guidance, support and reassurance. He should be able to visualize the optimum use of the building and its facilities, to inspire and stimulate cooperation between his teachers and to organize the school for the benefit of all the children. He must also resist the temptation to introduce too complex an organization which leads to excessive timetabling. The successful headteachers according to Arkwright *et al.* (1975) need to be good organizers, to have the ability to delegate and be committed to the type of building, so that their leadership can be both dynamic and democratic.

Some indication of how teachers view the role of the headteacher can be gleaned from a limited number of studies which have sought information on this topic. Angus (1975) and Kleparchuk (1970) report teachers as feeling that they need to be concerned with the quality of interpersonal relationships amongst staff members since staff relationships, good or bad, tend to be magnified in the open plan setting. Teachers desire a degree of autonomy and often feel they do not have it (New Zealand, 1977), and as such the head should indicate a willingness to give more responsibility to teachers and to teaching teams. He should provide, but not impose, expertise and direction, and help teachers achieve a sense of worth and dignity in their work. That this ideal is not always met is not perhaps surprising since it assumes that headteachers themselves enjoy a high level of interpersonal skill and no little expertise in open plan organization. That they do not is exemplified by the frustration and confusion reported by the New Zealand teachers due to the lack of leadership shown by headteachers.

*Work Load*

A surprising number of studies report adversely on increased work load and inadequate preparation time. The comments, emanating from different countries, are very similar. From Canada the findings of 10 studies all lead to the conclusion that work loads are considerably heavier in open plan schools, largely because of increased planning time. In turn this leads to increased stress and strain. The New Zealand teachers stated that work load was their major problem and 40 per cent of the South Australian teachers believed that their work load had increased to the point where their private lives were beginning to suffer. A similar message from the United States is gained from Murray (1971), who concluded that there was insufficient planning time and that heavy work loads were a major concern.

It might be thought that such factors would undermine morale but the evidence on this is equivocal. Levels of satisfaction can be influenced by many factors. It has already been reported that many teachers are more satisfied in team teaching organization, and there is also evidence that teachers who volunteered to work in open plan schools are more satisfied (Allen, 1976; Pritchard and Moodie, 1971). Similarly, teachers who have experience in working in such schools tend to have more positive attitudes, particularly those teaching younger children (Zeigler, 1973).

Those studies which have quantified satisfaction or preference for working in open plan schools provide a consistent pattern of reasonably high morale (South Australia; New Zealand, 1977; Fowler, 1970; Allen, 1972; Bennett *et al.*, 1975). But studies which have compared open plan teachers with those in conventional schools would indicate that satisfaction is higher in the latter (Broward Co., 1972a). However, there is clearly not a direct link between morale and action since a large majority did not favour a move back to self-contained classrooms. Allen (1976) also found satisfaction significantly higher in conventional schools but explained this in relation to teachers' need for structure. In general those teachers who said they were following open or informal approaches had significantly higher satisfaction than those who were not, but teachers with a low need for structure had higher job satisfaction in self-contained classrooms irrespective of the teaching approach adopted. The only findings opposing this trend were reported by Meyer and Cohen (1971) and it may be significant that all these teachers were operating in teams.

*Noise and Distraction*

Noise and distraction are considered together since to many teachers they are interrelated. Brunetti (1971) has argued that studies of the effects of noise on student and teacher performance are inconclusive at this point. Nevertheless there is no doubting the significance of noise as an adverse factor in the opinions of teachers and pupils in open plan schools. Studies which have focussed exclusively on open plan schools typically report that excessive noise levels constitute the most undesirable aspect of open plan schooling (Kruchten, 1971; Murray, 1971; Justus, 1971; Ledbetter, 1969; Bennett *et al.*, 1975; Strathclyde, 1976) and one which is related to disruption, disturbance and teacher stress. This was also the finding of the SEF6 (1975) study which, as a supplementary open question, asked teachers what advice they would give to teachers going into open plan for the first time. One in five teachers brought up noise and distraction and some gave specific advice – 'use ear plugs and tranquilisers'; 'make quiet corners'; or 'plan noisy times with another teacher'. When asked 'what is your major concern about working in an open plan school?' one third mentioned noise. Durlak *et al.* (1974), in a secondary analysis of an earlier SEF study concluded that although there is a problem of more noise to more people in open plan the problem is by no means non-existent in self contained classrooms. Nevertheless studies which have compared open and self-contained classes bear out the view that open plan areas are considerably noisier and that teachers see it as a greater problem (Zeigler, 1973; Halton Co., 1969; Broward Co., 1972b; Kyzar, 1971).

Teachers believe that distraction is affected by noise. In the South Australian (1976) survey, for example, distraction from noise was claimed to affect concentration, a view shared by Hersom and McKay (1971) and by Justus (1971) particularly in the areas of reading and mathematics. The teachers in the Cheek (1970) study also pointed to a link between noise, distraction and undesirable pupil behaviour. Noise would also seem to have effects on teaching. One quarter of the Pritchard and Moodie sample had had to make compromises to avoid disturbing others.

Data from pupils would seem to support teachers' perception on noise and distraction. Both Ledbetter (1969) and Halton Co. (1969) report pupils believing that noise was disrupting or distracting. The source of such noise was ascertained by Tedrick (1973) in a sample of over 800 grade 6 pupils. Over two thirds perceived noise in other parts of the area which disturbed them, caused by pupils and teachers or sounds from films, and 50 per cent perceived noise from TV, singing and music which was disturbing. It was also reported that these affected boys more than girls.

Noise was perceived by pupils as a problem in the SEF6 (1975) study of 22 schools, more particularly at elementary level. The source of the noise which most bothered them came from talking, movement and general noises in other classes. One fifth of pupils mentioned noise as something they would want to tell a visitor about, and most of these comments were negative. Similar findings were reported by Justus (1971).

Findings on perceived noise were inconsistent in the Traub *et al.* (1973) study because of the differing perceptions of the participants. Teachers and observers perceived more noise in schools with an open educational programme, but pupils perceived more noise in the less open programme schools. On this the authors suggested that many pupils are able to filter out or ignore noise and distractions when pursuing their activities. When schools were categorized by architectural openness no consistent trend was found. The observers perceived open plan schools to be noisier than the closed schools, but teachers did not. There was no difference in pupil perceptions.

Although agreeing that noise is more of a problem in open plan Brunetti (1971) argued that the type of activity taking place is more important than space, and that a high noise level does not necessarily result in distraction. In support of this he presented figures showing that 9 per cent of pupils in an open plan school with a traditional educational programme reported being distracted, compared to 27 per cent in an open plan school with an individualized programme, and 31 per cent in a conventional classroom. This would seem to support Durlak's claim that noise is a problem in open plan but is by no means non-existent in conventional classrooms. Brunetti also reported that some pupils felt noise to be a problem but were not distracted by it, while others reported being distracted by it but did not feel it to be excessively noisy. Clearly there are several factors involved in distraction including individual perception, social conversation, movement and noise.

Data from both the Tedrick (1973) and SEF6 (1975) studies would indicate that movement is less of a problem than noise as far as pupils are concerned. Nearly half of the SEF sample were never bothered by the movement of other people in their class group. Nevertheless it was claimed that the same pupils seem to be bothered regardless of the source and type of distraction and need a quiet environment in which to feel comfortable.

Brunetti believes that density may be more important than amount of space in considering noise, distraction and privacy. In this he is supported by the comments of Arkwright *et al.* (1975) and the SEF study. The authors of the latter study argued that crowdedness is more strongly related to every type of distraction from all sources and that providing more space or fewer pupils was preferable to the provision of elaborate acoustical treatment or partitioning. They added that falling enrolments may be a boon to open plan schools, a feeling implicit in the DES Building Survey (Great Britain, 1977a).

Space provision is also important when considering pupil need for privacy, although half the pupils in Brunetti's open plan sample said they could find an adequate place to study by themselves, whereas only one in four pupils in self contained classes could. In other words the conventional classroom provided less opportunity to separate off from the remainder of the class group. In the SEF study the proportion of pupils in open plan schools who reported sufficient privacy was somewhat lower at 34 per cent.

There is also an indication that familiarity with a certain kind of environment could alter perceptions. The children in the Bennett and Batley (1977) study who transferred to an open plan middle school from a conventional first school perceived noise to be a bigger problem than those who had transferred from an open plan first school.

In the only educational study to record sound levels Kyzar (1971) reported that the sound levels in conventional schools averaged 63 decibels whilst those in open plan averaged 70 decibels. It was thought that this difference would not affect performance. However Walsh (1975), an architect, would disagree. He quoted Miller (1974) on the effects of noise on people: 'Children have less precise speech than do adults and also their lack of vocabulary or different concepts of the rules of language may render speech unintelligible when some of the cues in the speech stream are lost. Thus adequate speech communication with children under thirteen years of age probably requires lower noise levels than those required for adults. It is possible though unproven that the language development of early childhood might be adversely affected because of noise. From this, difficulty in learning language and learning to read may ensue. One can only guess at how severe a noise must be to produce such effects. Nearly continuous sound levels in excess of 70 decibels might be required.' Welsh also quoted Japanese research to indicate that noise levels in the range 60–70 decibels produced various forms of emotional irritation, lack of motivation, disturbance of mental work, speech interference, reduced concentration and fatigue. The Japanese Ministry of Education has designated a maximum noise level of 55 decibels as the standard of exterior noise transmitted to classroom spaces. Similarly the Wilson Report in Britain (1963) argued that 55 decibels should be the only upper limit to be tolerated in buildings in which communication by speech is of great importance.

From his own research in open plan schools Welsh concluded 'high background noise levels are the major complaint in the use of open plan school facilities. They can cause discomfort, distraction, annoyance and interference with speech communication. The maximum background noise level in open plan schools should not exceed approximately 65 decibels.' At this level the maximum distance between teacher and pupil at which intelligible speech communication can occur is approximately 7 feet (2.13 metres). Yet in his own study it was quite common to observe noise levels in excess of 70 decibels in open plan elementary schools. He argued for sound absorbent surfaces or alternatively extra spaces or fewer pupils. But since the space required to maintain 65 decibels would be nearly double that currently provided in Britain this alternative appears unlikely.

*Discipline*

Although the teachers in the Cheek study perceived a link between noise, distraction and misbehaviour there is no other evidence to support this. Mister and McCann (1971) and the Halton Co. (1969) study both reported teachers believing that the maintenance of discipline was easy and that few discipline problems existed. On the other hand the New Zealand teachers reported that lack of discipline was a major problem.

Studies which have contrasted open and conventional schools also provide different viewpoints. In one study three quarters of teachers in open plan schools felt that discipline was not good enough whereas less than one half of teachers in self contained classes did so (Broward Co., 1972a). In Sweden, Gran (1971) reported that discipline and general behaviour was similar in both types of school although she added that some open plan schools did report a large number of pupils with behavioural problems.

*School Design*

Most teachers believe that the design of a building should not dictate organization, although some feel that it does. When specifically questioned on aspects of design or limitations of the building a large range of responses have been drawn. The Strathclyde and Cumbria studies are fairly typical in this respect. The Strathclyde teachers included lack of space generally, lack of audio-visual rooms, quiet rooms too small, lack of withdrawal areas, lack of storage areas, lack of soundproofing and poorly sited cloak/toilet areas. The responses of the Cumbrian teachers were similar, stressing lack of quiet areas, more space, poorly sited cloaks/toilets and inadequate storage. Dissatisfaction with storage and furniture seems worldwide (Fitzpatrick and Zani, 1974; Hersom and Mackay, 1971; New Zealand, 1977; South Australia, 1976).

Teachers usually have access to a practical/wet area although they are considered inadequate by some. Fitzpatrick and Zani for example listed three problems in their use: 1. their use as a thoroughfare prevents the full realization of their potential benefit; 2. they are too small; 3. more display and work tables are required. Similar arguments were made in the South Australia report and by Gran (1971) in Sweden.

The availability of alternative spaces seems to be a problem in many designs. The call for more withdrawal or quiet areas by the Strathclyde and Cumbria teachers is echoed by Fitzpatrick and Zani and Hersom and MacKay. The need for enclosed spaces capable of housing an entire class was a central recommendation of the New Zealand survey and was also mentioned by Fowler (1970) and Pritchard and Moodie (1971). Indeed, many designs in Canada and the USA, for example, comprise both open and closed spaces in approximately equal numbers. The availability of more space generally has already been cited and was quoted as the major disadvantage of open plan schools in the New Zealand and South Australia surveys, the reason being problems of overcrowding.

Concern at the quality of acoustics, lighting and ventilation have also been expressed, but it would be unfair to leave the impression that all comment has been negative. It has not. The Strathclyde teachers praised the provision of activity/resource areas and quiet rooms where they were provided, and commented on the flexibility of some designs which incorporated movable partitions. The Cumbria teachers also gave credit to the improved facilities.

It has also been felt that the faults highlighted could have been due to inadequate briefing of the architect and lack of consultation. The NUT (1974) argued that LEAs should engage teachers in the consultation process from the very beginning since, on their information, this was not happening. It did not see consultation as a mere matter of allowing headteachers to see already formulated proposals or finished drawings. This kind of contact should also be continued after the school has been completed in order to monitor the effect of what had been done. Lack of involvement in school design is not however a problem peculiar to Britain. In a Canadian context Beardsley *et al.* (1973) wrote 'A few principals have been involved in the overall planning of the school and others have been able to make minor adjustments prior to opening but for the most part – more so for teachers – the school building is a *fait accompli.*'

*Staffing and Training*

Fitzpatrick and Angus (1974) argued that 'for any school to function at its peak it must have at least three factors operating in its favour. It must have a rationale or purpose that is clear to all its members; it must have a staff consistent in its appreciation and endorsement of the rationale; and it must have a staff equipped as fully as possible with the pedagogical skills that are required to operationalise the rationale.'

A number of studies testify to the fact that teachers are not always clear about the objectives or purpose of open plan schools, or that they disagree with them (Bennett *et al.*, 1975; Cheek, 1970; Kaelin, 1970; Seidman, 1975). There are also many teachers who find the open plan environment inappropriate. Fitzpatrick and Angus for example argued that there are teachers fully competent in a self contained classroom situation who are unable to realize their teaching goals in the open plan school. In particular the mobility of children between teachers and the mismatch of professional expectation with their colleagues leave considerable tensions; for example, where teachers close off their areas as an act of withdrawal (cf. Busselle, 1972). It requires a substantial adjustment for many teachers to become used to being visible. Indeed 50 per cent of the teachers in the New Zealand survey pointed to their openness to public scrutiny as being the biggest factor in their feelings of greater stress.

The same message was broadcast by Beardsley *et al.* (1973). They argued that the absence of personal space defined by walls threatens many teachers' sense of territoriality: 'such teachers may find teaching in open spaces personally disastrous. Many teachers enjoy working in a protected environment in which areas of responsibility are clearly specified. However there are many others who would find this stultifying and frustrating.'

It is not surprising therefore that the selection of teachers has attracted considerable comment. Selection practices vary widely but there is general agreement that teachers appointed should be committed to open planning and that this is most likely to result from appointing volunteers. 90 per cent of Murray's (1971) sample felt this strongly, as did those in the Cheek (1970) and Hersom and Mackay (1971) surveys who also felt, along with Kaelin (1970), that there should be the opportunity to opt out of open plan both for teachers and pupils.

In addition to being committed volunteers they should also be appointed early (Cramer and Barnes, 1973), and staff development and curriculum planning should begin with the design of the building itself (French, 1972). Optimally (and optimistically) French also believed that in-service efforts should begin one year in advance, giving the teacher involved the opportunity to participate in the development of, and agreement with, the philosophy and statement of goals for the programme.

Teachers call for in-service courses because of their dissatisfaction with pre-service training. The same message emanates from many studies with depressing regularity. 'Teacher training is not helpful for teachers in open plan' (Allen, 1972); 'training for open plan is inadequate' (Murray, 1971); 'insufficient' (Pritchard and Moodie, 1971); 'badly needed' (Hersom and Mackay, 1971; New Zealand, 1977; Gran, 1971); 'a major problem' (Cheek, 1970); 'would be an excellent investment' (Zeigler, 1973). This same message also came from the probationers in the South Australia study.

The New Zealand study is the only one to sample college principals. These, it would appear, were uncommitted to open plan and held a cautious attitude to the development of open planning. Their sanguine comment was that there were insufficient open plan schools to allow practice. As a result most trainee teachers leaving college had no extensive knowledge, either practical or theoretical, of open plan education. The report recommended that colleges should provide courses which include cooperative teaching, open plan organization and personal relationships, and that opportunity be provided for teaching practice in open plan schools, and it called for the development of in-service courses for practising teachers.

Fitzpatrick and Angus (1974) outlined a similar list of skills including interpersonal relationships, sensitivity to the situation of colleagues, leader and follower skills, the orchestration of small groups, the ability to take advantage of the physical environment and familiarity with the rationale of open planning. Despite the felt need for more relevant training and attempts to delineate the skills required, few innovative training courses appear to have been developed. The one exception found is that by Gray (1977). He starts from the premise that teachers have to be prepared differently to teach differently and to provide educational practices appropriate to the fullest use of the open plan concept. Accordingly he focusses on five major teacher education goals: 1. Developing basic teaching competence; 2. Developing human relations competence; 3. Developing curriculum design competencies; 4. Developing team teaching competencies; and 5. Developing competencies for implementing open education practices in open areas. Clearly there is much to be done in this area.

**Summary**

There is always the danger of over-generalization from a mass of evidence of this type. Nevertheless teachers seem to see advantages in teaching in a team or cooperatively, provided that there is agreement about its composition and size. When this is achieved satisfaction among teachers is high. But there is also a great deal of concern about incompatibility due to problems of interpersonal relationships. These, together with frequent team changes can create low morale. The role of the headteacher is seen as crucial. He should be concerned with the relationships among his staff, have expertise in the organization of open plan schools, have the ability to delegate responsibility, giving the feeling of autonomy among teams and staff. Teachers do not always feel that sufficient leadership is provided.

Inadequate preparation time and heavy work loads are frequently mentioned as a fact of life but not ones which appear to affect morale, which, on the whole, appears to be reasonably high. It seems not to be as high as in conventional schools but a majority of teachers in open plan do not favour a return to self contained classrooms.

Noise and distraction figure prominently in the hierarchy of problems of open plan both for teachers and pupils. However, individual perceptions of noise differ, perhaps indicating differing thresholds of tolerance. Noise levels appear to be related to certain kinds of activity, amount of space, and density. Overcrowdedness was seen as one of the greatest problems. Sound levels have been rarely measured and there is some dispute as to what should be regarded as an acceptable level. A level of 65 decibels allows intelligible conversation to a maximum of seven feet (2.13 m) but it seems likely that levels substantially above this are typical in open plan primary schools. To ease this requires sound absorbent surfaces, more space or less pupils. Some teachers felt noise and distraction led to increased discipline problems but the evidence is equivocal.

Noise also came up in opinions about school design, but the biggest plea is for more space generally, together with more withdrawal or quiet areas, and better designed practical areas. A plea for more consultation on planning is made.

There is agreement that the open plan teaching environment is not suitable for all teachers and pupils, who should be given the chance to opt out gracefully. Staff should ideally be committed volunteers amply supported by in-service provision. There is universal condemnation of pre-service training, but little or no progress appears to have been made in this area.

**Pupil Attitudes and Personality**

*Attitude to School*

There is a consensus among teachers that open plan schooling facilitates social development of pupils by providing the opportunity for increased social contact with both peers and adults (Cheek, 1970; Fowler, 1970; Gran, 1971; Kaelin, 1970; Kruchten, 1971). The only note of caution was expressed by Gran, whose teachers were somewhat negative about the pupils' feeling of security. Teachers also believe that pupil responsibility is developed through greater independence and self reliance (Mister and McCann, 1971; Halton Co., 1969, Pritchard and Moodie, 1971; Kaelin, 1970; Zeigler, 1973; Bennett *et al.*, 1975). There is also a feeling that pupils enjoy working in the open area (Pritchard and Moodie, 1971; Fowler, 1970).

But what of pupils themselves? Fourteen studies were located which bear on this question. Many have been small-scale studies drawing samples from one or two schools, often carried out by research students in North American universities. Most of these studies have compared limited samples of children in open plan and conventionally designed schools. The greater proportion have found that pupils in open plan schools profess better attitudes to school and themselves (Halton Co., 1969; Beals, 1972; Beckley, 1972) although pupils in the Halton Co. study admitted wasting more time. On the other hand attendance was better and there appeared to be fewer discipline problems. However the largest study, of 1,000 pupils in open plan and 1,000 in conventional schools found no difference in attitudes to teacher and that the pupils in conventional schools held more positive attitudes to maths and language arts (Arlin and Palm, 1974). In another large study Spigel (1974) questioned 2,000 pupils in grades 2 and 7 about their attitudes to physical and non-physical aspects of their learning environments and found that pupils in conventional schools professed more favourable attitudes. Day (1974) provides one of the few longitudinal studies. He tested 198 pupils in two open and two conventional schools over a three year period. He reported more favourable attitudes among pupils in the open plan schools, and that these improved over the three year period.

The results are mixed and might be explained by the indication that attitudes in open plan have been found to vary by age. Townsend (1971) found better attitudes and feelings towards teachers and teaching programmes among sixth grade pupils in open plan schools, but not at second grade, where children from conventional schools expressed more positive attitudes. In another small study Daniels (1974) found that only in grade 4 were attitudes better in open plan schools. Jeffreys (1970) reported no differences in his sample of grade 3 and 5 pupils, and Stowers (1974) reported mixed findings. Attitude to school among boys was better in self contained classes but among girls they were better in open plan.

A major problem with studies on pupil attitudes, indeed of much of the research on open plan schools, is the naive implicit assumption that because the architecture is open so must be the teaching. That it is not has already been commented upon. This leads to problems of interpretation since it is not possible to ascertain whether it is the architectural arrangements, or the teaching practices they house, which relate to differences in attitude. Only two studies have differentiated between the two.

The first, a study of four schools by Wilson *et al.* (1969), found that the attitudes of pupils experiencing traditional teaching in self-contained classes were less positive than those in an open plan school with more open teaching. This would argue that the teaching approach rather than the design is the main factor. But this result was not supported by the most sophisticated study in this area by Traub *et al.* (1973). They classified the architecture of the school open, mixed and closed, and the teaching approach as more or less open on the basis of the DISC questionnaire. They found a moderately strong relationship between school design and attitudes to school, teacher, self and independence. Among eleven-year-old pupils those in open plan schools scored more highly on all these than did those in mixed or closed schools, and this was also true of eight year olds although the effect was less strong. There was no trend for attitudes in relation to differences in teaching approach. They also tested initiative, autonomy and responsibility to self among the eleven year olds and found that these were generally higher in open plan schools.

Allen (1976) extended this study by incorporating a measure of teachers' need for structure as well as classifying school type and teaching approach. 476 pupils in open plan and 346 in conventional schools were given a school sentiment index and a self appraisal scale, analyses of which indicated a strong and consistent relationship with one combination of variables. Situations in which a traditional teaching approach was offered in a self contained classroom by a teacher with a high need for structure yielded the highest scores on every sub-test of the pupil scales. Allen interpreted these findings in terms of the benefits pupils derive from a structured programme, such as lack of confusion and increased security.

*Self Reported Personality*

Ascertaining the personality characteristics of pupils in open plan and conventional schools has been a favourite pastime, particularly among doctoral and masters students. Unfortunately most have only tested on one occasion, making it virtually impossible to attribute any differences found to the type of school or teaching approach.

Self concept has attracted the most attention but the sample of schools have tended to be very small and no attempt has been made to ascertain the teaching approach.

Six of the nine studies located reported no differences between the self concepts of pupils in open and conventional schools (Ruedi and West, 1973; Black, 1974; Judd, 1974; Rudawski, 1974; Stowers, 1974; Daniels, 1974). One found differences favouring open plan. Lukasewitch (1976) tested 321 pupils who had been in their schools for at least two years and the results showed that pupils in open plan had a more favourable self concept in relation to school subjects. Heingartner (1972) presents mixed results, whereas Sackett (1971) found differences favouring conventional schools. He tested grade 6 pupils in three neighbouring schools, one of which was open plan, working on humanistic principles allowing maximum freedom to pupils, one of which was self contained, and the other of which was departmentalized. Both the latter ran traditional teaching programmes and their pupils gained higher self concept scores. But whether this effect relates to the openness of the architecture or the teaching is impossible to say.

The remaining studies which have focussed on single personality characteristics cover a wide range, from adjustment to risk taking.

McDaniel (1970) contrasted pupils on social and personal adjustment at first and second grade. Overall there were no significant differences but the trends were in favour of open plan pupils. On a related theme Grapko (1972) assessed security, consistency and independence and found these to be very much higher in conventional schools in grades 4 and 6. Six months later the open plan pupils in grade 4 had caught up a little but not at grade 6. The author contended that the open plan pupils were one year behind pupils in conventional schools on the measure of security.

Blumenthal and Reiss (1975) carried out a series of four replicated studies to show that open plan does not affect preference for delayed rewards. This they argued provided no support for those who would believe that open plan promotes permissiveness and impulsivity. Annifant (1972) on the other hand concluded from his study that open plan schools are more conducive to risk taking, but no account was taken of the teaching approach.

Reiss and Dyhdalo (1975) posed the question of whether pupils learned to be more persistent in open plan. In their second grade sample they found that in general they did, but those who did not learned considerably less. Non-persistent boys in open plan averaged 20 percentile points less on achievement tests than those in self contained classes. These results were congruent with those for fourth grade pupils on the basis of which the authors argued that certain types of children react negatively to open plan and that different options should be available so that significant harm should not be done to non-persistent (distractible) children.

Finally three studies have relied on published personality inventories covering a wide range of personality traits. Bell *et al.* (1976) used the Cattell Personality Questionnaire (CPQ) to test 43 pairs of children matched on IQ and sex from an open and a conventional school. Open plan pupils, following an informal teaching approach, were more mature, adventurous, thick-skinned, sober, controlled, relaxed and liked group action. Pupils from the conventional school following a traditional teaching approach were more emotional, enthusiastic, sensitive, individualistic and tense. Overall the open plan children were less anxious, but again it is not possible to differentiate openness of design and openness of teaching. LaForge (1972) in an equally small sample tested present and former pupils of one open and one conventional school with the CPQ and found no significant differences. Carbonari (1971) wished to find out change in pupil personality over one year in one school and divided his sample into those who had been in the school more than one year and compared them with those who had been in the school less than a year. He found that those who had been in school more than a year were more independent, lively, self reliant, extraverted and anxious.

*Curiosity and Creativity*

It is arguable whether creativity can be considered a personality characteristic, but it is included with curiosity because studies have tended to consider them together.

Wilson *et al.* (1969) gave tests of curiosity and the Torrance tests of creative thinking to pupils in four schools. One was open plan with an open teaching approach, one conventional with an open teaching approach and two conventional schools with a traditional teaching approach. No differences were found on curiosity, but the open plan pupils scored consistently lower on the creative tests. Traub *et al.* (1973) also found no differences in curiosity scores or on the figural creativity section of the Torrance tests. However, significant differences were found favouring traditional teaching approaches on verbal creativity. Taken together these two studies would indicate higher creativity scores associated with traditional teaching approaches, but Day (1973, 1974) found no differences in a follow-up study of pupils in two open and two conventional schools. The only other study located in this area is by O'Neill (1971) on creativity and self esteem among girls, where no differences were found overall.

*Friendship Patterns*

Two studies included an assessment of friendship patterns in schools of differing design. Traub *et al.* (1973) found that among eight- and eleven-year-old pupils those in open plan schools listed significantly less names of fellow pupils they would like to play with than those in conventional schools. In O'Neill's (1974) study boys aged eight to ten were asked to name five best friends. These revealed that the number of isolates were similar in both types of school; that ten per cent more pupils in open plan listed fewer than five friends; that children new to the district or school found it more difficult to make friends in the open plan schools; and that open plan pupils appeared to have a more altruistic conception of friendship. In a comparison study based on the analysis of stories written by these pupils, those in open plan schools told stories involving peers where there was more negative content than positive content.

These findings are supported by studies which have compared friendship patterns in classes experiencing informal and traditional teaching approaches but not in open plan schools. The largest is by Hallinan (1976). She found that in traditional classrooms there was a clear hierarchy based on popularity whereas in the informal or open classes there was a more uniform distribution of popularity probably brought about by the increased opportunity to become known. There were more mutual choices in traditionally taught classes and they tended to last longer. Because of this Hallinan wondered whether the increased interaction in the open classes made for more superficial relationships. Pupils in traditional classes also gave and received more choices. This, according to the author, poses a dilemma for teachers concerned with social development. While the open teaching approach has the advantage of decreasing the number of social isolates and of fostering a more uniform distribution of popularity, children in traditional teaching situations tend to have more friends, and more stable friendships.

**Summary**

The evidence reviewed does not lend itself to a coherent synthesis. Research on pupil attitudes is totally equivocal. Most of it has been inadequately conceptualized, failing to differentiate between teaching approach and school design. The two studies which did make this differentiation tended to disagree, partly, one suspects, because of the small and localized nature of the samples. Similarly, little can be said about differences in self concept in schools of differing design, and nothing can be said about the development of self concept. On the other hand there is some evidence to show that pupils feel more secure in self contained classrooms experiencing a traditional approach, and that under this approach creativity may be a little higher.

The most consistent picture is provided by studies of friendship patterns. Pupils in conventional schools tend to have more friends and to make friends more easily but from these studies it is not possible to assess whether this is a design or teaching effect. Evidence from research in conventional schools would indicate the latter.

Overall there appears to be no justification in accepting the generalizability of any of these trends, particularly since all were undertaken on the North American continent.

**Pupil Achievement**

Few surveys have included questions on teacher perceptions of pupil achievement. Those that did have tended to find that most teachers feel that pupils perform better or as well as those in conventional schools (Pritchard and Moodie, 1971; Fowler, 1970). The New Zealand teachers rated achievement as higher in the open plan school, a finding supported by Wilkinson (1973) in Britain. His sample thought that pupils produced work of a greater variety and of a slightly higher standard although they also felt that presentation of work had suffered. However the Cumbria teachers (Bennett *et al.*, 1975) were concerned about academic losses, as did those questioned in the NUT survey, who argued that open plan schools had not helped children to produce a higher standard of work.

There is also a feeling that only certain types of pupil benefit from open plan schooling. The Gran (1971), New Zealand and Wilkinson studies all isolate those of above average ability or gifted. In fact a large majority of the teachers questioned by Wilkinson believed that open plan schools were really only suitable for suburbs or districts that were socially and economically above average.

The type of child likely to be overlooked, or who might benefit from conventional schooling was characterized as quiet, shy, less able and aggressive by the Bennett *et al.*, Pritchard and Moodie and New Zealand studies. Surveys by teacher unions support these opinions. The Union of Women Teachers named younger children and most children with learning difficulties or emotional problems, arguing that the fear of large groups in great spaces 'is very real in insecure children. Yet we subject them to the terror of educational agrophobia when we fail to recognise that their sense of security is tied with a familiar room and a regular place in it.' The report concluded 'Members have expressed reservations as to the suitability of open plan schools and team teaching for children in disadvantaged areas.'

Are these opinions supported by research evidence? Longitudinal studies are considered first. These involve following groups of children through their schooling and testing for achievement at regular intervals. Indications of pupil progress can thereby be gained and, if properly controlled, changes in achievement can be attributed to the teaching approach experienced. In practice longitudinal studies comparing pupils in open plan and conventional buildings are limited by the smallness and unrepresentativeness of the samples. This is exemplified in the study by Bell *et al.* (1974, 1976, 1977), since this concerns the achievement of pupils in one open informal and one conventional traditional school in the same middle-class suburb. 57 pupils in the open and 112 pupils in the conventional school, all of whom had attended kindergartens following the same curriculum, were followed through the first years of elementary school. At the end of the first year there were no differences in number, but significant differences in reading favouring the conventional school. At this stage they were seven months ahead on word recognition, and twice as many of the open plan pupils were below reading norms. Since there had been no differences on pre-school variables, or on age or socio-economic status, the authors argued that the traditional learning situation was the cause of the difference, concluding that for a number of children the open environment provided an adverse educational situation.

The results of the second year testing revealed that the reading scores of the conventional group remained significantly better, but there were still no differences in number. At the end of the third year the conventional group was seven months ahead on reading, four months ahead in vocabulary and five months in maths computation. The authors contended that both schools had dedicated, well-trained teachers and as such it was difficult to account for the differences except in terms of the more informal approach adopted in the open plan school, and the open design itself with its many distracting influences. Their impressions from observation were that children not under close supervision in small groups in the open plan school wasted much time aimlessly wandering about, watching the movements of other classes and interacting without useful purpose with classmates.

Another longitudinal study by Burnham (1973a/b) used a slightly larger sample matched on IQ, location of school, teacher qualifications and average class load, but not on teaching approach. Testing over a three year period using standardized tests of reading and mathematics revealed no differences, as did the studies by Burnham (1971, 1973c) and Kennedy and Say (1971).

Two studies concentrated on reading performance only. McRae administered tests of reading at the beginning and end of the year to just 34 pupils in an open plan school and 34 drawn from conventional schools. At the beginning of the year the conventional group achieved significantly better scores. At the end of the year there were no differences in speed, accuracy or vocabulary, although the conventional pupils were still achieving better on comprehension. Moodie (1971) used the same tests on 48 open and 49 conventional school pupils who were transferring to the same secondary school. At the end of the elementary stage the conventional pupils scored more highly, but after five months in the secondary school no differences were recorded.

Although not strictly longitudinal, two studies followed up the same set of schools. Gathercole (1970) compared all the pupils in grades 4 to 8 in two new open plan schools over one year with the achievement of pupils in all other schools in the district. At grade 5, open plan pupils were achieving one year five months behind on the Canadian Test of Basic Skills; at grade 6 two months behind; at grade 7, one year one month behind; and at grade 8 two years five months behind. These adverse results were interpreted in terms of the newness of the schools. McPherson (1972) later matched three open plan schools in size, intake area and IQ scores. The same test was used on grade 8 pupils, the results of which showed significantly higher scores for the conventional pupils in vocabulary, and trends favouring this group for better work study skills, language, maths and reading.

On balance, longitudinal studies tend to favour higher achievement in conventional schools, although it should be borne in mind that the samples have been small, limited to the North American continent, and none have made any systematic attempt to describe the teaching approach, leaving it impossible to ascertain whether the better achievement is related to design or teaching methods.

Only three studies, only one of which was longitudinal, have classified teaching approach and design. Traub *et al.* (1973) report a study involving four designs involving two kinds of school intake. Type 1 schools housed a high proportion of pupils from English speaking homes (less than 15 per cent came from homes where English was a second language). These tended to be of middle-class suburban background. Type 2 schools housed a higher proportion of pupils from homes where English was spoken as a second language (30 per cent or more pupils were from this background which tended to be working class and inner city). Schools were also classified on school design into open, mixed and closed, and teaching approach as less open and more open based on the DISC questionnaire.

The results were interesting. Children in Type 1 schools showed no difference in achievement irrespective of school design and teaching approach. But in Type 2 schools the achievement of pupils was consistently higher in schools with less open (formal) teaching approaches. The differences were consistent across age levels and across all the sub-tests of the Canadian Test of Basic Skills. 'For every CTBS sub-test at each grade level the students in schools with less open programmes substantially outperformed the students with more open programme. This finding is the clearest and had the best statistical support of any finding in the present investigation'. In terms of magnitude the differences amounted to about six months.

The importance of this study is that it points to an interaction effect between teaching approach and social class/ability. The benefits of a more structured approach for low ability or low social-economic status children have also been found by Soar (1973) and Brophy and Evertson (1976). Rosenshine (1976) and Bennett (1978a) discuss this in more detail.

A recent Australian study found no interaction effects for pupil achievement but did so for self esteem (Angus *et al.*, 1979). This study related type of school design and teaching approach to pupil achievement and self esteem among fifth year primary children in 120 schools. Although the differences were not significant for written expression there were significant differences in maths and reading favouring conventional schools irrespective of teaching approach. On self esteem it was found that conventional schools favoured pupils of low social status and open plan schools high social status.

The other study to classify teaching and design was the more limited investigation by Lukasevitch (1976), again using the DISC questionnaire, and the CTBS test. Although in general she found little relationship between achievement and both design and teaching approach the trends were for a traditional teaching approach in either an open or closed classroom for achievement in reading comprehension, and for a traditional teaching approach in a self contained classroom for achievement in mathematics concepts.

The remaining studies have neither been longitudinal nor have they distinguished teaching approach or types of pupil. As such their value is limited. Six report findings favour conventional schools, two favour open plan, and another five report no differences.

Sackett (1971) contrasted an open plan school, with a humanistic approach favouring maximum pupil freedom and team teaching, with a neighbouring, conventional and departmentalized, school. The same basic curriculum applied throughout all schools in the district. Grade 6 pupils were tested on the Iowa Test of Basic Skills, the open plan pupils achieving poorly in comparison to the pupils from the other schools. Townsend (1971) carried out a similar study comparing an open plan, a conventional and a departmentalized school. Pupils in grades 2 and 6 were tested and achievement scores of open plan pupils were worse in more areas. Grapko (1972) compared achievement on the CTBS in one open and one conventional school and reported that pupils in the latter school scored more highly. However, he contended that this was due to the fact that more lower IQ pupils were in the open plan school. Warner (1970) studied only one school which had both open and self contained classes. The pupils in self contained classes achieved better in maths at grade 4 but no differences were noted at grades 2 and 3. Girls tended to perform better in the self enclosed environment whereas boys did so in the open area, a finding supported by the Broward County (1972a) study. They also found that at grade 8 all the significant differences favoured pupils in conventional schools. Better performance in maths in conventional schools was also reported by Stowers (1974) in a sample of 96 pupils drawn from four open and four conventional schools.

Allen (1974) assessed achievement using the Stanford Achievement Tests at grades 3 and 5. He found no differences at grade 3 but reported significant findings favouring open plan pupils in two sub-tests – word meaning and paragraph meaning. On the basis of his study Killough

(1971) maintained that after pupils had been in open plan school for at least two years they showed better achievement in most areas. The remaining studies located found no differences (Jeffreys, 1970; Read, 1973; Black, 1974; Spigel, 1974; Daniels, 1974).

**Summary**

From the research undertaken so far the trends favour higher achievement in conventional schools. But it would be rash to accept this as a final judgement. Samples have been small and unrepresentative and all were carried out in North America using fairly limited achievement criteria. Perhaps the one of greatest significance is the interaction of teaching approach on pupils of differing ability levels or social class background. There are also hints that an interaction may occur between school design or teaching approach and differences in sex.

**Conclusion**

Reviewers of research find themselves in a situation akin to that of ancient cartographers. They aim to map out an area as faithfully as possible from the information available, but are aware that incomplete information, and their own human fallibility, may distort the picture, and become conscious that much is still to be discovered. Reviews, like ancient maps, are therefore always interim statements and a reflection of a particular historical context.

The information available would indicate that although, as suggested in Chapter 1, there may be a symbolic link between open plan schools and open education practices the link in reality is a tenuous one. The reasons for this are many – confusion about rationale and purpose, inappropriate staffing, inadequate pre- and in-service provision, inherent drawbacks of open design and the heavy demands made on teachers, many of which could have been overcome early with constructive evaluation programmes. Nevertheless teachers must be given credit for resilience. Progress has been made with team and cooperative teaching approaches, morale is reasonably high and few would wish to return to a self contained classroom.

Studies so far carried out would indicate that the effect of open plan on pupil attitudes to school, self concept, curiosity and creativity is minimal, although there is a suggestion that security may suffer. The results of studies on pupil achievement are mixed but the overall trend appears to show that achievement on standardized tests favours pupils in conventional schools. But it is not possible to ascertain whether this effect is related to teaching approach or to school design, or indeed to an interaction of the two since rarely have they been differentiated. The acceptance of the assumption that open plan schools house a particular teaching approach has bedevilled the research, as indeed has the equally erroneous assumption that open plan schools are, as a group, homogenous. In fact the layout of these schools, their size, amount, type and orientation of space all differ to such an extent that it is inappropriate to regard them as a single group. Gran (1971) and Traub *et al.* (1973) recognized this and called for more precise ways of indexing architectural type. Future studies of the effects on pupils requires a more adequate conceptualization of the problem, including a longitudinal design incorporating a classification of both design and teaching approach, and allowing for interaction effects on pupil ability, social class background, sex and race.

Finally, the evidence which indicates that open plan schools vary widely both in design and in teaching organization should serve to undermine general and often misconceived stereotypes, and lead to the recognition that each school is in a very real sense unique.

*Chapter 3*

# *The Design of the Study*

By the middle of the 1970s open plan primary schools had become regular features of the educational landscape. Their numbers had increased progressively through the previous decade, but as in so many aspects of education this development had not been paralleled by any kind of evaluation. Little had been done to examine problems of teaching curriculum and organization despite concern expressed by professional associations. This study was therefore designed to provide an organized and comprehensive body of knowledge concerning problems, successes and practices in different types of open plan schools serving the age range 5–11 years. More specifically its aims were:

1. To provide a detailed, comprehensive picture of open plan schools as they are operating at the moment.
2. To ascertain where problems have arisen and the manner in which they have been overcome, or where they are still apparent.
3. To point out areas of successful teaching and curriculum practice as perceived by teachers.
4. To provide an objective record of the attitudes and opinions of teachers on a wide range of issues relating to the open plan environment.

The study can be considered in three stages – (a) Familiarization; (b) National questionnaire survey; (c) Observation and interview studies.

**Familiarization**

A previous small-scale study in Cumbria (Bennett *et al.*, 1975) had demonstrated that the term 'open plan schools' was a misnomer, giving the impression of homogeneity when heterogeneity was the rule. Such schools vary enormously in size, type and orientation of space as well as differing quite markedly in teaching approach. Familiarization with such diversity on a national scale was thus essential. This was achieved by selecting twenty-seven local education authorities and requesting visits to three schools which differed in architectural design, avoiding where possible 'show' schools. A minimum of four days was spent in each authority, three of which were spent in one day visits to schools, observing practice and talking to staff. The fourth day was spent with advisers and architects. A summary of the reports written of these visits is contained in a document entitled *Journeys into Open Space* which was circulated to all LEAs and to the schools visited early in 1976. This report also provided a basis for discussion with several teacher groups which were cooperating with the project team.

The familiarization exercise was invaluable in allowing an adequate conceptualization of the complex issues involved. It formed the basis of a classification scheme of open plan schools in addition to providing a solid foundation for the development of questionnaires and observation schedules to be used later in the study.

**A Classification of Open Plan Schools**

In an earlier questionnaire to LEAs definitions of open plan had been requested. These definitions varied since some were couched in terms of architectural design and others in terms of teaching behaviours which might be expected in such buildings. However, most were reasonably consistent with the following – 'An open plan school is one in which the teaching area is not divided into classrooms as such, but which provides home bases together with joint general purpose and specialist areas'. Although useful as a basic definition, it fails to encompass diversity in design. Indeed one authority felt it necessary to provide three definitions:

| | |
|---|---|
| Open Plan | Where the building design provides a large degree of openness with divisions provided only by means of loose furniture. |
| Semi Open Plan | Where the building is generally open but teaching spaces are defined by walls which have openings within them. |
| Flexible Open Plan | Where areas can be opened out or closed off easily by means of sliding screens. |

Although more specific, these definitions were still too broad to serve as a basis for adequate classification. A scheme was therefore devised which used the teaching unit rather than the school as the focus, since a number of teaching units of differing design can often be found within the same school. Two dimensions were used to account for differences in size of unit and the type of shared facility. These were, the number of teachers the unit was designed for, and amount of shared space.

*Number of Teachers*

(i) Designed for two teachers (Pairs).
(ii) Designed for three teachers (Triples).
(iii) Designed for four teachers (Quads).
(iv) Designed for five or more teachers (Multis).

*Amount and Type of Shared Space*

(i) Shared teaching space in addition to shared practical and/or enclosed areas such as quiet rooms (Type 1).
(ii) Shared practical and/or enclosed areas but no shared teaching space (Type 2).

Observations in the initial school visits suggested that this distinction between designs which

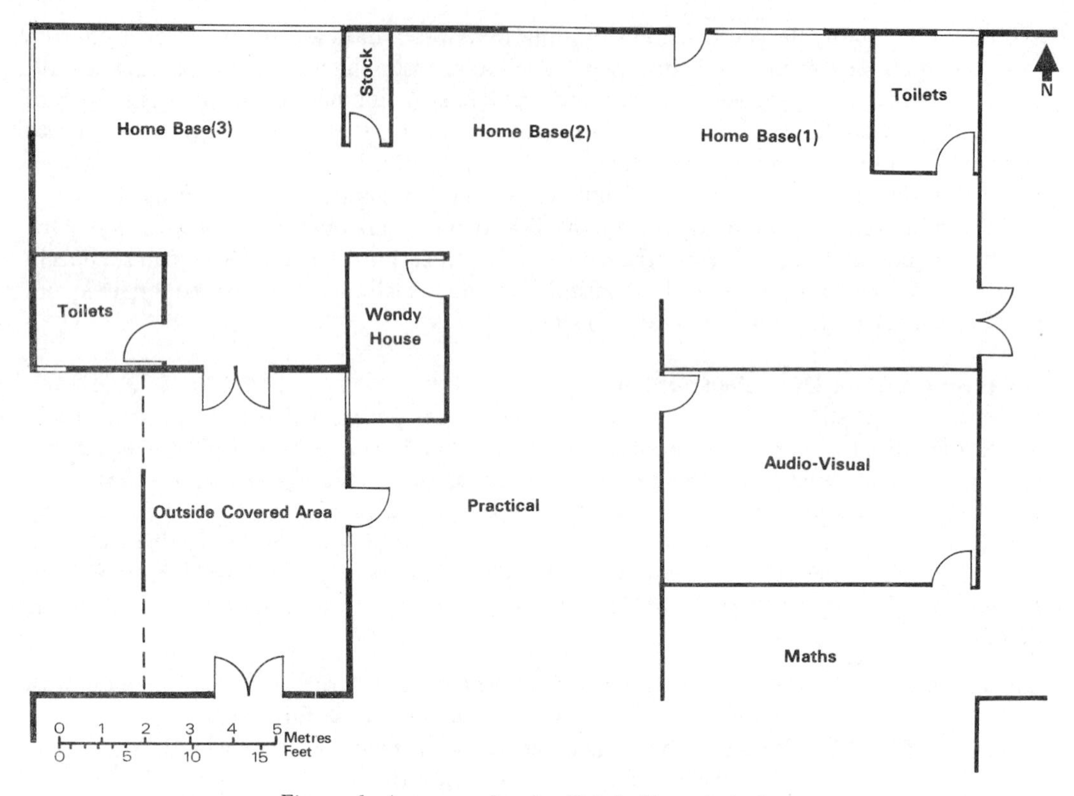


*Figure 1 An example of a Triple Type 1 design*

allowed shared teaching space and those which did not appeared to be crucial in terms of teaching organization.

The four sub-categories of Numbers of Teachers and the Type 1 – Type 2 distinction between types of shared space gave an eight-fold classification – Pair Type 1; Pair Type 2; Triple Type 1 and so on.

The simplified plans in Figures 1 and 2 serve to indicate how this classification scheme was used. Figure 1 shows an infant unit comprising three home bases all of which share the tiled practical/wet area together with two enclosures indicated as a study and a group room. There is a great deal of shared teaching space although this is a little curtailed for the teacher in home base 1 because of the siting of the store and study. The unit is designed for three teachers (and 120 pupils) and shared teaching space is available leading to the classification Triple Type 1.

Figure 2 shows a unit which is also designed for three teachers but in this instance each teacher occupies a classroom-sized bay each of which opens, through a door-sized opening, on to the shared practical/wet area. In addition they share a small enclosed quiet room. There is no shared teaching space available in this design other than use-specific spaces and it is thus classified Triple Type 2.

As might be expected, one of the trends noted in the initial school visits was for teachers in Type 2 units to operate more independently than those in Type 1 units, although this was by no means universal.

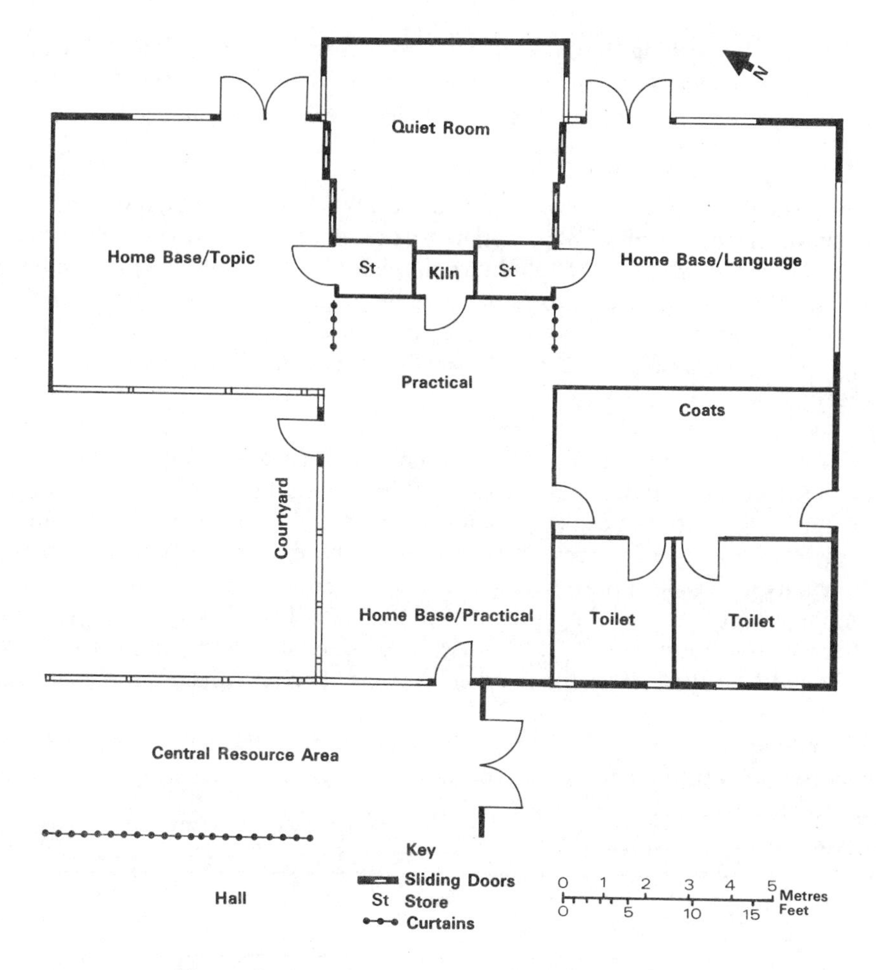


*Figure 2 An example of a Triple Type 2 design*

**Questionnaire Survey**

In an attempt to gain both breadth and depth it was decided to carry out a national survey by questionnaire, followed by observational and interview studies in selected schools.* Two questionnaires were developed, one for headteachers and one for unit teachers. The headteacher questionnaire contained sections on the school, pupils and staff, teaching and curriculum observation, consultation in design, record keeping, parents, pre- and in-service provision and aims and attitudes toward open plan. Headteachers were also requested either to forward a school plan or draw a scale plan on a matrix provided.

The teacher questionnaire included a number of the same questions, particularly on aims and attitudes, but more emphasis was placed on unit design and their perceptions of it, and

* Appendix E, *Instrumentation,* including the questionnaires, the interview schedules, the Learning Experiences Schedule, the Pupil Behaviour Schedule and the Use of Space Schedule, is available as a separate publication from the Schools Council.

further details of teaching and curriculum organization. Both questionnaires were professionally printed in a form suitable for machine reading by Document Reading Services after extensive piloting on over two hundred teachers in seventy schools.

*Sampling*

All headteachers of open plan schools in England and Wales were sent a questionnaire, as were class teachers in one third of all schools chosen on a random basis. More specifically the teacher sample was selected as follows. The full list, or population, of schools was provided by LEAs. This list was split, or stratified, into four lists containing infant, first, junior and primary schools. The schools in each list were then ordered randomly before selecting every third school, i.e. a sampling ratio of 1:3. In other words it was a stratified random sample selected systematically.

The full list numbered 2,370 schools. However, it soon became apparent that the judgements of LEA advisers and the perceptions of headteachers did not always agree. 338 headteachers wrote, often with an air of puzzlement, to explain that their school could not, on any basis, be considered open plan. This amended the population to 2,032. Of these 1,529 schools replied, giving a response rate of 75.2 per cent. This is a conservative estimate, since it assumes that all non-respondents were indeed open plan schools. This response was achieved after two follow up letters, the second incorporating a tear-off slip which asked the respondent to specify the reasons for not cooperating if they did not wish to do so. Over a hundred slips were returned, although one fifth of these did not state their reasons. The remainder did so, specifying the following reasons:

20 per cent stated that they were unhappy either: (a) with the questionnaire; (b) with all questionnaires; (c) with the open plan project; (d) with all projects.

| *Unit Type* | *Infant* | *First* | *Junior* | *Primary* |
|---|---|---|---|---|
| Pair Type 1 | 17.5 | 24.1 | 11.3 | 18.1 |
| Type 2 | 38.8 | 35.8 | 43.2 | 36.9 |
| Total | 56.3 | 59.9 | 54.5 | 55.0 |
| Triple Type 1 | 10.8 | 9.0 | 7.7 | 8.6 |
| Type 2 | 18.8 | 12.4 | 9.7 | 16.9 |
| Total | 29.6 | 21.4 | 17.4 | 25.5 |
| Quad Type 1 | 2.5 | 3.9 | 9.6 | 4.7 |
| Type 2 | 5.3 | 8.7 | 12.7 | 10.0 |
| Total | 7.8 | 11.6 | 22.3 | 14.7 |
| Multi Type 1 | 1.4 | 2.1 | 1.7 | 2.2 |
| Type 2 | 4.9 | 4.8 | 4.0 | 2.7 |
| Total | 6.3 | 6.9 | 5.7 | 4.9 |

*Table 1 Distribution of unit designs by type of school (%)*

19 per cent claimed that a new headteacher had just been appointed and it would have been unwise to complete the questionnaire with so little experience.

17 per cent said they were too busy, overworked or lacked secretarial support.

15 per cent stated that the school was currently being remodelled or extensively altered or was not yet open.

5 per cent claimed that a biassed picture would result because of large staff changes.

3 per cent said they had been discouraged by the attitude of the LEA.

Following the return of the questionnaires the teaching units were classified on the basis of the scheme outlined earlier. Table 1 shows the distribution of unit designs by type of school.

Not all headteachers returned a school plan so the trends apparent in Table 1 cannot be considered definitive. Nevertheless the two teacher unit is clearly the most prevalent design and is much more likely to be the more closed Type 2 variety in all types of school.

With the exception of junior schools the three teacher unit is the next most prevalent with the Type 2 design again more apparent. The imbalance between junior and infant schools is more marked among four teacher units. This is not too surprising considering that a one form entry school will normally have three infant and four junior classes, with multiples of these for larger intakes. The large multi unit is fairly rare, comprising some five or six per cent of all units. Here too the Type 2 design predominates. It is interesting, in the light of such evidence, to speculate on the popular stereotype of open plan schools as large, open structures.

**Observation and Interview Studies**

The entire second year of the project was devoted to observation and interview studies of selected schools. The emphasis here was on teaching and curriculum organization and use of space, a focus not only dictated by the research brief but also by the priorities of teaching staff and advisers interviewed earlier.

Three observation schedules were designed for these purposes. The first, called the Learning Experiences Schedule (LES) was developed to observe the activities of individual children. Its design resembles an activity log recording pupil activities every minute in the following categories:

| | | |
|---|---|---|
| (i) | the space occupied | e.g. Home base |
| (ii) | the curriculum context | e.g. Language |
| (iii) | the actual curriculum activity | e.g. Free reading |
| (iv) | the child's actual activity | e.g. Involved on task |
| (v) | the teaching/learning situation | e.g. Individual work |
| (vi) | the materials used | e.g. Book |
| (vii) | posture | e.g. Sitting |
| (viii) | the social scene | e.g. Not interacting with other children<br>Two teachers present in unit. |

In pilot observations it was found that two children could be observed concurrently. Thus each child was recorded every two minutes throughout the school day, excluding breaks and dinner time. In each unit six children were selected to represent the full ability range within the unit based on reading age confirmed by teacher perception. This allowed three girls and three boys of high, average and low ability to be observed. In order to control for age all observations were based on second year infants and second/third year juniors. This selection process was adopted to provide representativeness *within* the unit, but did not allow subsequent comparisons by ability *across* different units or schools because, in the extreme case, the high ability children in one unit could be at a similar level to the low ability children in another. Thus differences in patterns of activity by children of different ability can be validly ascertained within any unit, but not between units.

Observations from the second schedule, the Pupil Behaviour Schedule (PBS) provided a more general picture of pupils' activity within the unit. As with the Learning Experiences Schedule, location, posture, curriculum activity and pupil activity were recorded together with verbal interactions between pupils and between pupils and teachers.

The PBS was used to observe six children per day for four days, thereby providing information on twenty-four pupils per unit. These children were selected on the same basis as that outlined above for the LES. A time sampling procedure was adopted whereby each of the six children are observed every thirty seconds for five minutes in rotation. This cycle continued for the whole day.

The third schedule focussed entirely on use of space within the unit. This required scale drawing of the unit including furniture layout and the purpose for which each space was being used, i.e. teacher designated, not as indicated on the plan. For example the study in Figure 1 was in this instance being used as a Wendy House. Its designation on the Use of Space Schedule was therefore Wendy House. Each space was then observed every twenty minutes and a record made of the number of children occupying the space, their activities and the activities of any adults (teachers, ancillaries, parents). A location/activity matrix was then drawn up separately for morning and afternoon. This continued for three days.

The focus of the observational study was deliberately pupil-centred since it is only through the observation of pupil activities that the effects of a given organization can be perceived. This focus was balanced by long interviews with the headteacher and all the unit teachers. The interview schedules were designed to elicit information on aims and objectives, the teaching organization and how and why it had developed, curriculum organization, perceptions of design, the role of parents and attitudes to open plan. The headteacher interview touched on wider issues, including consultation in design, staffing, the provision of appropriate courses and his own role. All interviews were tape recorded and subsequently transcribed for analysis.

*Sampling*

The size of the observation sample crucially depended on the amount of time to be spent in each unit. A number of considerations were relevant here, including the number of pupils to be observed, the number of observations required to ensure reliability and validity, the constraint of having only one observer in a unit at any given time, and the additional time required for interviewing and drawing scale plans. Three weeks per unit was ultimately agreed upon, which, after deducting school holidays, enabled the three project officers to observe in twenty-three schools.

Which twenty-three schools? A statistical sample was inapplicable here, not only because the purpose of the observation was description rather than inference, but because a statistical sample would not have guaranteed the features demanded by the research brief. These were that schools covering the age range 5–11 be included, and that problems and successes be investigated. From the initial visits it became clear that more problems seemed to exist in large, open units and that team/cooperative teaching was a problematic area as far as teachers and advisers were concerned. The sample was deliberately chosen to allow an equal number of infant and junior units, and to provide a similar number of different sized units but concentrating on the more open designs. The sampling was, however, chosen to reflect the actual distribution of designs, e.g. proportionally more infant three teacher units, and four teacher junior units. The actual sampling plan is shown below.

| | | *Design Type* | | | |
|---|---|---|---|---|---|
| *Unit type* | *School type* | *Type 1* | *Type 2* | *Totals* | |
| Pairs | Infant | 1 | 1 | 2 | 5 |
| | Junior | 1 | 2 | 3 | |
| Triples | Infant | 4 | 1 | 5 | 7 |
| | Junior | 1 | 1 | 2 | |
| Quads | Infant | 0 | 1 | 1 | 5 |
| | Junior | 3 | 1 | 4 | |
| Multis | Infant | 2 | 1 | 3 | 6 |
| | Junior | 2 | 1 | 3 | |
| Total | | 14 | 9 | 23 | |

*Table 2 Observation sampling plan*

Twelve junior and eleven infant schools were chosen, including fourteen Type 1 and nine Type 2 designs. Unit size is fairly evenly split, the imbalance in triples being caused by the decision to examine two schools of identical design. These were infant Type 1 designs and account for the inflation in that cell. The inflation in the junior quad cell has already been commented on.

There is no way of knowing how representative this selection of schools or units is, even if the term representative could be defined adequately in this context. It would therefore be unwise to infer generality. They were chosen to highlight specific facets of open plan schooling and design and should be considered in this light.

The observations took place from September 1975 until July 1976 in eighteen local education authorities spread across England and Wales.

*Chapter 4*

# *The National Scene: Teaching and Curriculum Organization*

---

**Teaching Organization**

The message from previous studies is that although open plan schools provide a physical environment more conducive to teacher cooperation, there is no guarantee that cooperation will take place. Questions were therefore included to assess the extent of independent and cooperative teaching. The items were derived from organization observed in the familiarization stage of the study, supplemented by interviews with teachers and advisers. They were further refined following an extensive pilot study. Eight basic teaching organizations were isolated. At one extreme was the organization in which the teacher operated independently as she would in a conventional classroom box, and at the other extreme teachers spent most of the day in cooperative team teaching situations. The items are shown in Table 1. Both headteachers and classteachers answered these questions in relation to: (a) the organization(s) currently practised; and (b) the organization(s) they would ideally like to practice. In other words there was a recognition that for various reasons the current organization may not be the ideal. Also, since different organizations may be used for different aspects of the curriculum, or for parts of the school day, teachers were asked to respond to as many items as seemed appropriate, i.e. multiple responses were allowed. For this reason the columns in Table 1 do not add up to 100 per cent, unlike an earlier article by Bennett (1978b) where a different base was used. Tables A1 and A2 (Appendix A) present the responses of head and class teachers in infant, first, junior and primary schools. The pattern for first and primary schools is confounded by the fact that they house both infant and junior teachers. Thus, for the purposes of description and comparison the infant and junior sample is used and presented in Table 1.

The replies of the infant headteachers indicate that wholly independent teaching occurs in less than one fifth of schools, the most frequent organization being where members usually teach independently but cooperate a little with another teacher. Two fairly prevalent organizations, occurring in over one third of schools, are: where independent teaching is combined with some cooperative planning; and where teachers operate on their own for work in the basic

| Teaching Organization | Headteachers | | | | Teachers | | | |
|---|---|---|---|---|---|---|---|---|
| | Infant | | Junior | | Infant | | Junior | |
| | Actual | Ideal | Actual | Ideal | Actual | Ideal | Actual | Ideal |
| (a) Teachers operating independently | 18.7 | 7.6 | 20.1 | 6.2 | 26.4 | 15.2 | 28.6 | 14.0 |
| (b) Teachers mainly operating independently but cooperating a little with other teachers. e.g. reading story to two groups | 52.6 | 26.8 | 33.7 | 12.5 | 45.8 | 27.2 | 22.7 | 11.7 |
| (c) Teachers mainly operating independently but planning cooperatively. e.g. who teaches what, where and at what time | 37.6 | 28.7 | 41.8 | 26.7 | 16.2 | 11.2 | 24.0 | 15.5 |
| (d) Teachers operating independently for basic subjects but cooperating on project/topic work | 36.1 | 32.1 | 34.1 | 28.9 | 18.7 | 17.8 | 21.7 | 21.5 |
| (e) Teachers cooperating for basic subjects but operating independently for project/topic work | 8.4 | 7.6 | 14.3 | 9.2 | 2.2 | 2.9 | 8.2 | 6.2 |
| (f) Cooperative/team teaching planned on a day-to-day basis | 11.8 | 12.4 | 12.8 | 11.7 | 3.2 | 2.0 | 2.0 | 1.1 |
| (g) Cooperative/team teaching with each teacher specializing in certain areas of the curriculum | 12.4 | 16.1 | 22.0 | 26.4 | 7.0 | 9.4 | 14.9 | 16.5 |
| (h) Cooperative/team teaching with no teacher specialism | 14.7 | 17.6 | 17.2 | 15.0 | 12.6 | 12.2 | 9.0 | 9.6 |
| (i) Other/undecided | | 4.7 | | 4.0 | | 9.4 | | 10.6 |
| N = | 380 | | 273 | | 712 | | 759 | |

*Table 1 Actual and ideal teaching organizations of head and class teachers in infant and junior schools (%)*

skill areas but cooperate on projects and topic work. Team/cooperative teaching also occurs in over one third of schools (i.e. a combination of items f, g and h), a slight preference being shown for an organization without teacher specialism.

Headteachers were replying in terms of the whole school, whereas class teachers replied in terms of practices in their own unit. Some discrepancy is therefore to be expected. Teachers claim that independent teaching is more frequent than the headteachers had indicated. Over a quarter stated they were teaching wholly independently and far fewer, about one in six, were planning cooperatively or cooperating on project work. Only a fifth claimed to be team/cooperatively teaching, and here there is a much clearer preference for team teaching without teacher specialism.

The views of head and class teachers on ideal organization is similar in that both anticipate a decrease in independence. However, unlike their heads, the teachers do not foresee an increase in team teaching, and nearly one in ten are undecided about what form their ideal organization might take.

The pattern of response from junior headteachers indicates that there is somewhat less independent teaching and correspondingly more team/cooperative teaching in junior schools. About one half claim to be using some variant of team teaching, but here the most popular form is that involving teacher specialism.

But here too there is quite a marked discrepancy between the perceptions of the headteachers and their class teachers. Nearly one in three teachers state that they teach wholly independently, and aproximately one in five claim that they sometimes cooperate, either in planning or project work. The greatest disparity between head and teachers is in the frequency of team/cooperative teaching. Only one quarter of teachers state that they teach in this way, but they confirm the popularity of teacher specialism. Both heads and teachers view their ideal organization as a decrease in independent teaching. However, the comparison between actual and ideal organization may not be completely accurate since although most used multiple coding on actual organization, fewer did so in relation to ideal organization.

Replies to another item on the questionnaire show that 80 per cent of teams comprise two or three teachers and that the proportion of the school day devoted to team teaching varies from less than 5 per cent of the day to the whole day. On average those who team teach in both infant and junior schools do so for 35 per cent of the day.

The smooth running of organization based on teaming, indeed most organizations, appeared in initial visits to schools to be in part dependent on the amount of ancillary help available in the unit. In fact, some organizations depended quite clearly on the presence of an ancillary in specified spaces, e.g. stationed in a practical area, where the visibility of the practical area from the teaching area was poor. This allowed teachers to send groups of children into these areas, knowing that materials would be supplied and supervision given. Responses to the questionnaire showed that infant schools are better provided with such help. 65 per cent of infant teachers said they had ancillary help, against only 27 per cent of junior teachers.

*Teaching Organization and Design of Teaching Unit*

The design of teaching units varies enormously in open plan schools, often even in the same school. It is therefore important to ascertain whether teachers feel that organization varies in relation to the type and orientation of space available. In answering this question, it seemed more appropriate to analyse in terms of the age of children taught, i.e. 5–8 year olds and 8–11 year olds, rather than in terms of types of school, i.e. infant, first, junior and primary, since this gave a larger sample size. These analyses are therefore based on teachers of infant and junior age children, irrespective of the designation of their school.

Table A3 and A4 in Appendix A provide the full results, from which it can be seen that the apparent differences relate more to the openness of the unit (Type 1/Type 2) than to the number of teachers the unit was designed for. This is shown graphically in Figures 1 and 2.

Clear differences in organization in infant Type 1 and Type 2 units can be seen in Figure 1, particularly when considering the first two and last two organizations. In the more open Type 1 units, 57.7 of teachers indicated that they used independent teaching or independent teaching with minimal cooperation, whereas in the most closed Type 2 units, it is 79.6 per cent. This pattern is reversed when considering team or cooperative teaching. In Type 1, team teaching, with or without specialization is 27.9 per cent against 13.2 per cent in Type 2 units. There thus seems to be a clear link between openness in unit design and openness in teaching organization. This same pattern is apparent in large or small units. Variations in pattern in relation to size of unit only occurs in organizations (d) and (e), whereby cooperation for projects occurs slightly more often in the smaller Type 1 units than the larger ones. Cooperation in basic subjects on the other hand is somewhat more likely in the larger Type 1 units.

Variations in organization also occur in junior units although they are less marked than in infant units, as Figure 2 shows.
Independent teaching and independent teaching with minimal cooperation occurs 35.8 per cent in Type 1, and 56 per cent in Type 2 units. This is less than infant units, but is accounted for by the greater popularity of organizations (c) and (d) in junior units. The incidence of team or cooperative teaching is also higher, but the pattern remains – 30.3 per cent in Type 1 and 16.7 per cent in Type 2 units. It was indicated earlier that team teaching involving teacher specialism is more frequent in junior units and this is particularly noticeable in two teacher Type 1 units.

Another factor of interest in relation to unit design is the timetabling of space. This is less common in two and four teacher units, irrespective of openness, but is very prevalent in the more open triple and multi units. For example, in the junior multi Type 1 units, 85 per cent timetabled space, whereas only 11 per cent did so in Type 2 units. Possible reasons for this will be considered later.

*Pupil Groupings*
How are pupils assigned to teachers or classes? As might be expected from other recent studies, streaming, or allocation on the basis of ability, is fairly rare. It is least apparent at infant level, averaging 3.5 per cent to over 8 per cent at primary level. In the vast majority of cases allocation is done on the basis of age. However this does not necessarily imply a single age grouping. With the exception of junior schools the majority have implemented some form of vertical grouping as can be seen in Table 2.

The age span of such groupings varies, although that involving a four year range is rare. The most popular is a 1½–2 year span. Junior schools are out of step on this issue both in practice and attitude. This can be seen from Table 3, which shows the responses of headteachers to the question 'Do you favour vertical grouping of pupils?' The junior heads vote seven to three against, whereas the remainder are split 50:50.

These assignments and grouping arrangements tend to be school-based rather than teacher- or unit-based decisions. This leaves the teacher some freedom concerning whether or how to

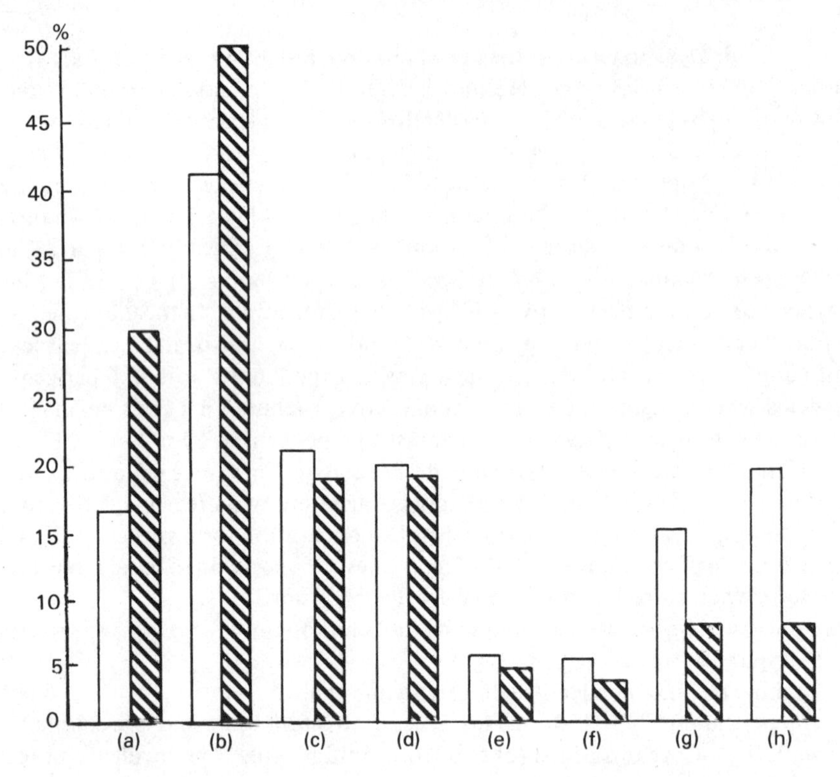


KEY
Type 1
Type 2

(a) Usually operate as an independent teacher

(b) Mainly independent but cooperate a little with other teachers

(c) Mainly independent but plan cooperatively

(d) Independent for basic subjects but cooperate on project/topic work

(e) Cooperate for basic subjects but independent for project/topic work

(f) Usually cooperative/team teaching but without a lot of prior planning

(g) Usually cooperative/team teaching with each teacher specializing in certain areas of the curriculum

(h) Usually cooperative/team teaching with no teacher specialism

*Figure 1 Teaching organization of infant teachers by design of unit (%)*

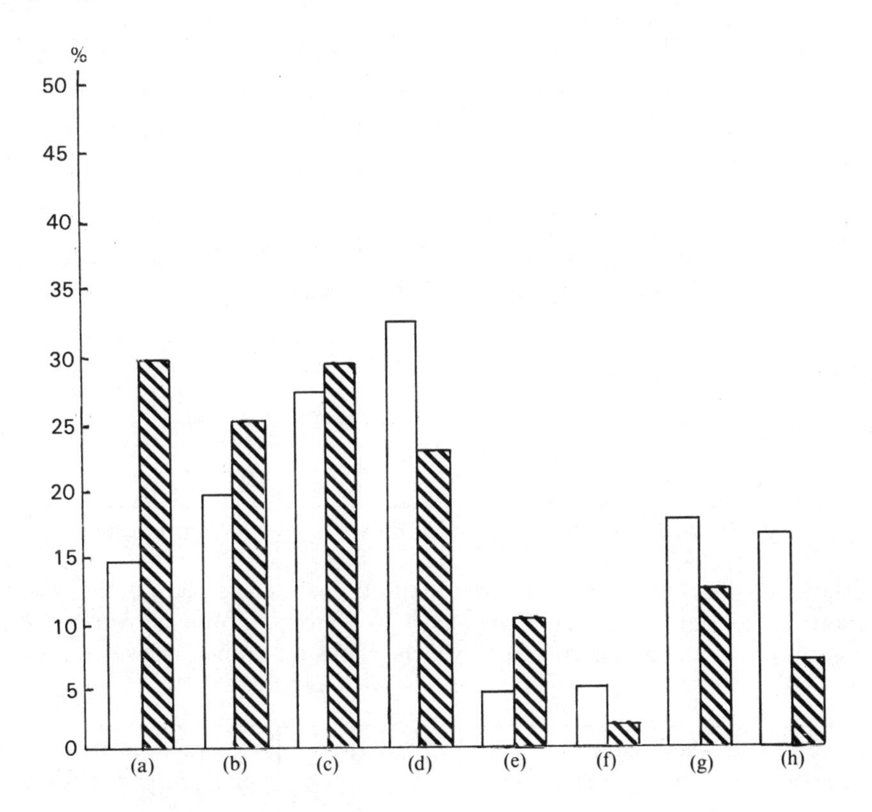


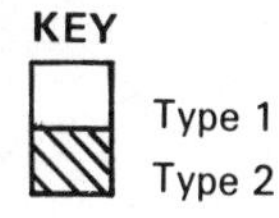


(a) Usually operate as an independent teacher

(b) Mainly independent but cooperate a little with other teachers

(c) Mainly independent but plan cooperatively

(d) Independent for basic subjects but cooperate on project/topic work

(e) Cooperate for basic subjects but independent for project/topic work

(f) Usually cooperative/team teaching but without a lot of prior planning

(g) Usually cooperative/team teaching with each teacher specializing in certain areas of the curriculum

(h) Usually cooperative/team teaching with no teacher specialism

*Figure 2 Teaching organization of junior teachers by design of unit (%)*

| | *Infant* | *First* | *Junior* | *Primary* |
|---|---|---|---|---|
| 1 year span | 48.3 | 41.9 | 64.5 | 34.2 |
| 1½ - 2 year span | 36.9 | 50.0 | 30.3 | 51.0 |
| 3 year span | 14.2 | 7.0 | 2.6 | 12.0 |
| 4 year span | 0.7 | 1.0 | 2.6 | 2.8 |

*Table 2 Age span of pupil groupings (%)*

| | *Infant* | *First* | *Junior* | *Primary* |
|---|---|---|---|---|
| Yes | 49.9 | 44.7 | 29.1 | 47.9 |
| No | 50.1 | 55.3 | 70.9 | 52.1 |

*Table 3 Percentage of headteachers in favour of vertical groupings*

group for work activities. In practice the vast majority of teachers place pupils in groups, although this does not imply that pupils then work as a group. Group size varies, the most popular being groups of 5 or 6. The criteria on which groups are formed also varies, as Table 4 shows.

| *Pupils placed for work by* | *Infant* | *Junior* |
|---|---|---|
| (a) age | 19.8 | 6.5 |
| (b) ability | 57.4 | 40.2 |
| (c) friendship | 24.7 | 34.3 |
| (d) random grouping | 41.4 | 50.9 |

*Table 4 Bases of group formation: infant and junior teachers (%)*

This pattern is somewhat surprising in that it shows that nearly 60 per cent of infant teachers group by ability for some aspect of curriculum. Dixon (1978) has also commented on this, claiming that open plan schools promote 'hidden streaming'. She argued that teachers take elaborate steps to conceal this grouping from parents to avoid having to justify themselves. Other interpretations are of course possible. If any justifications are required they are to be found in the Plowden Report which approved grouping within class on the basis of similar ability or attainment. It could be perceived to be the best compromise in individualizing instruction given current class sizes.

Nevertheless grouping by ability is used less by junior teachers where random grouping is most practised. The multiple responses to this item would indicate that groupings change for different activities.

**Summary**

The evidence gained would seem to support that found in earlier studies. There is no guarantee that, because a physical environment is provided which allows cooperative teaching ventures, such approaches will be used by teachers. In Britain many more teachers appear to be operating independently or with minimal cooperation than in team or cooperative groups. It is also clear that the design of the unit has an effect. There is much more independent teaching and less cooperative teaching in the less open Type 2 units. This general pattern could, of course, reflect an interim state which may change over time. Certainly many head and class teachers feel that less independence and more cooperation constitute the ideal.

**Curriculum Organization**

Previous studies have provided little information about how teachers in open plan schools organize the curriculum, although the Strathclyde study did point out the prevalence of what is termed here the split day – basics in the mornings and project, art and craft and so on in the afternoons. In the light of the paucity of information the questionnaire items on curriculum organization were derived from initial school visits and were refined after pilot studies. Seven basic arrangements were perceived. The first two are based on assignment systems. Pupils are presented with their assignments at the beginning of the day, or in some cases at the beginning of the week. In some instances the teacher determines the order in which these will be carried out but in others pupils are given choice as to the order. The third system has been termed the rolling timetable and consists of a number of curriculum activities which are repeated. A simple system would be maths, language, creative activities, followed by maths, language, creative activities . . . The number of activities comprising the curriculum varies.

The fourth organization is the split day referred to above, and the fifth a teacher-directed curriculum which is less rigid, varying as the teacher feels it necessary. The sixth and seventh are both thematically based, the first involving project/topic work chosen by the teacher, and the second the same system but involving a high degree of pupil choice.

The results for head and class teachers in infant, first, junior and primary schools are presented in Tables A5 and A6 in Appendix A, and the responses from infant and junior schools are presented in Table 5 overleaf.

The curriculum organization in infant schools as perceived by headteachers shows an emphasis on assignment systems and the split day. Fewer schools claim to be using a wholly thematic approach. The pattern provided by infant teachers does not show a wide divergence.

The ideal organization as perceived by headteachers is not too dissimilar to actual practice, although there is a trend to move away from the split day and teacher-directed approaches. It was not possible to ascertain the ideal organization from infant teachers because of a small printing error in the questionnaire which could have led to distortion.

Curriculum organization in junior schools shows quite a different pattern. The picture portrayed by headteachers shows the domination of the split day approach, used in seven out of every ten schools. Assignment systems are also used, but the rolling timetable variant is not favoured. Neither are thematic approaches, which are used in one school in six. This same pattern is true of junior teacher responses. The percentages here are lower since less multiple responses were given, as might be expected, since they were reporting on a more specific context.

The headteachers' views of their ideal organization are not dissimilar to actual practice, although there is a trend for more emphasis on thematic approaches at the expense of the split day.

| Curriculum Organization | Headteachers | | | | Teachers | |
|---|---|---|---|---|---|---|
| | Infant | | Junior | | Infant | Junior |
| | *Actual* | *Ideal* | *Actual* | *Ideal* | *Actual* | *Ideal* |
| (a) Pupils being given assignments at the beginning of the day or week to be carried out in the order given by the teacher | 21.3 | 15.0 | 27.8 | 19.4 | 14.5 | 12.8 |
| (b) As (a) but pupils given free choice as to the order in which they carry out assignments | 22.1 | 22.9 | 25.3 | 22.3 | 15.0 | 15.4 |
| (c) Pupils being assigned a basic curriculum consisting of a given number of activities which are repeated. Teachers sometimes call this a 'rolling timetable'. e.g. maths, creative work, English, followed by maths, creative work, English, etc. | 25.5 | 22.4 | 15.4 | 13.2 | 26.1 | 10.8 |
| (d) Basics being usually covered in the morning and creative activities/topic work in the afternoon | 41.8 | 31.8 | 69.2 | 49.1 | 36.4 | 63.2 |
| (e) Curriculum mainly taught by the teacher but varying from day-to-day | 28.7 | 16.8 | 25.6 | 17.2 | 22.6 | 20.8 |
| (f) Major emphasis on project/topic work (incorporating basics) mainly chosen by the teacher | 16.6 | 14.7 | 14.3 | 15.4 | 10.0 | 8.6 |
| (g) Major emphasis on project/topic work (incorporating basics) mainly chosen by the pupils | 8.2 | 9.7 | 3.7 | 5.1 | 3.7 | 0.9 |
| (h) Other/undecided | | 4.5 | | 3.7 | | |

*Table 5 Ideal and actual curriculum organization: headteachers and teachers in infant and junior schools (%)*

*Curriculum Organization and Design of Teaching Unit*
This analysis took the same form as that for teaching organization. Teachers were grouped into those teaching 5–8 year olds and 8–11 year olds, irrespective of type of schools taught in. The findings are less clear-cut than those for teaching organization.

Table 6 shows the organizations for each design of infant teaching unit, together with an average for Type 1 and Type 2 units. An inspection of these averages would indicate that whether the unit is more or less open would seem to make little difference. This is because the averages mask marked differences due to the size of the unit. Two, three and four teacher units can be taken together when considering infants because they share a similar organizational pattern. In each of these the split day is more prevalent in the less open Type 2 units, as is the teacher-centred approach. On the other hand there is a tendency for assignment systems to be more popular in the more open Type 1 units. There is little consistency when thematic approaches are considered.

Curriculum organization in the large units containing more than four teachers is quite different, presenting almost a reversal of the pattern found in the smaller units. Here the split day is more prevalent in the more open units and assignment systems in the more closed units. Also of interest is the comparatively high incidence of thematic approaches in both designs, more than double that of the smaller units. This reversal is difficult to explain. The large units are more difficult to organize and the organizations seen in initial visits varied widely. Some attempt to cope with large teaching teams whereas others break down the total space into smaller areas. In one school the head had bought wood from school funds to make this permanent, but others use screens or furniture for this purpose. The reversal in pattern is not apparent in junior units and may thus relate to the age of children taught.

In junior units (Table 7) there are consistent differences in organization in relation to the degrees of openness of the unit.

The split day and teacher-centred approaches predominate in the less open designs, whereas assignment systems and thematic approaches are more prevalent in more open designs. These patterns generally hold irrespective of size of unit, with the exception of thematic organizations. These vary markedly in relation to the number of teachers in the unit, presenting a pattern similar to that found in infant areas. They are more prevalent in two and three teacher Type 2 units, but in the large multi units they are very popular in the more open, and unpopular in the more closed units.

*Record Keeping*
The recent Green Paper (1977) came out strongly in favour of record keeping, arguing that clear and reliable records of progress are necessary if individual help and counselling are to be provided. 'The keeping and transmission of records should be systematic and understandable; they should be subject to clearly understood and agreed controls on what information is kept and what is not; and on what is disseminated and to whom; and full regard must be paid to the rights of parents, as well as those of teachers and pupils, to know what material is included.' They proposed that LEAs review existing practices covering the records themselves, arrangements for parents to see records and the currency the records should have.

An extensive investigation into record keeping was not considered necessary in this study since a project on record keeping is currently funded by the Schools Council at the National Foundation for Educational Research. Nevertheless items on record keeping were included in

| Curriculum Organization | Type | Pairs | | Triples | | Quads | | Multis | | Average | |
|---|---|---|---|---|---|---|---|---|---|---|---|
| | | 1 | 2 | 1 | 2 | 1 | 2 | 1 | 2 | 1 | 2 |
| (a) Pupils are given assignments at the beginning of the day or week and pupils carry out these assignments in the order given by the teacher | | 20.5 | 17.6 | 13.3 | 14.1 | 26.2 | 14.3 | 13.5 | 27.2 | 18.4 | 18.3 |
| (b) As (a) but pupils are given free choice as to the order in which they are carried out | | 16.5 | 13.0 | 17.2 | 13.4 | 18.7 | 12.6 | 13.5 | 24.3 | 16.5 | 15.8 |
| (c) Groups of pupils are assigned a basic curriculum consisting of a given number of activities which are repeated. Teachers sometimes call this a 'rolling timetable'. e.g. maths, creative work, English, followed by maths, creative work, English, etc. | | 18.9 | 17.8 | 26.6 | 20.3 | 17.8 | 17.7 | 16.2 | 17.5 | 19.9 | 18.3 |
| (d) Basics usually covered in the morning and creative activities/topic work in the afternoon | | 44.4 | 51.4 | 38.6 | 48.4 | 32.7 | 46.9 | 54.1 | 35.0 | 42.5 | 45.4 |
| (e) Curriculum mainly taught by the teacher but varied from day-to-day | | 19.2 | 22.2 | 21.9 | 27.5 | 21.5 | 22.9 | 24.3 | 16.5 | 21.7 | 22.3 |
| (f) Major emphasis on project/topic work (incorporating basics) mainly chosen by the teacher | | 7.1 | 9.2 | 8.2 | 4.7 | 3.7 | 6.3 | 19.8 | 16.5 | 9.7 | 9.2 |
| (g) Major emphasis on project/topic work (incorporating basics) mainly chosen by the pupils | | 0.7 | 2.6 | 5.6 | 1.9 | 1.9 | 1.1 | 3.6 | 5.8 | 3.0 | 2.9 |
| | N = | 297 | 455 | 233 | 320 | 107 | 175 | 111 | 103 | 748 | 1053 |

*Table 6 Curriculum organization of infant teachers by type of unit (%)*

| Curriculum Organization | Type | Pairs | | Triples | | Quads | | Multis | | Average | |
|---|---|---|---|---|---|---|---|---|---|---|---|
| | | 1 | 2 | 1 | 2 | 1 | 2 | 1 | 2 | 1 | 2 |
| (a) Pupils are given assignments at the beginning of the day or week and pupils carry out these assignments in the order given by the teacher | | 21.6 | 13.0 | 22.9 | 8.5 | 14.7 | 17.5 | 21.6 | 7.8 | 20.2 | 11.7 |
| (b) As (a) but pupils are given free choice as to the order in which they are carried out | | 29.3 | 18.0 | 22.9 | 21.5 | 25.3 | 12.1 | 12.2 | 18.2 | 22.4 | 17.5 |
| (c) Groups of pupils are assigned a basic curriculum consisting of a given number of activities which are repeated. Teachers sometimes call this a 'rolling timetable'. e.g. maths, creative work, English, followed by maths, creative work, English, etc. | | 14.4 | 9.0 | 18.1 | 7.7 | 7.4 | 13.1 | 16.2 | 9.1 | 14.0 | 9.7 |
| (d) Basics usually covered in the morning and creative activities/topic work in the afternoon | | 53.9 | 63.2 | 45.7 | 67.7 | 43.2 | 52.4 | 41.9 | 49.4 | 46.2 | 58.2 |
| (e) Curriculum mainly taught by the teacher but varies from day-to-day | | 18.0 | 18.0 | 15.2 | 26.9 | 16.8 | 27.2 | 25.7 | 33.8 | 18.9 | 26.5 |
| (f) Major emphasis on project/topic work (incorporating basics) mainly chosen by teacher | | 4.8 | 8.1 | 8.6 | 11.5 | 8.4 | 4.9 | 24.3 | 2.6 | 11.5 | 6.8 |
| (g) Major emphasis on project/topic work (incorporating basics) mainly chosen by the pupils | | 0.6 | 1.2 | 1.0 | 0.8 | 0.0 | 0.5 | 1.4 | 0.0 | 0.8 | 0.6 |
| | N = | 167 | 345 | 105 | 130 | 95 | 206 | 74 | 77 | 441 | 758 |

*Table 7 Curriculum organization of junior teachers by type of unit (%)*

the questionnaire. Analyses of these established that records were almost universally kept although there were differences in who they were kept by. In infant schools 85 per cent of teachers stated that only they kept records, whereas in junior schools 45 per cent of teachers indicated that records were kept by both teacher and pupil.

The type and frequency of record keeping varied between infant and junior teachers, as Tables 8 and 9 show.

| *Infants* | *Daily* | *Weekly* | *Termly* | *Yearly* |
|---|---|---|---|---|
| Basic skills | 59.0 | 31.7 | 21.6 | 4.4 |
| Project/topic work | 3.9 | 36.8 | 35.1 | 4.8 |
| Social/emotional development | 4.4 | 8.8 | 58.8 | 20.5 |
| Physical skills | 2.4 | 10.3 | 52.7 | 19.8 |

*Table 8 Type and frequency of record keeping: infants (%)*

| *Juniors* | *Daily* | *Weekly* | *Termly* | *Yearly* |
|---|---|---|---|---|
| Basic skills | 35.3 | 52.0 | 17.3 | 5.5 |
| Project/topic work | 4.0 | 42.3 | 38.5 | 5.4 |
| Social/emotional development | 1.6 | 5.4 | 43.9 | 37.9 |
| Physical skills | 0.7 | 7.9 | 33.6 | 41.0 |

*Table 9 Type and frequency of record keeping: juniors (%)*

Nearly six in ten infant teachers keep records of basic skills daily, almost twice that in junior schools. Junior teachers rely more on weekly records. Those on project work tend to be weekly or termly in both infant and junior schools, reflecting the longer time base of such activities. This is also true of socio-emotional and physical development, although in each case junior teachers are much more likely than their infant counterparts to record these yearly than termly.

Identical questions were asked of head and class teachers concerning the communication of progress to parents. Table 10 shows the frequency with which written reports are sent to parents as perceived by head and class teachers in infant and junior schools. The practices in these schools are quite different and in both instances the headteachers present a more optimistic picture.

Over sixty per cent of junior schools send a written report once a year and another one in five sends one twice a year. According to the headteachers only about 14 per cent of schools send no

| | *Infant* | | *Junior* | |
|---|---|---|---|---|
| | Head | Teacher | Head | Teacher |
| Once yearly | 34.1 | 24.3 | 67.1 | 60.3 |
| Twice yearly | 7.6 | 3.7 | 18.3 | 19.4 |
| Thrice yearly | 1.5 | 0.9 | 0.9 | 1.3 |
| Not at all | 56.8 | 71.7 | 13.7 | 19.1 |

*Table 10 Frequency of written reports: head and class teachers in infant and junior schools (%)*

written reports. The position is somewhat reversed at infant level, where the majority send no written report at all, and about one in three send one annually.

Is this because infant schools rely much more on face to face contact with parents? Table 11 shows the frequency with which parents are met.

| | *Infant* | | *Junior* | |
|---|---|---|---|---|
| | Head | Teacher | Head | Teacher |
| Once yearly | 26.3 | 36.4 | 21.3 | 33.6 |
| Twice yearly | 38.6 | 35.5 | 45.8 | 51.5 |
| Thrice yearly | 34.0 | 26.4 | 32.4 | 14.5 |
| Not at all | 1.1 | 1.7 | 0.4 | 0.4 |

*Table 11 Frequency of parental contact: head and class teachers in infant and junior schools (%)*

The answer would seem to be not. One third of both junior and infant schools see parents three times a year according to headteachers, but a greater proportion of junior schools see parents twice a year. Meetings between parents and teachers apparently occur less frequently. The discrepancy between the replies of head and class teachers is probably because parents tend to see the headteacher when a difficulty arises, rather than the class teacher. This explanation is supported by an analysis of extra comments made by the headteachers on their questionnaires. For example, 61 claimed that parents are welcomed at any time, 27 said that parents are seen by appointment or on request, and a similar number stated that parents are seen regularly according to individual requirements. It might be surmised that on most of these occasions the parent might see the head but not necessarily the teacher. These analyses brought one or two interesting practices to light – 'One hour is set aside for parents after school one day per week'; 'In addition to parents' meetings the school holds one "Fathers Evening" per year'; and 'all exercise books are sent home when complete'.

Nevertheless the evidence gathered would indicate that junior schools keep parents more informed about the progress of the children through written reports and formal parental contact than do infant schools, although informal contacts with parents, e.g. at the end of the school day, is no doubt higher at infant level. Evidence concerning the prevalence of parent–teacher associations supports the above evidence. Less than 30 per cent of infant schools have a formally constituted PTA, whereas nearly half of junior schools have one.

| *Activity participated in* | *Infant* | *Junior* |
|---|---|---|
| General help | 96.7 | 89.8 |
| Cooking, sewing | 95.0 | 87.6 |
| Library | 71.0 | 65.9 |
| Listening to pupils read | 71.3 | 79.5 |
| PE and games | 30.9 | 55.3 |

*Table 12 Frequency and type of parental participation in infant and junior schools (%)*

Findings on parental involvement provide a counterbalance. More infant than junior headteachers favour parental involvement in the day-to-day activities of the school – 72 per cent to 62 per cent, and more claim that parents actually participate, 65 per cent compared with 50 per cent. The activities in which parents commonly participate are shown below in Table 12.

It is claimed that between 5 and 10 per cent of parents participate and that headteachers prefer this participation to be on a regular basis by previous agreement.

Headteachers were also asked about any apprehension that parents may have felt about their children attending an open plan school. The extent of this apprehension did not vary across infant and junior level. One in eight parents were reported to be very apprehensive, one half somewhat apprehensive and the remainder not apprehensive. However, it was claimed that this had decreased or disappeared altogether in the majority of parents. It remains somewhat higher among parents of junior children, where 18 per cent of parents continue to be apprehensive.

When asked what the bases of this apprehension were heads replied that standards in the basic subjects, teaching methods and disciplines were, in that order, predominant. Parents obviously translated this concern into pressure on the headteacher for changes in organization. However, it is abundantly clear that this pressure had little effect in most cases. 98 per cent of headteachers claimed that no changes had been made in response to such pressure. This could of course be interpreted in a number of ways – that it was felt that the apprehension was unfounded, that heads are convinced in the efficacy of their current organization, that parents have no right to a voice in matters relating to curriculum and methods, or that the responses were based on bravado. This last alternative is included since in initial visits there were headteachers who had bowed to parental pressure, usually orchestrated by knowledgeable middle-class parents. The pressure was for more emphasis on the basic skills within a formally taught framework.

**Summary**

The organizational pattern is dominated by the prevalence of the split day, particularly at junior school level, as was the case in Strathclyde.

The relationship between design and organization is complex and differs at infant and junior level. In infant schools the size of the teaching unit was more important than openness, but this trend is reversed in junior units.

The data on record keeping indicate that records are invariably kept but that their emphasis and frequency varies in infant and junior schools. Junior schools tend to keep parents more informed of progress, both by written reports and parental contact. They are also more likely to have a PTA. On the other hand, parental involvement is higher in infant schools. Initial parent apprehension about standards of work and teaching methods appears to have died down in the main, although some have attempted to exert pressure for organizational change, with little or no success.

*Chapter 5*

# *The National Survey: Aims and Attitudes*

---

**Aims of Education**

Two recent studies have investigated the stated aims of primary school teachers (Ashton *et al.*, 1975; Bennett, 1976), but neither provided any information on the aims of teachers in open plan schools. A section in the questionnaire was thus devoted to this, in order to ascertain to which aims such teachers attach most importance, and, as a subsidiary question, to assess whether the stated aims of teachers in open plan schools differed from those in conventional schools. Fifteen aims were derived from the earlier studies, providing a balance between those relating to social and intellectual areas. Teachers and headteachers were asked to respond to each of these aims in terms of their importance on a five point scale, from 'of no importance' to 'of utmost importance'. Separate analyses were carried out for head and class teachers in infant, first, junior and primary schools.

Table A7 (Appendix A) presents the mean scores of each aim and a corresponding rank order for headteachers. For presentation the aims have been grouped in much the same way as in the Ashton *et al.* study. Thus, mean scores of 4.5 and above are designated 'of utmost importance'; 4.0 to 4.4 'of major importance'; 3.5 to 3.9 'very important'; and 3.0 to 3.4 'important'.

The importance which headteachers attached to the aims varied little in relation to type of school and are as follows:

*Utmost Importance*

To enable the child to develop as a happy, cheerful and well-balanced individual.

To equip the child with basic skills in reading, writing and number.

*Major Importance*

To encourage the child to be tolerant, respecting and appreciating the feelings and views of others.

To encourage the child to learn how to learn.
To develop in the child good attitudes to work.
To help children to learn to cooperate with each other.
To enable the child as an individual to come to terms with and live in society.
To inculcate good standards of behaviour.

*Very Important*
To develop the child's creative abilities to the full.
To help the child to find enjoyment in all aspects of school life.
To develop in the child a high level of oracy.
To encourage the child to conform to the accepted morals and values of our society.
To encourage self-expression.

*Important*
To promote a high level of academic attainment.
To prepare the child for academic work in the secondary school.

The relative importance of these aims as perceived by class teachers is shown in Table A8 (Appendix A). This shows that little variation exists in different types of school and that there is a high degree of congruency in the views of head and class teachers. For both, the aims of most importance relate to the all-round development of the child socially, emotionally and intellectually. However, it is interesting to ponder the seeming conceptual split in the minds of primary teachers of the development of basic skills on the one hand and the promotion of academic attainment on the other. Although the latter is seen as important, it appears at the bottom of the rank order, whereas the former appears at the top. It could be that the term academic has a particular connotation in teachers' minds.

The aims grouped under major importance are mostly in the social area relating to the development of caring, cooperative, empathic yet conforming behaviour. The two aims relating to school work bear on the development of good attitudes to work and learning how to learn. Both encompass the ideal of the independent learner.

The development of creative ability and the encouragement of self-expression come within the 'very important' category, together with the development of oracy. The two remaining aims relate to social and moral behaviour. Teachers wish their pupils to enjoy all aspects of school life within the confines of accepted moral values.

The two aims which consistently came lowest in the rank order, although still considered important, both related to academic work – the promotion of a high level of academic attainment and preparation for secondary school. Not surprisingly the average score for the latter aims was a little lower among infant teachers.

How do the aims of teachers in open plan schools compare with those of their counterparts in conventionally designed schools? Two sources for such a comparison are available. Ashton *et al.* (1975) gained a national sample of 1,513 infant, junior and primary school teachers for their *Aims of Primary Education* study, and Bennett *et al.* (1976) reported the aims of 468 top junior teachers in junior and primary schools in Lancashire and Cumbria, all in conventional buildings. A completely accurate comparison cannot be made because different numbers of aims were used in each investigation. Nevertheless since the aims in the present enquiry were derived from the above studies a measure of comparison is possible.

*Aims of utmost importance*

| *Aims* | *Open Plan Schools* | *Aims of Primary Education* | *Teaching Styles* |
|---|---|---|---|
| To enable the child to develop as a happy, cheerful and well-balanced individual | 4.5 | 4.5 | – |
| To equip the child with basic skills in reading, writing and number | 4.6 | – | 4.8 |

The average score for the first aim is identical in the current and *Aims* study, whereas the mean was somewhat higher for the basic skills aim in Teaching Styles. The difference is slight and could be confounded by the differing types of response required in that study, i.e. the scale varied from 'essential' to 'not important' rather than 'of utmost importance' to 'of no importance'. The aims in the Ashton study were much more specific, reading, writing and arithmetic being considered separately. 'Reading with understanding' averaged 4.5 and 'reading fluently and accurately' 4.3. Aspects of arithmetic tended to fall into the 'very important' category of that study, and writing clear and meaningful English lower still in the 'important' category. Nevertheless the indications are that few differences emerge among teachers in different schools on these two aims.

*Aims of major importance*

| *Aims* | *Open Plan Schools* | *Aims of Primary Education* | *Teaching Styles* |
|---|---|---|---|
| Tolerant, respecting and appreciating views of others | 4.2 | 4.0 | – |
| Encourage to learn how to learn | 4.2 | 3.6* | – |
| Develop good attitudes to work | 4.0 | 4.3* | – |
| Help children learn to cooperate | 4.1 | 3.9 | 4.0 |
| Come to terms with society | 4.0 | – | 3.9* |

The starred scores indicate that the aims were not stated in identical form but that the meaning appears to be the same. For example the counterpart of the 'learning how to learn' aim in the Ashton study was 'developing the ability to plan independent work and organise his own time'. It was in relation to this aim that the only discrepancy appeared, a higher rating being accorded in open plan schools.

*Very important aims*

| *Aims* | *Open Plan Schools* | *Aims of Primary Education* | *Teaching Styles* |
|---|---|---|---|
| Develop creative abilities | 3.8 | 3.6 | 3.7 |
| Enjoyment of school life | 3.9 | – | 3.9 |
| Develop oracy | 3.7 | 4.0*<br>3.2 | – |
| Conform to accepted morals and values | 3.6 | 4.4*<br>3.8 | – |
| Encourage self-expression | 3.7 | – | 3.8 |

The average scores for the 'very important' aims are similar in each study. The starred scores indicate that two similar items appeared in the Ashton study which relate to the question asked. For example, on oracy, the two similar aims were 'the child should know how to convey his meaning clearly and accurately through speech', and 'the child should know how to speak in a clear and fluent manner'.

*Important aims*

| *Aims* | *Open Plan Schools* | *Aims of Primary Education* | *Teaching Styles* |
|---|---|---|---|
| High level of academic attainment | 3.1 | – | 2.6 |
| Preparation for secondary school | 3.1 | | 3.0 |

These two aims were identical in this and the Teaching Styles study, allowing direct comparison. On this evidence open plan teachers tend to stress a high level of attainment slightly more than the junior teachers in Lancashire and Cumbria.

**Summary**

The hierarchy of the aims of head and class teachers in open plan schools are very similar and appear not to differ markedly from those of teachers in conventional schools. This is borne out by a remark often heard in open plan schools during initial visits, that the architecture of a school does not determine aims but may affect their implementation.

**Attitudes to Open Plan**

A number of earlier studies have ascertained the attitudes of teachers to open plan schools, and these, plus interviews in the familiarization stage of the study, provided a pool of items for the attitude section of the questionnaire. The 'Attitude to Open Plan' section in the teachers' questionnaire comprised forty-four items to which response was required on a five point scale ranging from 'strongly agree' to 'strongly disagree', high scores indicating disagreement. The mean scores for teachers in infant, first, junior and primary schools are presented in Table A9 (Appendix A). Type of school appears to make very little difference and all teachers are thus considered together. In the following description only those statements with which teachers most strongly agreed or disagreed are considered for the sake of clarity of interpretation. Three themes emerge, cooperation, demands and noise.

There is agreement that teachers have to cooperate in open plan units and that in the main the design of the unit enables this to happen. But clearly teachers have to be adaptable, share materials and problems, and as a result learn a good deal from each other.

There are many demands made on teachers. The statement with which there was strongest agreement was that a lot of organization is required. Organizational demands, including the necessity for agreement on methods and standards, are matched by physical demands. Teachers feel that excessive demands are made on their attention and that they feel very tired at the end of the day. Pupils have a lot of contact with teachers apparently but it is strongly felt that a smaller teacher–pupil ratio is essential not only to ease the demands placed on them but also because of considerations of space. It was strongly felt that there are too many pupils for the space provided.

Teachers were also concerned about children being distracted by noise spreading from one area to another. Consequently they are worried about keeping their own group quiet. Nevertheless despite the demands made on them and the problem of noise, job satisfaction appears to be high.

*Attitudes Towards Open Plan and Conventional Schools*

The general attitudes outlined above relate only to open plan schools and allow no basis for a comparison of attitudes in conventional schools. Since the design brief of this study did not include the questioning of teachers in conventional schools, another section on attitudes was included in the questionnaire which was only completed by heads and teachers who had taught in both types of school. This section comprised twenty-two statements to be answered on a five point scale of 'strongly agree' (1) to 'strongly disagree' (5) in relation to both open plan and conventional schools. The mean scores are presented in Table 1. On Item 1 for example headteachers tend to disagree that children are most independent and responsible in conventional schools and tend to agree that they are more independent and responsible in open plan schools. Teachers agree with this view, but somewhat less strongly. A mean score of 3.0 indicates the opinion that there is no difference. The scores for all head and class teachers are presented in Tables A10 and A11 (Appendix A) but since little difference is apparent in different types of school the scores of primary heads and teachers are taken as representative and shown in Table 1.

Their responses are described under two general headings, teaching and curriculum, and pupil work and behaviour.

*Teaching and Curriculum*

There is a very strong feeling among headteachers that teachers have more preparation to do, and that teaching is more of a strain in open plan than conventional schools. Teachers generally agree with this. But despite such demands, teaching is regarded as more stimulating in open plan although teachers feel more confident in the conventional classroom situation.

Despite the extra preparation, strain and diminished confidence, headteachers feel that open plan schools provide a better environment for the probationary teacher. Teachers are not as convinced about this, reflecting disagreements in the wider educational setting. In talking to teachers, advisors and teacher trainers in initial visits, there was evidence of a clear difference of

| | Headteachers | | Teachers | |
|---|---|---|---|---|
| | Conventional | Open Plan | Conventional | Open Plan |
| 1. Children are more independent and responsible | 3.6 | 2.3 | 3.3 | 2.6 |
| 2. Teachers have more preparation to do | 3.9 | 1.9 | 3.5 | 2.3 |
| 3.Bright children progress more | 3.0 | 3.0 | 2.8 | 3.3 |
| 4. Teaching is more stimulating | 3.5 | 2.3 | 3.3 | 2.6 |
| 5. Probationers benefit more | 3.3 | 2.6 | 3.0 | 2.8 |
| 6. The average child escapes notice more | 3.5 | 3.2 | 3.7 | 3.1 |
| 7. Standards of work tend to be higher | 3.0 | 3.2 | 2.8 | 3.5 |
| 8. Children are more easily distracted | 3.7 | 2.5 | 3.8 | 2.3 |
| 9. Children benefit more socially | 3.8 | 2.0 | 3.5 | 2.2 |
| 10. Teaching is more of a strain | 3.9 | 2.0 | 3.8 | 2.3 |
| 11. The dull child benefits less | 3.0 | 3.5 | 3.3 | 3.3 |
| 12. There are more discipline problems | 3.5 | 3.1 | 3.8 | 2.8 |
| 13. Parental involvement is easier | 3.6 | 2.3 | 3.5 | 2.6 |
| 14. There is greater continuity for children | 3.3 | 2.5 | 3.2 | 2.7 |
| 15. The curriculum is wider | 3.5 | 2.6 | 3.4 | 2.8 |
| 16. Community involvement is easier | 3.5 | 2.5 | 3.4 | 2.6 |
| 17. Teachers feel more confident | 2.6 | 3.2 | 2.7 | 3.2 |
| 18. More curriculum planning is required | 3.7 | 2.0 | 3.5 | 2.2 |
| 19. The timid/insecure child is better off | 2.8 | 3.1 | 2.6 | 3.4 |
| 20. The design dictates teaching method | 2.9 | 2.6 | 3.1 | 2.7 |
| 21. Keeping areas orderly and tidy is difficult | 3.7 | 2.4 | 3.8 | 2.4 |
| 22. It is possible to provide a wider variety of equipment | 3.7 | 2.2 | 3.6 | 2.4 |

*Table 1 Comparison of opinions of head and class teachers in primary schools (mean scores)*

opinion. Some feel that probationers should gain experience and build up confidence in normal classrooms whereas others argue that the presence of, and cooperation with, other teachers is of value in providing suitable teaching models and allowing exchanges of ideas about practice. Both arguments have intuitive validity but clearly more evidence is required.

Three items related to the design of the teaching unit. There was marginal agreement that design dictated teaching method more in open plan schools. There was much stronger agreement that keeping areas tidy and orderly is also more difficult. It is interesting to note in this context that some LEAs pay caretakers extra for working in open plan schools because it is felt they are more difficult to clean. On the other hand there was strong agreement that open units allowed the provision of a wider variety of equipment.

There is a broad measure of agreement between heads and staff on curriculum issues. Both feel that more curriculum planning is required in open plan, that the curriculum is wider and provides better continuity for children. It is also felt that a wider involvement with parents and the community is easier.

### *Pupil Work and Behaviour*

During initial interviews and visits to schools, opinions were frequently expressed about the effect of open planning on different groups of pupils – the bright, the dull, the average, the timid. As a result, statements concerning these groups were incorporated into the questionnaire. There is agreement between heads and staff on two of these and disagreement on the other two. Both are agreed that the average child does not escape notice in the open setting but that there is less chance of this happening in conventional buildings. Both also agree that the timid/insecure child is better off in conventional schools, an opinion held more strongly by teachers.

The disagreements concerning bright and dull children are not marked. The heads professed no opinion as to whether bright children progressed more in open or conventional schools, whereas teachers felt they did better in conventional schools. The opposite pattern occurs with regard to dull children.

When considering children in general there was common agreement that open plan benefits children socially, developing independence and responsibility. On the debit side it is admitted that they are more easily distracted and that there are more discipline problems, the latter felt more by teachers than heads. There was a slight tendency among headteachers to feel that standards of work tended to be higher in conventional schools. Teachers concurred with this view but somewhat more strongly.

*Teacher Perceptions of 'Teaching Unit Design'*

Teachers' evaluations of the design of their units is of central importance, not only in terms of current organization but also in terms of possible implications for future school design. Two

| *Facility* | *Infant* | | | *Junior* | | |
|---|---|---|---|---|---|---|
| | *Good* | *Adequate* | *Poor* | *Good* | *Adequate* | *Poor* |
| Heating in winter | 44.0 | 34.8 | 21.2 | 48.1 | 32.7 | 19.1 |
| Heating in summer | 37.9 | 46.8 | 15.4 | 38.5 | 48.8 | 12.7 |
| Artificial lighting | 63.9 | 30.4 | 5.7 | 59.0 | 35.6 | 5.5 |
| Natural lighting | 58.1 | 25.7 | 16.0 | 49.5 | 29.7 | 20.7 |
| Ventilation | 29.7 | 35.4 | 34.9 | 21.6 | 37.7 | 40.6 |
| Acoustics | 35.8 | 41.7 | 22.6 | 28.9 | 42.9 | 28.2 |
| Display | 42.9 | 37.6 | 00.0 | 36.5 | 38.9 | 24.6 |

*Table 2 Ratings of facilities by infant and junior teachers (%)*

sections in the questionnaire were devoted to this aspect. One was a rating of such facilities as heating and lighting, and the other a measure designed to elicit evaluative responses on the spaces and facilities in their unit.

Table 2 presents the ratings separately for infant and junior teachers.

The majority of teachers feel that the facilities listed are at least adequate, but their evaluations of the different facilities varies widely.

They are most happy about the lighting, particularly artificial lighting, although junior teachers less so than infants. One in five junior teachers rated natural lighting poor, for example. Heating is generally considered to be adequate.

Display and acoustics are perceived as adequate by eight in ten infant teachers, but again junior teachers are less enthusiastic. Ventilation is considered the least adequate by both groups of teachers, particularly junior teachers, 40 per cent of whom rate it poor. This is likely to vary in the different spaces in the unit. The ventilation in small quiet rooms was frequently adversely commented on. These comments most frequently occurred when quiet rooms were used for whole class activities such as watching TV. Whether architects foresaw such use is open to question.

*Evaluation of Spaces within Units*

Another scale, commonly known as a semantic differential, required teachers to rate spaces and facilities such as quiet rooms, practical areas and storage on eight bi-polar adjectives on a five point scale. These adjectives were noisy–quiet; restricting–not restricting; light–dark; small–large; adequate–inadequate; badly-sited–well-sited; visible–not visible and well-designed–badly-designed. Few differences were apparent for different types of school (see Table A12, Appendix A) and teachers are thus considered as one group for the purposes of description.

Quiet Rooms

These were perceived as very small, restricting, somewhat noisy and not too well sited. On the credit side they were seen as light, very visible, reasonably adequate and fairly well designed.

Teaching Area

Since teachers spend much of their time in the teaching area it might have been imagined that they would have had fairly definite views on design. It would not appear to be so. On the favourable side they perceived them to be highly visible and light but on all other aspects they were neutral, with junior teachers being slightly more critical. They saw the area as being rather small and restricting. Whether this is in part due to the large size of junior children, which is not taken into account in deciding space requirements, is difficult to say.

Practical/Wet Area

The evaluations are again somewhat neutral. They are perceived as slightly noisy and restricting and fairly small. These are balanced by the views that they are also light and fairly visible.

Storage

Strong views were expressed on storage, or lack of it, in initial visits. Teachers in general see them as restricting and small, but are fairly neutral on design, adequacy and siting.

Display

This facility was also included in the rating list, where three quarters of teachers felt it to be at least adequate. Information from the semantic differential indicates that it was seen as slightly restricting but light, visible and fairly adequate.

Cloaks/Toilets

It was probably a mistake to include both these facilities under one heading since in initial visits cloaks were a constant source of irritation, particularly the movable variety. In general these facilities were seen as noisy, small and restricting, although fairly light and visible.

Furniture

Very small, very noisy and somewhat restricting, although fairly adequate and reasonably well designed.

Hall
The hall was included since it is a space used by all children for certain activities. These are seen as fairly noisy, very light and adequate, although less so for juniors. They are fairly well designed.

**Summary**
As in previous research teachers are conscious of the extra demands made upon them and the problem of noise. Nevertheless, job satisfaction appears to be high and teaching is seen as stimulating. There is disagreement about the utility of open plan schools for probationary teachers and for certain kinds of pupils. The majority of teachers feel that the facilities offered are adequate, although a substantial minority felt that ventilation was poor. In general teachers' responses towards different spaces were fairly neutral, although quiet rooms and storage were seen as restrictive and small.

**Headteacher Attitudes to Team Teaching**
In view of the theoretical link between open plan buildings and team or cooperative teaching, headteachers were questioned about their views and attitudes towards this form of organization. Their responses are shown in Table 3 below.

| | | *Yes* | *No opinion* | *No* |
|---|---|---|---|---|
| (a) | Enables support to be given to less experienced teachers | 87.0 | 6.2 | 6.8 |
| (b) | Enables more efficient use of teacher skills | 83.1 | 8.1 | 8.3 |
| (c) | Can lead to personality clashes between teachers | 81.9 | 10.4 | 7.7 |
| (d) | Is of benefit to pupils | 73.3 | 14.1 | 12.6 |
| (e) | Can carry a less able/inexperienced teacher | 66.8 | 8.5 | 24.7 |
| (f) | Can place too great a load on one teacher | 61.3 | 12.5 | 26.2 |
| (g) | Causes problems if a member of a team is sick or leaves | 61.1 | 8.7 | 30.1 |
| (h) | Facilitates pupil supervision | 47.7 | 15.8 | 36.5 |
| (i) | Can have a deleterious effect on pupil/teacher relationships | 22.8 | 21.4 | 55.8 |

*Table 3 Headteacher attitudes to team teaching (%)*

There was wide agreement that team or cooperative teaching enables more efficient use of teacher skills, gives support to less experienced teachers but can lead to personality clashes. At least 60 per cent of headteachers also thought that team teaching is of benefit to pupils, is unlikely to cause a deterioration in pupil–teacher relationships and allows the school to carry a less able or inexperienced teacher. They did feel, however, that such an organization can place too great a load on a teacher and that problems are caused by teacher absence. They were somewhat ambivalent about this approach facilitating pupil supervision.

In a separate question 83 per cent agreed that they were in favour of teachers working in teams, given an appropriate building and staff, and a similar percentage indicated that their building was in fact suitable. Relating these views to actual organization indicates a large gap between attitude and practice in this area.

**Teacher Preferences**

*Open v. Conventional Buildings*

Job satisfaction would seem to be high in open plan schools, but it could of course be as high in conventional schools. In order to gain a comparative view a question was inserted which asked head and class teachers whether, other things being equal, they would prefer to work in an open plan or conventional school.

| | *Infant* | *First* | *Junior* | *Primary* |
|---|---|---|---|---|
| Open Plan | 56.8 | 52.5 | 54.0 | 48.9 |
| Conventional | 14.5 | 11.4 | 18.4 | 17.7 |
| No Preference | 28.7 | 36.1 | 27.5 | 33.3 |
| N = | 380 | 163 | 275 | 713 |

*Table 4 School preference: headteachers, by type of school (%)*

Table 4 shows the preferences of headteachers. About a half prefer open plan, whereas only one in six prefer to be back in a conventional school. This bears out the feelings expressed in initial visits, where headteachers indicated that they preferred the increased access open plan schools gave them to the teaching situation. This in turn led to a feeling of greater involvement.

Table 5 shows the preferences of class teachers, which form quite a different pattern. Overall, teachers are almost equally split three ways, one third preferring open plan, one third conventional and one third having no preference. Infant teachers, like their headteachers, prefer open plan most strongly, whereas more junior teachers prefer conventional to open plan schools.

| | *Infant* | *First* | *Junior* | *Primary* |
|---|---|---|---|---|
| Open Plan | 37.8 | 31.2 | 32.0 | 34.5 |
| Conventional | 25.0 | 30.4 | 36.6 | 28.1 |
| No Preference | 37.1 | 38.4 | 31.4 | 36.4 |
| N = | 712 | 395 | 759 | 1497 |

*Table 5 School preference: teachers by type of school (%)*

**Preference and Type of Unit**

It has already been shown that teaching and curriculum organization varies in different unit designs. Is this also true of teacher preference? To assess this, teachers were again grouped according to the age range taught. Tables 6 and 7 show preferences by unit design of infant and junior teachers respectively.

The results in Table 6 highlight an interesting paradox, this being that the most prevalent design, the more closed two teacher unit, is associated with the lowest preference among infant teachers. It would seem that the more open two and three teacher units are much preferred to

| | Pairs | | Triples | | Quads | | Multis | |
|---|---|---|---|---|---|---|---|---|
| Type | 1 | 2 | 1 | 2 | 1 | 2 | 1 | 2 |
| Open Plan | 39.9 | 27.6 | 41.1 | 30.1 | 34.0 | 41.9 | 41.1 | 41.2 |
| Conventional | 27.1 | 32.3 | 25.1 | 26.8 | 24.5 | 22.7 | 23.4 | 21.6 |
| No Preference | 33.0 | 40.1 | 33.8 | 43.1 | 41.5 | 35.5 | 35.5 | 37.3 |
| N = | 288 | 446 | 231 | 306 | 106 | 172 | 107 | 102 |

*Table 6 Preferences of infant teachers by design of unit (%)*

the more closed variety. This does not hold when considering larger units however. There is no difference in preference for open plan among teachers in multi (5+ teacher) units and a reverse trend is seen in four teacher units, whereby a greater preference is apparent in Type 2 designs.

| | Pairs | | Triples | | Quads | | Multis | |
|---|---|---|---|---|---|---|---|---|
| Type | 1 | 2 | 1 | 2 | 1 | 2 | 1 | 2 |
| Open Plan | 48.2 | 32.7 | 38.5 | 36.4 | 41.3 | 32.8 | 45.9 | 33.8 |
| Conventional | 23.2 | 33.7 | 32.7 | 32.6 | 28.3 | 34.8 | 24.3 | 32.5 |
| No Opinion | 28.7 | 33.3 | 28.8 | 31.0 | 30.4 | 32.4 | 29.7 | 32.5 |
| N = | 164 | 339 | 104 | 129 | 92 | 204 | 74 | 77 |

*Table 7 Preferences of junior teachers by design of unit (%)*

The most prevalent design in juniors is the pair Type 2 and here too it is associated with least preference. The pattern of responses of junior teachers is more consistent than among infants in that the more open units are associated with greater preference for open plan, irrespective of the size of the unit. This is seen most clearly in two teacher units where nearly one half prefer open plan schools. It may be that the less open units provide the worst compromise for teachers, giving neither the self contained autonomy of a conventional classroom nor the benefit of a truly open teaching environment.

In view of the teacher perceptions of space and facilities described in the last section it might be thought that preference might also vary in relation to the age of the school building. To gain an overall view of this, schools were grouped into three broad age spans – those built prior to 1971, those built in 1971–2 and those in 1973–5. Table 8 shows teacher preferences in relation to age of building.

| | Age of School | | |
|---|---|---|---|
| *Preference for* | Prior to 1970 | 1971–2 | 1973–5 |
| Open Plan Schools | 33.5 | 36.4 | 32.0 |
| Conventional Schools | 29.4 | 28.6 | 33.4 |
| No Preference | 36.9 | 34.9 | 34.6 |

*Table 8 Teacher preference by age of school (%)*

No clear trend is evident. Fewer teachers in schools built in the period 1973–5, a time of diminishing space, prefer open plan and more prefer conventional schools, but the differences are not large.

### Summary

Headteachers prefer open plan schools more than teachers do, and infant teachers tend to prefer them more than junior teachers. These preferences vary in relation to the design of the unit. In the main the highest preference is shown by those working in more open units.

### Consultation and Staffing

In Chapter 2 it was reported that the teacher unions in particular were concerned at the lack of constructive consulation with teachers. This was also the general picture gained from interviews in the familiarization stage of the study. In many instances there is an obvious reason for this; the head and staff are not appointed until after the building is well advanced or the original headteacher is not now in the school. In order to overcome this in the questionnaire, the item on consultation read 'If you are the first headteacher, at what stage were you consulted on building plans – not at all, initial architect's sketch plan, final planning or building stage'. A second question was included, asking at what stage they thought they should be consulted. The replies are presented in Table 9.

| | *Infant* | | *Junior* | |
|---|---|---|---|---|
| *Type of consultation* | Actual | Ideal | Actual | Ideal |
| Not at all | 53.2 | 0.3 | 40.3 | |
| Initial architect's sketch plan | 23.9 | 88.3 | 30.6 | 92.9 |
| Final planning stage | 12.6 | 10.3 | 17.1 | 6.4 |
| Building stage | 10.3 | 1.1 | 12.0 | 0.8 |

*Table 9 Stage of consultation of headteachers in infant and junior schools (%)*

Even when the question is limited to the original headteacher, the picture looks less than optimistic. Junior heads apparently gain more opportunity for consultation than infant heads. Over half of the latter were not consulted about design at all and less than a quarter were involved from the initial sketch plan stage. The large gap between actual and ideal practice is also evident in the table. All want consultation, the vast majority at the sketch plan stage.

In some authorities, a wider consultative net has been cast with the creation of groups of teacher representatives variously called 'consultative committees', 'building panels' or 'design groups'. Some have been short-lived because, according to some advisers, they tended to concern themselves with political rather than design issues. One suggestion which might circumvent such problems is to man these groups with head and class teachers who are already teaching in open plan schools. Experience of working in schools of differing design could then be shared.

The situation is clearer when the design is for a replacement or a modified school. Here the headteacher is usually invited to comment at the earliest stage. But how far heads are able to change the proposed design is more difficult to establish. The act of consultation does not automatically connote involvement in decision making. It became apparent in interviews with advisers that consultation was often seen as a diplomatic tool, as the following comments reveal. 'The fact of consultation itself is the key thing, not the design modifications that may result'; 'We usually aim to persuade them into certain ways of using the building rather than making major changes'; 'Consultation is seen as an exercise in diplomacy rather than in the expectation of plans being radically altered'. These views may be legitimate since a school is built for decades, not just for current users. A number of headteachers made this point, arguing that they are not qualified to make judgements since they cannot interpret plans into practical terms. One went even further and made a case for less consultation, arguing that progress comes from a few and if there was mass consultation then the mass would not advocate progress. Nevertheless, headteachers do feel strongly that they should be involved, and consultation for the sake of consultation is not likely to appease them.

Responses to the questionnaire about modification at the building stage indicate that many headteachers do manage to secure modifications, albeit minor ones. Of those who were consulted by the LEA 30 per cent claimed to have secured no alterations, whereas 60 per cent had negotiated minor works. The remaining 10 per cent had managed to gain major concessions.

One half of those questioned had requested modifications to be made since the school opened and a quarter had achieved some of these. It was not possible in a questionnaire to ascertain these changes in detail but a general picture is presented in Table 10.

| *Have the modifications made the teaching units –* | *Actual* | *Ideal* |
|---|---|---|
| More open | 39.2 | 23.8 |
| More closed | 60.8 | 76.2 |
| More adaptable | 43.2 | 56.1 |
| No difference | 56.8 | 43.9 |

*Table 10 Modifications to teaching units: all headteachers (%)*

The modifications received have tended to make the units more closed than more open and that, as far as they are concerned, is what the majority wanted. Over one half of the modifications apparently made little difference.

Some flesh can be hung on the skeletal questionnaire data by considering the modifications carried out in the schools used for the observational studies. At the planning stage the modifications were fairly minor, usually involving the movement of facilities from one space to another. In these schools the following were moved – a window, a cooker, the toilets, a kiln and potter's wheel, the secretary's reception bay and a stock cupboard. The remainder were modifications or additions to basic provisions – glass was put in a door, in a window, quarry tiles were provided under some of the sinks, moveable instead of fixed furniture was acquired, and in one atypical case, larger cloaks areas were conceded together with a repositioning of home bases.

A quarter of these schools had not managed to gain modifications since the school opened. Of those that had, a number were designed either to close off areas or to combat noise. Pinewood screens were obtained, curtains were added, doors were put on the hall to create a noise barrier, and extra soundproofing in the forms of carpets and ceiling tiles were acquired and fitted. Cloaks too appeared to be a constant source of irritation, particularly moveable trolleys. In some schools these have been banished in favour of coat hooks or pegs. Additional external work has also been carried out including the building of a shed for the caretaker, flagging, extension of the playground using funds provided by parents, and, in one instance, an open court has been made into a classroom.

These modifications were not dissimilar to those noted on initial visits. But perhaps the most serious modifications occur before the school is built, in an attempt to cut costs. One school had all its teaching areas reduced by six feet to meet increasing costs and this is not an isolated case. As one headteacher commented 'This school is a disaster – the prototype (which was good) was cut drastically in size'.

Finally, a large number of extras seem to have been acquired by some headteachers since the completion of the building, mostly fixtures and fittings. A number had acquired extra display facilities, carpeting and storage. Many had subverted the so-called '70 per cent rule' used by some authorities (cf. Hamilton, 1977) by acquiring extra furniture to enable all pupils to have a chair and desk. Also, many had purchased blackboards since some LEAs clearly felt them to be inappropriate in open plan schools and did not provide them.

*Staffing*

As was indicated earlier, the possibility of consultation depends upon the timing of the appointment of the headteacher. Policy varies widely. Some appoint a year before the school opens and others immediately before opening. Replies to the questionnaire show that 40 per cent were appointed immediately prior to opening and another 40 per cent one term before opening.

Teachers are usually appointed just before opening which could be considered doubtful practice, since 70 per cent of the teaching force in open plan schools have no previous experience in such schools, and of the remaining 30 per cent two thirds have no more than one year's experience. One LEA did admit that staffing is the most important yet intractable problem because of the 'simple scarcity of expertise in this field of schooling'. As a consequence some LEAs take greater care in the selection of teachers for such schools, but many do not, a fact regarded as unfortunate by many advisers.

Appointing practices vary widely. In some areas and for some posts headteachers appear to have complete autonomy, but at the other extreme some LEAs exert almost total control. Of more particular concern to open plan schools were suggestions that the teachers themselves should have some influence, particularly in organizations involving team teaching. A number of headteachers commented that applicants should be able to get on with existing staff or have the personality which will fit in with the atmosphere of the school.

**Teacher Training**

Headteachers are particularly unhappy at the products of teacher training. In answer to the question 'do you think that Colleges of Education provide the right kind of training for teachers in open plan schools' only 7 per cent gave an unqualified 'yes'. Over 50 per cent gave a categorical 'no'.

For those who replied that they did not feel colleges provided the right kind of training, an open-ended question was included to allow them to state which aspect could be improved. These replies were analysed and can be summarized in two broad categories – what skills are required, and how they might be achieved.

*Skills Required*
The most frequent response was that students should be trained in the management and day-to-day organization of a unit. More specifically, students should be trained in the planning and practice of cooperative/team teaching. Not simply the organizational skills, but a recognition of, and expertise in, the interpersonal relationships necessary, stressing particularly the concepts of cooperation, team work, flexibility and versatility.

Other requirements relating to teaching organization were that students should be trained in the understanding and use of various teaching methods. Stress was placed on knowing how to organize an integrated day, and to plan individual and group work so that all pupils are purposefully employed. The necessity for detailed planning of work in a mixed ability situation was frequently mentioned, as was training in the assessment and recording of individual work and progress.

On curriculum it was desired that the students recognized the importance of a structured curriculum as the basis for optimum learning, and requested specific training in the teaching of basic skills, particularly reading.

In a more general context, it was felt that the abilities to share, prepare and use materials, equipment and visual aids were important as was the ability to maintain discipline.

*How the Skills Could Be Achieved*
The most popular view is that students can best be taught how to teach by actually being in a teaching situation. There were many calls for more visits to open plan schools during training and for more frequent and longer periods of time spent on teaching practice in such schools, although it was recognized that students needed experience in conventional schools also. The headteachers recognized that there are probably insufficient schools for this purpose but there were complaints that colleges are reluctant to send students to open plan schools for practice, or that they only sent first and second year students, or only mature students. Much concern was expressed about the apprehension students express about working in open plan schools. It was felt that this was based on ignorance because of a lack of knowledge in colleges, which in turn led to 'terrible rumours', and pre-conceived ideas based on fiction.

In order to gain experience in team teaching it was suggested that students be allowed to work together in mock teams on teaching practice. One head claimed that offers to have more than one student for this purpose had been rejected. Others felt that this same experience could be gained by working with an experienced teacher. In general it was argued that teachers felt less than involved with the assessment of teaching practice and thought that more use could be made of staff expertise. Other, more radical, suggestions included the view that all students should spend time in schools as unqualified teachers prior to entry into college, and that the third year of training should be completed after a few years' experience in schools.

The opportunity was taken to conjecture about the suitability of college staff. Many felt that tutors need the direct experience of teaching in open plan settings and if they do not have it, should be given it, by secondment if necessary. Those without such experience were considered unsuitable to advise their students. A few even felt that college tutors were prejudiced against open plan schools. Finally, a large number argued for greater liaison between tutors and headteachers, clearly feeling that a more cooperative venture would benefit students in training.

There were also suggestions concerning the college curriculum. It was felt that students should have a more vicarious experience of reality by having discussions with, and attending talks given by, heads and staff on all aspects of open plan philosophy. More attention should be given to broad-based subjects. Students should have more experience working with individual children, including those having learning difficulties. Selection for college should be stricter and the attainments of the students in the basic skills should be improved.

The comments by headteachers communicate concern that many of the managerial and organizational skills necessary for open plan schools are not present in the products of teaching training. They stress the centrality of experiencing actual practice and in working with teachers and children rather than working with theories. This thread of practicality is possibly best summarized by one head who wrote 'Maybe there should be a return to the name Teacher Training College – and colleges should do just that!'

*In-Service Training*

In-service training is of course one way of overcoming scarcity of expertise, but initial visits led to the conclusion that in-service training with particular reference to open plan was very variable and often sparse, although there were exceptions. One of the reasons given for this state of affairs is the lack of expertise among advisers and college staff. To assess the situation on a national basis a question on in-service training was included in the questionnaire. Table 11 documents the replies received from infant and junior headteachers.

| | *Infant* | *Junior* |
|---|---|---|
| Visits to other schools | 81.7 | 69.4 |
| Teacher centre courses | 72.6 | 69.4 |
| Discussion groups | 60.7 | 52.4 |
| Longer courses | 34.7 | 33.9 |
| On-site training with advisory staff | 28.0 | 25.3 |
| ATO/DES courses | 41.6 | 42.9 |
| In-school training by head | 73.2 | 67.2 |

*Table 11 Types of in-service courses provided (%)*

Visits to schools are a popular provision, closely followed by in-school training by the headteacher, and courses in teacher centres. Self-help discussion groups also figure prominently. ATO/DES courses, longer courses provided by the authority and on-site training with advisory staff are less frequently offered. The large majority of heads felt that all these options were useful.

Interviews with the headteachers in observational schools bear out this general picture. According to them provision of courses ranged from none to a 'good selection'. When provided, the quality also varied widely, 'some courses are very good, some hopeless'. Nevertheless all commented on the keenness of teachers to attend courses and many believed that in-school courses were of most value. Suggestions included the headteacher giving continual in-service training within the school, or extending invitations to advisers, other headteachers and college lecturers to visit the school to discuss particular issues or share experience. These activities should, however, be balanced with outside courses to avoid the staff becoming inward-looking. Day courses were preferred, even though these created problems of cover or replacement. Courses provided after school were attended by tired teachers and were thus felt to be less effective.

**Summary**

There is a clear gap between the amount and type of consultation accorded headteachers and that which they desire. Even when consultation is offered, there is evidence to suggest that the motives are often political rather than based on a genuine desire to assure constructive involvement. Some modifications have been achieved at the planning stage although most have been of a minor nature. This is also true of modifications made after the school has opened. The most serious modifications as far as headteachers are concerned occur in response to costings, since these have sometimes seriously reduced space and/or distorted the original design.

Procedures for the appointment of staff vary widely but of more concern to headteachers is the quality of teachers recruited straight from training. Over half are dissatisfied with the way teachers are trained. They would prefer a much greater emphasis on classroom management skills, and abilities relating to the teaching of basic skills. They are concerned at the lack of knowledge of students about open plan schools and the lack of practice in such schools. It is felt that the balance between academic and practical work is wrong and the centrality of actual practice and of working with teachers and children rather than theories were stressed. The provision and quality of in-service courses also varies markedly. School based in-service courses are viewed with most favour, balanced with external day courses.

**Conclusion**

The questionnaire survey was undertaken to provide a broad but shallow picture of organization and attitudes in open plan schools. The findings are broadly those of other surveys. Practice is diverse. Although it can be said that team or cooperative teaching is not widespread and that the split day is the most common form of curriculum organization, teaching approaches vary widely between schools and often within the same school, and appear to be related to the design of the teaching unit.

As in other surveys, teachers are concerned about noise and heavy work loads but morale appears to be relatively high, although headteachers have a greater preference for such schools than do teachers. On the other hand there was a greater consensus on aims, which appear not to differ from those of conventional schools.

There appears to be little constructive consultation on design of schools with teachers, as the NUT booklet indicated. But the overriding concern is with the quantity and quality of pre- and in-service courses, particularly the former. Again this is not restricted to Britain, but is a worldwide weakness.

The questionnaire data is based on teacher perception and is limited in terms of the detail that it is possible to achieve. The observation and interview studies described in the next chapters are complementary but allow a more detailed description of actual, as opposed to perceived, practice.

*Chapter 6*

# *Teaching Organization*

---

Although the open plan concept embodies the notion of teachers cooperating together in aspects of their work, it was seen from their responses to the questionnaire that team or co-operative approaches were less popular than operating independently or with minimal cooperation. However, this kind of general information gives little flavour or feel of the complexities of the actual organizations in units, or of the factors involved in the choice of a particular organization. The purpose of this chapter is therefore to move from the general to the specific.

Each of the observed units is considered separately in a search for both common and unique elements. These brief descriptions provide an indication of the wide variety of organizations adopted, but present little information about how such organizations came into being. The second section of this chapter therefore presents two studies of organizational history, recording the changes that have been made and the reasons why they were made.

Descriptions of how teaching is organized in 23 units would be extremely space consuming, and therefore a form of shorthand is used. For each unit observed a sketch plan of the design is provided along with a symbolic representation of the basic organization (see below). Underneath the sketches is given the type of school, intake area, design type, number of children and teachers designed for, and current enrolment.

To take the first unit described as an example: type of school – First; intake area – Urban/multiracial; design type – Multi Type 1; number of children designed for –320; numbers currently on roll – 311 (shown as 320 (311)); number of teachers designed for – 8; actual number in unit – 11 (shown as 8 (11)). If only part of the unit was observed this is indicated, e.g. Years 1 and 2. The designed and actual amount of space per pupil is also provided.

The key for the representation of the organization is as follows. The single age class group is shown as an open square □, and the teacher by a dot ●. Where classes are working together for certain activities but not as a team they are ringed by a broken line, e.g.

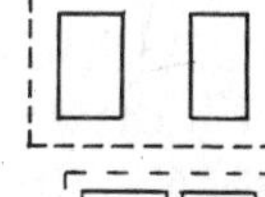

or if vertically grouped across two years:

Hatching is used for team teaching, e.g. if two teachers are teaming with two horizontally grouped classes then it is represented as follows:

Partial hatching is used for situations where team teaching is adopted for part of the day. The representation opposite shows three teachers with vertically grouped classes teaming for part of the day:

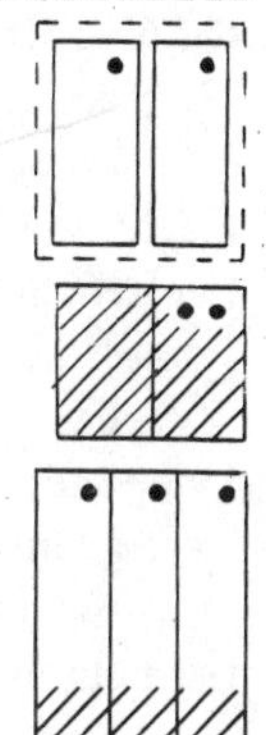

**Key and Scale for all Outline Plans in this Chapter**

| | | | | | |
|---|---|---|---|---|---|
| •••••••••• | Curtains | HB | — Home Base | K | — Kiln |
| ---------- | Adult Eye-level Screen | QR | — Quiet Room | R | — Remedial Reading |
| -·-·-·-·- | Moveable Partitions | AV | — Audio Visual | WH | — Wendy House |
| -•-•-•-•- | ½ Wall 160 cm high | T | — Toilets | HT | — Head Teacher |
| —•—•—•— | ½ Height Screen | S | — Store | DH | — Deputy Head |
| ▽▽▽▽▽ | Sliding Doors | C | — Coats | 1.5 cm = | 5 metres |
| | | CK | — Cooking | 1.4 cm = | 15 feet |

## Infants

Infant units are considered first, beginning with four units where independent teaching was usual.

Unit U

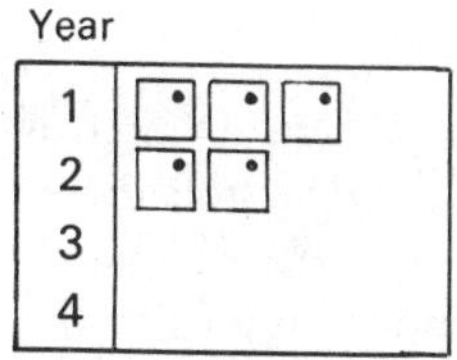


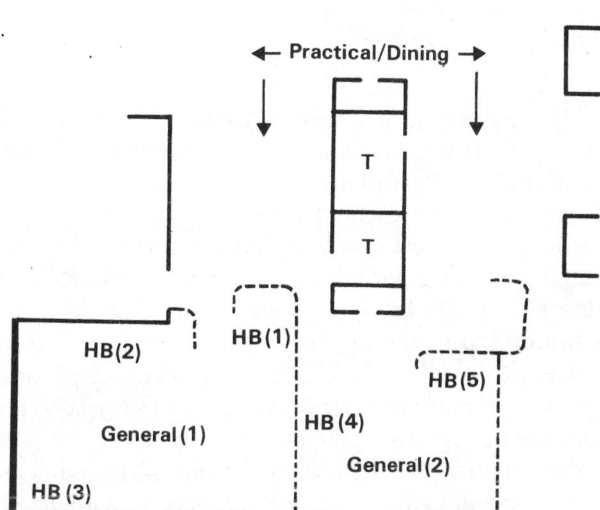


First School Urban/Multi-Racial
Multi Type 1 320(311) 8(11)
Years 1 and 2 2.0 m² (2.1 m²)

Unit U houses the first two years of a first school serving an urban area with a multiracial intake. The school was designed for 320 children and 8 teachers but at the time of observation housed 311 children and 11 teachers. It was designed with a teaching area of 2.0 sq. m (21.5 sq. ft) per child, but the actual space per child at the time of observation was 2.1 sq. m (22.6 sq. ft).

The teaching unit observed comprised one large open area divided by screens into general teaching area 1, with three teachers of five-year-old children, and general teaching area 2 with two teachers of six-year-old pupils. They shared a practical/dining area with the rest of the school, because of which it was timetabled throughout the day.

As can be seen from the diagram, each teacher had a register group with which she worked independently of other teachers. The only sharing was of materials. Within each class children were grouped by ability. The split day was in operation comprising basic skills teaching in the morning and other activities in the afternoon, work being assigned to groups or individuals at the beginning of each session.

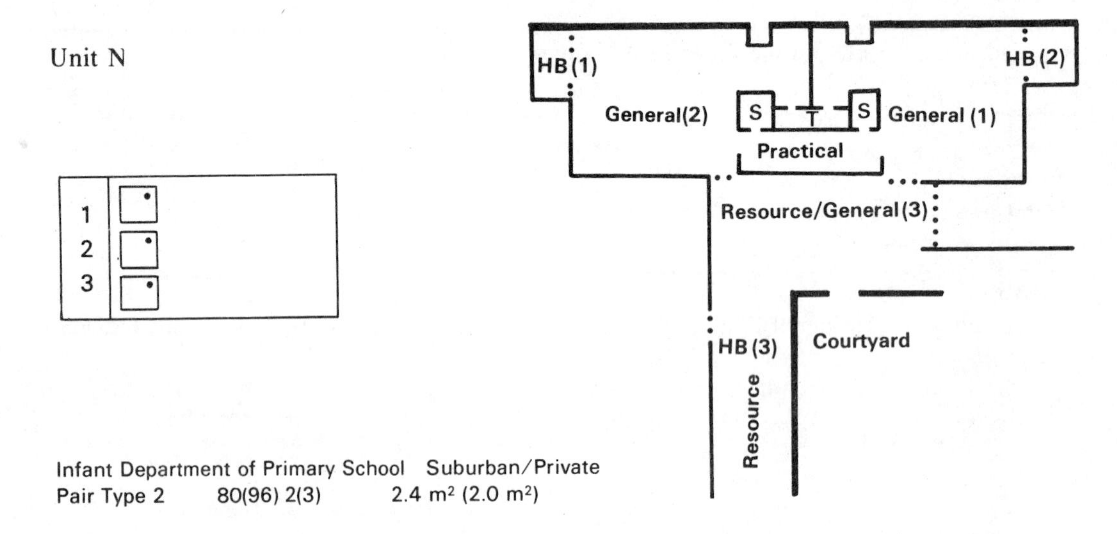


The general teaching areas in Unit N are of classroom size. A small practical area is shared as is a resource area bordering on to an internal courtyard. The unit is overcrowded, housing 96 instead of the planned 80 pupils, in three classes, necessitating one extra teacher. Each home base contains one teacher and her class, the remaining teacher with the reception class using the resource area as a home base and general area. The three teachers work independently with a single age class group cooperating only for music. Within each class the children are divided into five groups based on ability. The school day is divided into four periods, two in the morning and two in the afternoon, one being a quiet period followed by an activity time.

Unit S was undercrowded, housing 87 of the planned 115 children. The three teachers each had a small home base area and shared three general teaching areas of differing size (one being used for maths) and a practical area. Each teacher operated independently, although there was some cooperative planning and sharing of space and materials. Within each class the children were placed into one of four groups based on ability. The teachers worked with the class as a

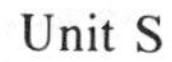


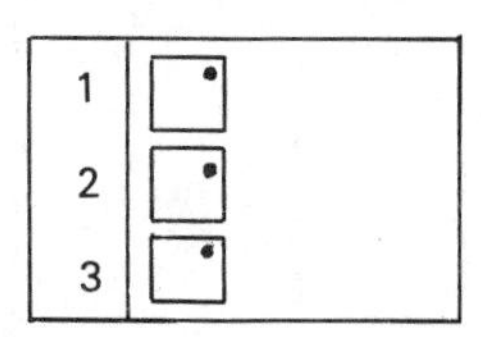


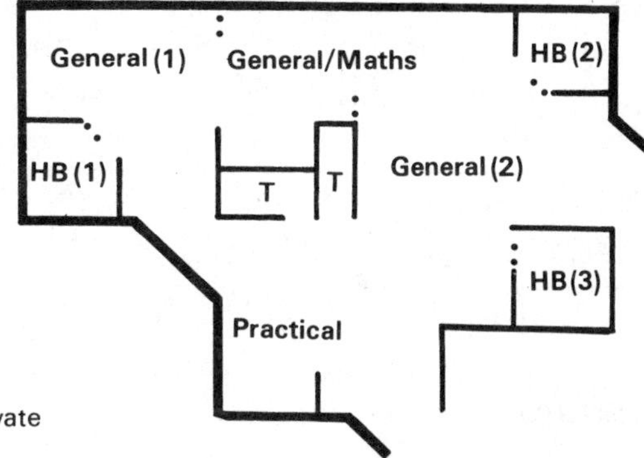


Infant Department of Primary School Suburban/Private
Triple Type 1 115(87) 3(3) 2.2 m² (2.9 m²)

whole at the beginning of each session but then gave daily assignments covering reading, writing, number and craft. The children could choose the order in which they completed these tasks.

The final unit in this group, Unit P, utilized a vertical grouping arrangement.

Unit P

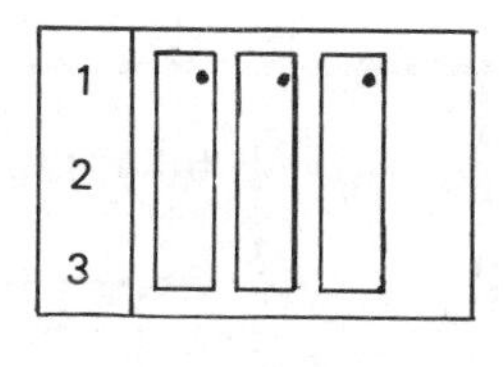


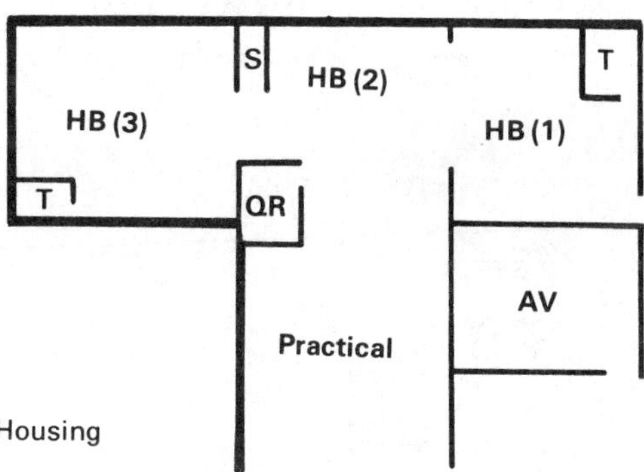


Infant Department of Primary School Suburban/Mixed Housing
Triple Type 1 120(122) 3(4) 2.0 m² (1.9 m²)

The available space consisted of an open general teaching area, the home base areas being only partially delineated by short lengths of wall. They also shared a large enclosed AV room, a practical area and a quiet room. Three of the teachers had a vertically grouped class covering years 1, 2 and 3 for which they were responsible for all areas of work. The fourth teacher withdrew all the children by age, banding for topic, reading and maths. Within their class groups children were grouped by ability and assigned work for one or two days. The children had choice in the order in which they completed their tasks.

*Partial Cooperative Teaching*

Three units were in a midway stage between independent and cooperative teaching. In the first, Unit O, classes worked together for certain activities whereas in Units Q and T part of the day is spent in teams.

Unit O

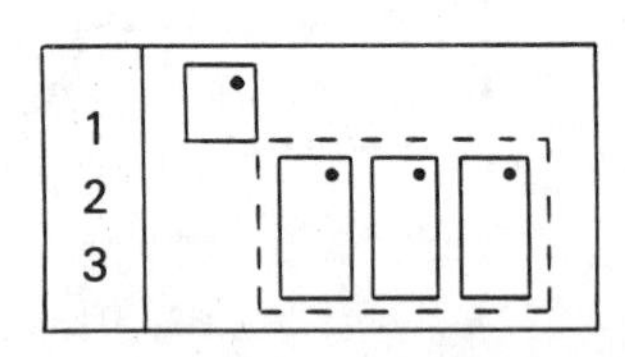


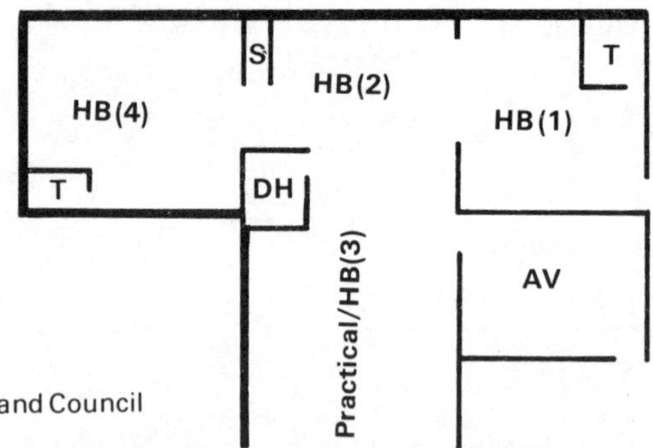


Infant Department of Primary School Suburban/Private and Council
Triple Type 1 120(117) 3(4) 2.0 m² (2.0 m²)

Unit O has four teachers working in a three teacher unit, as in Unit P. In fact these are identical units. One of the four teachers works independently in home base 1 with the reception class. The other three teachers have a vertically grouped class of six and seven year olds which they take for news, PE, story writing, reading and maths tests. In addition, they each take single age groups for practical and mechanical maths, handwork, topic, story and RE. Since there are only two home bases for three teachers one uses the practical area as a base. All space but home base 1 is timetabled, both teachers and children moving to different spaces during the day. A split day is in operation.

In Unit T there is a tentative move toward team teaching.

Unit T

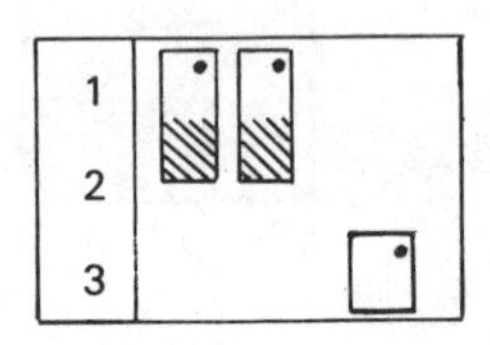


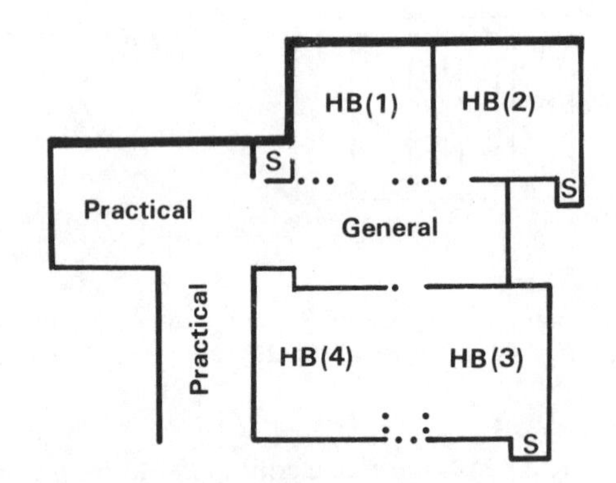


Infant Department of Primary School Rural/Mixed
Quad Type 1 120(75) 4(3) 2.1 m² (3.4 m²)

The space available comprises four home bases (two of which are more open than the others), a shared general teaching area and a practical area. Although designed as a four teacher unit it currently houses three. These teachers have their own register groups and work independently for most of the day. However, the two teachers with the vertically grouped younger children team for one hour per day, one teacher specializing in maths and the other in language.

The school day is broken into four periods. Children are grouped by age and ability and assigned work at the beginning of each work period. A full time ancillary works with groups from all three teachers all day in the practical area.

Unit Q

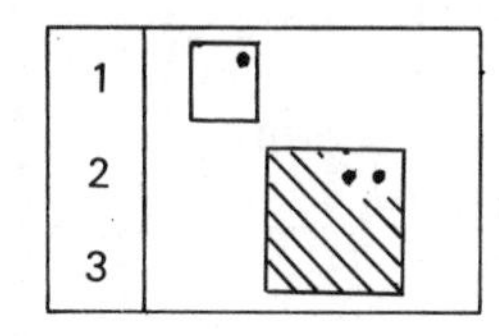


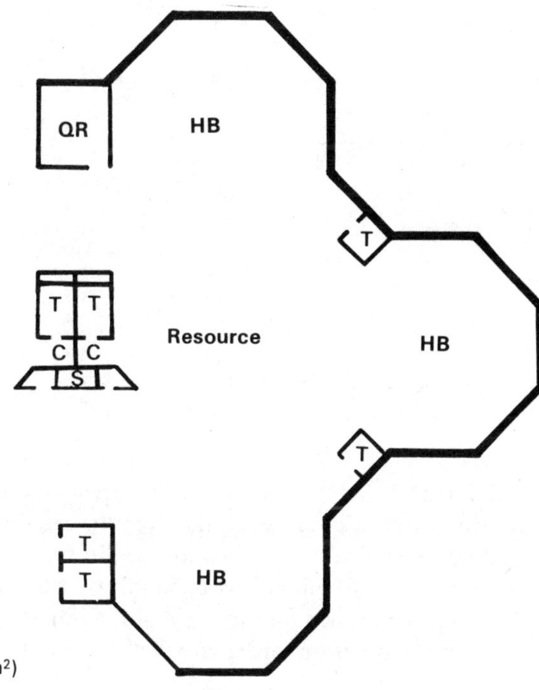


Infant School Suburban/Multi-Racial
Triple Type 2 120(94) 3(3) 3.4 m² (4.3 m²)

In Unit Q there is more team teaching but again only two of the three teachers participate. The building comprises three class sized home bases each opening on to a central practical/ resource area. A small quiet room is also shared.

Each teacher has a register class and the reception class stays with the same teacher all day. The other two team teach with their vertically grouped classes. One teacher takes responsibility for maths and the other for language. In addition each offers a range of work covering art, music, drama and PE.

The school day is broken into three sessions, and groups of children spend two sessions with one teacher and one with the other. They are broken into six groups based on ability.

The remaining four units are all characterized by team teaching organization.

In Unit M there are two small home base areas, a shared general teaching area, a shared practical area and teachers have a share in another small enclosed room. The two teachers work as a team. Each has her own register group of five and six year olds but the classes are combined in six work groups according to age and ability. One teacher takes all the children for maths and the other for English. This continues on a termly basis, at which time the teachers change specialisms, i.e. the maths teacher takes English and vice versa. Both teachers share craft and PE but music is shared with another unit in the school. A rolling timetable or workwheel is in operation covering the following areas – reading, craft, writing or finding out, practical maths, choice and number.

Unit R has less pupils and more teachers than designed for. They share three partially closed areas (home base 1, home base 3 and art/craft), five general teaching areas of varying size and two enclosed quiet rooms. The teachers work as a team, each teacher taking responsibility for number, writing and project for one day. These activities are located in specific areas of the

Unit M

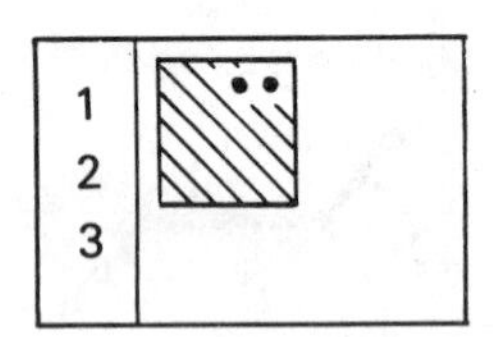


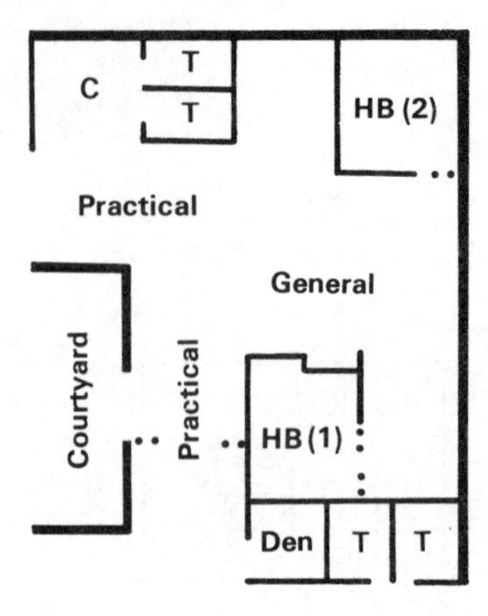


Infant School Suburban/Private
Pair Type 2 80(52) 2(2) 2.0 m² (3.1 m²)

unit. Each teacher takes a specific group of children in the relevant area and remains available for any other children using the area during that day.

Children are in different groups for different activities. They are assigned to a register group on a random basis but are grouped for work activity on number ability. For word building the children are grouped on the basis of reading ability. They are assigned work for the day and given choice as to the order in which they complete it.

Unit R

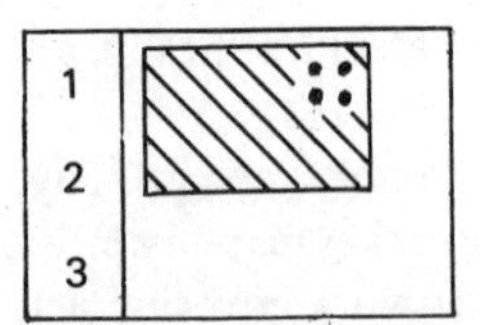


Infant School
New Town/Council Housing
Triple Type 1
120(96) 3(4)
2.1 m² (2.6 m²)

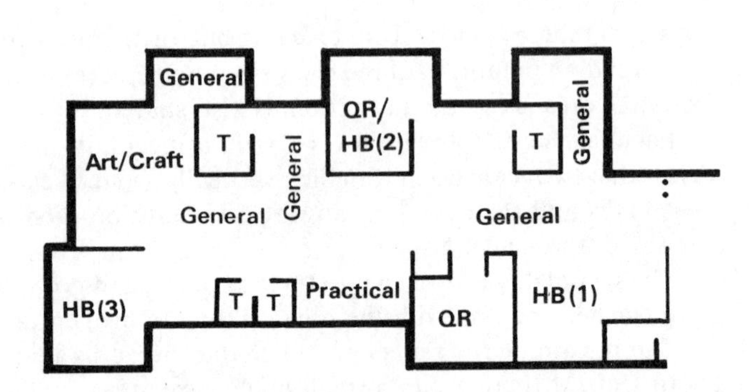


Like Unit R, Unit V had less children and more teachers than designed for. Six small home bases were available, two general teaching areas, two small practical areas and a resource area all surrounding a central courtyard. The teachers operate in two teams of three whilst the seventh teacher works in the resource area. One team comprises 4 to 6 year olds and the other 5 to 7 year olds. Each teacher in the team is responsible for one area of the curriculum – topic, number or reading, and writing – for one week. Responsibilities then change. In addition each teacher has a registration group of mixed age for story and 'checking work' times. The seventh teacher takes children from the younger team in the mornings and the other team in the afternoons for language and maths.

At the beginning of each session children select from the work areas available but return to their home base at the end of each session.

Unit V

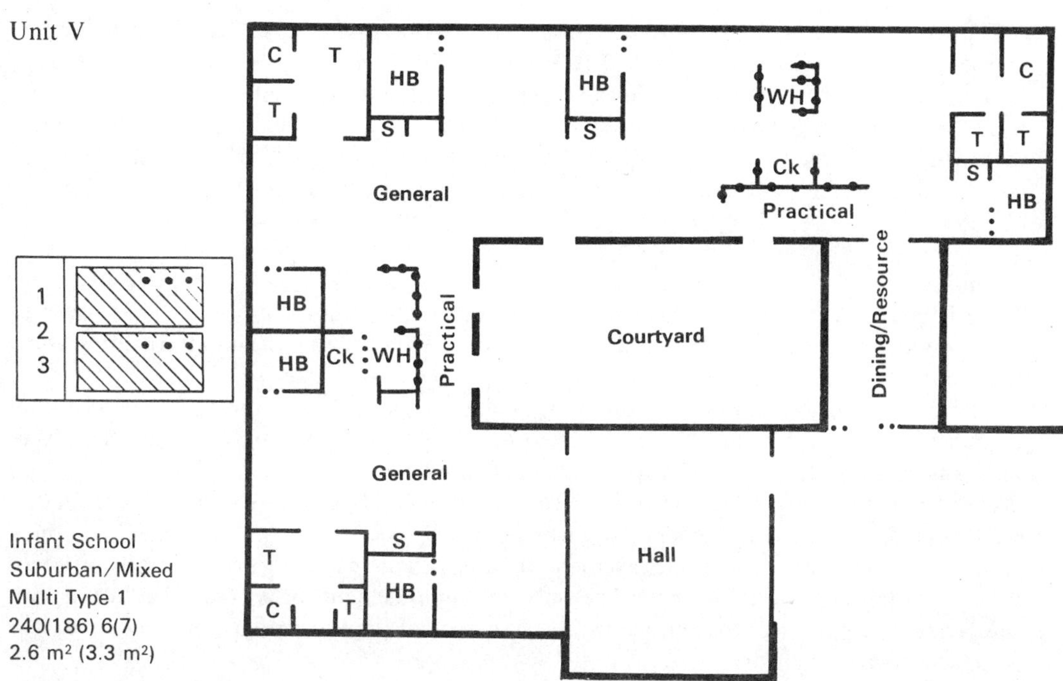


Infant School
Suburban/Mixed
Multi Type 1
240(186) 6(7)
2.6 m² (3.3 m²)

Unit W was also substantially under-pupilled. The design allowed for three teacher areas. Each unit was planned for three teachers and had a small enclosed quiet room and a general teaching area. In addition two further general teaching areas were shared by the whole school.

Unit W

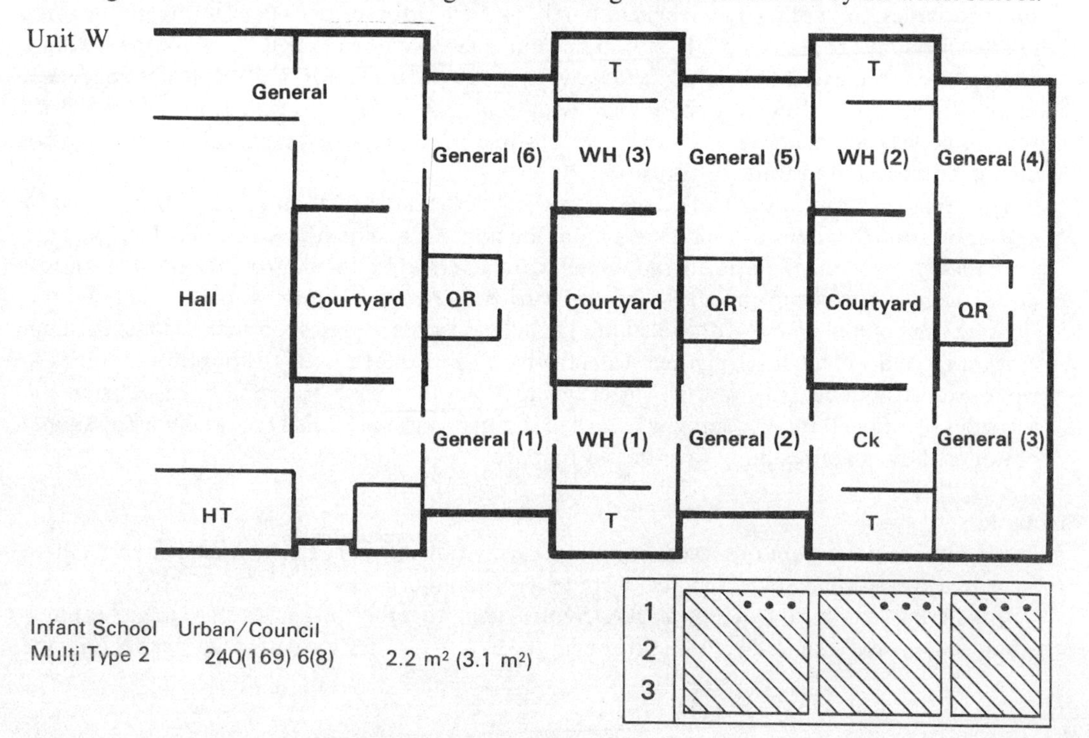


Infant School Urban/Council
Multi Type 2 240(169) 6(8) 2.2 m² (3.1 m²)

The teachers were in three teams, two of three teachers and one of two, each with a full time ancillary helper. Each teacher had a register group of mixed age (5–7 years) for whom they were responsible for work and progress. In each team one of the adults usually supervised everyone while the others worked individually or with small groups from the register class. The teachers share PE, drama and music on a termly basis. The accent is on the individual child who can select what he wishes to do and where he carries it out throughout the day (see Case Study 1, Chapter 10).

**Summary**

The foregoing descriptions of the infant units observed demonstrate the wide variety of organization and designs. Although there are common elements it is the unique features which stand out.

The teachers in four units were operating independently. But comparisons of this small group shows many differences. Some adopted single age pupil groupings whereas others were vertically grouped; the mode of work assignment varied from at the beginning of each session to every two days; some allowed pupil choice in the order and place of work but others did not; some organizations gave teachers responsibilities for specific groups of pupils but others preferred a 'floating teacher' arrangement. Finally, each teacher worked within different constraints imposed by the design. The only common element, other than the fact that an independent organization was in operation, was that all pupils were grouped by ability for some aspects of their work.

Three units were in a transitional stage between independence and cooperation. One common feature was that in each unit one teacher was teaching independently whilst the rest were attempting more cooperative ventures. In one unit classes were changed or joined for some activities, in another two teachers taught as a team for an hour per day and in the third two teachers taught as a team all day. In one unit space was timetabled necessitating teachers and children to move throughout the day, whereas in the other two units the same space was retained. One broke down the school day with two sessions, one three sessions and the other four. One was fortunate enough to have full-time ancillary help. such variations might of course be expected in units in transition.

The remaining four units had in common the fact that a team teaching organization was in operation. But this does not indicate a common approach. The only common elements here were that all were under-pupilled and, in the main, overstaffed in relation to the design, and all pupils were vertically grouped. Team size varied from two to four teachers, some with a floating teacher and others with substantial ancillary assistance. Responsibilities for curriculum areas showed a widely differing time scale, from one day, to one week to one term. In some the work was structured with a workwheel whereas another gave free pupil choice from the activities on offer. Pupil groupings also differed. Such variety should serve to blunt any simple notion of how team teaching operates in practice.

**Juniors**

Twelve junior units were observed. In this instance four were organized independently, three were in a transitional stage and five were team teaching.

In Unit B two general teaching areas were provided, together with an enclosed quiet room, a practical area and a shared resource area near the hall. It was designed as a two teacher unit but

Unit B

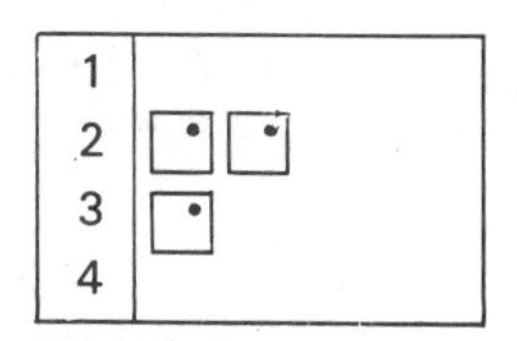


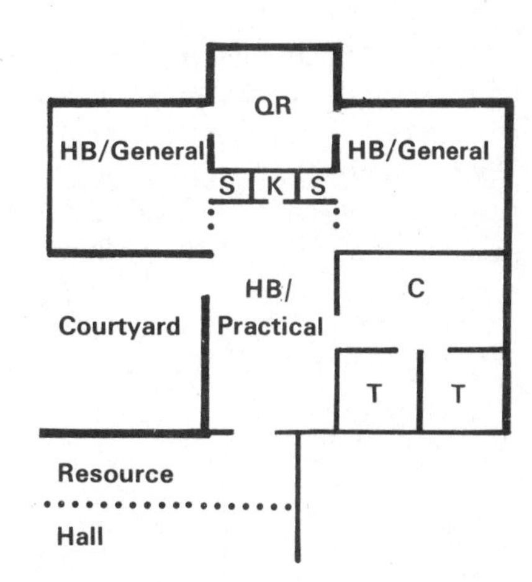


Junior School Suburban/Council
Pair Type 2 80(86) 2(3) 2.0 m² (1.9 m²)

accommodated three at the time of observation. The three teachers each had a register class group of single age which they worked with throughout the day. The extra teacher meant that the practical area was used as a home base necessitating all spaces to be timetabled. Each teacher and his or her class used each area once a day.

Each teacher was responsible for a curriculum area – language, maths or topic. However, their responsibility lay not in teaching but in providing equipment, materials and display. The children were grouped on a random or a social basis and are not allowed choice of work or location.

Unit E is a four teacher unit comprising an enclosed AV room, an enclosed room of classroom size, a general teaching area, a practical area and a shared library.

Unit E

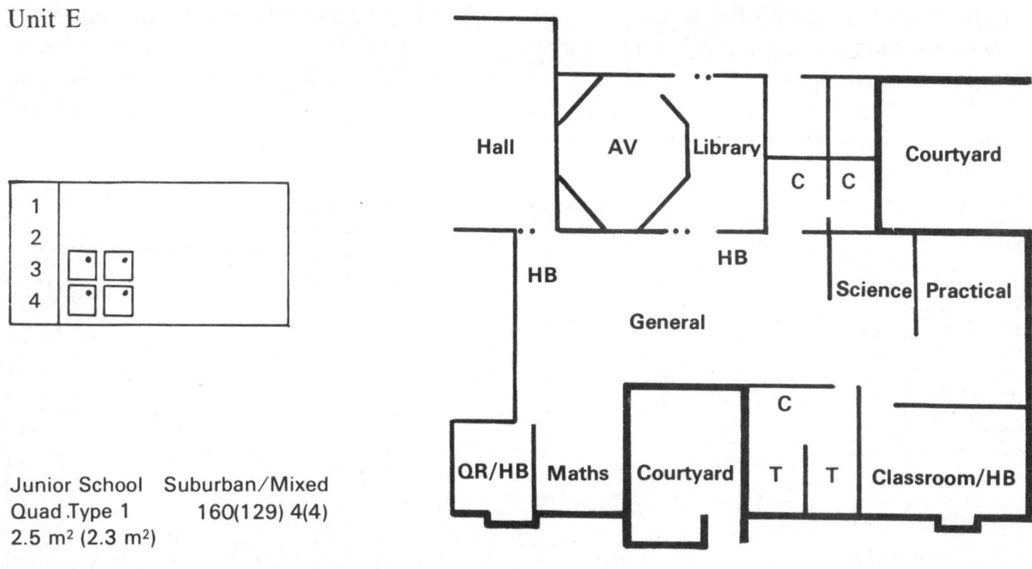


Junior School Suburban/Mixed
Quad Type 1 160(129) 4(4)
2.5 m² (2.3 m²)

The four teachers each had a register group of single age which they worked with throughout the day. This arrangement was broken on one day a week when the two third year teachers cooperated for art and language work. The space was organized on a use-specific basis incorporating an area for maths, one for science and so on. Because of this the spaces were timetabled – children and their teachers moving spaces for different subjects. The school day was in four sessions, but on three mornings a week all the children in the school were grouped by maths ability for work on Fletcher maths. Every teacher in the school had, on these mornings, responsibility for teaching one of these ability groups. In addition children were also grouped on maths ability within their own class group for all work with their own teacher.

Unit C

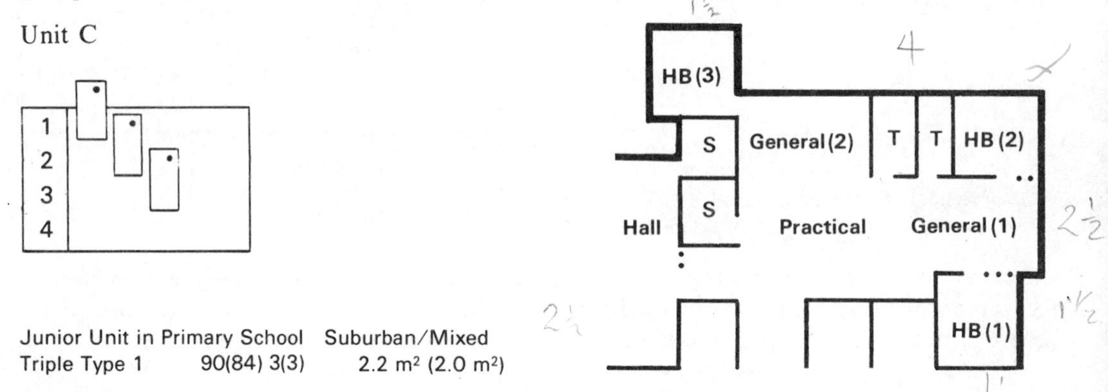


Junior Unit in Primary School Suburban/Mixed
Triple Type 1 90(84) 3(3) 2.2 m² (2.0 m²)

Three small home bases, two shared general teaching areas and a practical area comprised the accommodation in Unit C.

Each teacher had a vertically grouped class covering a two year range, which they worked with all the time. The only things shared were space and materials. Within each class children were grouped into between three and five groups based on ability. Assignments were allocated weekly but a daily requirement for maths, English and environmental studies was imposed.

Unit F comprises four small home bases opening on to the general teaching area and cookery/practical area, with shared use of an AV room, also acting as a home base. The unit was designed for four teachers but housed five. Each had a register group covering a two year span, and was responsible for assigning and checking their group work throughout the day.

Unit F

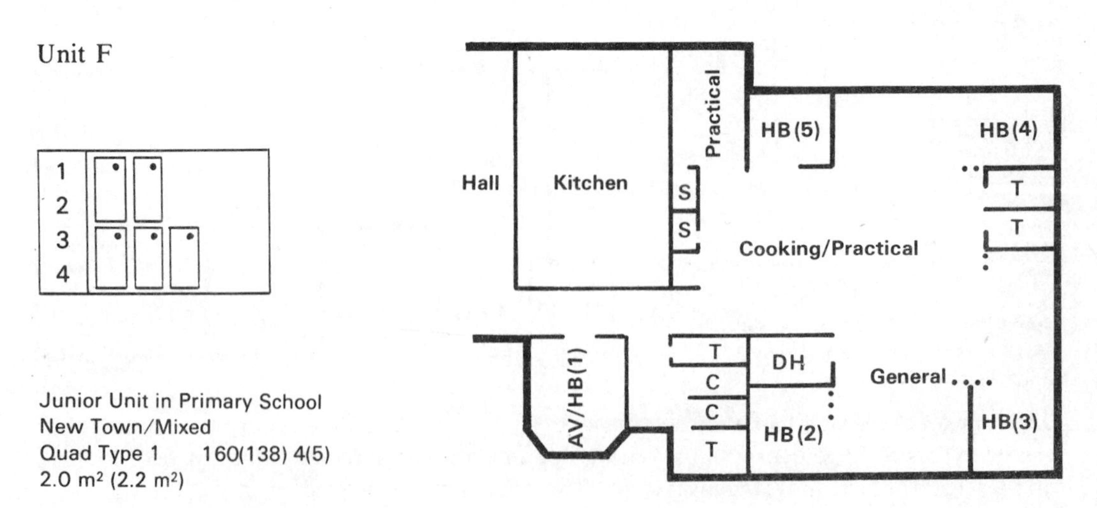


Junior Unit in Primary School
New Town/Mixed
Quad Type 1 160(138) 4(5)
2.0 m² (2.2 m²)

Teachers also helped in checking children's work when assigned by another teacher. Some of the classes were grouped by ability. Work was assigned on a weekly basis and children had an assignment book for this purpose. The book was checked at the end of the week. Some choice of order of work was allowed.

The organizational factor shared by the following group of units is the move towards cooperation whereby classes or teachers work together for some aspects of the curriculum.

Unit J

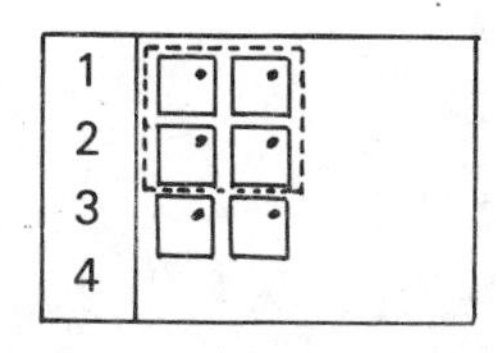


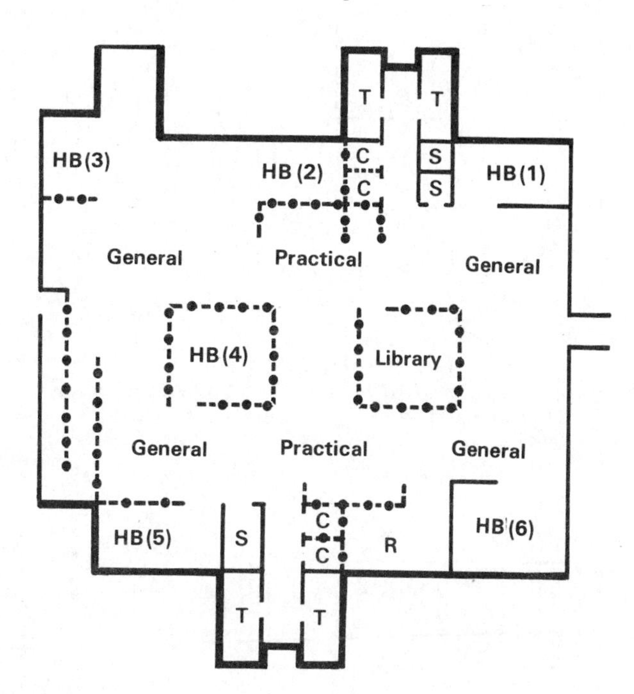


Junior Unit of Primary School
Urban/Council
Multi Type 1 320(141) 8(7)
1.6 m² (2.7 m²)

Unit J is a large open area housing 7 teachers and only 141 children. The space available and its use is shown. Six of the seven teachers had a register class of single age. The two third year teachers worked independently, whereas the four teachers with first and second year groups kept their own class for PE, art, swimming and the six weekly options (which included art, drama, science and needlework), but cooperated in maths and English. The seventh teacher withdrew small groups from the whole unit for remedial reading. The children were grouped by ability for basic skill work.

A part team teaching arrangement existed in Unit G. The four teachers each had a register group comprising third and fourth year and they worked with their group each day until 10.30 a.m. on maths, language, reading and handwriting. After 10.30 a.m. each teacher was responsible for a curriculum area for half a term, in this instance art, topic, maths or language. Each of these activities was allotted a specific space. A team leader was appointed who was responsible for calling weekly planning meetings. After 10.30 a.m. the children were allowed to select their area of work.

Although the representation of organization of Unit H looks similar to Unit G there are differences both in its operation and in space use. In this design for four teachers each is provided with a home base and quiet room, all opening on to a shared practical area.

Unit G

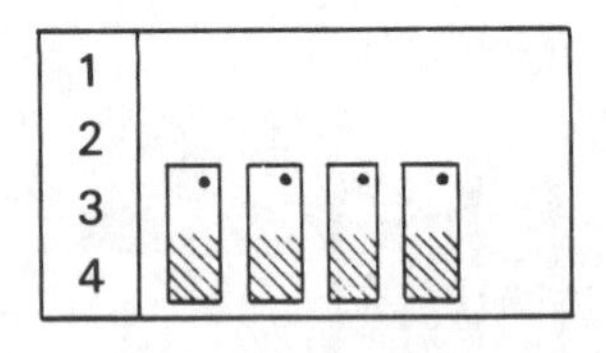


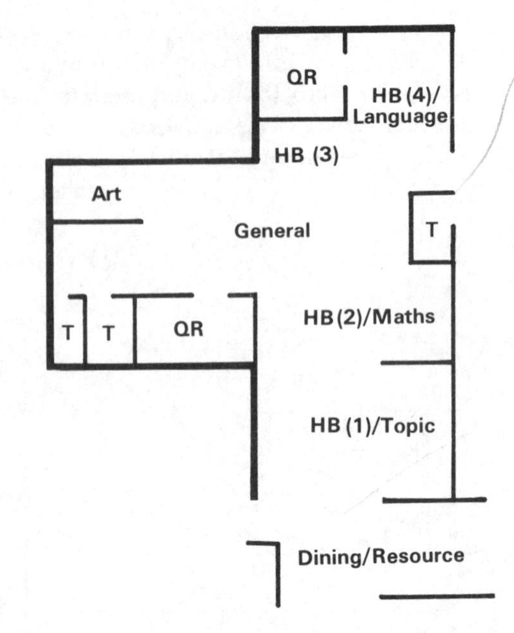


Junior School New Town/Council
Quad Type 1 160(120) 4(4) 1.95 m² (1.95 m²)

Unit H

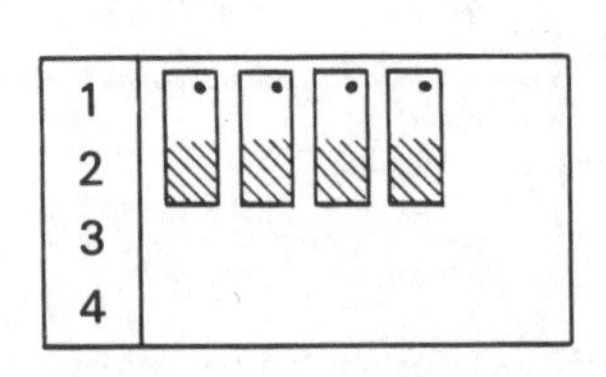


Junior Extension of First School Suburban
Quad Type 2 160(120) 4(5)
2.1 m² (2.9 m²)

Four of the five teachers had a mixed age register group for which they were responsible, for reading, PE, swimming, poetry, story and discussion, in addition to setting and checking their work through the day. In addition each of the five teachers was responsible for a curriculum area – maths skills, home skills, study skills, language and art/crafts. Each of these took place in a specific area. The teachers met every day for cooperative planning. A theme for the whole unit was taken for each half term.

Children were placed into 8 groups based on age and ability for maths, and each teacher had one first and one second year group twice a week. Monday and Wednesday afternoons and Friday morning were structured times, but during the rest of the week children chose their work in consultation with their register teacher.

The final group comprised those with varying kinds of teaming arrangements.

Unit A

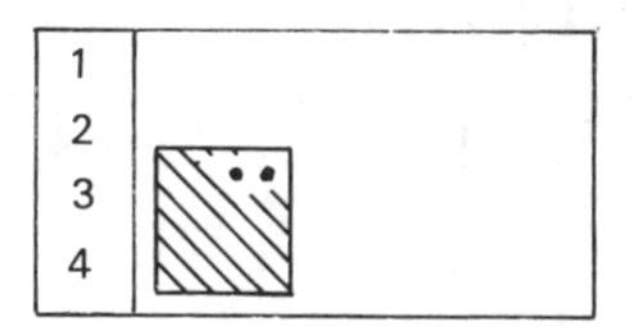


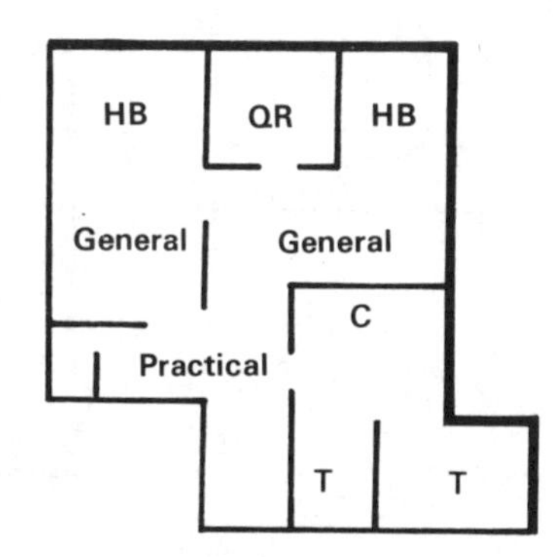


Junior School Suburban/Army
Pair Type 1 70(43) 2(2) 1.8 m² (2.9 m²)

Unit A was a paired unit, the two teachers sharing two general teaching spaces in which the home bases, a quiet room and a practical area were sited.

Each teacher had a register group of mixed third and fourth years which they took for creative writing, dance and movement. The children were grouped by ability for maths, each teacher taking a top, middle and low group for half a term for maths, English and creative work.

Work was organized around a workwheel each day, comprising topic, maths, SRA, handwriting, art/crafts, sound sense/dictionary. Children moved every three quarters to one hour, in a group, to use-specific areas.

Unit D

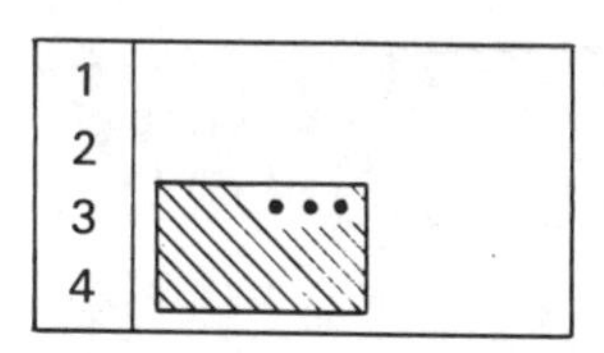


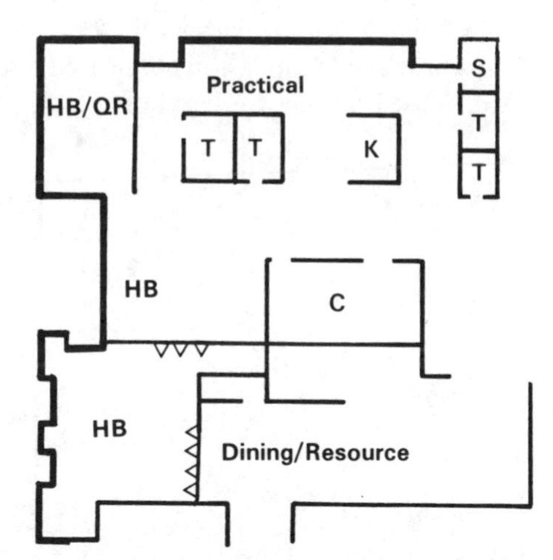


Junior Unit in Primary School Suburban/Mixed
Triple Type 2 80(85) 3(3) 2.2 m² (1.9 m²)

Unit D was a slightly over-pupilled three teacher unit with three partially enclosed home bases one of which doubles as a quiet room. The practical area was shared with another team of three teachers.

Each teacher had a register group of two years' span which they took for reading. In addition each teacher specialized throughout the year in one curriculum area, teaching all children in the unit in either maths, language or music. A fourth taught art and handwriting for both this and the other junior unit.

The children were set for maths and had a timetabled curriculum of music, art, language, maths, environmental studies and choice.

Unit K

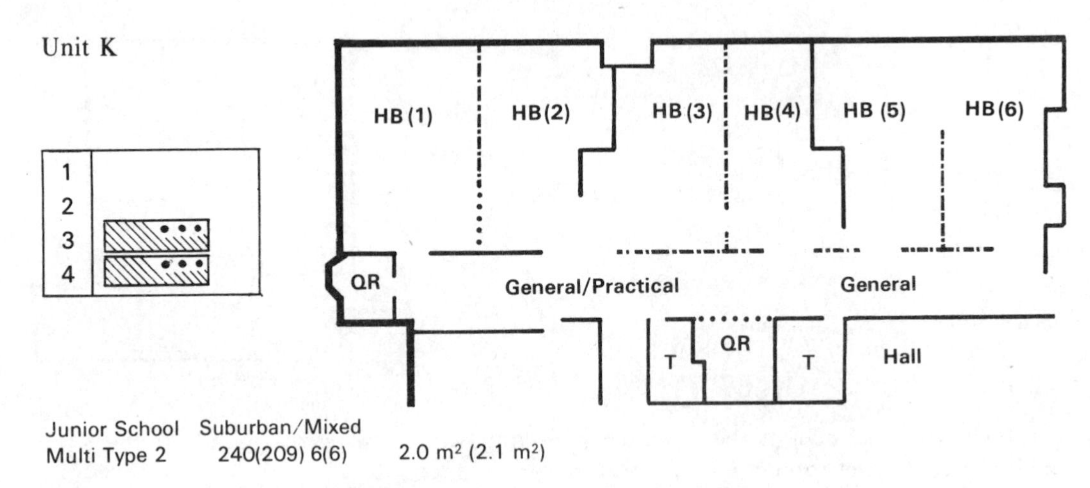


Junior School Suburban/Mixed
Multi Type 2 240(209) 6(6) 2.0 m² (2.1 m²)

Unit K is of linear design comprising six class size bases divisible by floor to ceiling partitions. They shared a general/practical area, an enclosed quiet room and a partially enclosed space.

The teachers each had a register class of single age and worked in two teams of three – all third years and all fourth years. Each teacher took one of three ability groups based on English and maths for half a term in each subject. Topic work was done in mixed groups and PE in maths groups (see Case Study 4, Chapter 10).

In Unit I the home bases were small and curtained off from the general teaching areas. The rest of the accommodation comprised a four sided practical area, a small enclosed room and a studio used by the whole school.

Unit I

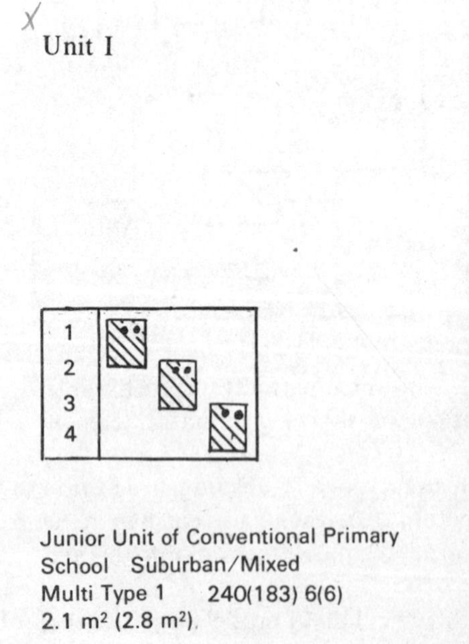


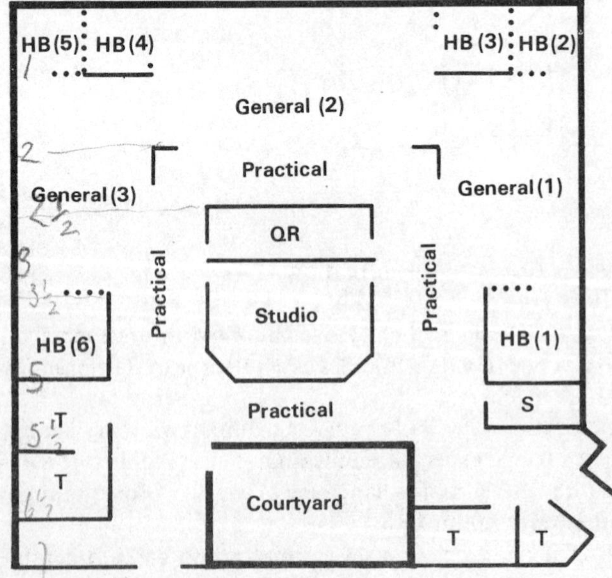


Junior Unit of Conventional Primary School Suburban/Mixed
Multi Type 1 240(183) 6(6)
2.1 m² (2.8 m²)

The six teachers worked in three teams of two – each of the teams having groups of a two year span. Each teacher had a single age register group which they taught reading. The two teachers worked together all day grouping children by ability for certain aspects of their work. The six teachers planned and worked as a team of six once a week, when they offered different workshops continuing for half a term. The assignment system was operated, work being assigned for 1–3 weeks depending on the child's ability.

Unit L

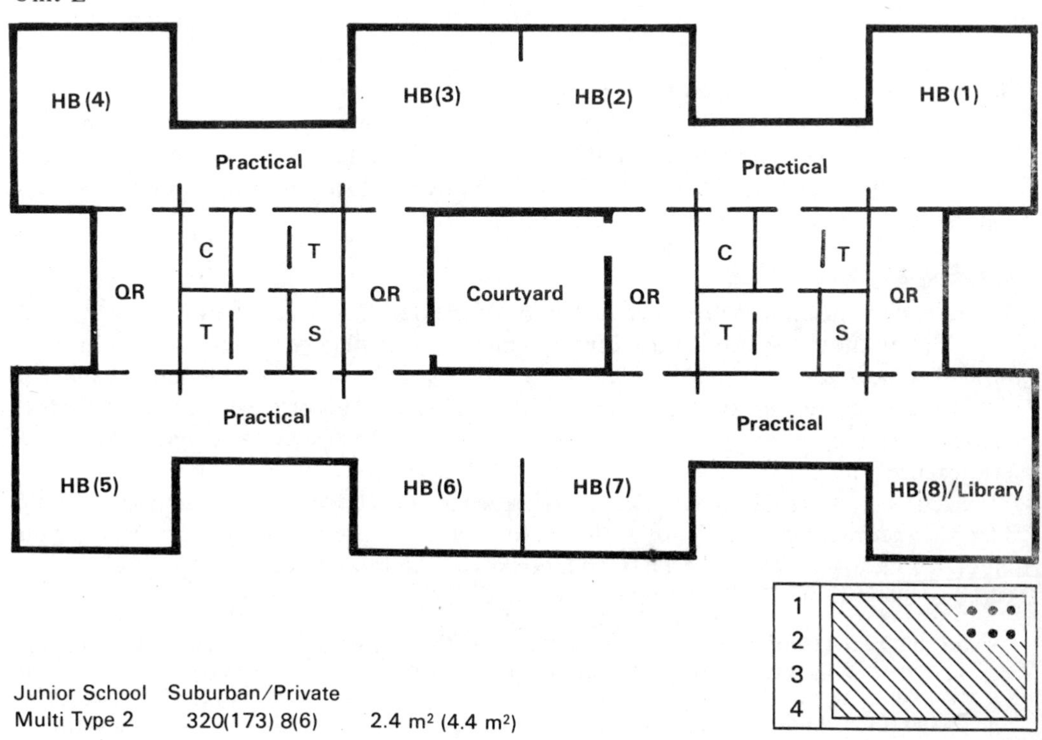


The final Unit is L, a very under-pupilled unit. Built for eight teachers, it was used by six teachers who each had a register group of first to fourth years and team in different ways for different subjects. For basic skill activities the children were grouped by age, but in vertical groups for core activities. Core time is when the child selects an area for two weeks – teachers specializing in science, art, maths, language and reading. Project work was done in half termly topics where teachers work in two teams of three.

**Summary**

Variety in organizational patterns in junior units matched that found in infants. Of the four units organized for independent teaching two utilized single age grouping and two vertical grouping. Two had weekly assignment systems, the others did not. Two timetabled space necessitating constant movement of teachers and pupils, and pupil grouping arrangements varied widely.

Wide variety in grouping was also apparent in team teaching organizations, from specific age to four year spans. Team size varied from two to six teachers, and length of teacher specialization for a given curriculum area varied from half a term to a full year.

It was argued in Chapter 3 that the units chosen for observation were not representative of all open plan units. This is true in the sense that more team teaching organizations were included, but the fact that each of the twenty-three organizations observed included unique elements, or combinations of elements, casts doubts on the whole notion of representative sampling of units or schools.

## Changes in Organization: Two Case Studies

Organizations are not static. They evolve and become modified in response to a number of factors. In order to highlight these factors the organizational history of two units is presented based on information acquired in interviews. Two three teacher units have been chosen, one infant (Unit O) and one junior (Unit D).

### *Unit O*

The present organization is presented earlier in the chapter. Basically there were four teachers one operating independently with reception children, the other three having a registration group of 6 and 7 year olds to which they teach various aspects of the curriculum. In addition single age groups were arranged for other curriculum areas. This organization meant that the practical area had become a home base requiring timetabled space and frequent movement of both teachers and children.

The school was a replacement. Thus all the teachers moved from an old Victorian building where they operated independently with vertically grouped classes. Being together in the old school had its advantages since the teacher could have 'dummy runs' in the old building. The head described this as follows:

> our old school building was . . . one open area with three screens . . . which seldom worked . . . the screens were pretty well permanently closed but the children still went from one classroom to another in order, for example, to go to the toilet, so teachers were not unaware of children from other classes . . . however, when this new building was first mooted, for a period of perhaps two years we deliberately adopted a policy of opening the screens and having two classes working together to find the snags, and at the same time we developed some team teaching . . . for a shorter time there was more or less the same staff as I have now.

The perception of the deputy head was similar:

> the infants were all together in the old building (as opposed to the juniors in split sites) and because it was already screened we put all the screens back and had a dummy run with the new situation. In that time we were able to see where . . . I'd gone wrong really . . . there was too much horizontal streaming and we were finding that because I'd streamed it that much we weren't able to have the readers heard in the same way – because the teachers were left with a colour group when they ought to have had their own classes. They should have been responsible for hearing their own children read in their own home bases but it wasn't working right . . . we used to do it for PE too . . . we thought at the outset that the children ought to be more of the same age in the PE group but we scrubbed that when we came here because we found it wasn't working out.

When the school moved:

> at first we had a reception class separate with two vertically grouped classes and then we started taking children in all at the same time in September so we had two vertically grouped classes of reception children together with young middle infants and two other vertically grouped classes of middle and top infants. This year we've started this way.

In those early days the teachers felt the need for screens or curtains and put their large blackboards across the area as dividers: 'We put up the board between . . . we felt too insecure . . . we put the blackboards up . . . but gradually found we didn't need them.'

Originally the four classes were arranged in four spaces, i.e. three in the three teaching bases and one in the large AV room, but this was changed due to the internal environment of the AV room which had no windows.

> until very recently we had one class in the large quiet room and it was a bit claustrophobic so we've moved out of there . . . the class now registers there and the classes take turns to use that as a study room for quiet lessons – the infant teachers certainly take it in turns to have its use. One of the classes uses it for registration and as a cloakroom but they move out so that other classes or groups can use it.

Also at this time the three vertical classes were colour banded according to age for several subjects: 'it was too much we thought . . .we ended up with a vertical registration time and little else so we gave up quite a lot of the colour banding.'

The triple problems of the size of the intake of reception children, the need to use the AV room as a base, and colour banding children throughout the day, led to organizational modification.

The youngest children admitted in September were grouped into a separate reception class with one intake in September, and the remainder were vertically grouped. These three vertically grouped classes timetabled the four spaces so that no one had to suffer the AV room for long periods, necessitating a good deal of movement. The colour banding scheme was also adopted.

> Each teacher has a mixed class of thirty children and . . . they are separated into three groups according to age for various activities – not everything. They separate for practical number, handwork, topic work, sounds, some PE and storytime.
>
> In this system each teacher takes their own class for news, story-writing, reading, work cards, some PE and storytime.

The teachers feel that they have 'adapted many things to suit the building' and although they are reasonably happy with the current organization 'none of us would ever be against changing again if we felt that something needed changing – if somebody had a fresh idea or thought the school could be organized a better way'.

The head's view was that:

> I don't think that we have ever reached perfection; we look for change and, indeed, as the staff changes new ideas or fresh skills are brought. We do change – we've changed our organization of the infant department three times in the few years that we've been in the building . . .

*Unit D*

The current organization involves each teacher having a vertically grouped register class which they take for reading. But each teacher also specializes throughout the year in maths, language or music and takes all the children in this area. A fourth teacher, shared with another unit, teaches art and handwriting. In other words team teaching with specialization.

This was not a replacement school and had the advantage of evolving as the school numbers gradually rose. The large six teacher unit, split into two three teacher units sharing practical and resource areas, began with two teachers and, 'the head teaching full time. Then had four teachers, then five teachers (as numbers rose) and then last year and this year six teachers. Last year the six teachers worked as two separate teams using some of the same areas, e.g. art area and resource area.'

Initially the organization called for one teacher to take maths, one language and the other art with all the children, but as numbers rose the organization of the space had to change. As the head pointed out,

> the architect's intention was two teachers at the top, two teachers down the bottom and two teachers in the middle. That was my target at one point. There again, I think I would go for that regardless of the building because of this two year age band, rather than the design of the building. I think if it was just one big room I'd still have that, but now we've got instead of 2 + 1 + 2, 3 + 3, but then there's a cross matching on the 1 + 1, one music specialist and one art specialist and they cross, so I've got departmental specialists.

The organization requiring teacher specialization remained, but problems began to occur with the shared practical area. Each team (i.e. lower and upper juniors) taught art to their own children, but, as the art specialist pointed out:

> . . . the art area was getting in such a mess I didn't know whether I was coming or going. I was supposed to be looking after equipment and I'd go round and find things missing and I didn't know where things had gone, it was just absolutely chaotic at times and I think they felt that the noise level would be less if there was somebody round there all the time doing it and we just got together and decided that with the number of children and the way we were organized if would be best divided out into time. I trained to do art anyway so I went into the art area . . .

But this decision affected the organization in both teams and meant a cross hatching of art and music specialists. The art and music specialists work in both teams as well as having their own home base group. At this point the upper junior team became three vertically grouped classes of mixed ability, but setted on maths ability for work groups. How their day is spent is explained by one teacher as follows:

> . . . the children spend the first hour of each day within those base groups, a base group teacher is responsible for pastoral care, development of handwriting skills and reading skills. During that hour two mornings a week there is an assembly which takes out about 20 minutes of that time. The children at ten o'clock change to the different work areas and the upper school is divided into two main work areas, the maths work area and a language or English work area, the third area either being art or the dining area where children would go mostly for choice sessions. At ten o'clock the children divide and change into those areas and go into their work groups. We found considerable difficulty in the teaching of mathematics to a wide range of ability groups and the children are in fact setted for maths in those groups so that each group consists of a vertical group of third and fourth year children but they have been divided according to ability so though whilst each group is mixed ability in fact as far as mathematics is concerned, each group could be divided into two sub-groups for the teaching of mathematics. The children then follow a timetable. The curriculum is quite wide, the timetable caters for music, art, language, mathematics, environmental studies and we also include in the timetable choice periods which are periods when the subject content is not laid down but children

> have the opportunity to choose and organize their own time. We also lay emphasis on the fact that children, if they've completed their mathematics or language work, are not tied to that area. With that member of staff's permission they can go from that, say, to the language area if they have language to complete. This rarely hapens because the children seem to . . . have more than enough to cope with within the allotted time. During afternoons the timetable is slightly more complicated because two afternoons a week children from the upper school go to the art area. The art specialist in the junior department covers both upper and lower school so in other words the group from upper school are taken by a lower school teacher and one of us is released to take children in lower school. And so two afternoons a week two of us in fact take it in turns to split the afternoon in two if you like, and take it in turns to go into lower school and deal with their environmental studies down there. The third member of the team also comes into contact with lower school because she takes them for music, she's the music specialist. Once a week on a Friday morning when the upper school music specialist is taking lower school group the reverse is true. A member of the lower school team in fact supervises an upper school choice period which is considerably more difficult because those children may be involved in anything up to five or six activities and that period lasts one hour.

The main determinants of the organization as far as the staff were concerned were the numbers of children and the way the space was designed. As the head explained, 'We were working very much on an individual approach type of organization and the timetable was rather fluid. As our numbers have grown it's become more rigid rather than less, despite the fact that we're more experienced, but numbers have forced this on us'.

The organization is designed to cut the amount of movement down to a minimum. The timetable allows all groups to move at the same time. Even so, the problem is not solved entirely.

> Because we've got so many children we have more difficulties than I think we would have normally with less numbers and we have to have our curriculum organized in a more formal way than we would if we didn't have so many children. And so disadvantages are that, say in my area there, you have the continual movement through and if you're trying to take a lesson rather than the children working individually, it can be rather distracting.

**Summary**

Clearly two cases studies cannot highlight all the factors involved in the modification of organizations. Two factors come out sharply however – the interaction of pupil numbers and the design of space. In both cases these appear to have led to organizations that are more rigid than the staff wished, involving strict timetabling of space. Very different organizations are possible in both instances, and it is perhaps constructive to contrast Unit O with its twin design Unit P, and note the organizations adopted (see Case Studies, Chapter 10). Most teachers appear open to the possibilities of change if new ideas arise, and no doubt visits to other schools on an in-service basis are designed to facilitate the process. It is hoped that the brief descriptions provided here will play the same role.

*Chapter 7*

# *Curriculum Allocation and Pupil Involvement: 1. Infants*

## Introduction

Investigators of classroom practice do not simply walk into classrooms and begin to observe. Classroom settings are extremely complex, requiring the observer to adopt a specific focus. This focus is provided by theories, implicit or explicit, which delineate which aspects of classroom practice are most worthy of consideration. Since many perspectives are available it behoves the investigator to make clear his focus and the theory from which it is derived.

Harnischfeger and Wiley (1978) have recently argued that for too long research on teaching has focussed on isolated and oversimplified factors: 'We believe that the major reasons for this deplorable situation lie in the fact that empirical investigation has been too specific and minute in focus, and that theory has either been too gross to guide research or completely lacking.' They contended that models or theories which integrate pupil and teacher activities in ways which take account of the content of the teaching–learning process, i.e. the curriculum, are difficult to find, but point to three models which can. With the exception of Carroll's (1963), these are of very recent origin, i.e. Bloom (1976) and their own (1975). Each focusses on pupil activities and how teachers influence learning directly by the allocation and use of time. Bennett (1978a) has recently adapted the Wiley/Harnischfeger model and assessed its utility and implications for teaching. Two of the central elements of the model are curriculum allocation – the amount of time teachers devote to different areas of the curriculum, and pupil involvement – the use which pupils make of that time. The importance of these two factors is that they vary markedly in schools and are related to pupil achievement. Indeed Westbury (1977) defines teaching as the management of the attention and time of students vis-à-vis the primary educational ends of the classroom.

## Curriculum Allocation

For the purposes of observation a coarse and a fine-grained classification of curriculum activities was adopted. For the latter the specific curriculum activity the children were allocated was recorded, and these were then grouped into areas of experience in a similar manner to that employed in the HMI Working Paper on Curriculum 11–16 (Great Britain, DES 1977c). These were mathematics, language, environmental studies, aesthetics, physical, social and moral education. To these was added administration and transition. These included the movement of pupils to spaces, general tidying up, waiting for instructions for a new curriculum activity, queueing up for the purpose of moving to a new location and so on. Definitions of these areas

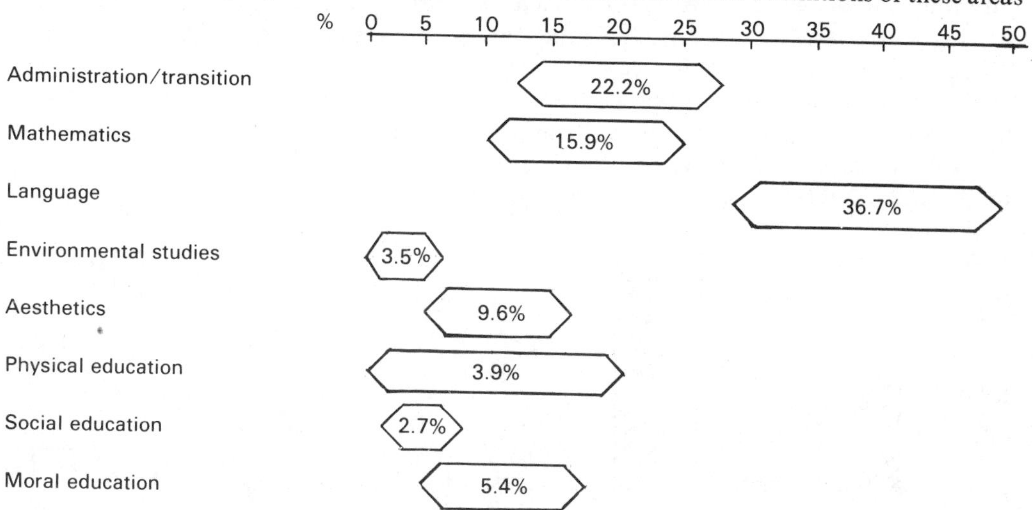


*Figure 1 Percentage of time allocated to curriculum areas: infants (average and range)*

of experience can be found in the glossary and, in more detail, in the supplement available from Schools Council.

The Pupil Behaviour Schedule provided data on 264 middle infant pupils in eleven units varying in size, degree of openness and organizational pattern. Figure 1 (and Table B1 in Appendix B) presents the percentage of time allocated to each curriculum area in infant units.

Figure 1 shows the average amount of time spent on activities as well as the range of time across the eleven units. For example, on average 22.2 per cent of the school time was taken up by administration and transition activities, but in one unit it was as low as 12.4 per cent and at the other extreme it was as high as 26.9 per cent (Table B1 presents the findings for each individual unit). Transition, rather than administration, accounts for the bulk of this – 17.8 per cent of the 22.2 per cent. That nearly a quarter of school time is taken up by essentially non-curricular activities may surprise some but is in line with other studies on open plan schools. Some researchers have termed this wasted time and used it as an index of teacher management competency (Gump, 1974) but many teachers would not accept this view, arguing for example that a task such as infants learning to tie shoelaces after PE is a relevant educational activity for infants. Nevertheless in the terms of this study it is non-curricular.

As might be expected, the bulk of curriculum time is consumed by language activities, averaging 36.7 per cent, but large variations are evident, being as low as 28 per cent and as high as 48 per cent. Thus, at the extremes, children in one unit were given the opportunity to be involved in language activities nearly twice as frequently as those in another.

Mathematics is accorded the next priority, with nearly 16 per cent of school time, but here too large variations are apparent, ranging from less than 10 per cent to nearly 25 per cent.

Aesthetics, which includes art and craft, making music and drama, accounts for nearly 10 per cent on average, with a range of 6 to 17 per cent.

As can be seen from Figure 1, very little time is given to environmental studies, social, moral and physical education. The range in physical education is rather large, but is largely due to one unit which, in the week of observation, made use of the fine weather to practice for a forthcoming sports day. If this is discounted the remainder of the units devoted between none and 4.7 per cent of the time to this area.

The marked variations in the time teachers allow for different curriculum areas indicates that infants gain quite different educational diets in different schools and units. This might be called curriculum balance, and Figure 2 plots the curriculum profile for Units T and U (see Table B1) to illustrate the differing curriculum emphases.

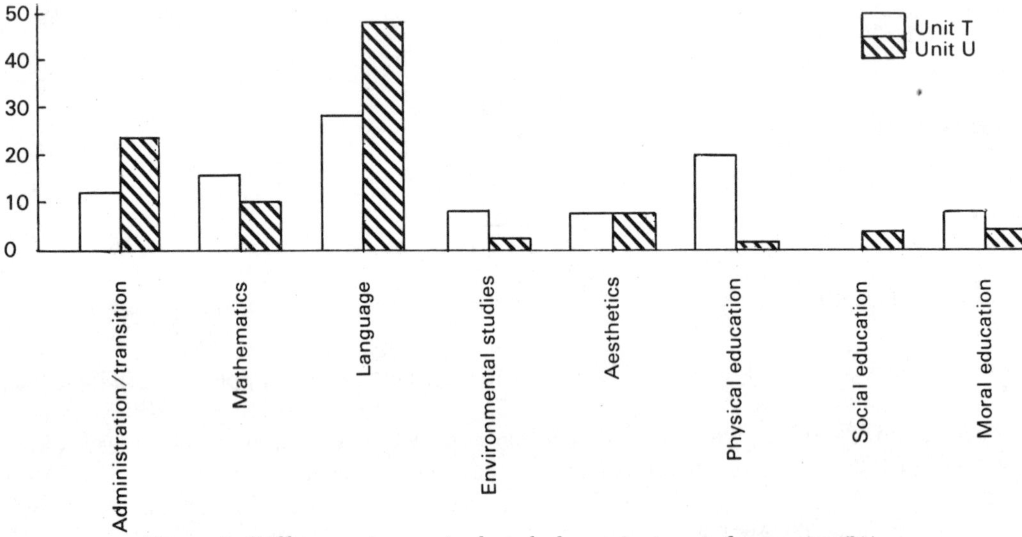


*Figure 2 Difference in curriculum balance in two infant units (%)*

Unit U consumes considerably more time in administration/transition and language, and Unit T more in mathematics and considerably more in physical education. Since these results are based on four days' consecutive observations they would indicate by inference that, using a 25 hour week norm, Unit U spent $2^1/_2$ hours more on administration and transition, $1^1/_2$ hours less on mathematics, 5 hours more on language and $4^1/_2$ hours less on physical education. But the balance achieved in one week may or may not be representative of that achieved over one month, one term or one year. No relevant research appears to have cast light on this issue although it can be imagined that the balance might differ in different terms due to a number of factors. One of these could be the weather, since more outside activity is possible at certain times of the year. Unit T, for example, was observed during the summer term in a period of hot weather, and advantage was taken of this to extend PE and games. The differences in curriculum balance shown in Figure 2 are thus accurate for the week observed, but it cannot be said that they are typical of the overall balance achieved. To assess that would require a longitudinal study.

**Pupil Involvement**

If curriculum allocation is conceived as the opportunity a teacher provides for pupils to study a given curriculum content, then pupil involvement can be conceived as the use the pupil makes of that opportunity. Pupil involvement is considered a very important factor in pupil learning, and a growing number of studies have confirmed this (Bennett, 1978a). Indeed Bloom (1976) goes so far as to say that the involvement of pupils is the clearest indicator of the effectiveness of instruction, and is seen to be influenced both by the teacher's management competencies and pupils' levels of application or motivation.

Two indices of pupil involvement were computed to answer two equally valid questions. The first, hereafter called overall involvement, was designed to answer the question 'What proportion of the school day are pupils involved in their work?'. The second, curriculum involvement, answered the question 'What proportion of the school day available for curriculum activities are pupils involved in their work?'. The first index uses as its base the total time available minus breaks for lunch and playtime, but includes administration and transition time. In the second, administration and transition is discounted.

*Overall Involvement*

Figure 3 presents the findings for all infant units and for Type 1 and Type 2 units. The shaded areas indicate non-involvement. 22.2 per cent of the non-involvement is in administration and

| | *All* | *Type 1* | *Type 2* |
|---|---|---|---|
| *No. of Units* | 11 | 7 | 4 |
| *No. of Pupils* | 264 | 158 | 96 |
| Administration/transition | 22.2 | 23.4 | 20.3 |
| Non-involvement | 16.4 | 16.4 | |
| Maths | 10.3 | 9.6 | 11.5 |
| Language | 28.3 | 29.0 | 28.4 |
| Environmental studies | 2.9 | 2.7 | 3.5 |
| Aesthetics | 8.0 | 9.0 | 6.3 |
| PE | 8.6 | 2.3 | 5.8 |
| Moral education | 2.5 | 2.7 | 2.2 |
| Social education | 5.3 | 5.0 | 5.6 |

*Figure 3 The infant day: mean percentage overall involvement*

transition time. (NB If pupils were given an activity to do in administration time, this was classified as involved.) Pupils were not involved on allocated activities for 16.4 per cent of the time. Thus, on average, pupils are involved for 61.3 per cent of the time. In other words, 3 of the 5 hour day, or 15 of the 25 hour week are characterized by involvement on curriculum activities.

There are few differences when unit design is considered. The more closed designs spend less time on administration and transition and slightly more on mathematics and physical education, but less time on aesthetics. Overall involvement in the more closed Type 2 unit is 63.3 per cent compared to 60.3 per cent in Type 1 units.

*Curriculum Involvement*

Curriculum involvement is an index of level of involvement within the time allocated to curriculum activities. Thus, administration and transition is discounted. Table B2 (Appendix B) presents the results for each of the eleven units and also for units of differing design. Figure 4 presents the averages and ranges of involvement by curriculum area. For this analysis, social and moral have been combined.

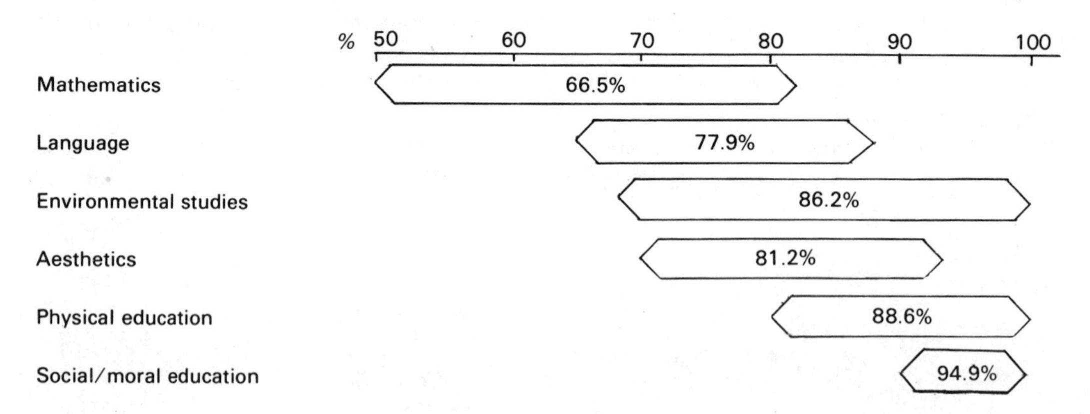


*Figure 4 Percentage curriculum involvement by curriculum area: infants (average and range)*

The average involvement across all curriculum areas is 79.1 per cent with a range of 71.1 per cent – 89.5 per cent, but as Figure 3 shows, this varies considerably. The average for mathematics is the lowest at 66.5 per cent and ranges from 50 per cent in one unit to over 80 per cent in another. Language shows the next lowest involvement at 77.9 per cent, ranging from 64 per cent to 89.5 per cent. The average for environmental studies is high and the range wide, one unit recording 100 per cent involvement, but little time was devoted to this area. Highest levels of involvement occur in physical education and social/moral education. These are not surprising since physical education activities are usually teacher-directed and paced and those in the social/moral area also tend to be paced, e.g. assembly, singing and so on, but also more passive.

Curriculum involvement is slightly higher in the Type 2 designs – 79.6 per cent to 78.8 per cent, but these differences are minimal.

Having considered curriculum allocation and curriculum involvement separately, it is instructive to consider their combined effect. To illustrate this, Units N, R and W (Table B1 in Appendix B) are examined in Table 1 following in relation to mathematics.

| | *Allocated* | | *Involvement* | |
|---|---|---|---|---|
| | (%) | *Time (mins)* | (%) | *Time (mins)* |
| Unit N | 14.6 | 219 | 50.7 | 111 |
| Unit R | 23.6 | 354 | 58.9 | 208.5 |
| Unit W | 14.1 | 211.5 | 81.6 | 172.6 |

*Table 1 A comparison of three units on allocated, involved and actual time*

In Unit N, 14.6 per cent of the time was allocated to mathematics which, using a 25 hour week, equates to 219 minutes. However, pupils were observed to be involved for only 50.7 per cent of that time, leaving only 111 minutes actual working time – some 22 minutes per day. The involvement rate of 50.7 per cent is an average across all 24 children observed and masks variations among pupils. Some spent considerably more time than this and others considerably less. Of interest here is that some units allocate considerably more time to mathematics, as in Unit R, but the actual time pupils spend on mathematical activities depends on pupil levels of involvement. In comparing Units R and W it can be seen that there is a substantial difference in the time allocated, but because of the high involvement rate in Unit W, the difference in actual time spent in mathematics is not large. The term curriculum balance was introduced when considering curriculum allocation, but these figures would point to wide discrepancies between the balance planned for and the balance achieved. What is missing in this study, indeed the vast majority of studies of classrooms, is any judgement as to the quality of the activities in which pupils engage. Such judgements about the quality of the task, the materials, the sequencing and pacing of the task, the nature of teacher feedback and so on, will be very difficult to make, but clearly headway must be made in this direction in future studies of classroom processes.

Other activities, not in themselves related to the curriculum, are essential if children are to carry out task requirements. For instance a child may be confronted with a problem he cannot solve or a word he cannot spell and seeks the aid of the teacher. If the teacher is busy he may have to wait for attention. Before a pupil can begin to paint or colour a picture he has to obtain the necessary materials. If a pupil is asked to read to the teacher he has to find his reading book. Similarly before changes of activity pupils are required to clear away the materials they have been using. Waiting, preparation and clearing away are all necessary and legitimate activities which can be time-consuming. It has already been shown that time devoted to administration and transition accounts for over 20 per cent of the school day and that this varies considerably between units. A breakdown of both transition time and curriculum time in terms of these activities and also in terms of the movement they entail is therefore of interest. Table 2 indicates the extent of waiting, preparation, clearing away and movement during transition in the different units. The figures presented do not summate to total transition time since some of these activities could occur at the same time or in conjunction with other behaviour.

It can be seen that, on average, pupils spent between 4 and 9 per cent of the school day during periods of transition, waiting for signals from the teacher before changing activity and/or location. For example, teachers signal the end of an activity and this is followed by a flurry of movement as pupils clear away and possibly obtain materials for the next activity. If a change of location is required, pupils form queues adjacent to traffic flow areas. There they can wait until the last pupil is ready and a further signal is received from the teacher which allows them to proceed to their next destination. Further waiting may then occur before children are allowed to enter a different space. The figures in Table 2 show that more time was spent waiting during transition periods by children in Unit U. In this large open unit children were required to queue, to change location and queue for morning milk.

| *Mean Percentage* | Type 1 | | | | | | | Type 2 | | | | Type 1 | Type 2 | All (11 units) |
|---|---|---|---|---|---|---|---|---|---|---|---|---|---|---|
| | M | O | P | R | S | U | V | N | Q | T | W | | | |
| Waiting | 7.3 | 7.1 | 6.6 | 5.9 | 6.6 | 9.1 | 6.6 | 7.0 | 7.3 | 4.0 | 6.0 | 7.0 | 6.1 | 6.7 |
| Preparation | 1.7 | 1.0 | 1.3 | 0.8 | 3.4 | 1.0 | 1.5 | 2.9 | 1.2 | 1.2 | 1.5 | 1.5 | 1.7 | 1.6 |
| Clearing away | 2.1 | 0.8 | 0.9 | 0.7 | 2.1 | 1.3 | 1.6 | 3.1 | 1.2 | 0.8 | 3.5 | 1.4 | 2.1 | 1.6 |
| Movement | 5.5 | 5.0 | 6.0 | 4.1 | 6.6 | 3.9 | 5.4 | 3.8 | 3.2 | 3.7 | 11.7 | 5.2 | 5.6 | 5.3 |

*Table 2 Transition: percentage waiting, preparation, clearing away and movement in relation to type of unit*

A great deal of movement was observed during transition in Unit W. Since choice of activity was almost totally unrestricted in this unit, pupils tended to change activity on their own instigation more frequently than in other units.

As already shown, somewhat more transition was observed in the more open Type 1 units. Although on average pupils were more often observed waiting in these units, extra transition time does not appear to be related to extra movement, possibly because distances involved in changes of location tend to be covered in a very short space of time and most movement during transition takes place in connection with preparation or clearing away.

A breakdown of movement and work-related activities during curriculum time is given in Table 3. It can be seen that the amount of time that pupils were observed waiting to see the teacher varies from 1.0 per cent in Unit W to 5.1 per cent in Unit V. In this last unit, queues of up to 10 children were frequently observed waiting to see the teacher for interpretation of mathematics work cars. In general, relatively little time was spent on preparation and clearing away, although this can be seen to vary between the different units. Much greater variation is apparent with regard to movement during designated curriculum time – from 3.2 per cent to 11.1 per cent. A comparison between Type 1 and Type 2 units reveals little difference with regard to time spent in waiting, preparation, clearing away or moving during curriculum activities.

| *Mean percentage* | Type 1 | | | | | | | Type 2 | | | | Type 1 | Type 2 | All (11 units) |
|---|---|---|---|---|---|---|---|---|---|---|---|---|---|---|
| | M | O | P | R | S | U | V | N | Q | T | W | | | |
| Waiting | 2.0 | 3.2 | 4.3 | 5.0 | 3.4 | 3.5 | 5.1 | 4.9 | 2.4 | 2.4 | 1.0 | 3,8 | 2.7 | 3.4 |
| Preparation | 0.8 | 2.2 | 2.6 | 1.9 | 1.1 | 1.4 | 3.3 | 2.6 | 4.1 | 3.2 | 2.0 | 1.9 | 3.0 | 2.3 |
| Clearing away | 0.2 | 1.0 | 2.1 | 1.5 | 0.5 | 0.7 | 1.9 | 0.7 | 1.1 | 0.2 | 0.6 | 1.1 | 0.7 | 1.0 |
| Movement | 4.2 | 4.7 | 7.0 | 9.8 | 8.1 | 6.2 | 7.4 | 3.2 | 4.9 | 5.0 | 11.1 | 6.8 | 6.1 | 6.5 |

*Table 3 Curriculum: percentage waiting, preparation, clearing away and movement in relation to type of unit*

*Active/Passive Curriculum*

If, as indicated in Chapter 1, the move towards a more progressive or open education is related to the development of open plan schools, it is of interest to analyse these data in the light of concepts underlying that approach. The model adopted here is that by Bussis and Chittenden (1970), who categorize four types of schooling, based on the twin dimensions of teacher and pupil involvement in content and process. Their model is reproduced below (Figure 5).

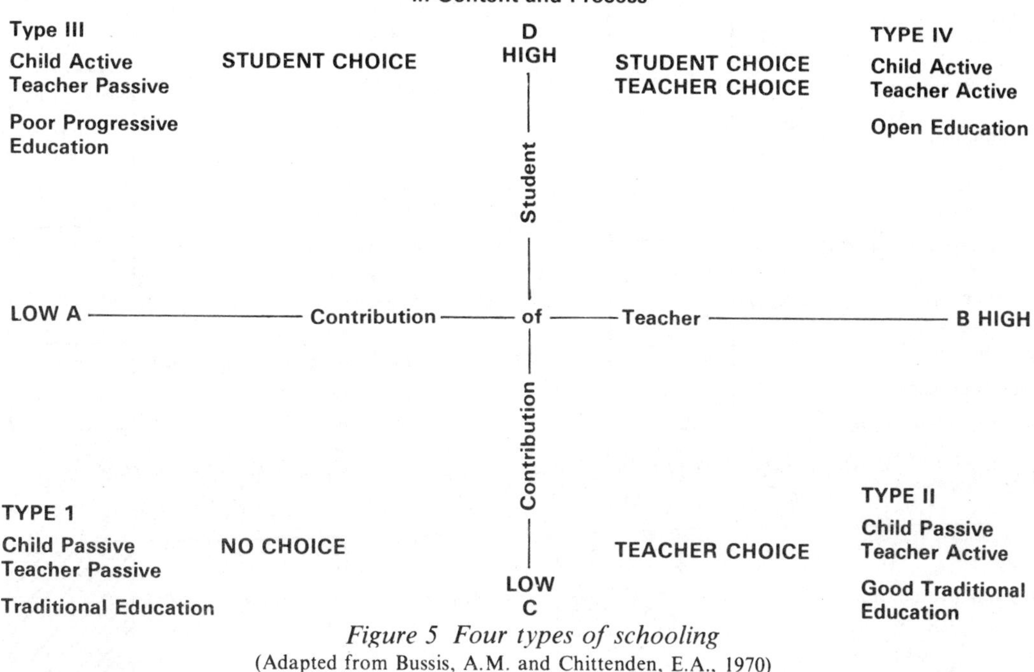


*Figure 5 Four types of schooling*
(Adapted from Bussis, A.M. and Chittenden, E.A., 1970)

In a later publication, Bussis, Chittenden and Amarel (1976) describe open education as an approach which is characterized by a high input from teachers and pupils alike. They argue, not against the logical organization of subject matter, but for diversity of approach based on individual pupils who differ in the way that they learn similar things. Thus curricular decisions are made by open education teachers on the basis of information gained from pupils' own decisions and choices about learning.

As outlined in the previous chapter, many different variations of teaching organization were encountered on observation in the 11 units, but in only five of these units was there an element of choice available to pupils. In four of these units (P, R, S and N) choice was available to pupils in association with an assignment system where pupils were allotted tasks for the day but could choose the order in which they were to be carried out. In the fifth unit (W) pupils had almost totally unrestricted choice of activities which were then guided and structured by members of the team. These would be categorized at the high end of pupil contribution in the above model and are thus categorized as having an active curriculum to be consistent with the model.

Figure 6 shows differences in curriculum allocation in those units whose curriculum was designated active and passive.

Active
N = 120
Administration/
transition
24.9
Maths
15.9
Language
37.6
Environmental studies
2.6
Aesthetics
10.0
PE
2.7
Social education
3.5
Moral education
2.9
Passive
N = 144
Administration/
transition
20.2
Maths
15.7
Language
36.0
Environmental studies
4.2
Aesthetics
9.3
PE
4.9
Social education
2.1
Moral education
7.5

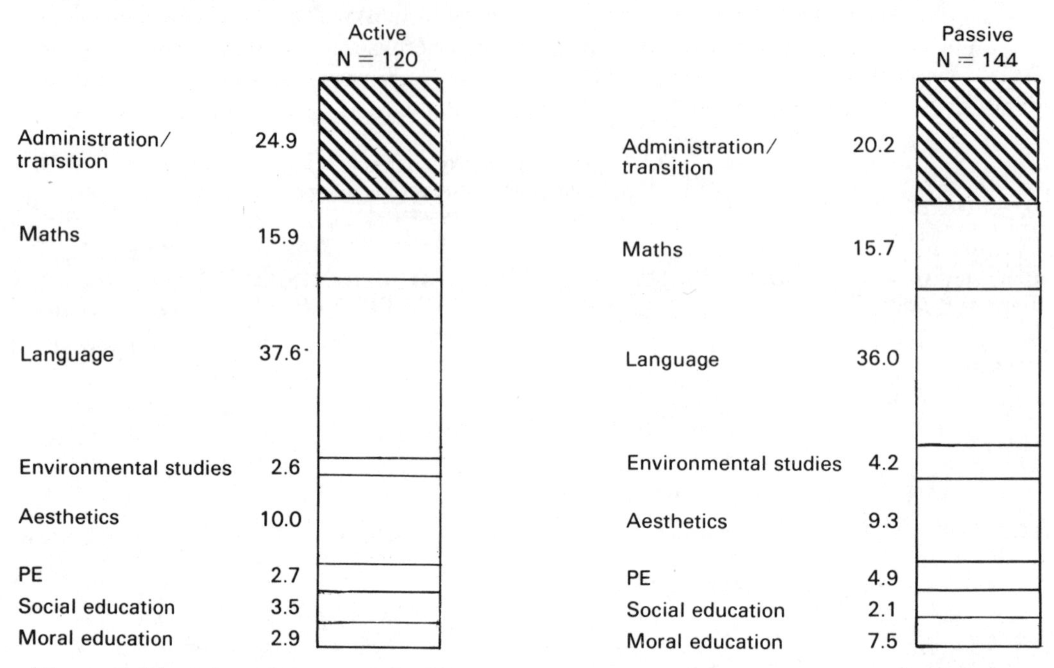

*Figure 6 The infant day: curriculum allocation in relation to pupil choice (average %)*

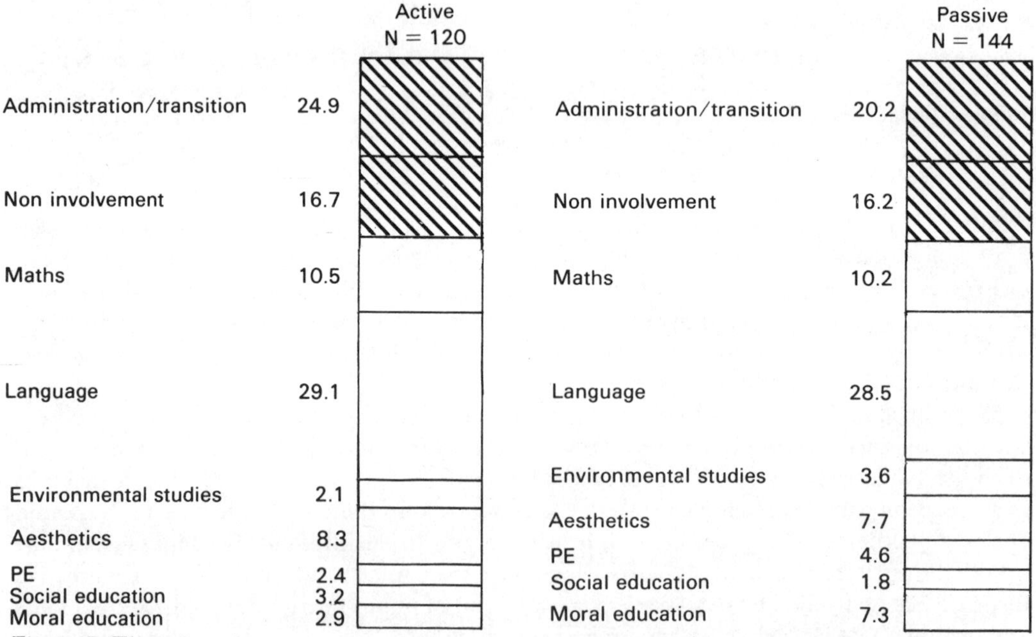

Active
N = 120
Administration/transition
24.9
Non involvement
16.7
Maths
10.5
Language
29.1
Environmental studies
2.1
Aesthetics
8.3
PE
2.4
Social education
3.2
Moral education
2.9
Passive
N = 144
Administration/transition
20.2
Non involvement
16.2
Maths
10.2
Language
28.5
Environmental studies
3.6
Aesthetics
7.7
PE
4.6
Social education
1.8
Moral education
7.3

*Figure 7 The infant day: overall involvement in relation to pupil choice of activities (average %)*

It can be seen that in those units where pupils had some degree of choice a greater portion of the school day was expended on administration and transition. Little difference is evident between the two sets of units with regard to the apportionment of time for work in the basic skills, but more time was allocated to PE and moral education in those units characterized by a passive curriculum.

Overall involvement is shown in Figure 7, where it can be seen that it is lower in the active curriculum units – 58.4 per cent to 63.7 per cent – a function of the increased administration/transition time.

Table 4 gives the figures for mean curriculum involvement for those units giving a degree of choice of activity and for those units where no choice was given, i.e. the active versus passive curriculum. Social and moral education have been combined for these analyses since they constitute only a small proportion of curriculum time.

| | *Mean percentage curriculum involvement* | |
|---|---|---|
| | Active N = 120 | Passive N = 144 |
| Mathematics | 67.8 | 65.5 |
| Language | 77.2 | 78.5 |
| Environmental studies | 86.1 | 86.3 |
| Aesthetics | 81.6 | 82.8 |
| PE | 89.8 | 87.3 |
| Social and moral education | 94.6 | 95.1 |
| Total curriculum | 77.9 | 80.0 |

*Table 4 Mean percentage involvement within curriculum area for active and passive curriculum*

On average curriculum involvement is slightly higher in units adopting a passive curriculum, but varies in differing curriculum areas. It would therefore seem that allowing pupils a degree of choice does not significantly affect their involvement, although there may be an increase in transition time.

**Curriculum Activities**

Perhaps the major problem encountered by the classroom observer is that of deciding whether or not a pupil is 'involved'. This may be quite apparent when pupils are actively engaged, as for instance in measuring or painting, but when the teacher is addressing the whole class or a group of pupils and the desired response is that of 'listening', involvement has to be assumed unless there are clear indications to the contrary. Similarly these observations tell us nothing about the quality of involvement. Since observations made during curriculum activities of a largely passive nature would most likely show a high rate of involvement, it is of interest to know the kind of activities in which pupils are involved. Table B3 in the Appendix lists the specific activities and involvement of pupils by type of unit and for those units which had an active and passive curriculum.

The figures in the table would indicate that pupils in Type 1 units were allotted more time for computation, practical maths, reading to the teacher, use of reading schemes, writing, listening to story, musical activities and television. Pupils in Type 2 units (where only the practical area was shared) appear to have spent more time in class group discussion and small group work with the teacher. Sand and water activities, making, drama, social play and sports were also more frequently observed in these units. Recourse to field notes made during observation would seem to indicate that although there were considerable differences in the extent and variety of materials used in different units, these did not appear to be related to unit design.

Further examination of the table reveals that pupils who were given a degree of choice with regard to activities were more frequently observed using practical aids to mathematics, using sand and water, reading books of their own choice, playing language games, writing on subjects of their own choice, drawing, music and movement, using large apparatus in PE sessions and engaging in social play. Pupils in other units were more frequently observed in whole class direct teaching sessions, computation, copying, listening to story, reciting, making, drama, singing, making use of small apparatus during PE sessions and engaging in sports activities. In this instance recourse to field notes on the use of materials indicated that although there was little difference in the extent to which standard texts were used for maths and language work, more use was made of the blackboard in units where no choice was given and pupils were more frequently observed using identical templates when involved in making models or doing collage. More use was made of dressing up materials in the active units.

*Teaching/Learning Situation*

Further information relating to the active/passive dimension of curriculum is afforded by observations of the teaching–learning situation made using the LES observation schedule. Two basic distinctions were made when recording activities in the context of the teaching–learning situation. The first related to whether activities were paced by the teacher, as for instance in story, singing or direct instruction. The second related to group size. For example 'small group work' is used to describe the situation when a small group of pupils are working in close proximity on the same or similar tasks. A breakdown of the teaching/learning situation by curriculum context and type of unit is given in Table B4 in the Appendix. (NB These observations were taken in a different week.)

Examination of the figures in the table reveals little overall difference in the amount of teacher-paced activities according to type of unit, although the distributions differ slightly. More direct teaching to small groups was observed in Type 2 units and more direct teaching to larger groups was observed in Type 1 units. A somewhat larger percentage of observations was made of small group work in Type 2 units.

With regard to the teaching of mathematics little difference is evident in the extent of teacher-paced activities, but group sizes can be seen to vary. More direct teaching to small groups was observed in Type 2 units and more individual and whole class direct teaching in Type 1 units. More observations were made of small groups of pupils working on similar tasks in Type 2 units but more individual work was observed in Type 1 units.

Observations made during language activities also reveal a similarity of approach between Type 1 and Type 2 units. Whole class direct teaching linked with individual or small group work appeared to predominate in both situations.

In the context of environmental studies a greater percentage of observations was made of small groups of pupils working on the same or similar tasks in Type 2 units with more direct teaching to one or more classes being observed in Type 1 units. It must however be remembered that these figures relate to a very small proportion of allocated curriculum time.

The dominant mode with regard to the teaching of art and musical activities during observations made in Type 1 units was that of direct teaching to class-sized or even larger groups linked with individual and small group work. Such teacher-paced activities were relatively infrequent in Type 2 units, where a much greater percentage of observations was made of pupils working on individually assigned tasks.

For the majority of observations made during physical education activities in Type 1 units, class-sized groups were seen to be working on similar tasks, often paced by the teacher. In Type 2 units, direct teaching to class-sized or larger groups featured prominently.

The figures for social and moral education, which also relate to only a very small proportion of allocated curriculum time, indicate that activities under these headings tended to be teacher-paced and were carried out in larger groups as in assembly or hymn practice, with some small group work of a social character.

A further analysis of the teaching/learning situation in relation to degree of pupil choice was carried out. The results of this analysis are given in Table B5 in the Appendix. These reveal large differences in the teaching/learning situation when units are divided on the active/passive dimension. On average 35.4 per cent of curriculum time was expended in direct teaching in units where pupils were given choice, but in the other units 46.4 per cent of curriculum time was spent on teacher-paced activities, the difference being mainly accounted for by a greater percentage of whole class direct teaching. Although there was little overall difference in the amount of small group work, pupils who were accorded a degree of choice of activities were more frequently observed working on individually assigned tasks whereas pupils in the other units were more often seen working as a class on the same or similar tasks.

During observations in the units where pupils had choice, the dominant approach to the teaching of mathematics was one where pupils worked either on individually assigned tasks, or with a small group of other pupils who were likewise engaged. 13.8 per cent of time allocated to mathematics was spent in direct teaching to groups of differing sizes. In the other units 24.7 per cent of time was spent in direct teaching, mainly to small groups of pupils. Although individual and small group work also featured in these units there were also numerous occasions on which class-sized groups were to be seen undertaking similar work.

Differences in approach can also be seen with regard to the teaching of language skills. More direct teaching, mainly to class-sized groups, was observed in units where pupils had no choice of activity (48.5 per cent), supported by small group, whole class and individual work. In the units where pupils were allowed some choice, direct teaching, mainly to class-sized groups, accounted for 39.1 per cent of time. This was accompanied mainly by individually assigned tasks with some small group work. This pattern is closely echoed with regard to the small proportion of curriculum time allocated to environmental studies.

A somewhat different picture is presented with regard to the teaching of aesthetics. Direct teaching to class-sized or larger groups accounted for 38.5 per cent of time allocated to this area of the curriculum in units where pupils had choice. This was accompanied by individual and small group work. In the other units direct teaching accounted for only 24.3 per cent of time, individual and small group work was also largely in evidence, but some whole class work was also observed.

In units where pupils had choice the teaching of social skills was largely by whole class direct teaching and small group work. In the other units small group work was also common.

Since assignment systems rarely extend to the teaching of physical skills, it is not surprising that in both sets of units physical education was largely undertaken in class-sized groups often paced by the teacher. Similarly activities classified under the heading of moral education were almost entirely teacher-directed in all units.

So far the descriptions provided do not appear to reveal any major differences in either curriculum allocation, involvement or specific curriculum activities when units are compared on design. However, there are indications that teaching organization, which may be linked to design, has a considerable bearing on the time expended on administration and transition, on the kinds of curriculum activities available to pupils, the context in which these activities are undertaken and on the materials provided. These will be taken up in Chapters 9 and 10.

*The Social Situation*

Although only a small portion of the school day is specifically allocated to activities designed to encourage the development of social skills, social encounters form an integral part of a child's experience in school. Implicit in the concept of open education is the assumption that flexibility of pupil grouping and greater freedom of movement enable children to interact with others. Cognitive, personal and social learning is assumed to be facilitated through interaction with both adults and peers.

In some of the infant units, especially those in inner city areas with a large immigrant population, much stress was laid upon the acquisition of language skills. In Unit W, for example, the development of language skills was the stated aim underlying all curriculum activities (the reader is referred to the case study in Chapter 10). In recording pupil interaction the observer was required to decide whether exchanges were positive or negative in character.

Table 5 shows the extent of observed pupil–pupil interaction in the different units, the mean interaction by type of unit and the mean interaction for those units in which pupils were given some choice with regard to activities.

Considerable variation is apparent in the extent to which pupils were seen chatting to peers. Pupil interaction in 10 of the 11 units ranged from 12.0 to 18.5 per cent of the school day, but in Unit W, where pupil choice was almost unrestricted and where special emphasis was laid on the development of language skills, pupils were observed discussing activities or making social exchanges for nearly one third of their time in school. The extent to which negative exchanges was observed also varied considerably between the different units. More arguing, pushing, snatching or other such anti-social behaviour was observed in Units U and W, both of which were in inner city schools, but these exchanges should be considered proportional to the total level of interaction, which in Unit W was very high. It can be seen that with the exception of Unit W there would seem to be little difference in level of pupil interaction that could be attributed to type of unit. Similarly, with the exception of Unit W there is little evidence that pupils spend more time in discussion when they are given choice as to the order in which they carry out their tasks.

*Pupil–Adult Contact*

Contact between pupils and adults was recorded in one of two categories depending on who initiated the contact thus distinguishing between teacher intervention and pupil consultation. Table 6 indicates the extent to which pupils consulted teachers or other adults, together with the extent to which teachers or other adults initiated exchanges with pupils.

| | Type 1 | | | | | | | Type 2 | | | | | | | | |
|---|---|---|---|---|---|---|---|---|---|---|---|---|---|---|---|---|
| | M | O | P | R | S | U | V | N | Q | T | W | Type 1 | Type 2 | Pupil* choice | No choice | All |
| Positive | 15.9 | 14.8 | 18.3 | 14.0 | 16.4 | 15.1 | 11.8 | 14.1 | 16.2 | 11.6 | 31.5 | 15.2 | 18.4 | 18.4 | 14.7 | 16.4 |
| Negative | .2 | .3 | .2 | .4 | .5 | 1.1 | .2 | .3 | .9 | .5 | 1.4 | .4 | .8 | .5 | .5 | .5 |
| Total | 16.1 | 15.1 | 18.5 | 14.4 | 16.9 | 16.2 | 12.0 | 14.4 | 17.1 | 12.1 | 32.9 | 15.6 | 19.2 | 18.9 | 15.2 | 16.9 |

*Table 5 Percentage pupil–pupil interaction in relation to type of unit and pupil choice (mean percentage)*

| | Type 1 | | | | | | | Type 2 | | | | | | | | |
|---|---|---|---|---|---|---|---|---|---|---|---|---|---|---|---|---|
| | M | O | P | R | S | U | V | N | Q | T | W | Type 1 | Type 2 | Pupil* choice | No choice | All |
| Pupil initiated | 2.9 | .8 | 2.0 | 3.5 | 2.8 | 1.9 | 3.1 | 1.8 | 4.2 | 1.8 | 2.7 | 2.4 | 2.6 | 2.8 | 2.2 | 2.5 |
| Teacher initiated | 1.7 | 3.0 | 3.5 | 4.1 | 1.4 | 2.3 | 2.7 | 2.2 | 2.7 | 1.8 | 6.2 | 2.7 | 3.2 | 3.6 | 2.3 | 2.9 |
| Total | 4.6 | 3.8 | 5.5 | 7.6 | 4.3 | 4.2 | 5.8 | 4.0 | 6.9 | 3.5 | 8.9 | 5.1 | 5.8 | 6.4 | 4.5 | 5.4 |

*Table 6 Percentage pupil–adult interaction in relation to type of unit and pupil choice (mean percentage)*

* units P, R, S, V and W

Across all units the average amount of pupil–adult contact was 5.4 per cent with individual unit variations from 3.5 – 8.9 per cent. Little difference can be seen in relation to type of unit, but it would appear that pupils tended to gain slightly less contact with adults in the more teacher-directed units (4.5 per cent) than in those units where pupils had choice (6.4 per cent). However, the presence of other adults, parents or aides, was more usual in these units and in Unit W which was part of a community school, parents were frequently seen helping with activities and talking to children. Thus the increased contact is perhaps not related to the presence of pupil choice.

Teacher-initiated contact is low at 2.9 per cent but is somewhat higher in the active mode, particularly so in Unit W, but the design of the unit appears not to have an effect on this.

*Non-Involvement*

Tables 2 and 3 broke down transition and involvement in curriculum activities by type of unit. The extent of these activities in active and passive units is shown in Table 7.

| | *Transition* | | *Curriculum* | |
|---|---|---|---|---|
| | Active | Passive | Active | Passive |
| Waiting | 6.3 | 7.0 | 3.8 | 3.1 |
| Preparation | 1.7 | 1.5 | 2.2 | 2.4 |
| Clearing away | 1.8 | 1.6 | 1.3 | 0.7 |
| Movement | 6.8 | 4.2 | 8.7 | 4.7 |

*Table 7 Non-involvement – transition and curriculum (%)*

Table 7 breaks down the amount of non-involvement behaviour in periods of transition and curriculum activities for both active and passive curricula.

From this it may be seen that curriculum organization affects circulation. Where pupils are operating in an active curriculum a continuous flow of traffic results, whereas in the passive mode peaks and troughs of traffic flow result. The effect of differing circulation flow may of course depend on the unit design and on furniture placement.

**Summary**

The observational data revealed large differences in the time allocated to differing curriculum areas. The balance achieved by teachers thus varies markedly, as does the time which teachers consume in managerial activities. Indeed such procedural activities take up more time than does non-involvement on the part of pupils. In comparison with other studies, the average figure of 22 per cent for administration and transition is high, although involvement rates are comparable. When allocation and involvement are considered together there is often a marked discrepancy between the teacher's allocated curriculum balance and that actually achieved.

There was no strong *a priori* reason why allocation and involvement should be associated with unit design, except that large open units might be more difficult to organize and administer. The finding that more time was spent on administration/transition perhaps fits in with this view. However in most other analyses the differences were slight. In considering the notion of the active/passive curriculum the results suggest greater procedural time in active curriculum, but allocation to basic skill areas and pupil involvement differences were slight.

Differences were found at the level of specific activities, whereby in active curriculum there was, as the name suggests, more active participation aligned with a greater use of a diversity of materials.

Analyses of the teaching/learning situation revealed that more direct teaching, especially to class-sized groups, was observed in passive units, and more individual assignments in active units. Much more movement in both transition and curriculum time was characteristic of active units. The increased movement dominating active curriculum may have implications for circulation and furniture placement.

**Case Studies**

Research is often criticized for concentrating on the average rather than the individual. Two case studies are therefore included here, which plot pupils' days. These children were observed using the LES schedule and are analysed in two ways – by breaking down pupil activities in relation to the LES categories, e.g. the spaces used, the activities engaged in and so on, and a synthesis in the form of a process chart is also included. From this chart, the pupil's activities at any minute of the day can be ascertained.

**'James'**

James is a six-year-old pupil in an all open plan primary school in the North West of England. The school serves a mixed catchment area, taking children from a council housing estate, older terraced property and modern, owner-occupier estates. The school was built as a one form entry primary school to cater for 280 children. At present it has 181 on roll, and has fewest children in the upper age range.

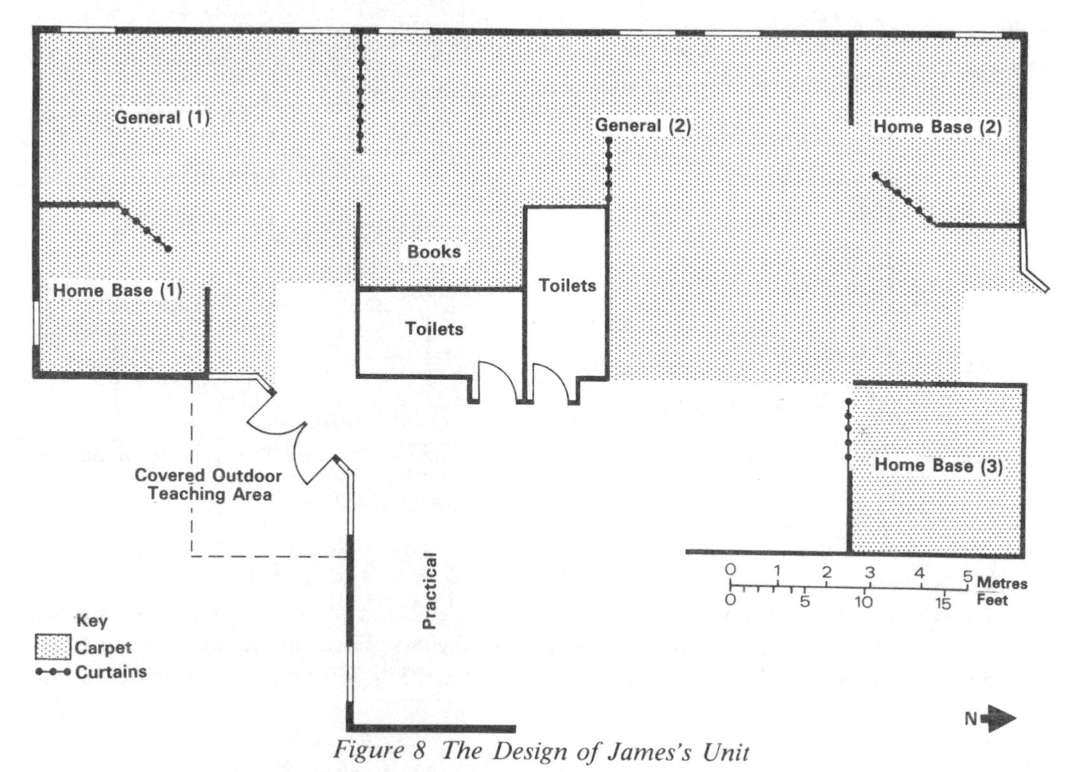


*Figure 8 The Design of James's Unit*

The infant part of the school, catering for 87 children at the time of observation (see plan – Figure 8), is classified as a three teacher Type 1 design. The three teachers enjoy the help of a nursery nurse, so staffing can be described as more than adequate. Children are allocated to home base groups by age, with all children spending at least two terms in the reception group and a full year in top infants.

The middle infants group, of which James is a member, is grouped roughly by ability for the purpose of assigning tasks, but the children are then able to choose when they do each activity, subject to certain constraints – for instance the use of the wet area – broadly a mixture of pupil choice and teacher direction. Teachers are each responsible for the work of their own home base groups, although the children are not kept separate in the physical sense – space is shared. This is especially true of the two teachers who work in closest propinquity (reception and middle), though all three share the library, maths area and wet area. Children may approach any of the staff for help and similarly all the staff have some jurisdiction over all the children. Cooperative planning is in evidence for curriculum purposes and for the use of the wet area. Day-to-day cooperation takes place on an ad hoc basis.

In general, the unit has a happy, purposeful atmosphere, children have a good level of task involvement, and their work is of a fairly high standard, though all the teachers tend to stress social rather than cognitive aims.

*The Pupil's Day*

Discussion of the various dimensions of the pupil's day follows the format of LES observation schedule. Discussed first, then, is the physical scene, the spaces used by James during the day (see Figure 9).

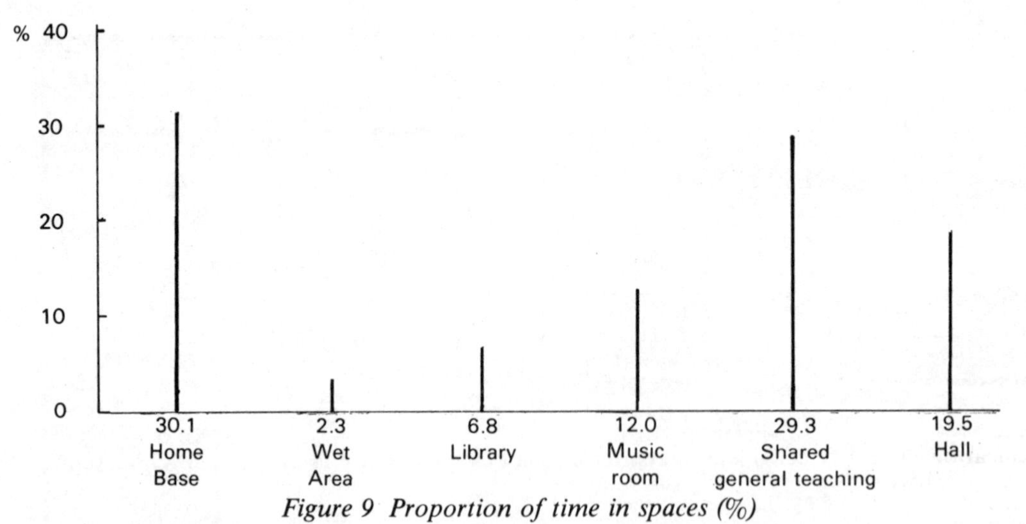


*Figure 9 Proportion of time in spaces (%)*

Physical Scene

James spent the greater part of the day in the small home bases and the shared general teaching area, these each accounting for about 30 per cent of the day. His activities in the home bases include play in the Wendy House, free writing and copy writing. The home base is also the scene of administration time, teacher/class discussion and some transition time.

The shared general teaching area was used by James for free writing, copy writing and watching a TV programme.

The third most used space by James was the hall which was the scene of a music and movement and singing class lesson. The least used spaces were the music/AV room, where James listened to a story at the end of the day, the library corner where he did some practical maths, and the wet area which James entered only briefly to fetch materials and to help another child with his apron.

The distribution of time across curriculum areas is shown in Figure 10.

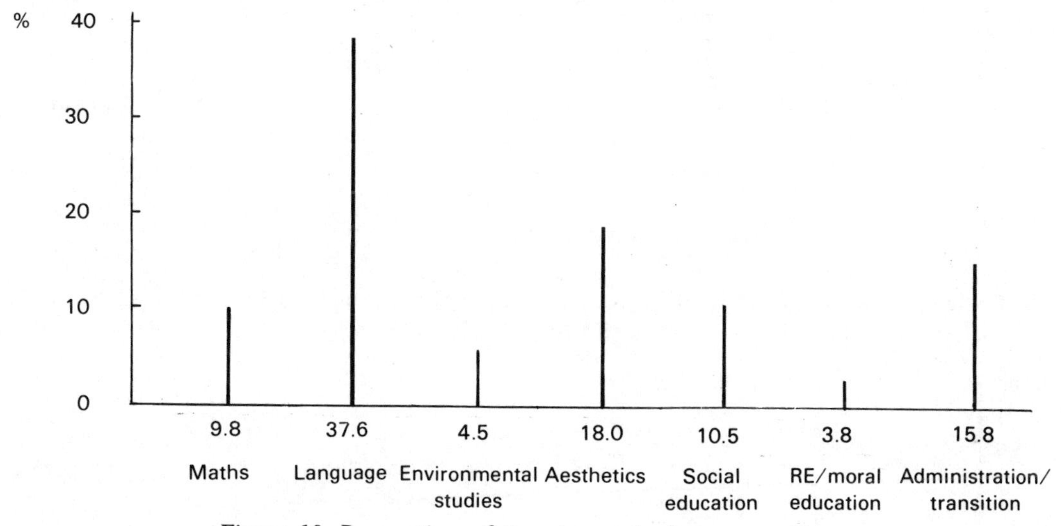


*Figure 10 Proportion of time in curriculum areas (%)*

Gross Curriculum Context

All the maths work done by James was of a practical nature involving the use of maths equipment, working from a work card. Language was by far the most frequent curriculum context, under which are subsumed copy writing, free writing, listening to a story and a brief period of whole class spelling activity. Another period of whole class teacher-directed activity was concerned with a teacher-directed discussion about the squirrels which had been seen taking food from the bird-tables, this being subsumed under environmental studies. Aesthetics included a period of music and movement and a TV programme. The bulk of the period of social education (10.5 per cent) was taken up by play in the Wendy House, while RE (assembly) accounted for 3.8 per cent.

Non-curriculum time, here described as administration/transition, accounted for 15.8 per cent, a low figure, compared with the average for the infant LES sample.

The actual curriculum activities subsumed under the above mentioned curriculum contexts are shown in Figure 11.

The central part of this case study is James's high level of task involvement, 67.7 per cent, which compares favourably with a mean score over the whole LES infant sample of 53.7 per

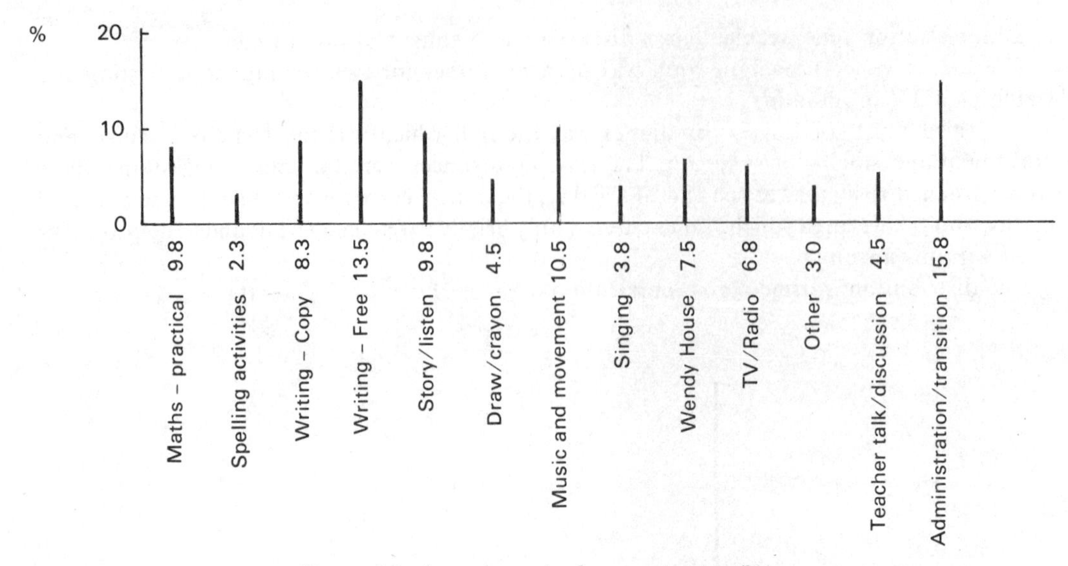


*Figure 11 Actual curriculum activities (%)*

cent and the unit LES average of 63.5 per cent. James's level of task involvement, together with his behaviours when not involved, is shown in Figure 2.

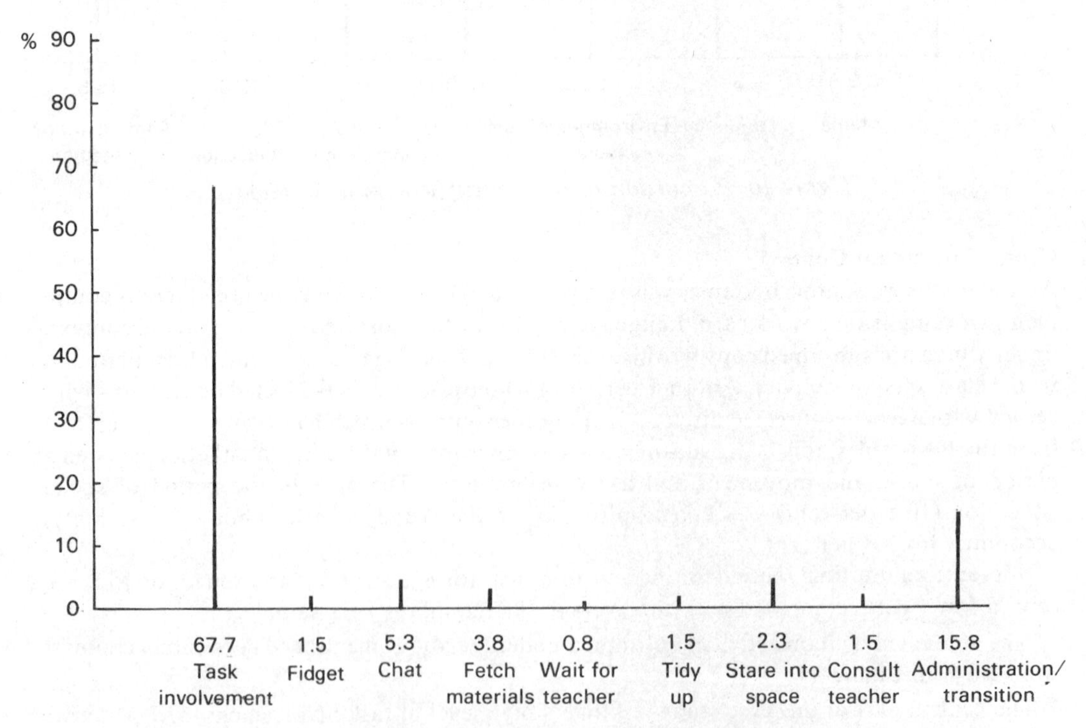


*Figure 12 Level of involvement (%)*

Actual Activity

The low level of administration/transition time in this case study is typical of the children studied in this unit, which showed a mean level of administration/transition of 15.3 per cent and must be seen as a factor in James's high involvement rate. The mean task involvement score in James's unit is 63.5 per cent, so James's score is not very different from that of his peers. The unit was well organized, children were clear about their tasks and well trained in the use of the unit, materials were all readily available, and all the areas were visible and easy to supervise. Although cooperative or team teaching as defined in this book weas not in evidence, there was cooperative and thorough planning and preparation of the unit. The teachers regarded themselves as a team and, in that their groups used the same spaces and resources, a measure of ad hoc cooperation was essential to their form of organization. In general, teachers were highly professional in their approach, clear about their aims and thorough in their organization and planning; this seems to be reflected in the constantly purposeful behaviour exhibited by the children.

It is probably a truism to say that very young children need variety in their school day – variety of activity, of teaching situation, and perhaps of space. Variety in all three is in evidence here. There is a balance between individual, group and whole class activity and between pupil-paced and teacher-paced activities (see Figure 13).

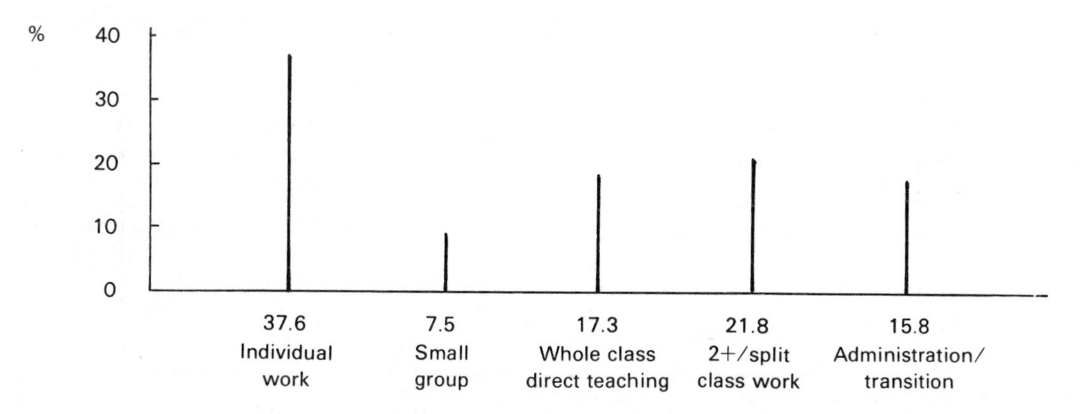


*Figure 13 Teaching/learning situation (%)*

Teaching/Learning Situation

Reference to James's process chart (Figure 17) shows clearly that activities in general continued for less than half an hour and that there was a fairly frequent change in the teaching/learning situation, except for an extended period of individual work in the afternoon.

Periods of administration/transition are not infrequent – eight during the day including those at the beginning and end of the sessions, but they are generally brief and those which involve the movement of the children from the unit to another part of the school, e.g. to the hall or the AV room, are managed speedily.

James sustained periods of task involvement over all his curriculum activities except for free writing, when his work was punctuated by bouts of chatter and fetching and putting away materials. This can fairly be described as James's least structured work situation, and perhaps indicates that a measure of structure and direction are important. Or the answer might also lie in the nature of the task itself.

Over the whole LES infant sample, it does seem to be the case that where direction and structure are minimal, task involvement tends to be lower. This is not to say that heavily structured and directed situations are appropriate to the teaching of all young children.

Earlier in this case study balance was mentioned, the balance between direction and choice, between the times when work is individual and pupil-paced and those in which the child's activities are mainly or wholly directed. It would seem to be a fair assumption that where activities are of a whole class, wholly directed nature, little account can be taken of children's individual needs and differences, consequently enhancing the probability of tasks being inappropriate to the child. Case Study 2 illustrates the point – a predominance of whole class work and massive teacher direction goes hand-in-hand with low involvement levels. In James's case, there *is* balance between the teaching/learning situations, these being in the main appropriate to the tasks in hand, while within each curriculum activity the tasks themselves were appropriate to the child.

The other dimensions of the pupil's day recorded by LES are shown in Figures 14, 15 and 16 below.

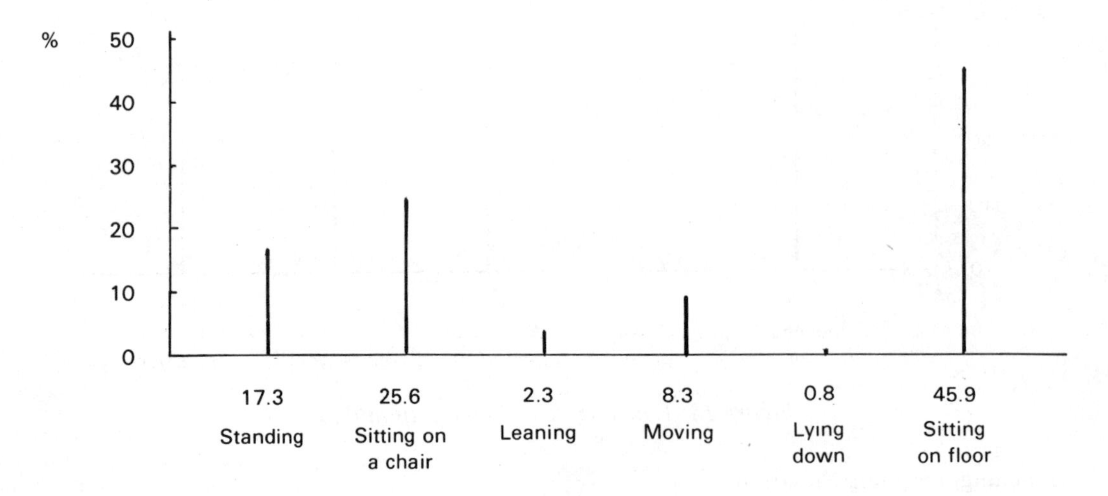


*Figure 14 Posture (%)*

Posture

The posture chart shows that James spent 25.6 per cent of his time sitting at a table, and 45.9 per cent sitting on the floor. The latter figure is unusually high and is accounted for by the fact that the small home bases and the AV room were minimally furnished – children sat on the floor during registration, class discussion and storytime. The fact that that part of James's day was taken up by a TV programme, during which he sat on the floor, also enhances this figure.

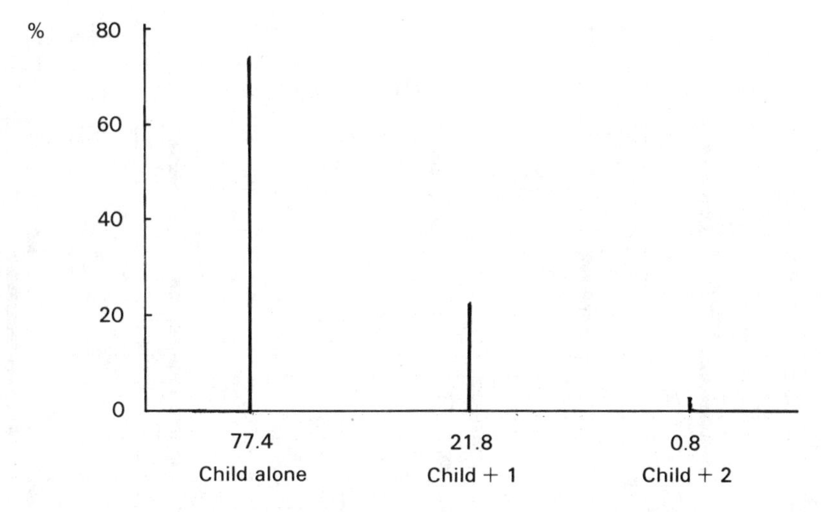


*Figure 15 Interaction with peers (%)*

James's interaction with peers, both work and non-work related, accounts for 22.6 per cent of the day. During the remaining 77.4 per cent, James did not interact with other children. 5.3 per cent was spent in contact with his home base teacher (see Figure 15).

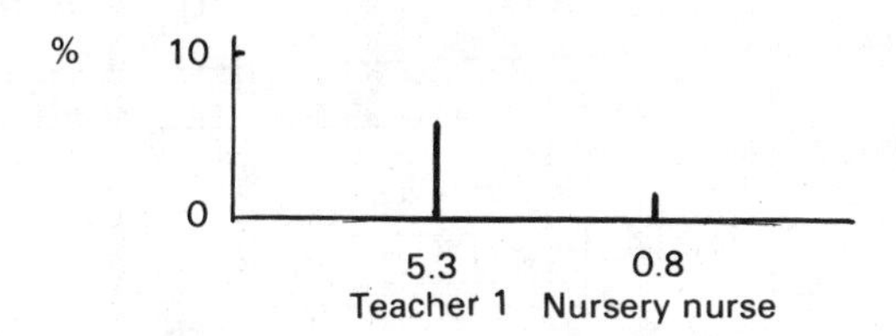


*Figure 16 Contact with teacher/ancillary (%)*

Process Chart

The process chart (Figure 17) provides a complete and continuous record of James's day. It can be read both horizontally and vertically. For example, if the interest is in the spaces used, it can be easily demonstrated that for the first 48 minutes he was in the home base and that he then moved to the hall. Also, his activity at any time in the day can be traced by reading vertically. For example, at the fortieth minute he was in the home base; the curriculum context was social education, the actual curriculum activity being play in the Wendy House; he was involved in that task, the teaching/learning context being small group work. Note particularly the substantial periods of task involvement, since this is in contrast to the next case, that of Daniel.

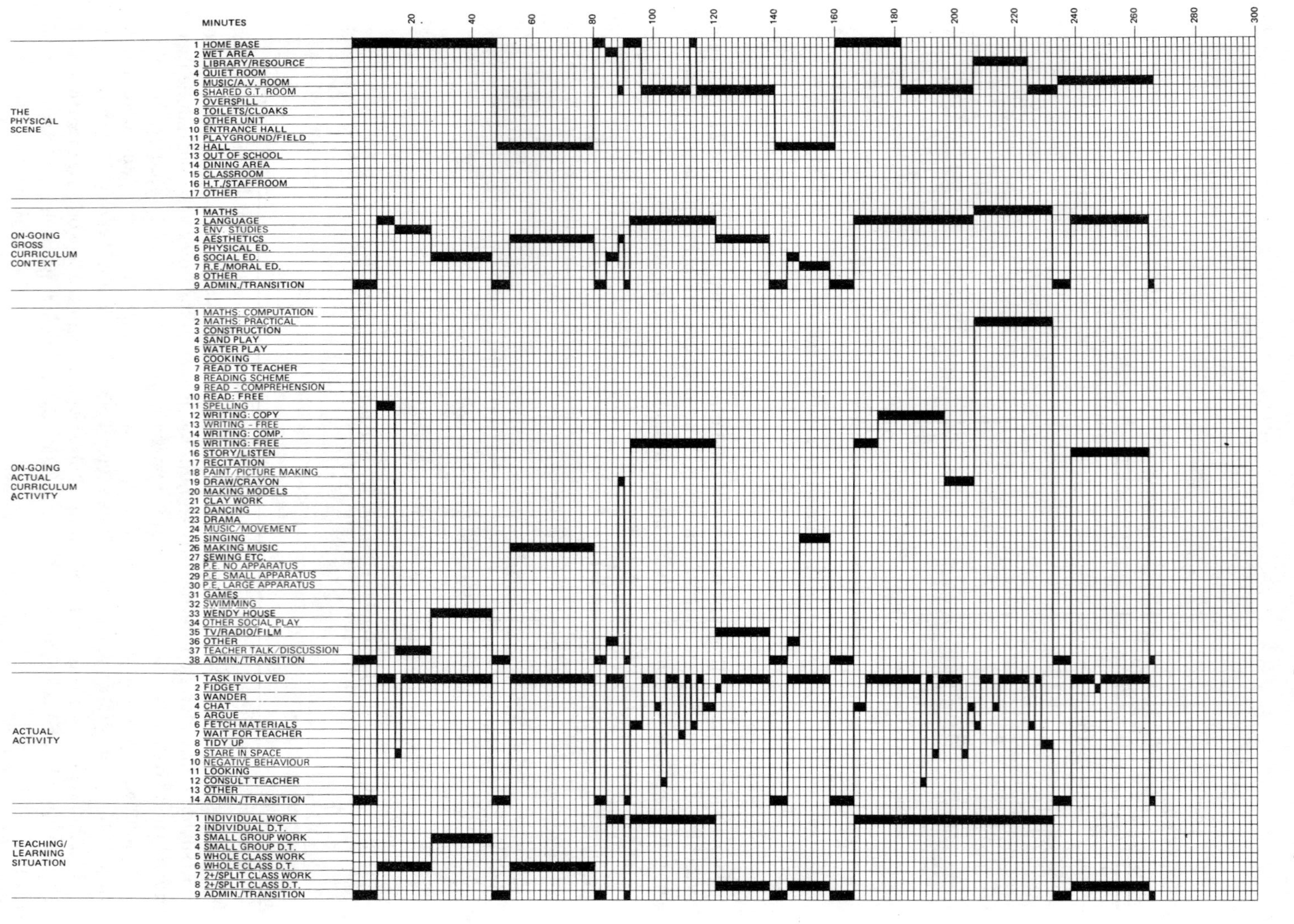

*Figure 17 Learning Experiences Schedule Process Chart: 'James'*

**'Daniel'**

Daniel is a six-year-old boy who is a pupil at an all open plan primary school situated in a fairly remote rural area. The infant part of the school consists of a four teacher Type 2 unit (Figure 18), though it was, at the time of the observation, housing only 75 children and three teachers. Children are allocated to teachers on the basis of age. There are 22 'middle' infants in Daniel's class who are allocated to groups within-class by reading ability. Daniel's group is ranked third. Daniel's teacher and the reception class teacher operate a team teaching system during part of the mornings, one taking responsibility for all the children's maths and the other for the language work. At other times, teachers operate independently. The curriculum emphasis in Daniel's class is very much on language, especially reading.

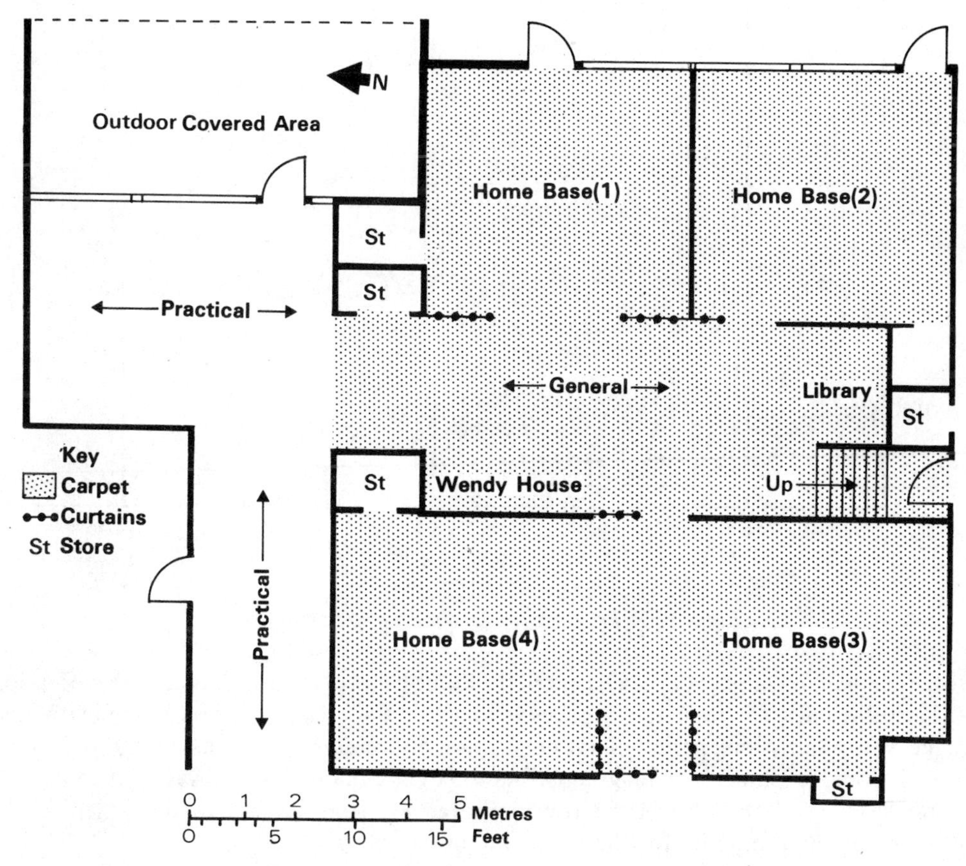


*Figure 18 The Design of Daniel's Unit*

The teacher responsible for middle infants reports some difficulties in supervising the children when they are not all in the home base. The spaces are rather fragmented. The wet area, for example, is both out of sight and largely out of hearing from the home bases and this may well be the cause of a rather high incidence of negative behaviour in this unit. However, activities were continued over long periods of time, perhaps too long for young children to sustain a high level of interest and involvement, and children were very dependent on teacher direction in most of their curriculum activities.

*The Pupil's Day*

Physical Scene
The spaces used by Daniel are shown in Figure 19.

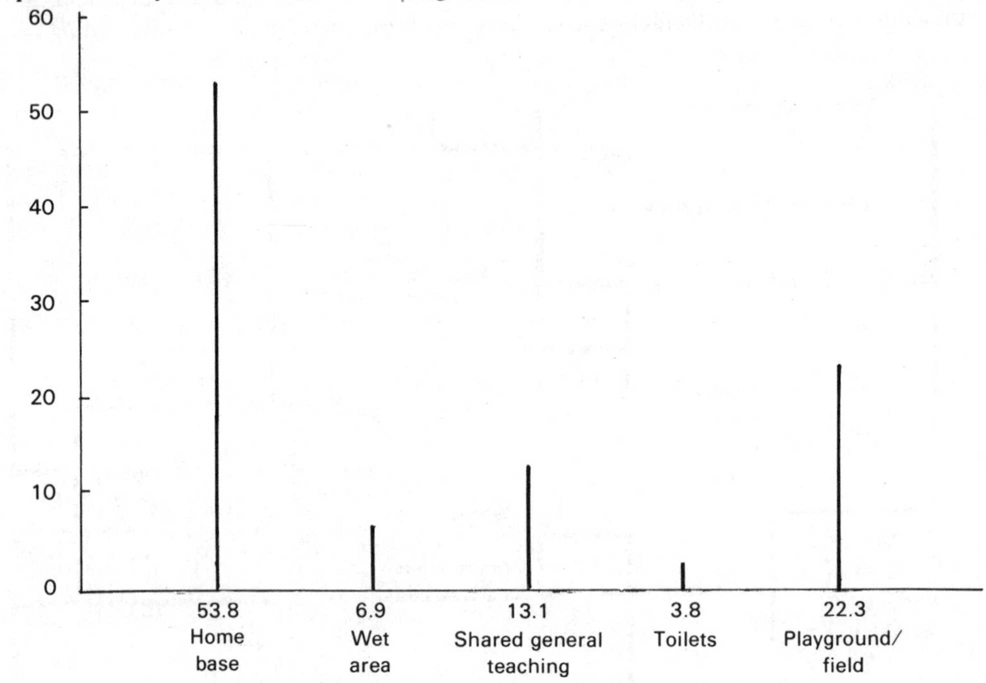


*Figure 19 Proportion of time in spaces (%)*

More than half of Daniel's day was spent in the home bases of his own class and the reception class. The principal activities in these spaces were within the curriculum contexts of maths and language, with a fairly long period of administration, followed by a class 'assembly' at the start of the day. Some of Daniel's language activities took place in the shared resource area outside the home base. The latter part of the afternoon was spent on the school field, where all the infant children had a practice for the forthcoming school sports day.

Gross Curriculum Context
The distribution of time in curriculum areas shows that administration/transition took up 20.0 per cent of the time. This is a rather inflated figure for this unit and is due to the lengthy process of organizing the children for the sports practice. In fact the average administration/transition time for this unit is low, 14.0 per cent compared with the average of 20.7 per cent for all infant units. For the same reason, the allocation of time to PE is artifically high (see Figure 20).

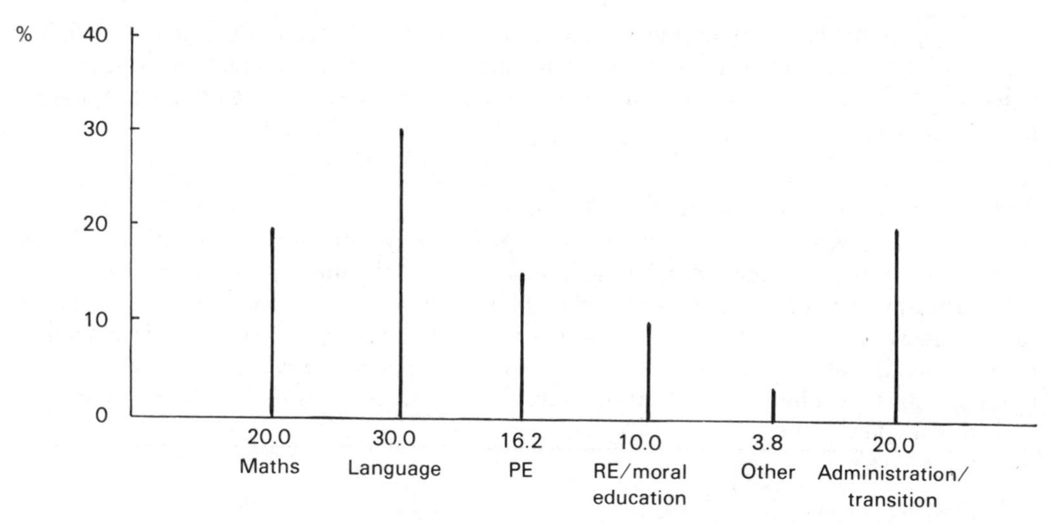


*Figure 20 Proportion of time in curriculum areas (%)*

The time allocated to basics – maths and language – accounts for exactly half the day, 30 per cent being allocated to language-related activities. The absence of aesthetics from Daniel's day is accounted for partly by the difficulty of supervision of the wet area, which effectively limited such activities to the times when a small group of children could be supervised by the ancillary assistant, and partly by the effect of the long sports practice. The time allocated to RE/moral education is high at 10.0 per cent, when compared with an average of 6.6 per cent over all infant units.

Actual Curriculum Activities

The actual curriculum activities subsumed under the curriculum contexts described above are shown in Figure 21.

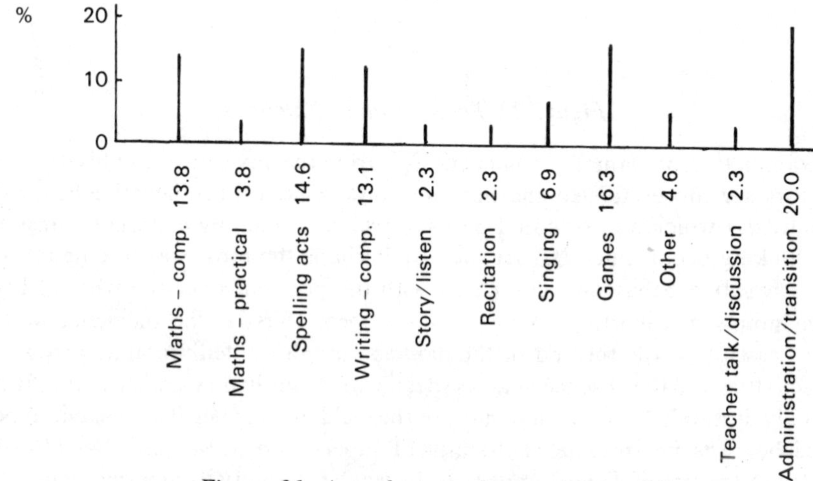


*Figure 21 Actual curriculum activities (%)*

The concern for basics expressed by the class teacher is reflected in the actual curriculum activities experienced by Daniel. Most of his maths was formal computation rather than practical work, while his language work was dominated by spelling activities and simple English exercises.

Actual Activities

Actual activities are shown in Figure 22. The outstanding feature of Daniel's day is his very low level of task involvement. At 32.3 per cent this compares very unfavourably with the mean LES score of 53.7 per cent over the whole infant sample and the unit average of 52.3 per cent. Administration/transition time for Daniel's day is close to the mean for all infant units, so it can be stated clearly that his low task involvement score is not a function of reduced curriculum time. In fact, if Daniel's level of task involvement is computed as a percentage of curriculum time (i.e. total time minus administration/transition time), a score of 40.9 per cent is gained, an exceptionally low figure.

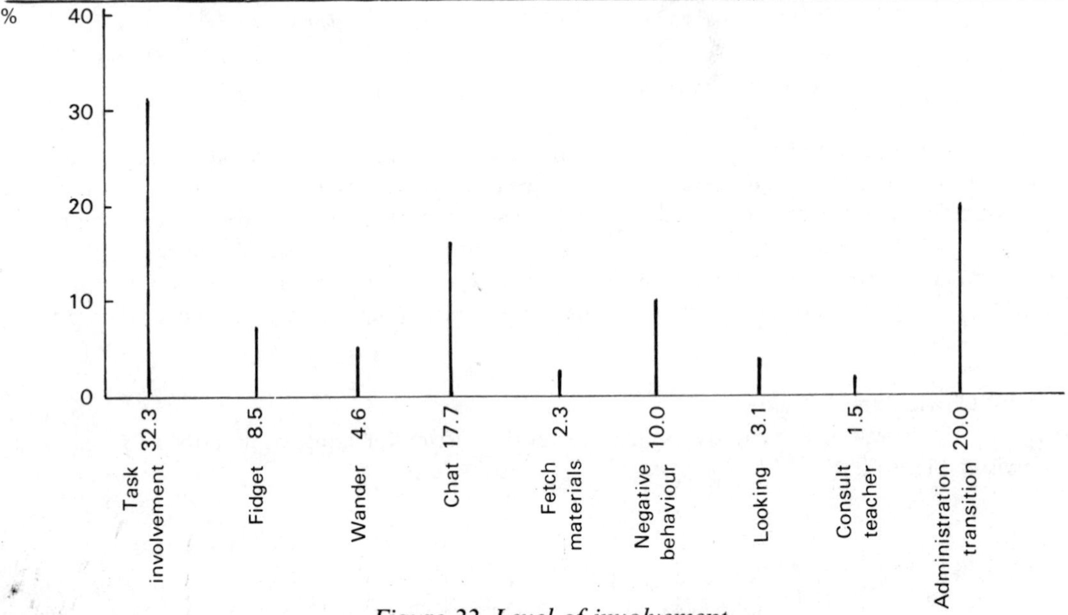


*Figure 22 Level of involvement*

Further examination of Daniel's actual activity during the day shows that his principal non-task behaviours are those labelled chatting (non-task-related talk), negative behaviour and fidgeting. Activities which are, or could be, task related – fetching materials, consulting the teacher and looking occur much less frequently. Perhaps the most startling figure is that of 10.0 per cent negative behaviour, compared with 0.8 per cent over the whole LES infant sample. Two points are worth making in this respect. Firstly, the incidence of negative behaviour increases towards the end of the day, as though the tedium of a narrow range of curriculum activities and the absence of tasks specific to the individual child eventually result in revolt. Secondly, it should be noted that many of the incidences of negative behaviour occurred when the teacher was not present. Difficulty of supervision in this unit has already been mentioned. It is a feature of Type 2 units that the teacher's ability to supervise more than one space at a time is severely restricted, leading to either one or other of several undesirable outcomes – the underuse of less visible areas, constraints on certain curriculum activities, higher incidence of children's activities being unsupervised, and overcrowding in home bases. These problems are overcome to some extent where nursery nurses, ancillary assistants or parents are used, but none of these are necessarily adequate surrogates for the teacher.

Teaching/Learning Situation

The distribution of teaching/learning situations through Daniel's day may also contain possible explanations for his low level of task involvement and the high incidence of negative behaviour. The bulk of the day was spent on whole class activities – the class either being taught directly or carrying out the same or similar tasks at the same time (see Figure 23).

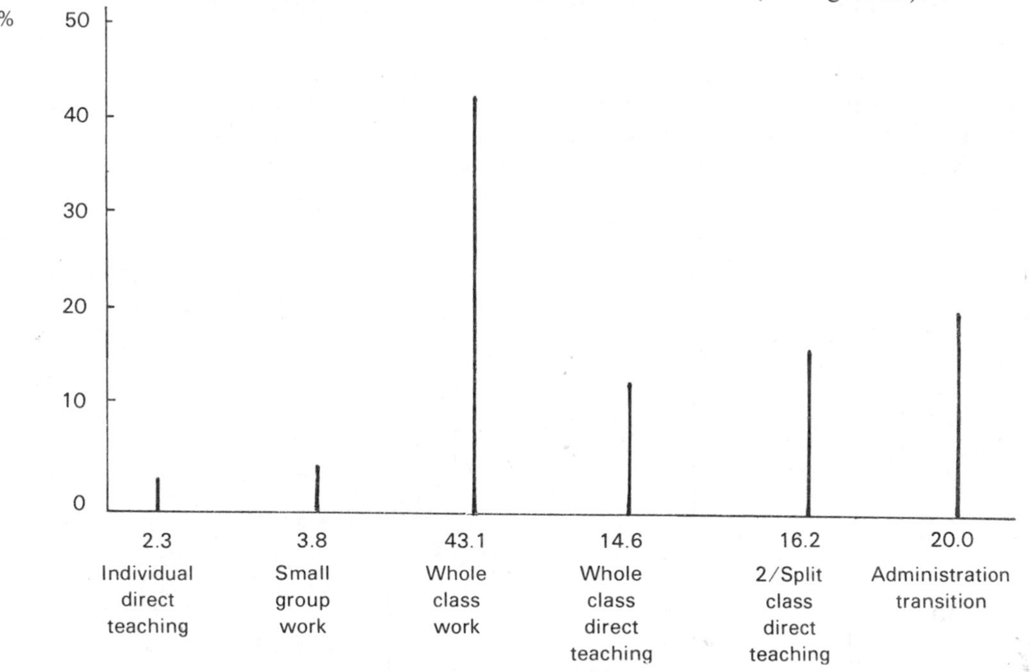


*Figure 23 Teaching/learning situation*

It does seem probable that the needs of individual children are less likely to be met in a regime of this kind. Daniel is, for his class, a lower ability child, thus inappropriateness of task could be a major factor in his low task involvement.

The pattern of involvement in differing teaching/learning situations in the whole infant sample is shown in Table 8.

Thus, in contrast to the junior sample (Chapter 8) where involvement in individual work is much higher than that in whole class work, there is little difference between these teaching/learning situations in the LES infant sample. It may be that rather more teacher direction, implicit in whole class work, is required at the infant level. However, to examine in isolation the ranks of teaching/learning situations and involvement over-simplifies the picture. To repeat a point made earlier, the question of balance seems to be crucial to the sustaining of high levels of

| *Teaching/learning situation* | *% Involvement* |
|---|---|
| Individual direct teaching | 90.4 |
| Whole class direct teaching | 81.8 |
| 2+/split direct teaching | 78.3 |
| Small group direct teaching | 71.5 |
| 2+/split work | 64.3 |
| Small group work | 60.9 |
| Whole class work | 59.2 |
| Individual work | 57.1 |

*Table 8 Involvement in differing teaching/learning situations: whole infant sample (%)*

task involvement. Thus, where a pupil's day contains a variety of teaching/learning situations and a variety of curriculum activities, involvement levels tend to be enhanced.

Other information provided by the LES is summarized briefly here.

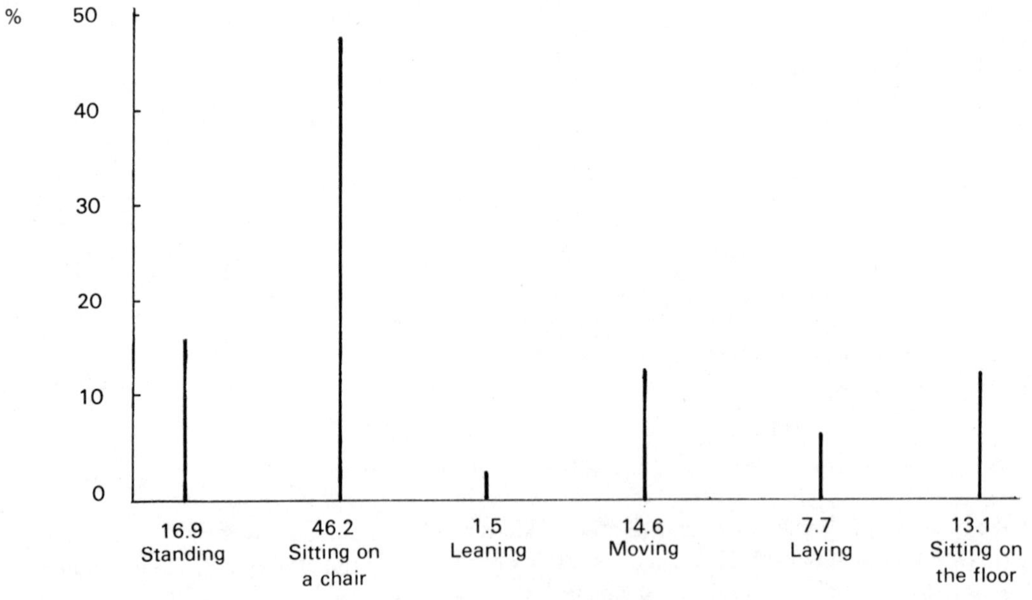


*Figure 24 Posture*

The posture chart (Figure 24) shows that Daniel spent nearly half of the day seated at a table, though a good deal of this was during administration/transition time.

Interaction with peers and teachers is shown in Figures 25 and 26.

Daniel spent more than half his day interacting with other children. It is noteworthy that less than 40 per cent of these interactions were task related. Contact between Daniel and his teachers was comparatively frequent. Most of these were of a disciplinary nature however.

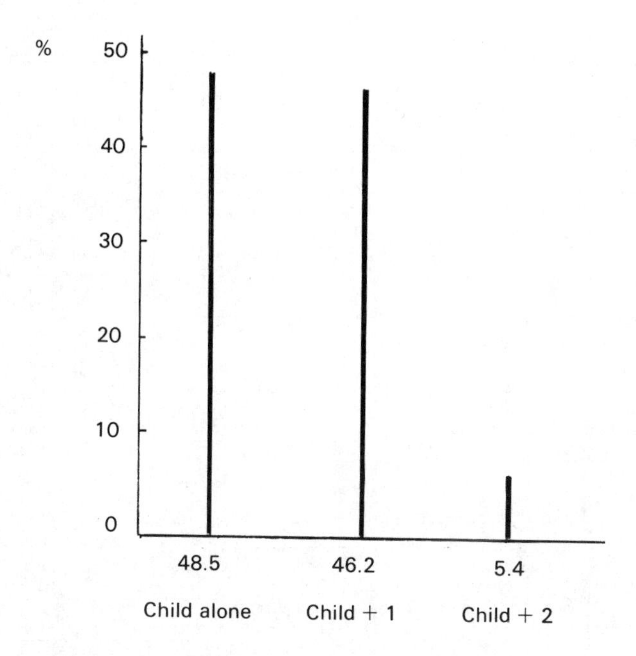


*Figure 25 Interaction with peers*

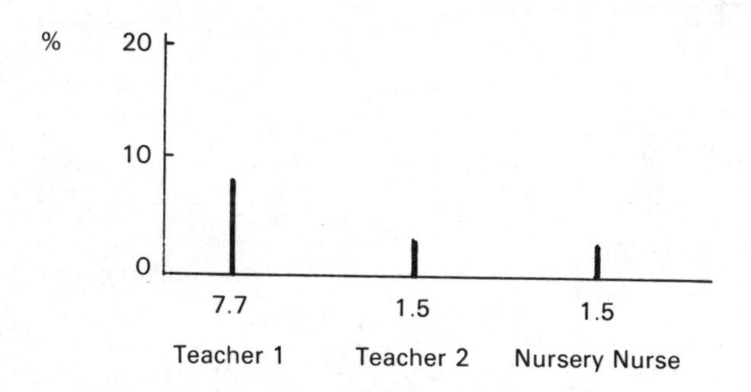


*Figure 26 Adult contact*

Process Chart
Daniel's process chart provides a continuous record of his activities (Figure 27). Note in this instance his lack of sustained involvement, in contrast to that of James.

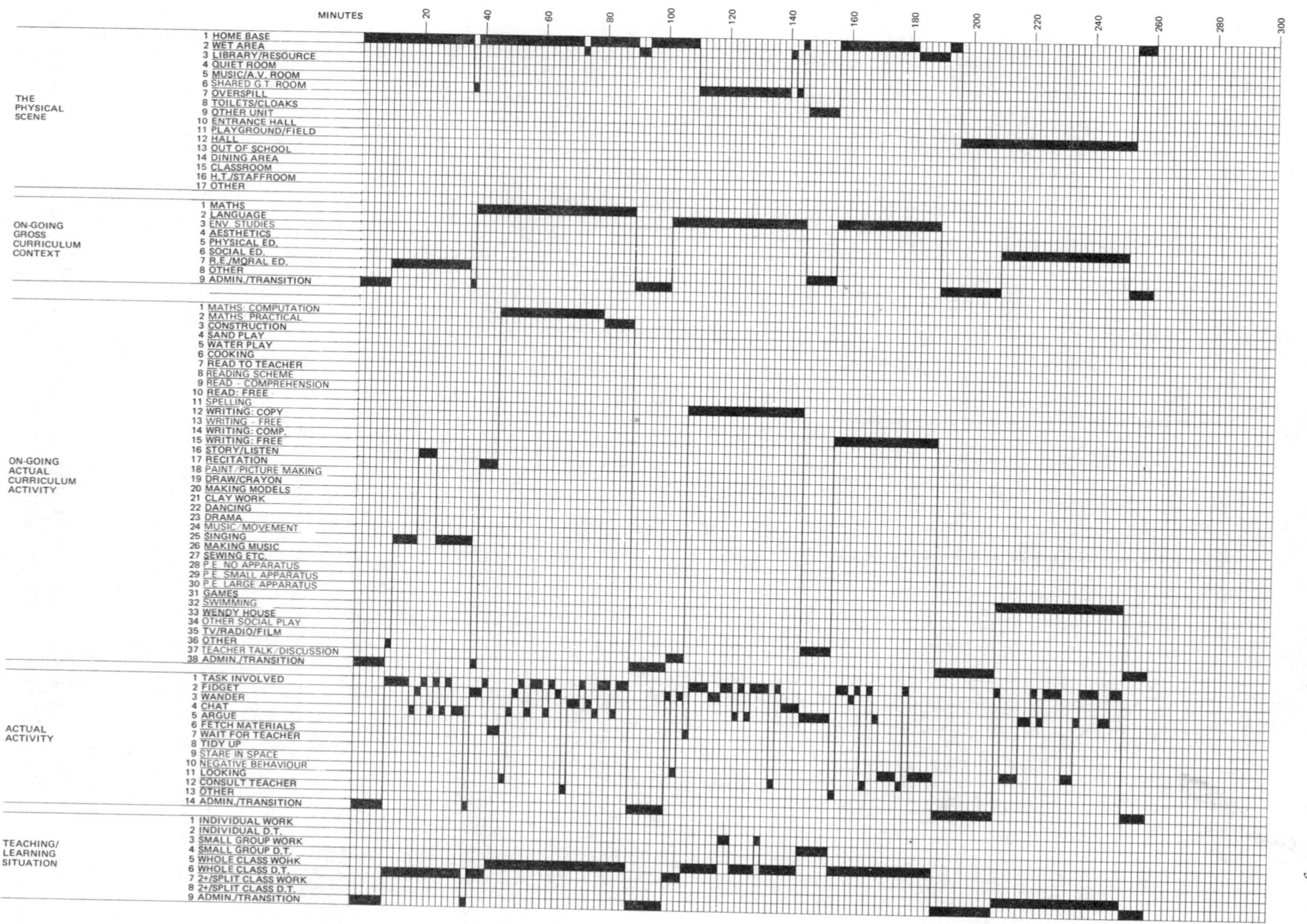

Figure 27 Learning Experiences Schedule Process Chart: 'Daniel'

*Chapter 8*

# *Curriculum Allocation and Pupil Involvement: 2. Juniors*

---

**Curriculum Allocation**

The findings presented here are again based on the Pupil Behaviour Schedule. 288 middle junior pupils were observed in 12 open plan units, varying in size, degree of openness and organizational pattern. Figure 1 shows both the average percentage of time in different curriculum areas and the range. Thus, administration/transition takes up 13 per cent of time on average, but varies across units from 9 per cent to 17 per cent of the school week. As with the infants, transitional activities account for most of this, averaging 11.6 per cent with a range of 8.5 per cent to 15.7 per cent.

The amount of time allocated to mathematics is a little higher than in infant units at 17.1 per cent, but the variation is wider, from 9.2 per cent to 26.5 per cent. At the extremes, therefore, children in one unit were given three times the opportunity to study mathematics than were pupils in another unit.

Language again accounted for the largest portion of time, averaging 30.7 per cent. This is less than at infant level, but the range is again wider, from 16.6 per cent to 46.4 per cent, so here too some children have three times the opportunity of others to participate in language activities.

The largest difference between infant and junior curriculum is seen in the area of environmental studies, averaging 13.2 per cent in juniors and 3.5 per cent in infants. The range is enormous, varying from none at all to nearly 30 per cent.

Time devoted to aesthetics is similar at infant and junior level, averaging 10.3 per cent in the latter, the range being 2.3 per cent to 17.7 per cent. On the other hand, much more time is spent on physical education at junior level, i.e. 9.4 per cent, compared with 3.9 per cent at infant level. Again the range is wide. Social and moral education are given little emphasis in both infant and junior units.

It was argued in the infant chapter that in the light of the marked variation in time allocated to different curriculum areas, quite different educational diets were being offered. In fact this situation is more extreme at junior level. Clearly there is no such thing as *the* primary school

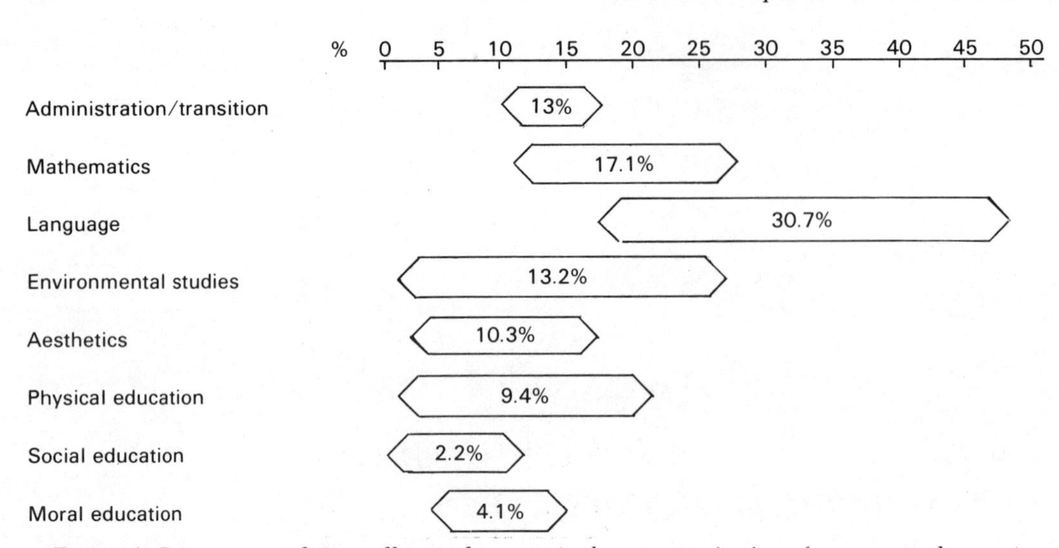


*Figure 1 Percentage of time allocated to curriculum areas: juniors (average and range)*

curriculum, but an enormous number of primary school curricula each achieving a different balance.

Figure 2 has been drawn to illustrate the balance achieved in two of the junior units.

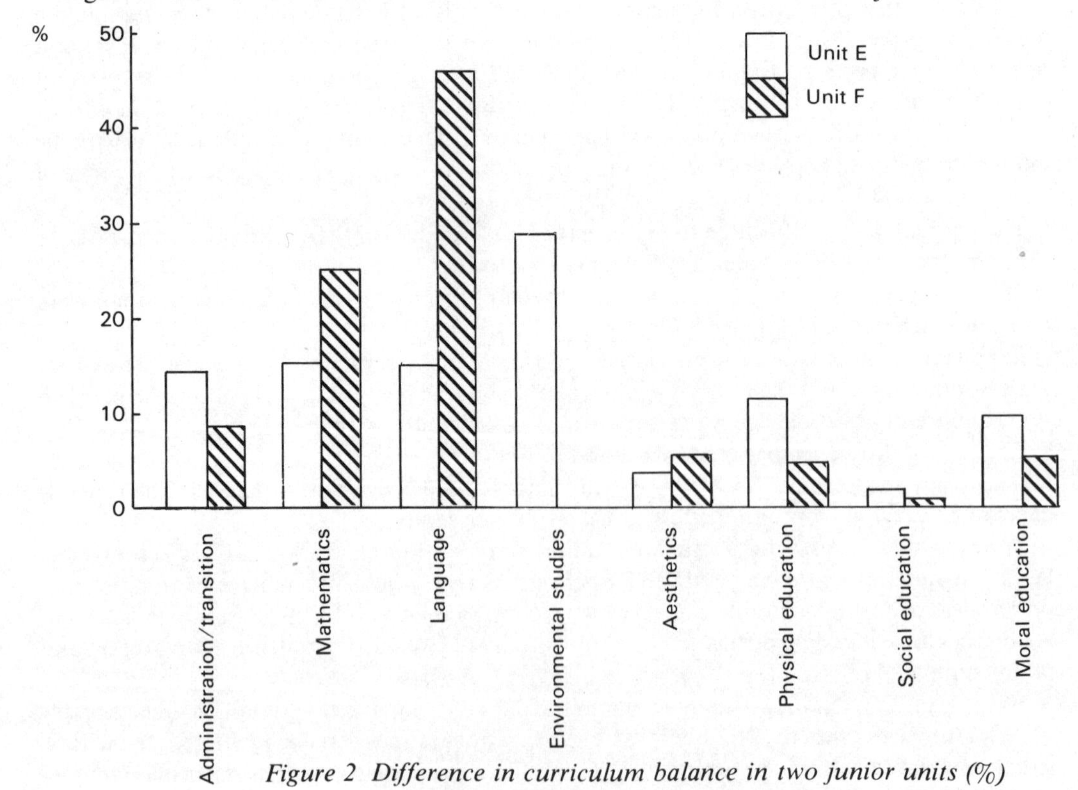


*Figure 2 Difference in curriculum balance in two junior units (%)*

There is little difference in administration/transition time, but in Unit E, 14 per cent of the week is allocated to mathematics and 25 per cent of the time in Unit F; 3½ hours compared to 6¼ hours per week. In language, the disparity is even more marked, 16.6 per cent to 46.4 per cent – just over 4 hours a week – in Unit E and over 11½ hours in Unit F. There is also wide disparity in time allocated to environmental studies. There was none at all in Unit F, but over 7 hours in Unit E. There is no suggestion here that one teacher provides a better balance than the other, but it should be kept in mind when evaluating these figures that different patterns of allocation have been found to relate to differing patterns of achievement.

Analyses were also performed to assess whether differences in allocation related to unit design. At infant level there was little relationship. In the junior units – however, there were some clear differences recorded. In the less open Type 2 units, more time was allocated to language, environmental studies and aesthetics. This was balanced by more physical education in Type 1 units (see Figure 3). However, this is simply a descriptive statement. It cannot be said that these differences can be attributed to differences in design. Nevertheless, these differences were apparent across a two week period using different observation instruments.

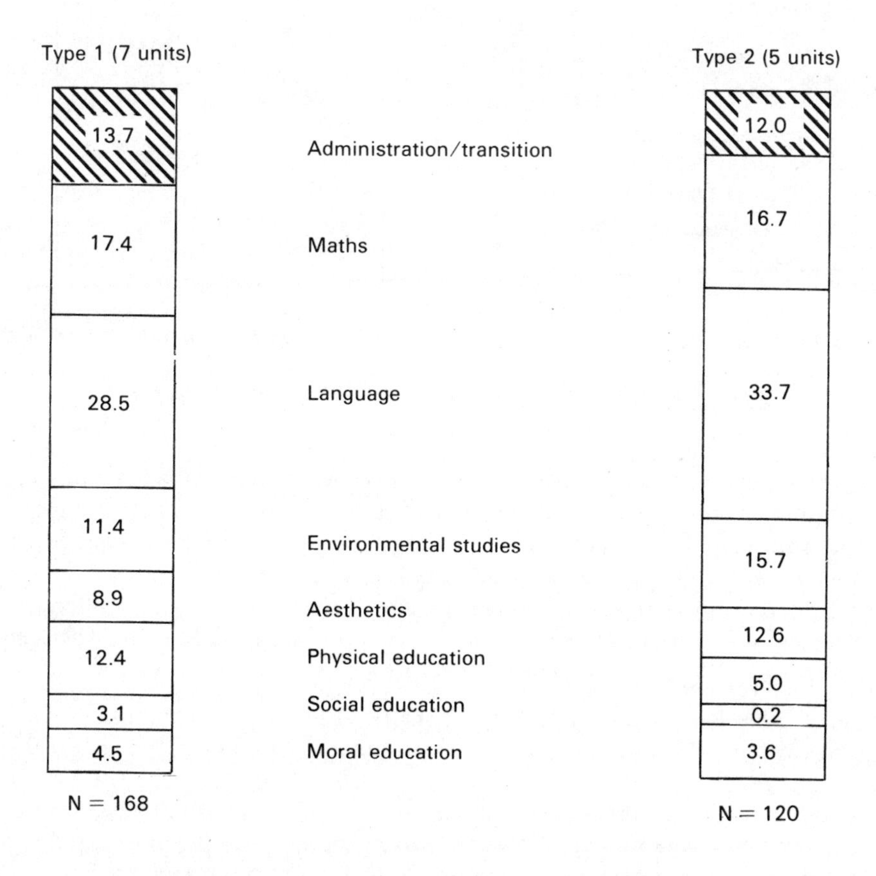


*Figure 3 Mean percentage curriculum allocation*

## Pupil Involvement

*Overall Involvement*

What proportion of the school day is spent involved on curriculum activities? Figure 4 shows overall involvement as a proportion of the school week for all junior units and for those of Type 1 and 2 design. The shaded areas indicate non involvement.

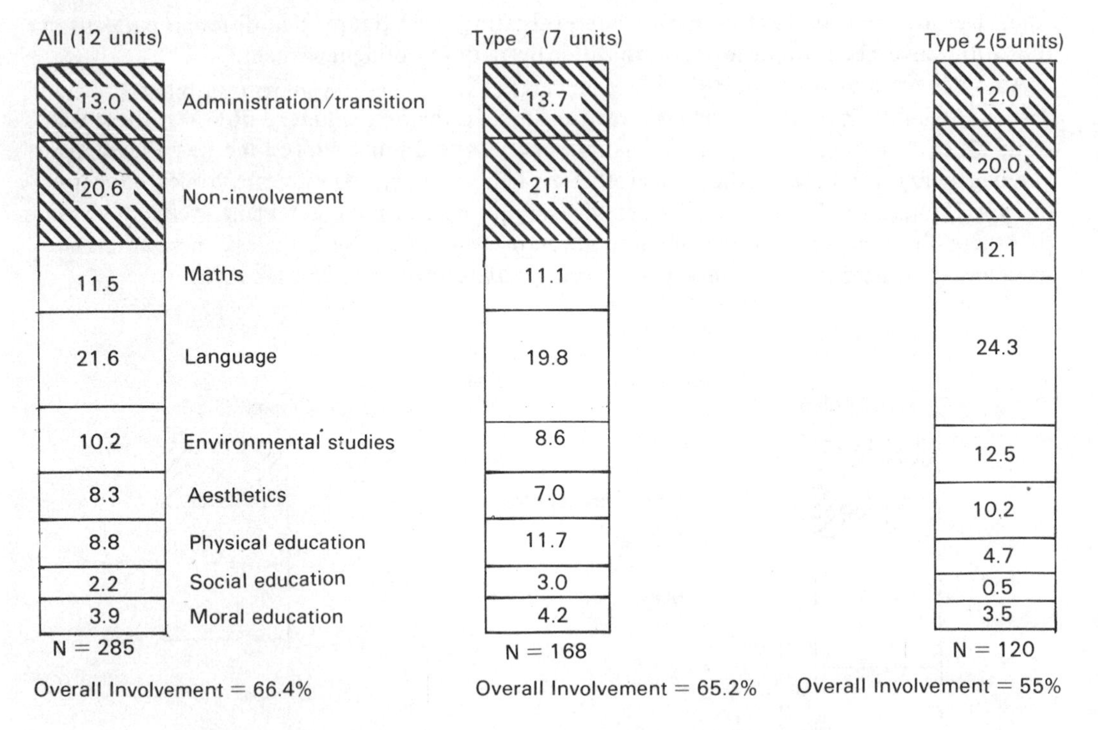


*Figure 4 The junior day: mean percentage overall involvement*

Pupils are not involved for just over one third of the week. This is made up of 13 per cent administration/transition time and 20 per cent of the time when pupils are not involved on allocated activities. This latter is slightly higher than in the infant sample. On average therefore, pupils are involved for 66.4 per cent of the time available.

When considering unit design, involvement is higher in the less open units, a difference which is to some extent a function of the extra administration/transition time in Type 1 designs.

*Curriculum Involvement*

Figure 5 and Table B8, Appendix B, present the findings for curriculum involvement, i.e. involvement within the time available for curriculum activities. This index discounts administration/transition time.

The average involvement across all curriculum areas was 76.2 per cent but varied markedly. Mathematics and language show the lowest involvement and also the most extreme ranges. Average involvement in mathematical activities was 67.9 per cent but varied from less than 60

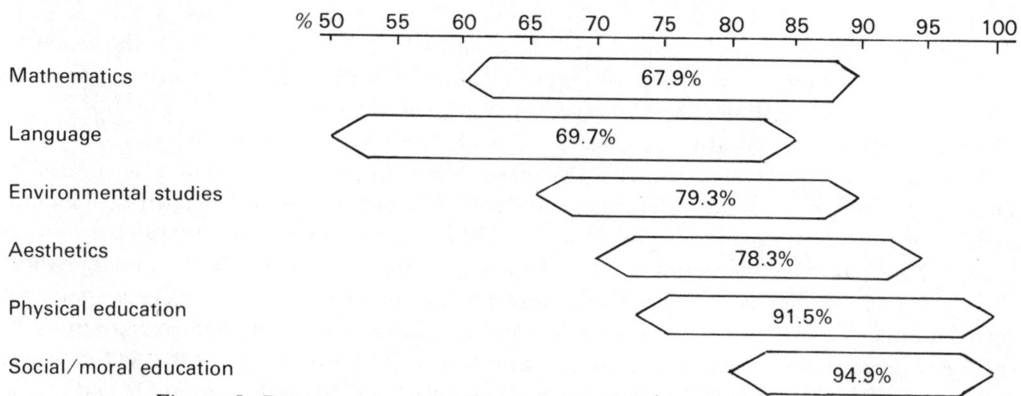


*Figure 5 Percentage curriculum involvement by curriculum area*

per cent in one unit to nearly 90 per cent in another. Similarly with language. The average was 69.7 per cent but was less than 50 per cent in one unit and nearly 85 per cent in another. The pattern of involvement follows that of infants with physical, social and moral showing the highest levels. However it is worth commenting on the average for PE since it highlights observational problems that occasionally arise. On one occasion the observer was put in a dilemma since the class observed was split into halves, one half going to the swimming baths and the other half into the hall. Since it was clearly impossible to observe both halves the observer stayed in the school and had to assume involvement out of the unit. In fact there would have been considerable transition time. This average will therefore be slightly inflated. Analyses were also undertaken to assess if there were differences between boys' and girls' involvement, but these were minimal.

The combined effect of allocation and involvement can be seen in Table 1 below where Units A, H and F are compared (see also Table B6).

Pupils in Unit A were allocated least time for mathematics – 138 minutes or just over $2^1/_4$ hours per week. This contrasts with the allocations in Units F and H, where it amounts to $6^1/_4$ and $6^2/_3$ hours respectively. When involvement is taken into account actual working time on mathematics reduces to less than $1^1/_2$ hours per week for Unit A pupils or about 17 minutes per day. The similarity of allocated time in Units F and H turn into a considerable discrepancy on actual working time since pupils in Unit H achieve a 90 per cent involvement rate against less

| *Unit* | *Time allocated* | | *Involvement* | |
|---|---|---|---|---|
| | *%* | *mins* | *%* | *mins* |
| Unit F | 25.0 | 375.0 | 58.4 | 219.0 |
| Unit H | 26.5 | 397.8 | 89.9 | 357.6 |
| Unit A | 9.2 | 138.0 | 62.6 | 86.4 |

*Table 1 Comparison of units F, H and A on allocation and involvement (%)*

than 60 per cent in Unit F. Thus the former achieve an actual work time of nearly 6 hours per week against just over $3^1/_2$ hours per week in Unit F. Pupils in Unit H were thus involved on mathematics for over 70 minutes per day compared to 17 minutes per day in Unit A.

Differences in pupil involvement are thought to be a function of both the teacher's managerial competence and the pupils' application and motivation. But factors other than these may have affected the performance of pupils in Unit F where, for example, in the observed week the temperature reached 26° C each afternoon.

Table B8 also provides the average involvement levels for pupils in units of differing design. Over all curriculum areas the difference is not large, 77.2 per cent in the less open Type 2 units, and 75.5 per cent in Type 1 designs. However, differences within curriculum area are sometimes substantial. In mathematics pupils in Type 2 units are involved 9 per cent more than those in Type 1, and in language over 4 per cent more. On the other hand, children in Type 1 units are involved more in aesthetic, PE and social/moral education. Of the possible explanations for the higher involvement in mathematics and language in Type 2 units, one is that in four of the five units pupils were taught by teams of teachers who were specialists in mathematics and language. In two of these units aesthetic subjects were also taught by specialist teachers. Table 2 provides the results for the four units with specialists in mathematics and language and for the two units with specialists in aesthetics. It can be seen that in each case the average involvement levels are higher.

| | Type 1 | | | | Type 2 | | | | Team teaching with subject specialism | | | | Overall mean |
|---|---|---|---|---|---|---|---|---|---|---|---|---|---|
| | Min | Max | Mean | N | Min | Max | Mean | N | Min | Max | Mean | N | |
| Mathematics | 58.4 | 72.9 | 64.2 | 7 | 63.4 | 89.9 | 73.2 | 5 | 67.5 | 89.9 | 75.7 | 4 | 67.9 |
| Language | 49.4 | 80.2 | 67.9 | 7 | 64.0 | 84.4 | 72.2 | 5 | 66.6 | 84.4 | 74.3 | 4 | 69.7 |
| Aesthetics | 67.9 | 87.6 | 79.6 | 7 | 67.2 | 94.8 | 76.5 | 5 | 70.1 | 92.8 | 82.6 | 1 | 73.3 |
| Whole curriculum | 67.7 | 83.7 | 75.5 | 7 | 71.5 | 87.0 | 77.2 | 5 | | | | | |

*Table 2 Juniors: % involvement, average and range, within curriculum area*

Although the sample is far too small to make generalizable claims, the link of specialist teaching and higher involvement has intuitive appeal, and is worthy of further study.

A further insight into such findings can be gained by considering the teaching/learning situation from the LES schedule (Table B7). The dominant approach in mathematics in the more open units was by individually assigned tasks and working in small groups. Individual tasks were also frequently noted in Type 2 units, although the most prevalent form was the whole class involved on the same or similar tasks. There was considerably less small group work.

There was more variety of approach in the language area. In Type 1 units individual work was again the most prevalent form, closely followed by small group work and the whole class engaged on the same work. Direct teaching to the whole class occurred for 10 per cent of the time. In Type 2 units, however, a quarter of the teaching was to the whole class, and whole class work and individually assigned tasks made up a substantial amount of time.

During environmental studies small group work predominated in Type 1 units, but was only 5 per cent in Type 2 units, where individually assigned work was the norm together with whole class teaching. Individual work also characterized aesthetics in both units although direct teaching to the whole class featured more strongly in Type 1 units. Of interest also is the great diversity in the incidence of whole class work. This was entirely missing in the more open units but fairly common in the less open units.

Social and moral areas were dominated by direct teaching to large groups, e.g. assembly, in Type 2 units and was strongly featured in Type 1 units, but here a greater variety of approaches were common.

Overall there was much more whole class teaching work and more class teaching combined with less small group work in the less open units.

**Non-involvement**

The type of non-task activities involved in both transition and curriculum time are shown in Table 3. Total transition time varies from 8.6 per cent to 15.7 per cent, both, as it happens, in two-teacher units. Unit A (15.7 per cent) was under-crowded with 43 pupils and 2 teachers, and Unit B was overcrowded with 96 pupils and 3 teachers. The overcrowding in Unit B meant that one class occupied the practical area as a home base, and space was timetabled. Each class had use of each area at some period of the day. In order to ensure a smooth transition pupils were highly organized to collect materials from their trays on entry, and follow prescribed routes to their destination.

As at infant level waiting and moving were the major activities in transition, averaging 4.3 per cent and 3.7 per cent respectively. Movement was also the major activity within curriculum time, with preparation and waiting each taking up 3 per cent of the time. Few differences emerged in these types of activity in units of different design.

**Specific Activities**

Depending upon the context in which they are undertaken, activities may have differing underlying objectives. An activity such as 'drawing' can be undertaken in order to promote mathematical skills or as an aid to language development. Similarly, 'measuring' may be required within other areas of the curriculum than mathematics, as for instance when pupils are assessing plant growth. A list of observed actual activities showing percentage involvement and non-involvement for both types of unit is given in Table B9 in the Appendix.

A large degree of similarity is apparent between the more open and the more closed units in the range of observed activities, but it is also clear that there are differences in the extent to which activities are undertaken. In the more open units, computation, drawing, and reading, using schemes of work such as SRA, featured more prominently, whereas in the less open units other activities, such as the reading of library books chosen by pupils themselves, painting, clay work or the writing of stories or news were more often seen. Observations also revealed that in the more closed units children worked more from the blackboard, work sheets or cards, with less use of standard texts in the teaching of maths and language, and that they did more practical work with less use of reference books in the teaching of environmental studies.

A greater emphasis placed on physical education is also evident in the more open units. Based on a five hour day, the 11.2 per cent devoted to physical activities would mean that on average each pupil would spend about three quarters of an hour of the school day either in the hall, on the playing fields, or in the swimming pool.

*The Social Situation*

Although only a small portion of the school day is specifically allocated to activities designed to encourage the development of social skills, social encounters form an integral part of a child's experience in school. Implicit in the concept of open education is the assumption that flexibility of pupil grouping and greater freedom of movement enable children to learn how to interact with others. The teaching/learning situation may be structured in such a way that cooperation and discussion is facilitated or controlled. It would seem plausible that group work might stimulate more task-related discussion than individual work and that in a team teaching situation children would have contact with a greater number of teachers. Table 4

| *Transition* | Type 1 | | | | | | | Type 2 | | | | | N = 168 | N = 120 | N = 288 |
|---|---|---|---|---|---|---|---|---|---|---|---|---|---|---|---|
| | A | C | E | F | G | I | J | B | D | H | K | L | Type 1 | Type 2 | All |
| Waiting | 4.3 | 2.8 | 7.3 | 3.8 | 2.7 | 3.6 | 7.1 | 3.4 | 3.7 | 4.6 | 3.9 | 4.8 | 4.5 | 4.1 | 4.3 |
| Preparation | 4.3 | 2.9 | 1.9 | 1.6 | 1.0 | 1.7 | 1.2 | 1.0 | .5 | 1.9 | .9 | 1.4 | 2.1 | 1.1 | 1.7 |
| Clearing up | 2.6 | .5 | 1.5 | .9 | .8 | 3.3 | .7 | .6 | .6 | .6 | 1.4 | .17 | 1.5 | 1.0 | 1.3 |
| Movement | 4.2 | 3.6 | 3.5 | 2.4 | 4.2 | 5.3 | 3.3 | 2.4 | 2.4 | 3.4 | 5.3 | 3.9 | 3.8 | 3.5 | 3.7 |
| Transition | 15.7 | 9.8 | 12.8 | 8.7 | 11.1 | 12.8 | 13.7 | 8.6 | 10.0 | 11.9 | 12.1 | 11.6 | 12.1 | 10.8 | 11.6 |
| *Curriculum* | | | | | | | | | | | | | | | |
| Waiting | 2.8 | 1.4 | 3.1 | 3.0 | 1.2 | 1.7 | 3.3 | 1.4 | 2.0 | 2.4 | 2.6 | 3.0 | 2.4 | 2.3 | 2.3 |
| Preparation | 2.4 | 2.6 | 3.6 | 4.7 | 3.2 | 3.6 | 2.3 | 3.8 | 4.4 | 1.1 | 1.9 | 3.3 | 3.2 | 2.9 | 3.1 |
| Clearing up | .1 | .5 | .6 | .4 | .3 | .7 | .5 | .5 | 2.6 | .10 | .3 | 1.0 | .4 | 1.1 | .7 |
| Movement | 3.6 | 1.9 | 3.9 | 5.5 | 4.1 | 5.8 | 3.6 | 2.6 | 7.9 | 2.4 | 4.8 | 5.3 | 4.1 | 4.6 | 4.3 |

NB Waiting, preparation, clearing up and movement do not necessarily summate to total transition 'time' as these activities could be tallied concurrently.

*Table 3 Individual unit profiles: non-task behaviour during transition and curriculum time*

| | Type 1 (7) | | | Type 2 (5) | | | All (12) |
|---|---|---|---|---|---|---|---|
| | Mean | Min | Max | Mean | Min | Max | Mean |
| *Pupil–pupil* | | | | | | | |
| Task-related | 8.7 | 5.6 | 11.3 | 10.0 | 7.3 | 12.0 | 9.3 |
| Social | 10.0 | 7.3 | 13.2 | 7.9 | 3.9 | 9.5 | 9.1 |
| Negative | .3 | – | .9 | .3 | – | .5 | .3 |
| Total | 19.1 | 15.3 | 24.9 | 18.1 | 13.6 | 22.0 | 18.7 |
| *Pupil-Teacher* | | | | | | | |
| Pupil initiated | 1.6 | 1.1 | 2.2 | 2.3 | 1.8 | 3.3 | 1.9 |
| Teacher initiated | 2.0 | 1.0 | 3.5 | 1.8 | 1.1 | 3.6 | 1.9 |
| Total | 3.6 | 2.2 | 5.6 | 4.1 | 2.9 | 6.0 | 3.8 |
| *Watching* | | | | | | | |
| Pupils | 12.7 | 8.1 | 16.2 | 8.9 | 6.5 | 10.6 | 11.1 |
| Teacher | 12.4 | 7.3 | 23.9 | 12.3 | 8.5 | 15.8 | 12.4 |

*Table 4 Pupil–pupil and pupil–teacher interactions in Type 1 and 2 units (mean percentage of the school day)*

indicates the extent to which pupils in both types of unit interacted with each other and the nature of that interaction – work-related, social or negative.

Contrary to what might be expected, slightly more work-related interaction was observed in the less open units. Since little difference was found in observed frequency of individual work between the two types of unit the possibility must be considered that discussion and cooperation are equally facilitated when class-sized groups are tackling similar tasks or when small groups of pupils are similarly engaged.

In contrast to the findings with regard to work-related discussion or cooperation, observation revealed that more social non-work exchanges took place between pupils in the more open units. In keeping with this finding pupils were also more often seen watching their peers in these units. There was little difference overall between the two types of unit in frequency of observed negative behaviour.

In view of the differences between the more open and the less open units concerning the amount of small group, direct and whole class teaching, it might be expected that differences would also emerge on analysis of observation made of teacher–pupil contact. The results of these analyses are also given in Table 4. It can be seen that pupils were observed to have slightly more contact with teachers in the less open units. It would also appear that there was a difference in the pattern of those contacts. In Type 1 units contact between teachers and pupils was more often instigated by teachers themselves, but in Type 2 units pupils were more often seen seeking consultation with teachers. In view of the dominance of team teaching in the less open units it was not surprising to find that on average pupils in these units had contact with a greater number of adults.

Finally, although not a specific focus of interest, analyses were computed to ascertain whether any differences in curriculum allocation or involvement occurred due to teacher absence. Absentees were noted for a total of nine days in three units through the year, a situation usually covered by the headteacher. The overall involvement of the pupils was a little lower than average but this could be a function of the small number of observations made. In looking at allocation it would seem that there is a greater emphasis on basic skills by teachers standing in. Fewer activities were observed in environmental studies and in aesthetics. Taken together these findings suggest that although teacher absence tends to constrict curriculum activities it does not have too deleterious an effect on involvement.

**Summary**

The pattern of curriculum allocation at junior level shows differing emphases to that in infant units. The time devoted to language is less with a corresponding increase in environmental studies and physical education. But the range is wider. In some units pupils are given the opportunity to study mathematics and language three times as often as those in other units. The level of pupil involvement is also wide, and when taken together allocation and involvement provide an indication of the actual as opposed to the notional curriculum balance. As was shown in the examples the actual balance achieved varies markedly.

One major difference between infants and juniors is the link between involvement and unit design. It might be thought that the more open units require more teacher management skills and this could be reflected in the greater administration/transition time and the lower involvement observed in Type 1 units. In common with infants the two curriculum areas which comprise approximately half the time available, mathematics and language, also show the lowest involvement. It is here also that large differences can be seen in units of differing design, the more open Type 1 units achieving lower involvement levels, by up to ten per cent in mathematics. One of the possible reasons for this could be the team teaching organization adopted incorporating teacher specialisms in Type 2 units.

In comparing these data with those gathered in other studies there are similarities. The questionnaire study of teachers in Lancashire and Cumbria by Bennett (1976), the interview studies by Bassey (1978) in Nottingham, and by Ashton *et al.* (1976) in the *Aims of Primary Education* study, all show large differences in time allocated to differing curriculum areas and these are supported by observational studies in the United States. The findings on pupil involvement also tie in with previous research although direct comparisons are not possible. Most studies have observed pupils in intact lessons. Thus, what we have called transition in curriculum activities, have been included, but not transition between activities. Nevertheless it would appear that involvement levels found in this study are no worse and on occasion are a little better than others reported.

**Case Studies**

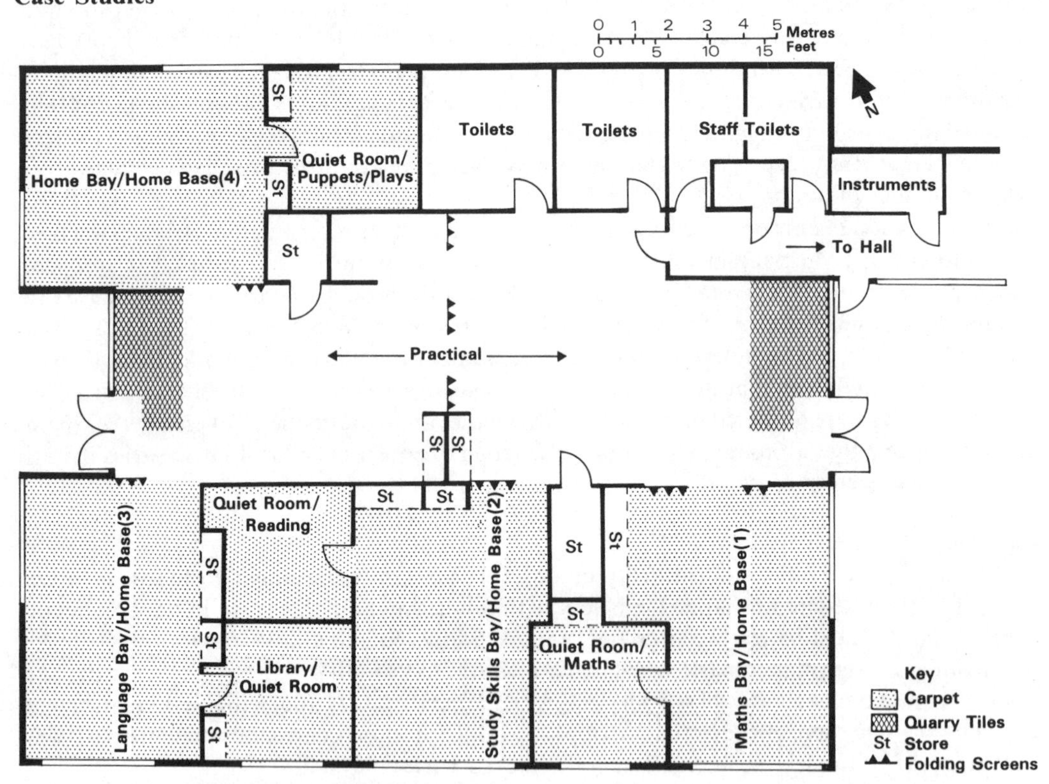


*Figure 6· The Design of Jane's Unit*

**'Jane'**

This case study, of a second year junior girl's day, has been selected as an example of high involvement. Jane is a pupil in an open plan extension to an existing first school, serving a suburban area in the South of England.

The unit, though designed as a Type 2 four teacher unit, is in fact staffed by five teachers, with the headteacher frequently involved both in planning and as an ad hoc 'extra' teacher (Figure 6). The unit houses 120 children, about two thirds of the school's 7–9 age group. Organized on a cooperative teaching basis, each teacher has pastoral and reading responsibility for a home base group, overall responsibility for a curriculum use-specific area of the unit and responsibility for the teaching and follow-up activities of two maths groups, to which children are allocated by age and ability. There is no other ability grouping. Work is organized on a thematic basis and reflects the headteacher's belief that children's learning should be informed by experience. The unit is organized to provide the maximum availability of relevant and appropriate activities and experience, relating, in various curriculum contexts, to the current theme. In the course of a day, a child is expected to have done some mathematics, written work and associated practical work, but is largely self-directing as to when each piece of work is done. Children are able to follow up particular interests within the theme, which is regarded as 'a starting point, not a straitjacket'.

Teachers meet daily to discuss progress, fill any gaps in current provision and to make any changes which are perceived to be necessary. The freedom and self-direction which the children enjoy depends for its success entirely on the complex underlying structure of curriculum and teaching roles within the unit. Standards of work seem very high, children are highly motivated, and exhibit an unusually high rate of involvement.

*The Pupil's Day*

The various dimensions of Jane's day will be considered following the format of the LES observational instrument.

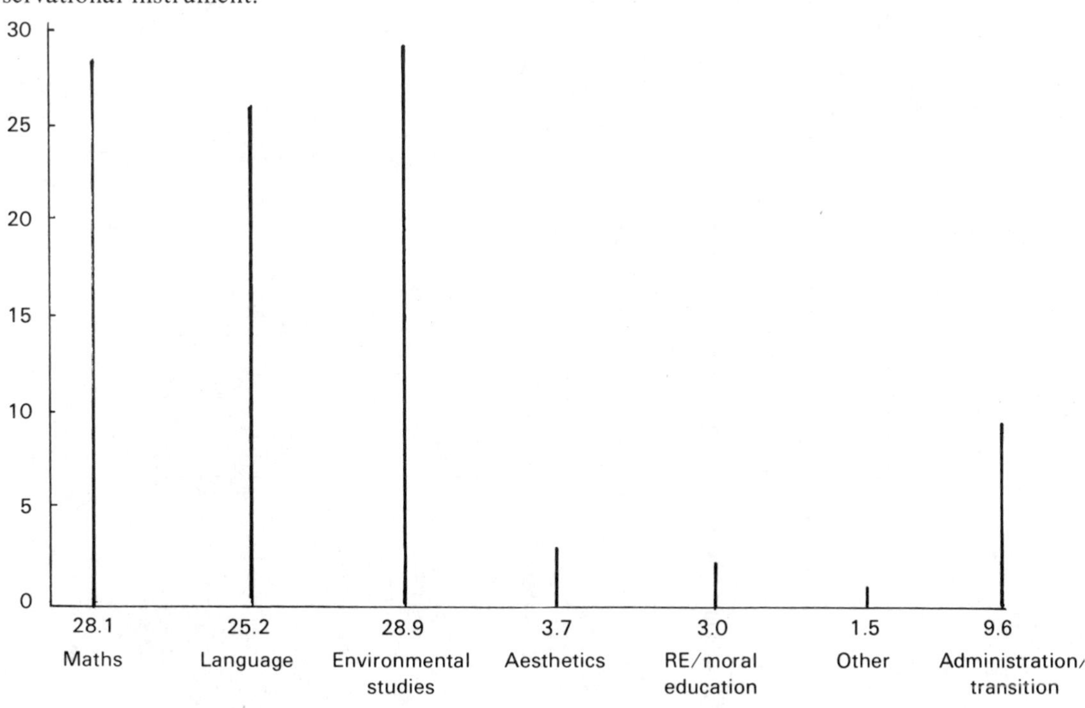


*Figure 7 Proportion of time in curriculum areas*

Physical Scene
Jane spent 86.7 per cent of her day in the use-specific home bases of classroom size. The activities in these spaces included computation, needlework and free writing related to the current theme, reading and class discussion. 5.9 per cent of the day was spent in one of the quiet rooms listening to a story. Of the remaining time, 3.0 per cent was spent in the hall (assembly), 3.0 per cent in the wet area and 1.5 per cent out of the unit. Jane's activities in the spaces reflect clearly the organization of space in the unit – her maths being done in the maths base, etc.

Gross Curriculum Context
The distribution of the day between the various curriculum contexts is shown in Figure 7. It would be misleading to discuss these figures in terms of allocated time, because of the high level of pupil self-direction in this unit. Jane herself was largely responsible for the above allocation of time to curriculum contexts. The major curriculum areas, maths and language, each account for rather more than a quarter of the day, with a further 28.9 per cent devoted to activities related to the current theme ('The Victorians'). The administration/transition time of 9.6 per cent is rather high for this unit, and compares with 15.9 per cent over all the junior units studied.

The proportions of time devoted to the actual curriculum activities subsumed under the gross curriculum contexts are shown in Figure 8.

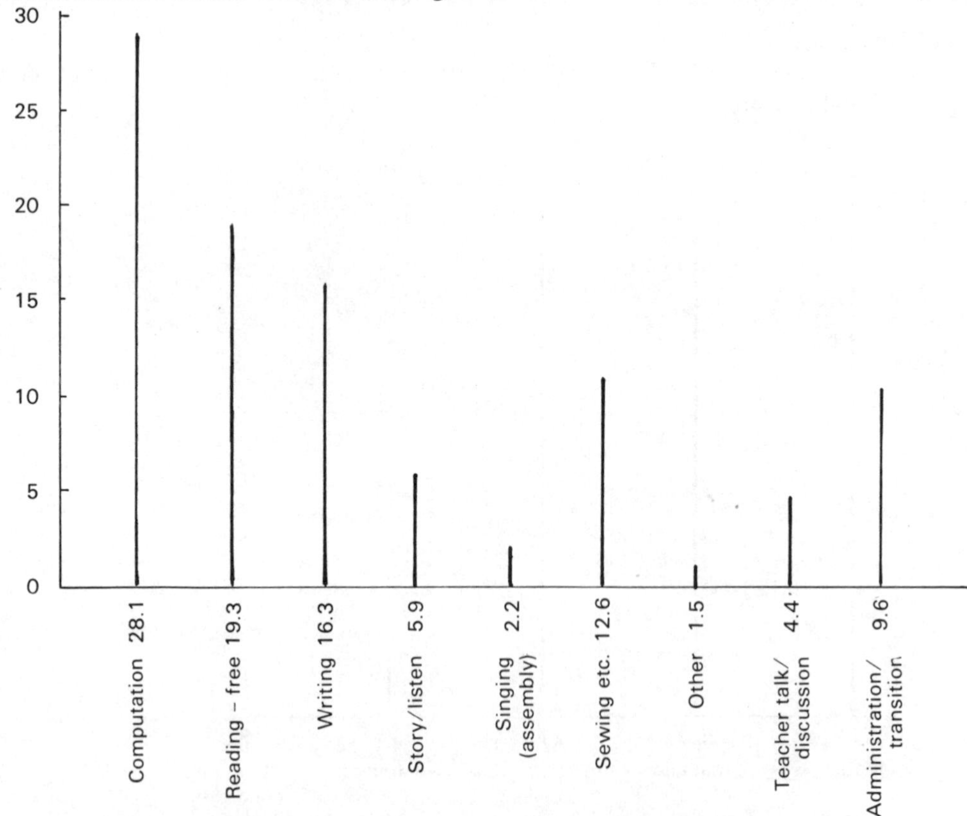


*Figure 8 Actual curriculum activities*

These figures indicate that of the whole day, 63.7 per cent was devoted to work in the 'basics'. The level of actual involvement is shown in Figure 9.

Overall involvement accounts for 71.0 per cent of the time – a very high level of involvement which compares with an average 69.2 per cent for this unit and 52.3 per cent over the whole junior sample. It should be noted that if time spent fetching materials and consulting the teacher, both clearly work-related activities, is added to the involvement score, a figure of 77.0

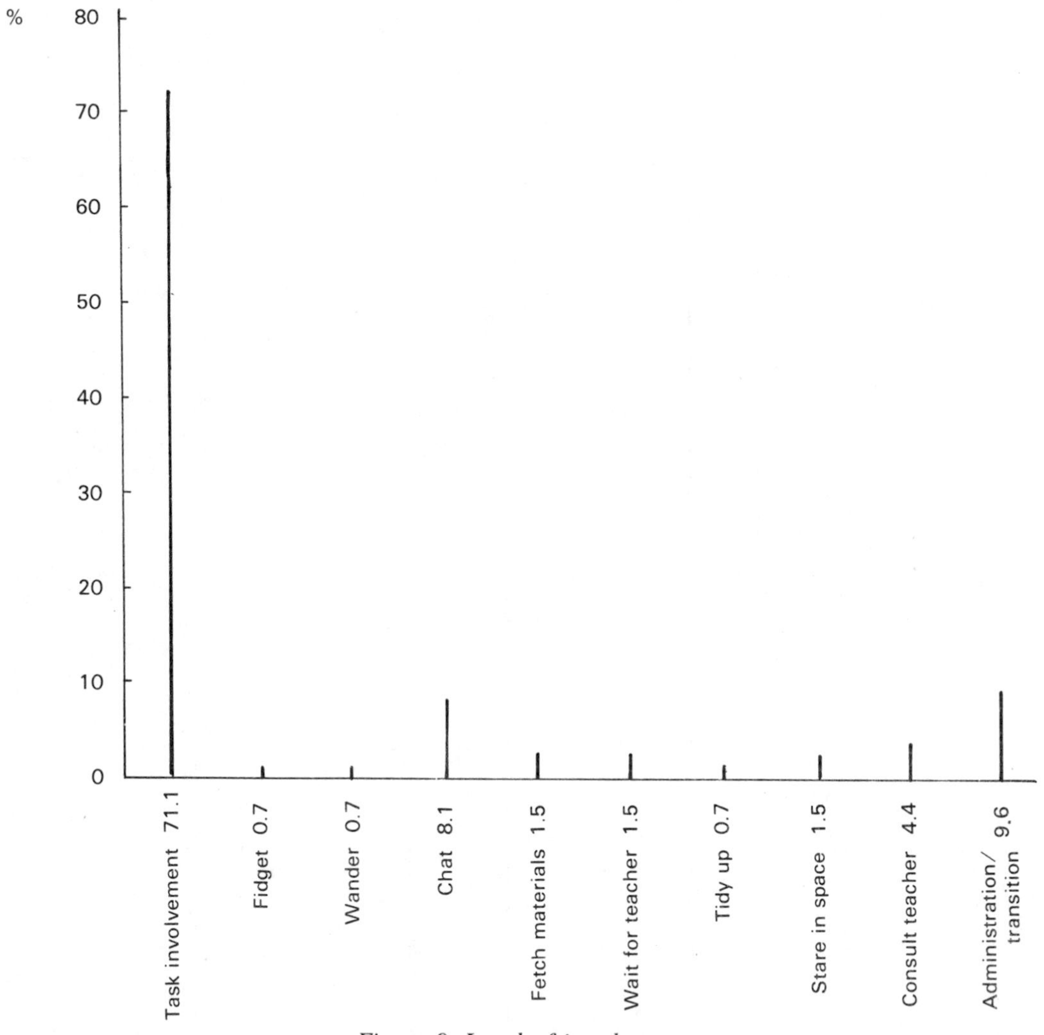


*Figure 9 Level of involvement*

per cent is obtained. Further, if task involvement is computed as a percentage of curriculum time (i.e. curriculum involvement rather than the whole day) a task involvement score of 89.3 per cent is obtained. This, while not the highest individual involvement rate found in this unit, is exceptionally high. Why is this the case? It cannot be said that the organization of this particular unit necessarily generates the high level of task involvement. Similar styles of teaching organization observed in other units do not achieve such high scores. The fact of pupil self-direction, and individual work (see Figure 10), the fact of an extremely well-organized and carefully planned team teaching system and of thorough and continuous curriculum planning all have a bearing on the pupil's interest and motivation.

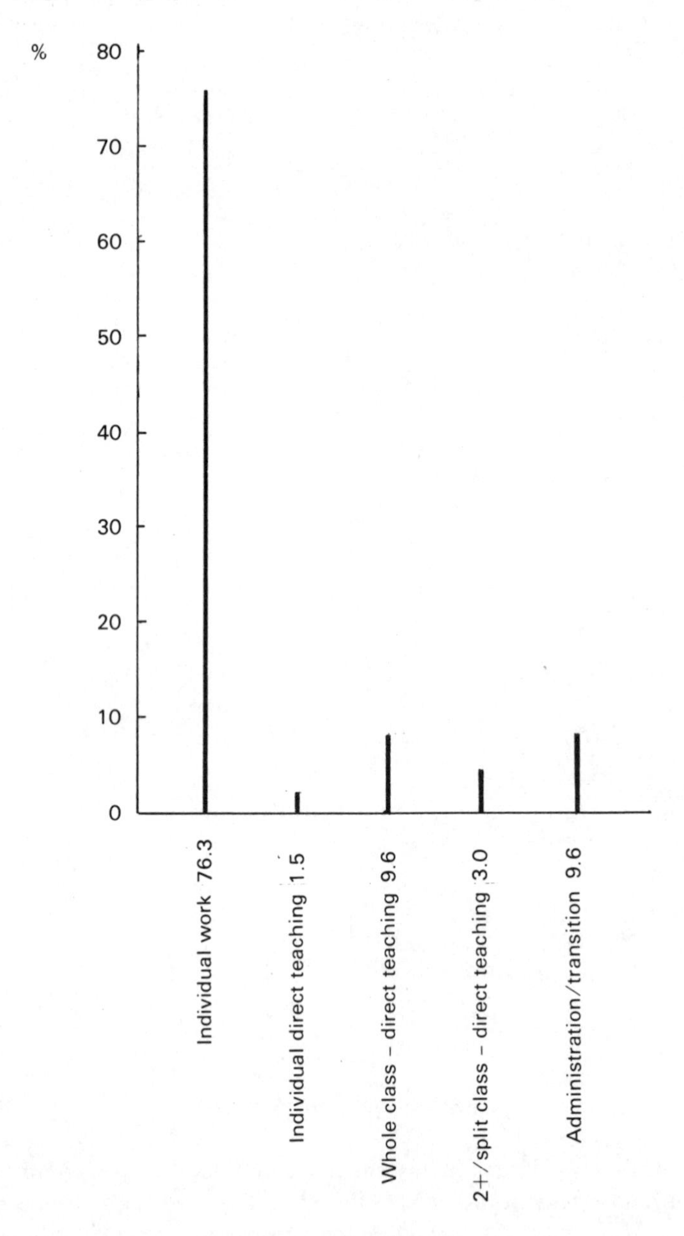


*Figure 10 Teaching/learning situation*

It should also be added that there is in this unit considerable concern for quality, which is manifested in the content and the appearance of the children's work. The same excellence is apparent in the displays and organization of materials by the teachers. This, combined with planning, day-to-day preparation and overall professionalism, seems to maintain the children's motivation and generates high levels of involvement. It should also be noted that the amount of administration/transition time for this child is comparatively low, at 9.6 per cent; which has an obvious effect on the time available for curriculum activities and, presumably, an effect on interest and motivation.

Another factor worthy of mention is the generous staffing level. The staffing level, at 24:1 (not unusual in the schools studied) not including the frequent involvement of the head and the presence of parents, means that pupils have ready access to teachers. Waiting for teacher is a comparatively rare occurrence in this unit and accounts for only 1.5 per cent in Jane's case. The staffing level also ensures adequate levels of supervision in all spaces – which would not necessarily be the case if the unit were staffed by only the four teachers it was designed for.

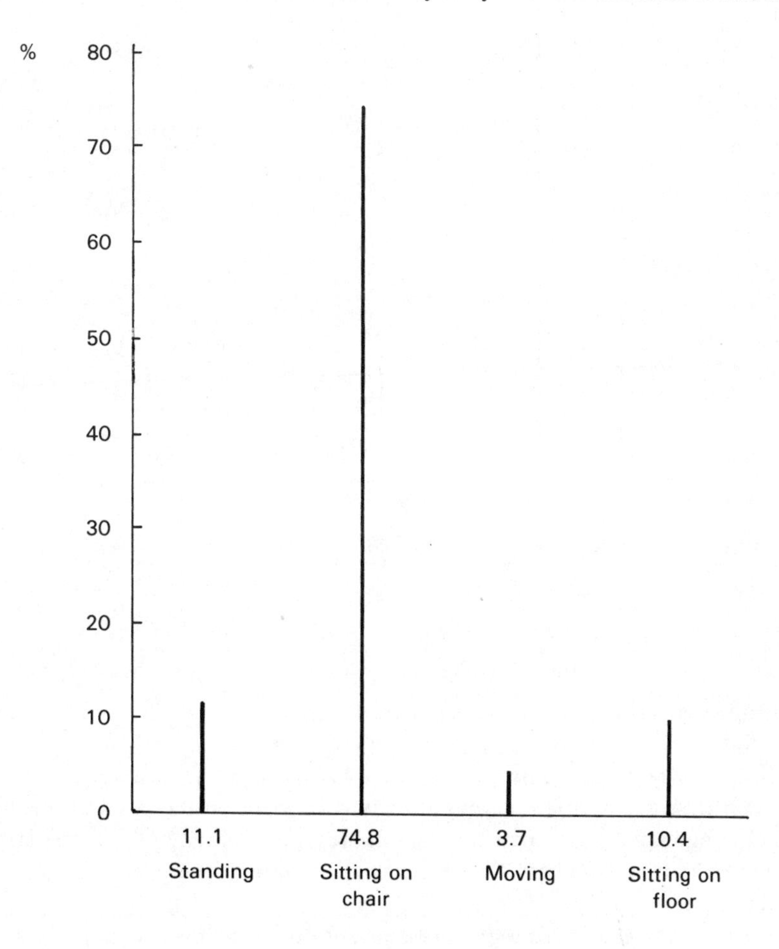


*Figure 11 Posture (%)*

Finally, it should be recognized that the unit itself is perceived as being of exceptionally good design and spacious by the teachers who staff it, and was similarly regarded by the members of the Project research team.

The other dimensions of the pupil's day, presented in quantitative form, include posture and social interactions. The former (Figure 11) shows that Jane spent most of her day seated. Only 3.7 per cent was spent moving around the unit – a reflection both of the low administration/transition time and her high task involvement score.

Jane's interactions with other children (Figure 12) account for 22.2 per cent of observations, including both work-related and non-work-related interactions. She had a total of 12 recorded teacher contacts and had, over the whole day, access to all five teachers, the head and one parent.

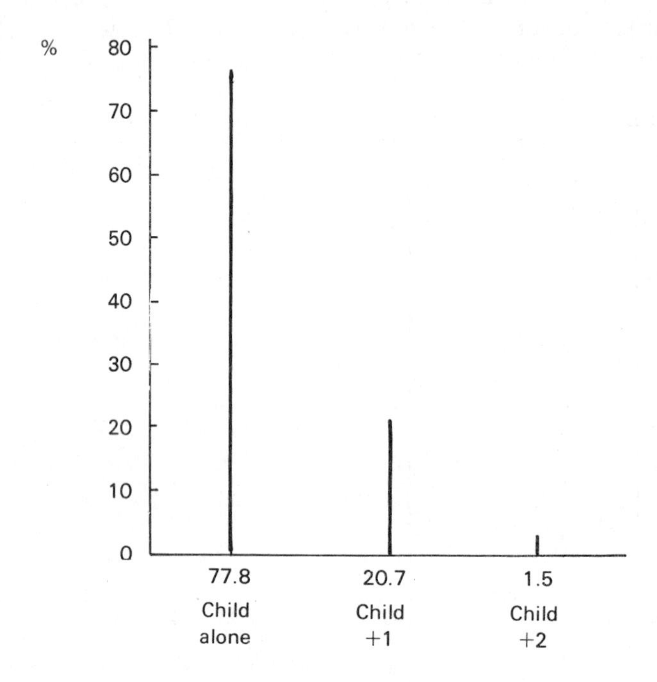


*Figure 12 Interaction with peers (%)*

Thus far, Jane's day has been considered in terms of frequencies, or quantitative data. Perhaps more interesting is the consideration of her day as a process. From Figure 13 it would seem that each of Jane's curriculum activities was sustained over a fairly long period of observation. Her task involvement shows a fairly consistent pattern of sustained periods of involvement varying between about 10 and 14 minutes, punctuated by fetching materials, consulting the teacher and social chat. The last is fairly equally distributed between the various curriculum activities.

Contact with teachers amounted to 9.9 per cent, most of which was with one teacher. There was no contact with parents or ancillaries.

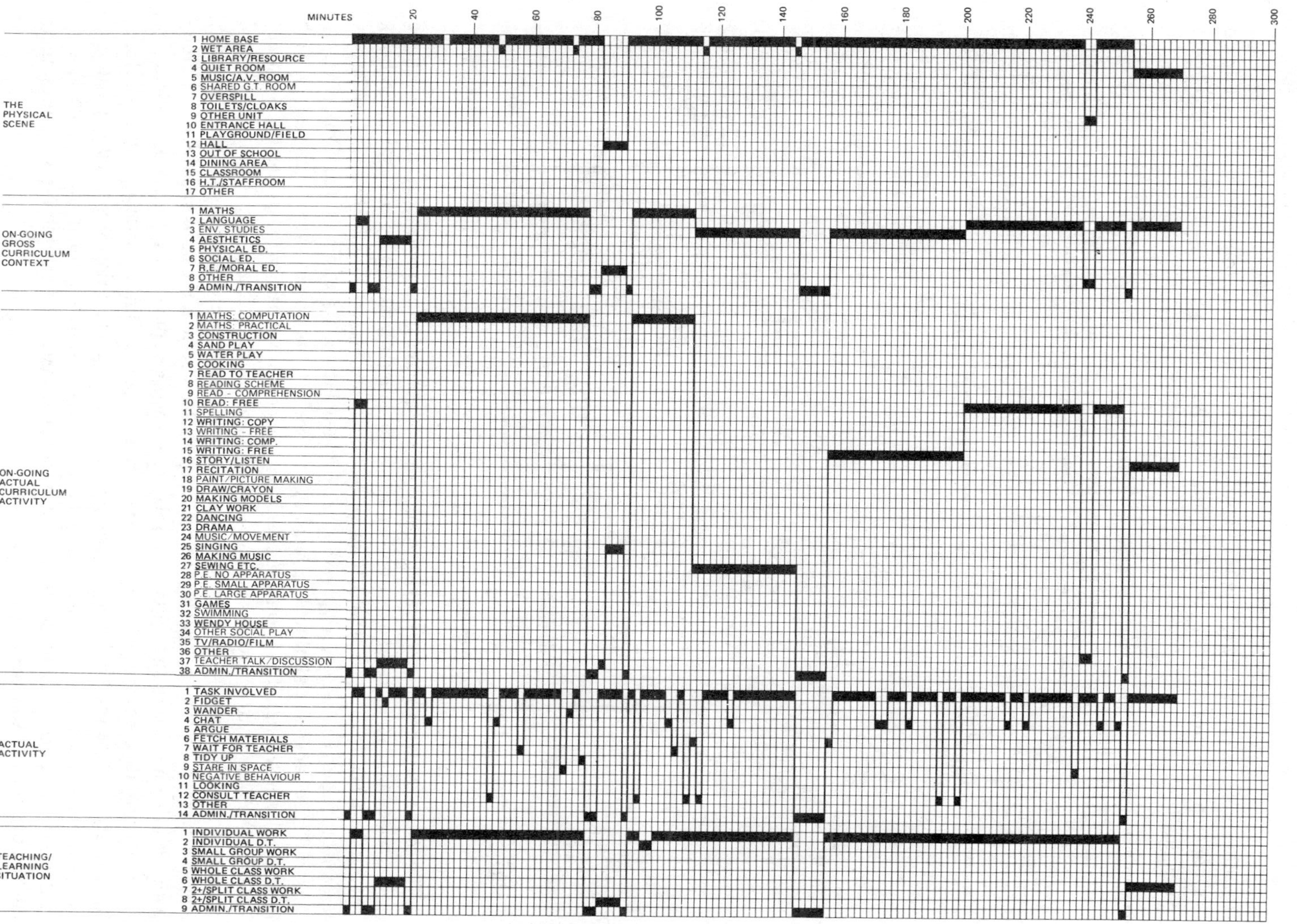


*Figure 13 Learning Experiences Schedule Process Chart: 'Jane'*

**'Tracey'**

The subject of this case study is 'Tracey', a third year junior girl in a four teacher, Type 1 unit in an all open plan junior school in the Midlands. Tracey has been selected as an example of low involvement.

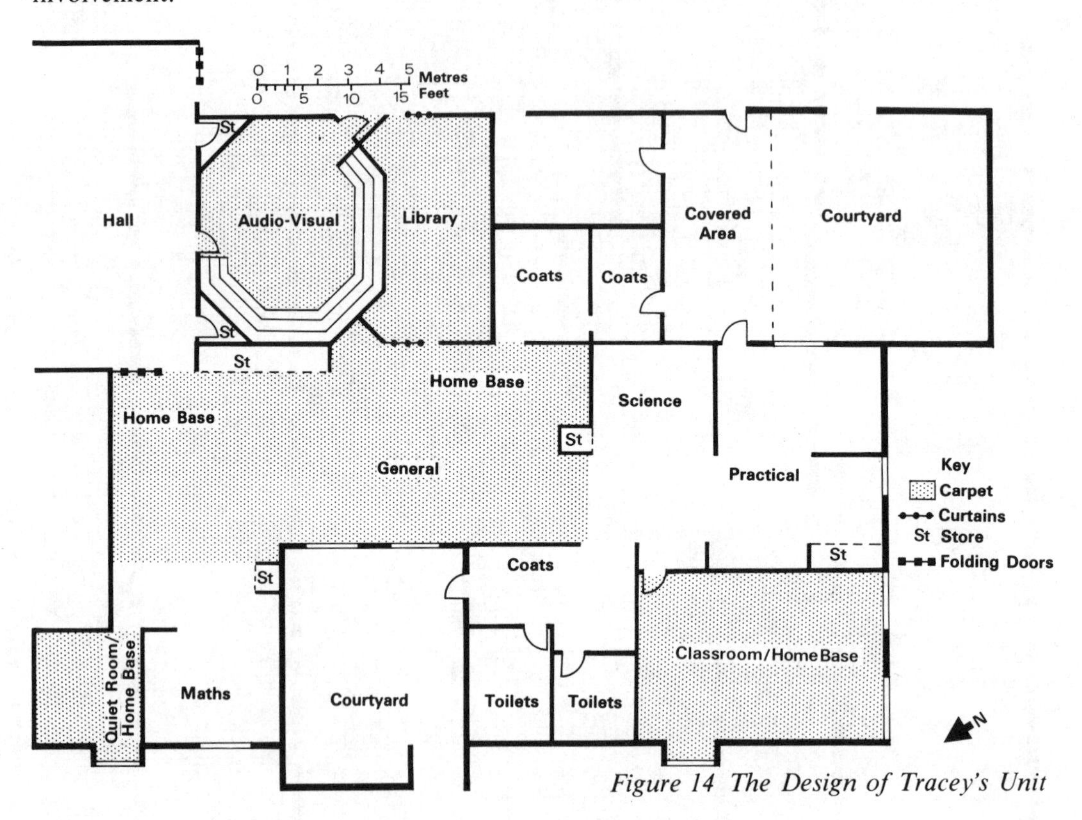


*Figure 14 The Design of Tracey's Unit*

The school, a two form entry junior school, serves a mixed catchment area, children coming from a wide range of social backgrounds, and was built as a replacement for an existing school. The headteacher describes a period of transition in which staff were 'highly resistant' to the new building. The current level of cooperation between teachers in the unit is limited. Children from the whole age range are allocated to maths groups which take place three times weekly, each group with one teacher. There was an interchange of children between the two teachers of third year juniors over part of some Tuesdays. The two teachers of fourth year children operated independently. Essentially the unit operates on a one-teacher–one-class basis. All the teachers stated a marked preference for the one traditional classroom in the unit, and this space along with the other areas was shared between classes on a timetabled basis; teachers, children and materials moved *en masse* at set times through the day. Curriculum activities did not, therefore, necessarily relate to the kind of space being used. For instance, if the class was doing comprehension and was timetabled for the wet area, then it did comprehension in the wet area. Within each class, teaching is on a whole class teacher-directed basis, all the pupils carrying out similar curriculum activities at the same time.

In general it is fair to say that there is evidence of a clash between the teaching styles and preferences of the teachers and the open nature of the unit. It is clear from the questionnaire and interview data that many headteachers feel that buildings need not dictate teaching style and organization. However, it would seem that the evident dissonance between the building and the organization of teaching and curriculum is one factor in the low level of task involvement exhibited not only by Tracey, but by all the target pupils in this unit.

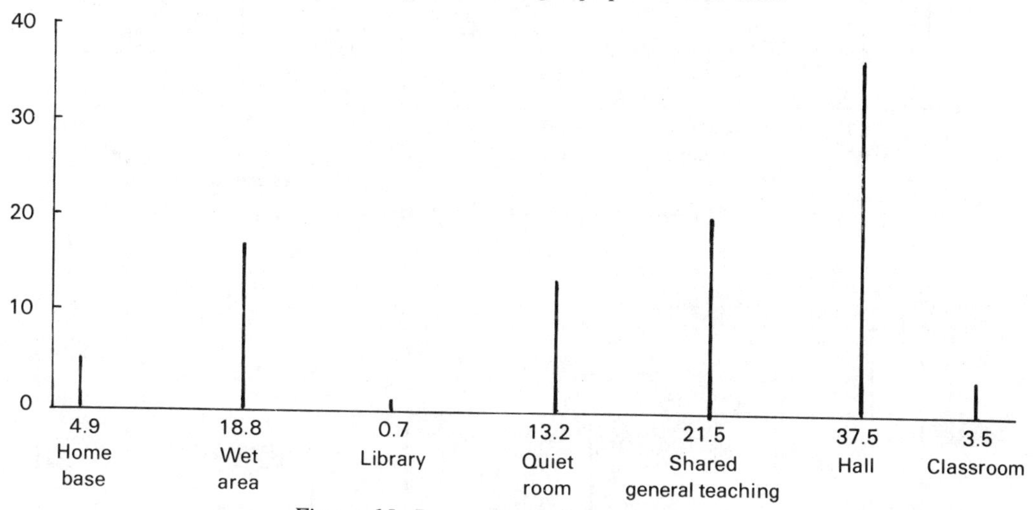


*Figure 15 Proportion of time in spaces*

*The Pupil's Day*

As in Case Study 1, the various dimensions of Tracey's day are considered following the format of LES.

Physical Scene

Tracey's day was split mainly between the hall, the wet area, the small quiet room and the shared general teaching space (Figure 15).

The hall, which accounts for 37.5 per cent of Tracey's day, was used for a long period of assembly and hymn practice and for a PE lesson. Her sole curriculum activity in the wet area was computation. The quiet room was used mainly for free reading and the shared general teaching area for free writing. A good deal of time was spent in moving the class from one space to another, including one movement of the whole class only ten minutes before the end of the school day.

Gross Curriculum Context

The allocation of time to different curriculum activities was fairly typical of that found over the whole junior sample, with 18.1 per cent allocated to maths and 29.2 per cent allocated to language (Figure 16).

Aesthetics is comparatively low and RE/moral comparatively high, due to the hymn practice and assembly mentioned earlier. Administration/transition accounts for 25.0 per cent of total observations: an exceptionally high figure. The reasons for this are discussed below. The actual curriculum activities subsumed under curriculum area are shown in Figure 17.

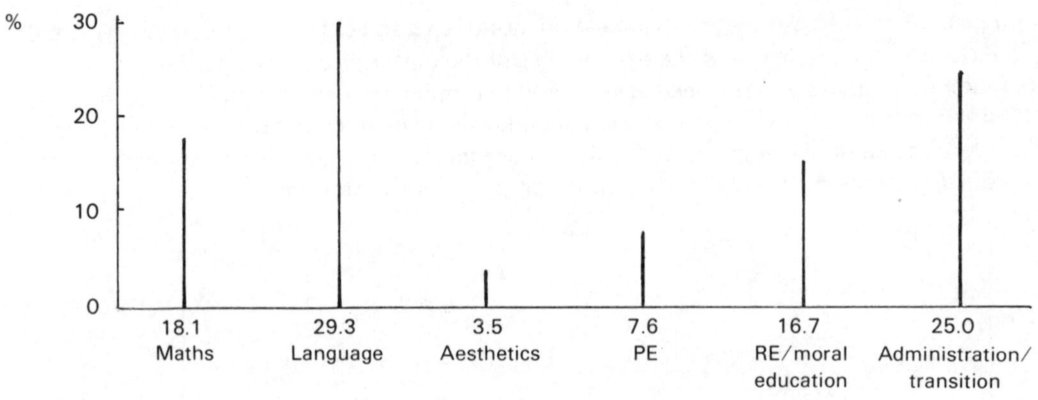


*Figure 16 Proportion of time in curriculum areas (%)*

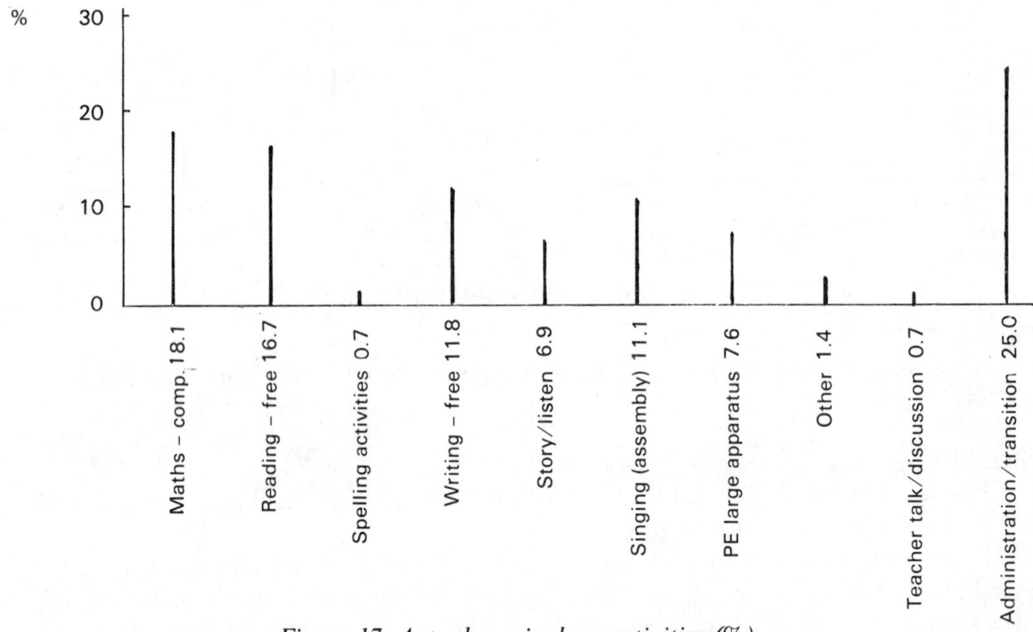


*Figure 17 Actual curriculum activities (%)*

Actual Activity

The focus of this case study is Tracey's low level of overall involvement, which accounts for only 27.1 per cent of her day as seen in Figure 18. This compares with the average in her unit of 35.1 per cent and with the average of the junior sample of 52.3 per cent. Tracey's involvement was not the lowest recorded in this unit.

Two main questions arise: firstly, how did Tracey spend the time when she was not involved and secondly, how can her low level of involvement be accounted for? In answer to the first of these questions, a sizeable proportion of the school day was swallowed up by administration/transition, 25.0 per cent, compared with an average of 15.9 per cent over the whole junior sample. One quarter of the school day was not therefore available to Tracey for curriculum activities. It is thus appropriate to examine her level of involvement in curriculum time, taking administration/transition time out of reckoning. Her level of curriculum involvement was 41.2 per cent – still very low compared with Jane in the earlier study and with the figure of 63.0 per cent for the whole junior sample. The undesirable effects of the high level of administration/transition must therefore be compounded by other factors. It is clear from Figure 18 that much of Tracey's time was spent in non-work-related chatter and almost as much fidgeting. Taken alone, the 'chat' score may indicate that Tracey is one of those incurable chatterboxes – but the level of the score for fidgeting indicates that other possible reasons must be considered.

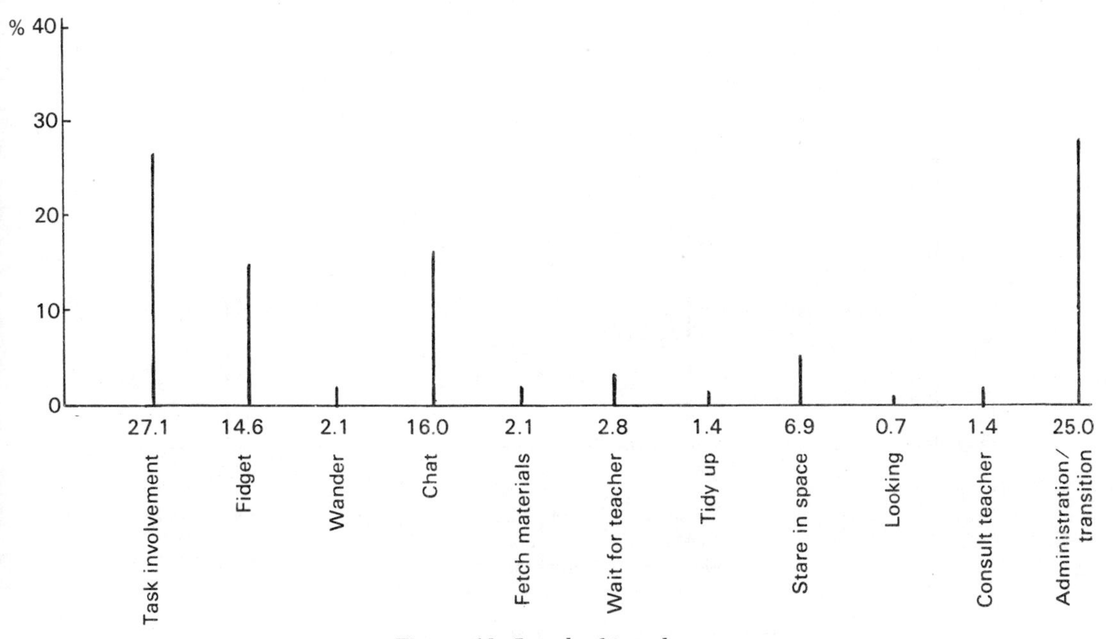


*Figure 18 Level of involvement*

Unfortunately her level of motivation, the appropriateness of tasks and quality of supervision cannot be answered by the observations taken, but the observer was left with the impression that little account was taken of children's individual needs, that children were largely teacher-dependent and curriculum activities almost wholly teacher-directed, and that the teacher's role seemed to consist of setting tasks from text books and then maintaining order – policemanship rather than pedagogy – but these *are* impressions. It should be added that involvement levels in the unit as a whole were generally very low, a mean of 35.0 per cent against 52.3 per cent over the whole junior sample.

The breakdown of Tracey's day in terms of teaching/learning situation is shown in Figure 19.

The second most frequent teaching/learning situation here is 2+/split 'class direct teaching', which occurred during assembly and hymn practice. Typically, this generates a fairly high involvement level at 72.8 per cent but in Tracey's case this was more a period of chatter and fidgeting than involvement.

Finally in this section, note must be made of the fact that Tracey comes within the lower ability range in this school and it seems likely that the interaction of ability level and that of predominance of whole class teaching could be one of the reasons for Tracey's low level of involvement. The danger of the needs of lower ability children being at least partially overlooked in whole class work exists and this may well explain in part Tracey's score. Process data relating to those pupils categorized as of lower ability in each school tends to show that task involvement is sustained for only relatively short periods of time and that they take longer to

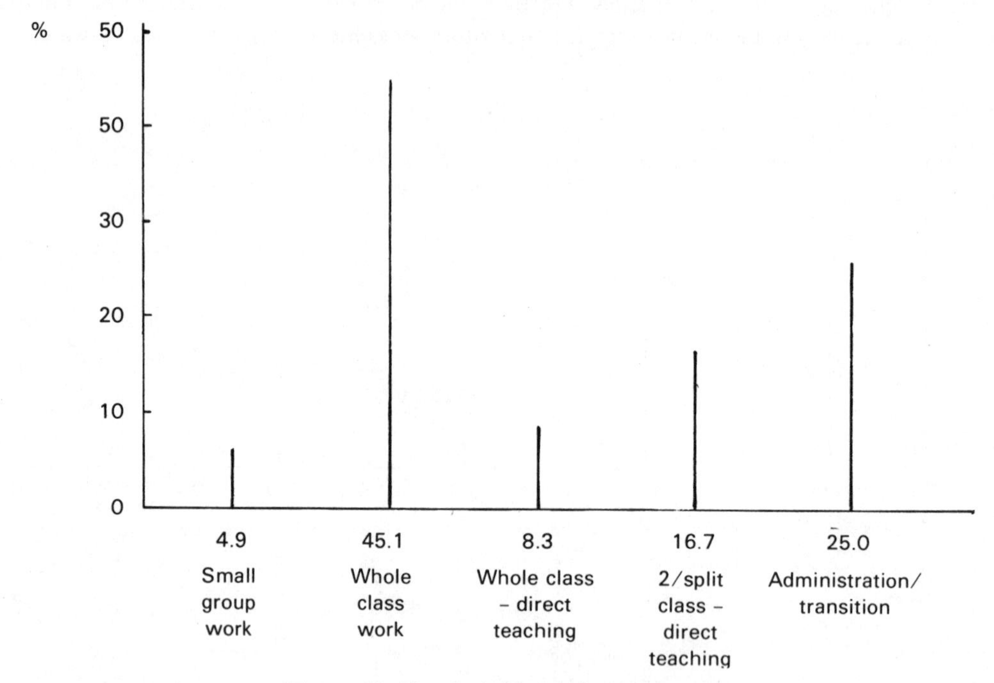


*Figure 19 Teaching/learning situation*

'settle down' after a transitional period. The organization of this unit involved regular major periods of transition when whole classes – teachers, pupils and belongings – move on to their next appointed space. It is, on the one hand, clear that teachers are paying a high price in wasted time for their share of the traditional classrooms. On the other hand disruption, disturbance and lack of continuity would seem to be deleterious to pupil involvement levels and especially to those of lower ability children.

The other dimensions of Tracey's day which are presented in quantitative form are concerned with posture and social interactions. As to the former (Figure 20), Tracey spent most of her day seated at a desk or work surface (50.7 per cent) and on the floor (31.3 per cent).

Tracey spent rather more of her day interacting with peers than Jane, though far fewer of her interactions were task-related. Contacts with teachers were far fewer than Jane's (Figure 21).

The process chart of Tracey's day (Figure 22) provides an interesting basis for comparison with Jane's day in Case Study 1.

It should first be made clear that the items in Section 1, the Physical Scene, refer to varieties of space. Thus Jane did not spend most of her day in one home base, but in fact four home bases – all the same variety of space. The spread of allocated time and curriculum activities does not

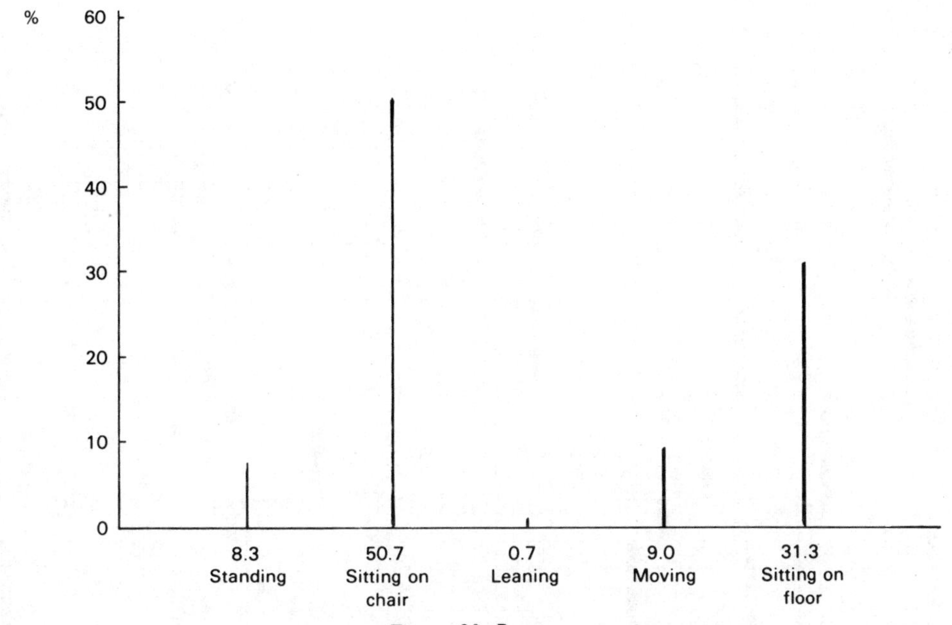


*Figure 20 Posture*

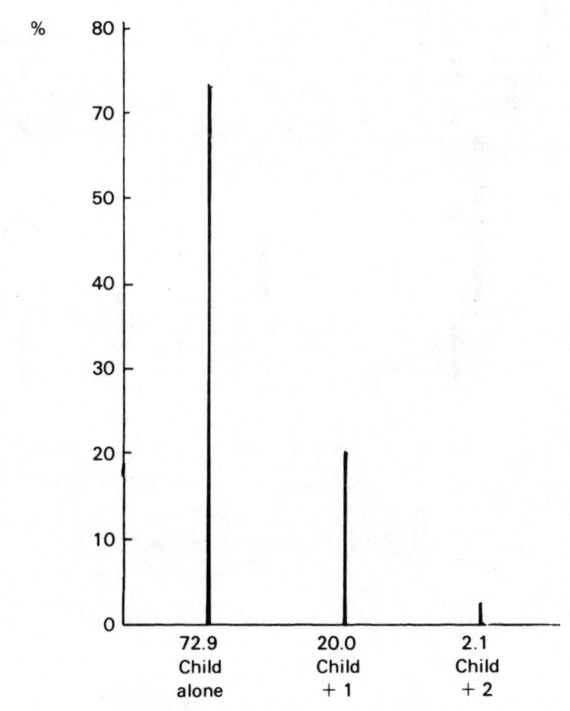


*Figure 21 Interaction with peers*

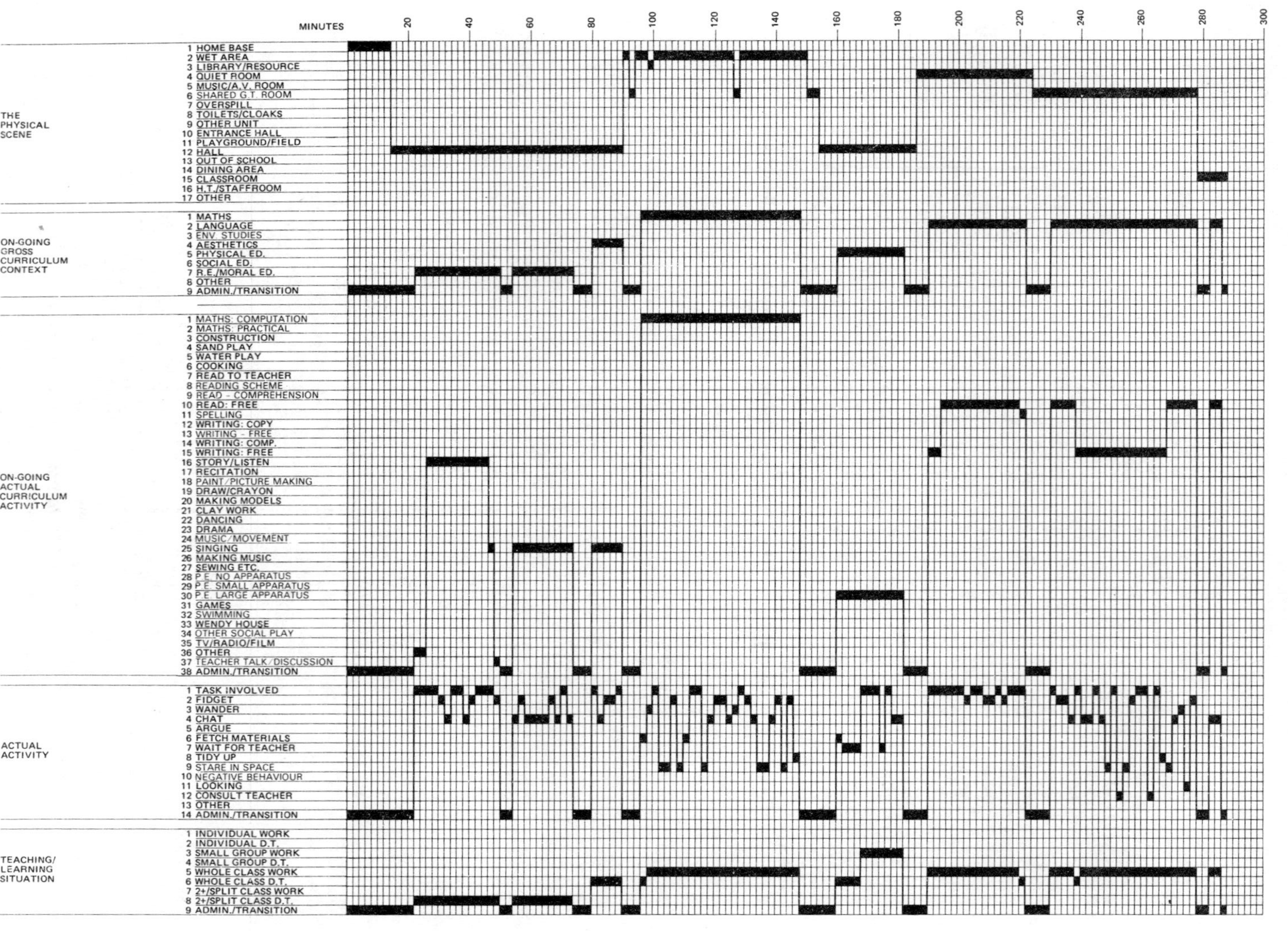


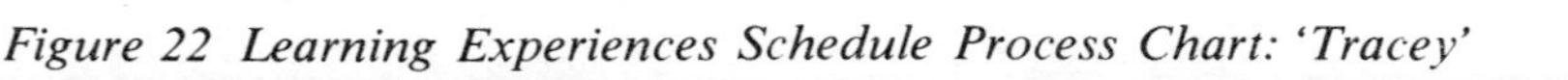
*Figure 22 Learning Experiences Schedule Process Chart: 'Tracey'*

differ greatly between the two case studies, except for the huge difference in the amount of administration/transition time. Similarly, the number of changes in actual curriculum activity is about the same. It is in the task involvement/non involvement section, 'actual activity', that the differences are most marked. Jane's periods of sustained task involvement are much longer than Tracey's, and the non-work behaviours less frequent and briefer.

Finally, Section 5 shows clearly that Jane's 'individual work' situation was sustained for long periods covering most of the day, when she was able to direct her own activities. Tracey's day is clearly very much more fragmented regarding the teaching/learning situation in which she found herself, and virtually entirely teacher-directed.

Tracey had very little contact with teachers, comprising only 2.8 per cent, and none with other adults.

*Chapter 9*

# *Use of Space*

---

**Introduction**

The argument presented in Chapter 1 asserted that of all the influences impinging on the early development of open plan schools the educational rationale was pre-eminent. Nevertheless, there is also evidence to indicate that cost limits have become a critical factor over the last decade. In interviews with architects it was often stated that a conventional school cannot be built under current cost limits, and it would appear that very few schools of conventional design have been built since the early 1970s.

Cost limits have eaten into the amount of space provided in schools. Here teacher perception is matched by DES statistics. Figure 1 shows the average areas per pupil from 1968 to 1976. In 1968 when open plan buildings began to proliferate the average space per pupil was 3.81 $m^2$ (41 $ft^2$) but fell to a little over 3.0 $m^2$ (36 $ft^2$) in the period 1974/5. However, these averages mask large variations. In the latter period variation in area ranged from 2.5 $m^2$ to 4.2 $m^2$ (27 to 45 $ft^2$) (DES, 1977). The DES study admitted that many recently built schools have been significantly smaller than the recorded average and that this has prejudiced their effective use. It was also admitted that standards of finish are well below those considered desirable or suitable and concluded 'there is evidence that owing to a combination of circumstances including cost inflation the areas per pupil achieved in some of the primary schools built in recent years are inadequate'. The report accepted that in schools built to a standard of less than 3.7 $m^2$ (40 $ft^2$), which includes the majority of schools built this decade, the curriculum and teaching methods have been constrained.

Given the general lack of space in open plan schools, what do teachers perceive to be the major problems in the use of space which is available? From interviews with teachers it became clear that two types of space were perceived as particularly problematic – quiet rooms and practical/wet areas. This chapter therefore focusses on these areas and the possible reasons for such problems, before addressing the more general question of what factors impinge on the use of available space.

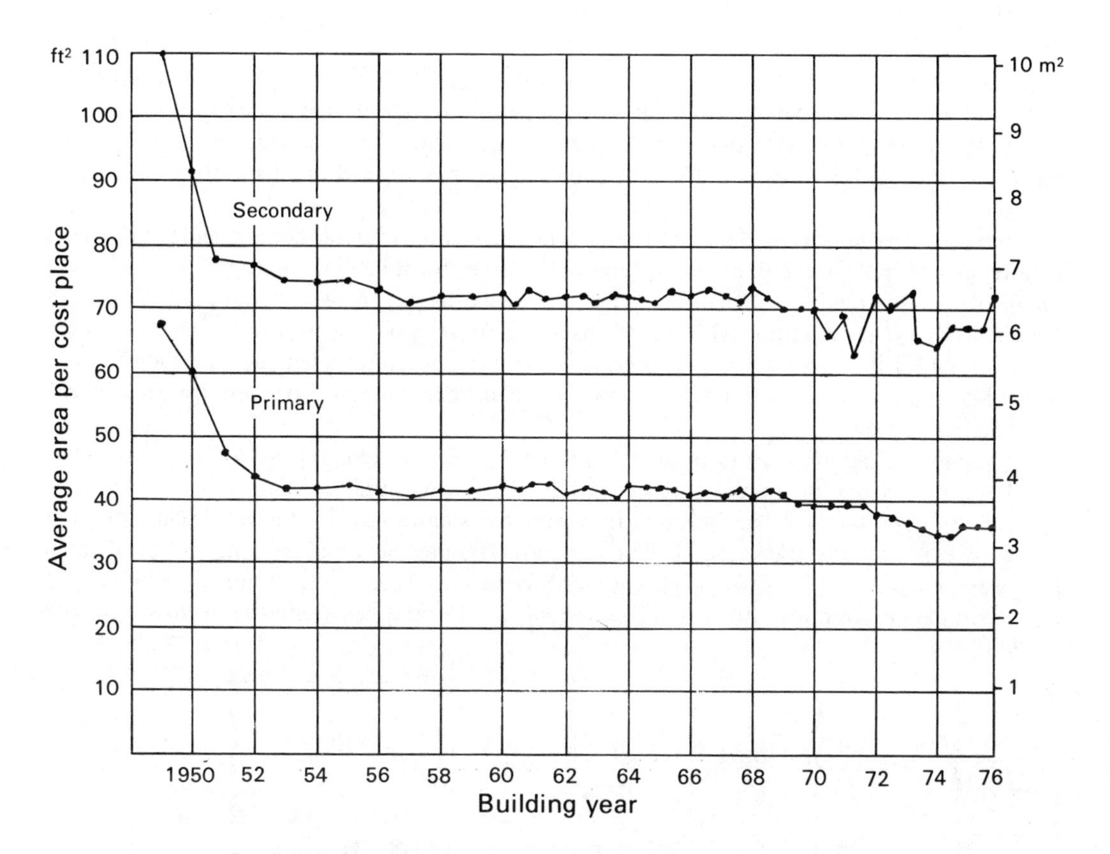


*Figure 1 Average areas per cost place in primary and secondary schools 1950-76*

Source: DES and Welsh Office *A Study of School Building*, HMSO 1977, p.57

**Use of Available Space**

In order to assess the use made of the available spaces by both teachers and pupils a Use of Space Schedule was developed and used to observe 30 teaching units in the 23 schools studied. 14 were infant and 16 junior units. In order to gather the information a scaled drawing was used on which was indicated the differing spaces as identified by the teachers in the unit. Each of those spaces was then observed every 20 minutes through the whole day for a total of three days. Records were made of the number of pupils and teachers in each space and the activities on which they were engaged.

Valid comparisons of space use across units were impossible to make because of differences in design, type of space available, number of pupils and teachers in the unit and spatial density. The actual amount of space per pupil available in the units observed, for example, varied from less than 2.0 $m^2$ to 4.5 $m^2$ (21.5 to 48.4 $ft^2$). Fifteen of the units were under-pupilled and were therefore less constrained in terms of organization, usage and movement. The following descriptions are therefore based on averages.

*Quiet Rooms*
These are defined as rooms of varying size but not larger than 32 $m^2$ (344.46 $ft^2$), having four walls and a door and located within the teaching unit. Originally they were conceived to be a self contained room of less than classroom size for the purposes of small group teaching or for noisy activities such as music or TV which could be carried on without distracting children in the rest of the unit.

From the observations made, quiet rooms tend to be smaller in infant units and tend to have a more specific purpose, e.g. used as a Wendy House or for remedial reading. Junior teachers on the other hand tend to use them more for class teaching purposes, and they contained more TV and audio-visual equipment. The patterns of use are very diverse and are presented in full in Tables 1 and 2 in Appendix C. Of interest is the average use of such rooms which in both infant and junior units is very low – ranging between 4 per cent and 5 per cent for both pupils and teachers.

What are the major factors in such underuse? Siting would appear to be paramount. Teachers in only one of the units observed felt them to be satisfactory in this respect.

Teachers' complaints, other than that they were too small to use for the whole class or large groups, were related to the siting of the room in relation to the other teaching spaces. Rooms that were only visible through a glazed door were felt to be poor because visibility and supervision of children was difficult. The same was felt about quiet rooms that were too cut-off

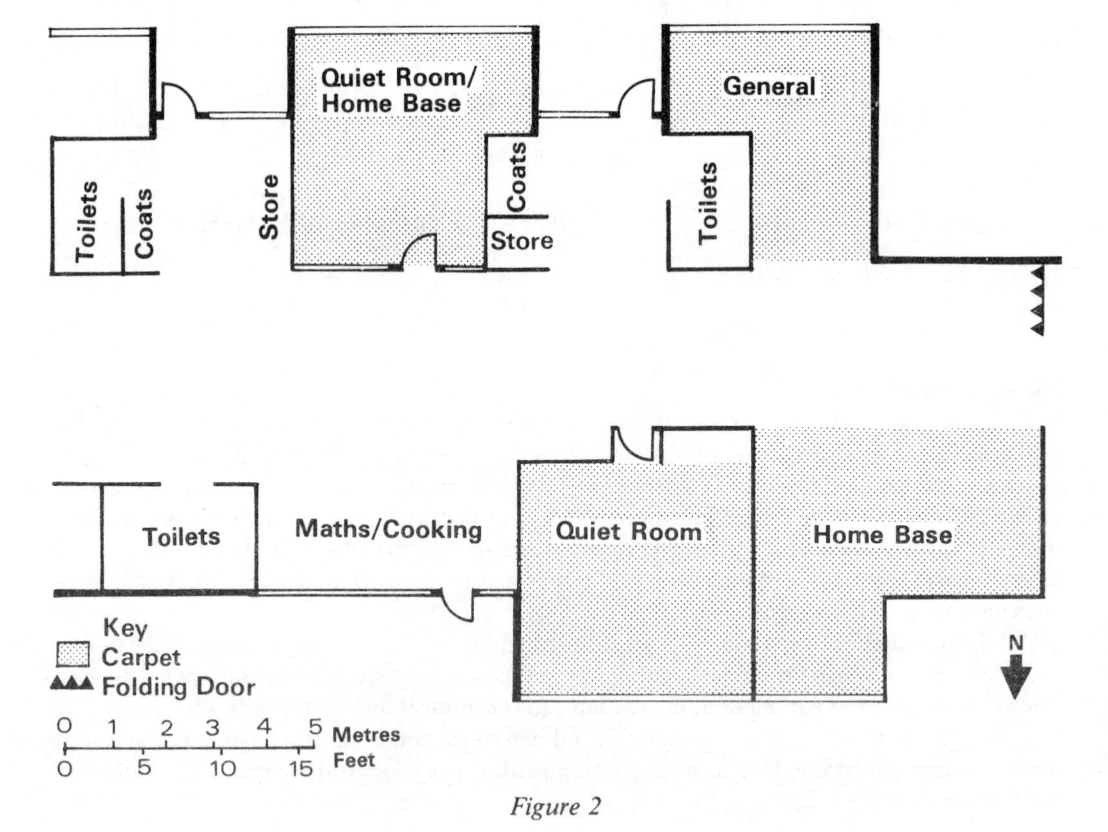


*Figure 2*

from the mainstream of general activity. These rooms were used minimally by both children and adults. The problem of where to place a quiet room is a difficult one. Because of its very nature, i.e. an enclosed room for either very noisy or quiet activities, it is necessary that it has to be away from, or cut off from, other working areas. The solution is probably in the degree of separation combined with potential visibility.

The only unit where teachers felt that their quiet rooms worked well had two rooms of a reasonable size (20 m$^2$ (215.28 ft$^2$)).

These two rooms were on either side of a central link area that was used constantly by teachers to get to the other areas on either side of the rooms. This meant that they could check easily and frequently through the glazed doors what was going on in the quiet room (see Figure 2).

The shape of a quiet room also seemed to have some bearing on whether the room was workable or not. An oblong space was seen as difficult whereas a square of a reasonably good size was liked. Rooms that were situated centrally with a door at either end, presumably to aid communication across, were found to have the opposite effect and acted as a block (see Figure 3 below).

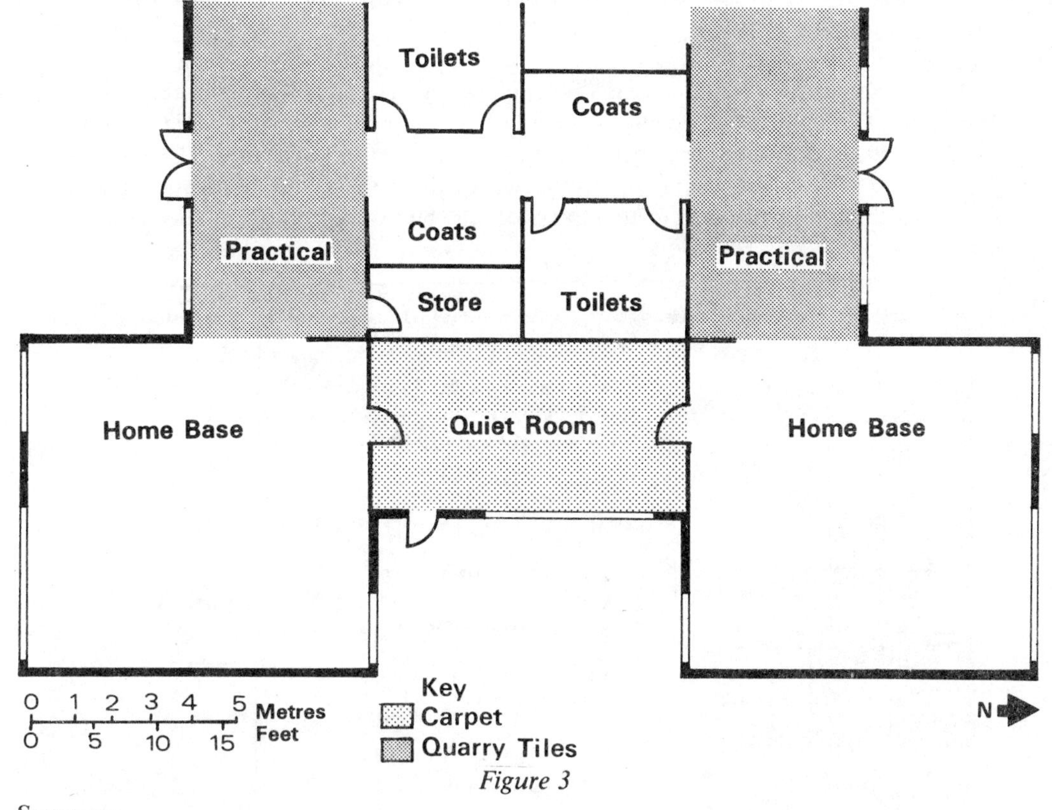


*Figure 3*

*Summary*

Quiet rooms that are square and large enough to take the whole class sitting on the floor and placed centrally for easy supervision would seem to be the most satisfactory from the teacher's point of view.

*Practical Areas*

Practical/wet/messy areas are defined as those areas which have sinks and a floor finish that is suitable for wet activities such as quarry tiles or vinyl tiles, and is situated within the teaching unit. Sometimes the practical area includes a cooker, but where additional cooking areas, used only for this purpose, have been provided, they have not been included.

More use was made of these areas in infant schools, 8.4 per cent and 13.2 per cent for pupils and teachers respectively, but less, at just over 6 per cent, for pupils and teachers in junior units. As expected the most usual pupil activities undertaken in these areas included painting, constructing, drawing and writing. Teachers were most frequently observed in individual teaching and group teaching although there was a good deal of time spent in organizing materials and general supervisory activity.

In the majority of the units this area was used for many specific activities, although in one or two instances it was utilized as a home and teaching base due to overcrowding or lack of space in the remainder of the unit (see Case Study in Chapter 10 for example).

Of the practical areas observed, two thirds were heavily used by the whole of the unit for circulation purposes. In other words they were major thoroughfares which caused congestion, distraction and noise. The siting of these areas thus constitutes a major problem.

*Siting Practical Areas*

The placement of an area that must cater for spillage and mess as well as being able to contain a wide variety of equipment, especially at the infant level, and enable large-scale projects to be worked on and left out, is one that rarely seems to be satisfactory to the user. The practical area appears in a variety of sites, the majority of which are difficult to work in practice. Placing the area around a central courtyard or toilet and storage block is common, as shown in Figure 4 below.

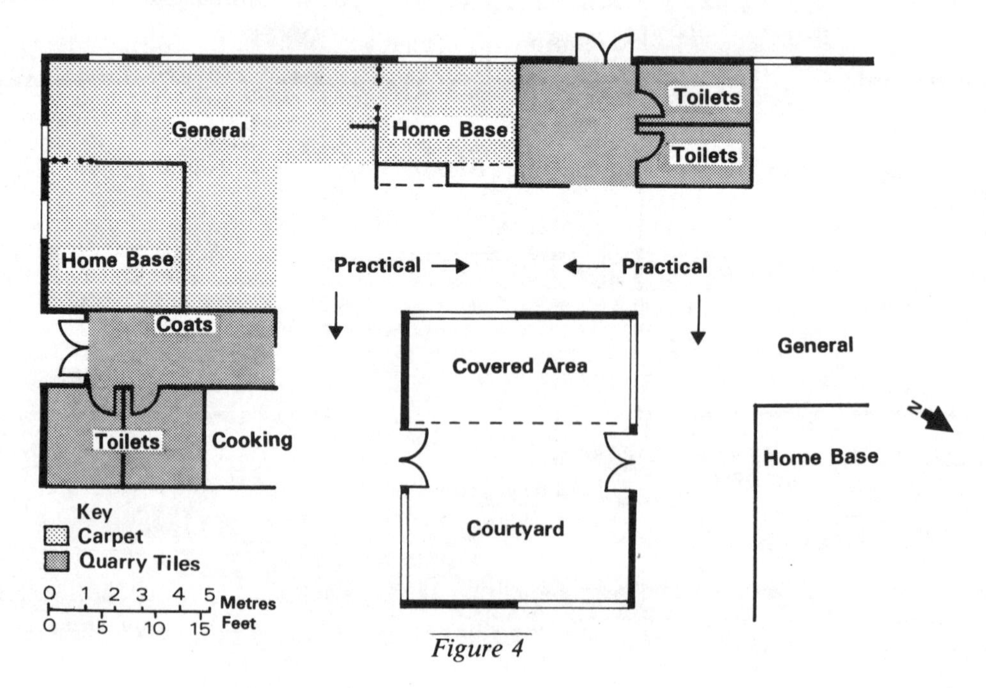


*Figure 4*

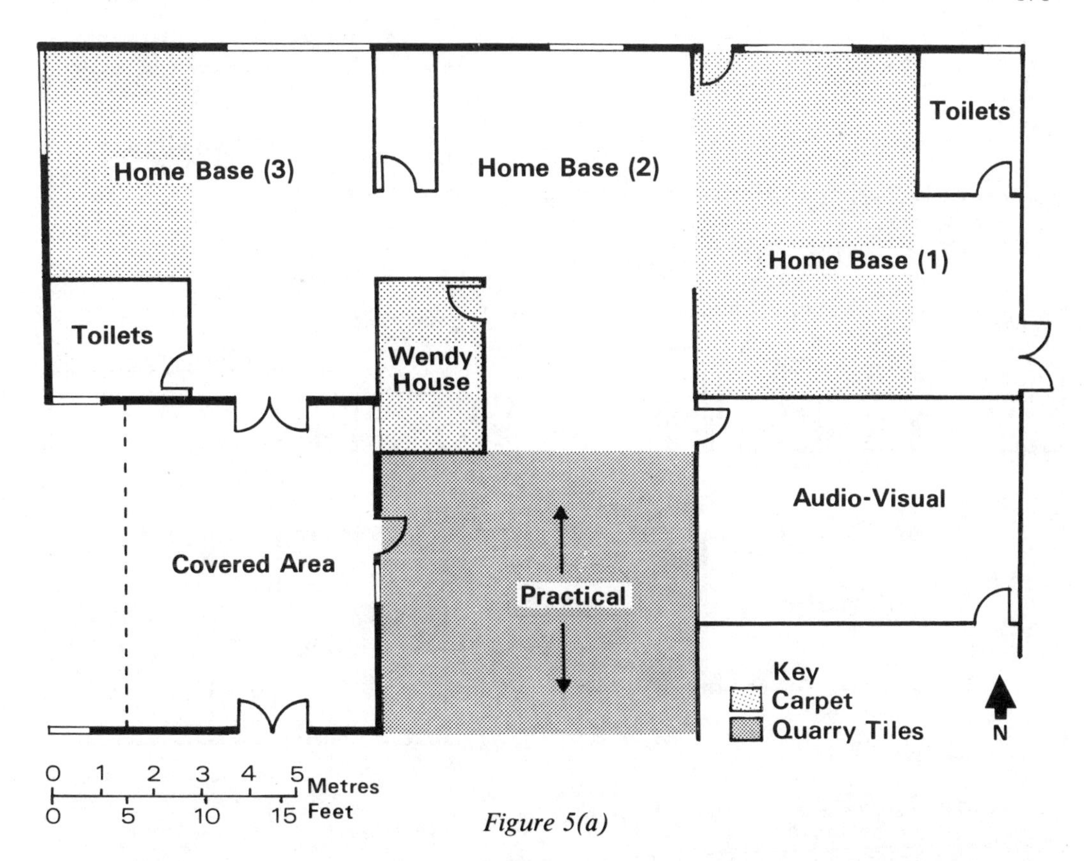


*Figure 5(a)*

This can work well when areas are sufficiently wide to allow circulation and work space plus storage of materials and work. But if the area is used for dining and has the toilets in the centre, or if the practical area is small and the only way through to other parts of the school, it becomes a disaster area with continued disturbance and distraction. On the other hand placing it at the end or on one side away from traffic does not necessarily work better because it can become too cut-off from the general activity areas, and is consequently underused. Siting the practical area in the centre of the general teaching space, as in Figures 5(a) and (b), sometimes works well and at other times does not. The teachers felt that the design of (a) was poor because access and visibility for them was limited, and that (b) was unsatisfactory because from the two end teaching spaces the practical area was not visible. From observations and teacher interviews it is clear that in siting practical areas, visibility from the general teaching spaces, circulation and access are the key features.

**Summary**

From the 'use of space' observations, the way in which teachers and children used space was different in every instance even when the design of the unit was identical. Quiet rooms were used mostly for quiet activities but were generally felt to be unsatisfactory, either because they were too small to use for a variety of purposes, or too cut off from the rest of the areas to make adequate supervision possible. Practical areas were used as expected for art and craft activities,

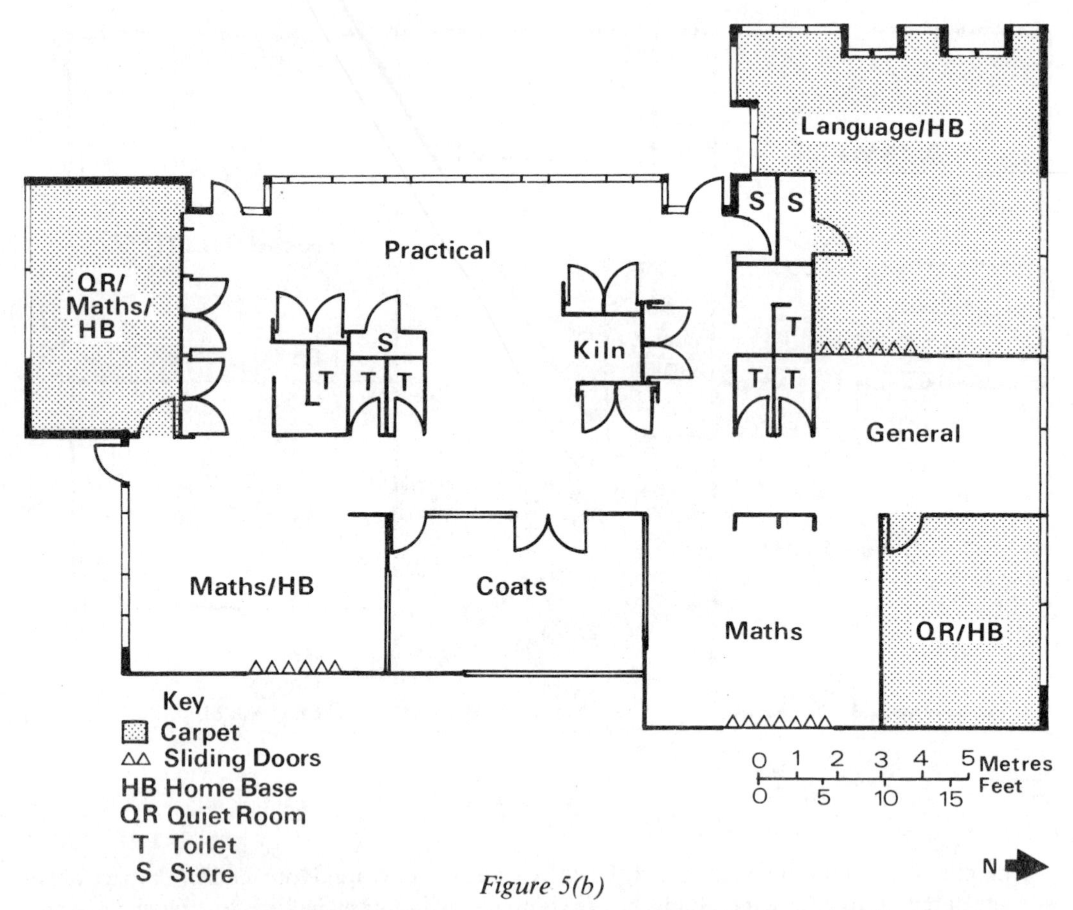


*Figure 5(b)*

but the majority were positioned so that circulation and therefore organizational problems were inevitable.

**Influences on the Use of Teaching Space**

What is it that determines or influences the use of teaching space? As with any problem the causes and influences are complex and difficult to unravel, each aspect interacting with another, and from this interaction develops the way in which the space is perceived and utilized by teachers. Because the interactions involve people and not just static buildings, the picture continues to change and evolve. Stating the ideal, Jakob Bronowski has said, 'A building is not a beautiful shell, and neither is it a functional shed. A building is a coherent solution of a problem in living.' There would only be a minority of educators that would say that their school was a 'coherent solution of a problem in living'. Many more would say that it was the very opposite. There are others, however, who would say that the building is unimportant, arguing that the people working within the building are a more important factor. Nevertheless, there is little doubt that the design of the spaces can either enable or inhibit different forms of teaching organization. As can be seen from Figure 6, the design is the initial influence and affects to varying degrees the organization. The position of different spaces is important for ease of supervision and visibility and the degree to which spaces fit this criteria often governs their use.

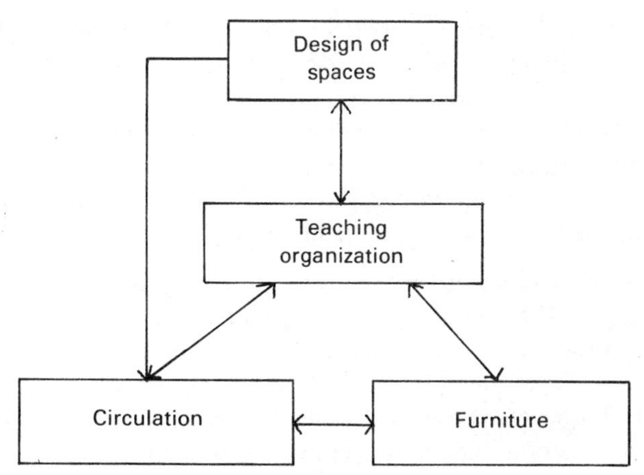


*Figure 6 Influences on the use of space*

As has already been seen, the size of spaces can affect what happens within them. If they are of an inadequate size their use is severely limited; if they are too large and undifferentiated they can be wasted. Often it is not so much the spaces themselves that cause the design to be satisfactory or not, but the link or connecting spaces between areas. These spaces can in the best designs create a unity and flow, but in the worst cause obstruction and backwaters.

*Design of Spaces* is influenced by the quality of communication between the architect and educator; by the skill of the architect to interpret his clients' needs, by teacher feedback or evaluation of the design and by environmental factors such as acoustics, lighting, heating and fire regulations.

*Teaching Organization*
In addition to the design of the spaces, factors such as the aims of the teachers, the previous experience of the headteacher and his staff, the number of pupils and teachers using the building and the amount and type of furniture all determine to some extent the organization adopted. It became clear from the interview studies that teachers in replacement schools were often able to practice new kinds of organization in their old building, which took into account the design of the new school they would be moving to. Nevertheless, in all the sample schools organizational changes had been made as teachers adapted to the possibilities and constraints of the design.

*Furniture* is influenced by the organization and style of teaching used; by the amount and type of furniture; by the numbers of children using the unit; and by the circulation routes.

*Circulation* is determined by the design of the school and unit as well as by the organization used; and by the placement of furniture.

Each of these factors is considered in turn.

*Design of Spaces*
Costs alone have not totally determined the design of schools. Architects and educators alike both point to the shifting patterns of primary education embodying changes in the kind and size of pupil groups, the extended range of pupil activities and the different relationship

between teacher and taught. Alternative physical settings to the conventional classroom were felt to be desirable which, ideally, should give pupils a sense of confidence and security as well as providing the opportunity for initiative and exploration. Adaptability and flexibility are also crucial to enable the provision of a range of different activities, and to provide adequately for a range of different organizations. To achieve these a variety of spaces – large and small, noisy and quiet, clean and messy, inside and outside, are required. The mixture of these spaces needs to be varied according to the age of the children:

1. a home base area that will accommodate the whole class comfortably;
2. a more general area, where children from different classes can mix, make contact with teachers other than their own and utilize shared resources;
3. smaller extensions of the general area suitable for small groups and away from the distractions of the larger general area, for specialized use, e.g. crafts, home economics;
4. an enclosed room or rooms suitable for either quiet or noisy work;
5. an outside covered work area.

A vexed question for both the architect and educator is to decide what the appropriate balance of these spaces might be. It would be easy to come up with an exact formula, but the danger of this is that it would make designs rigid and stereotyped, instead of each design taking into account the particular needs of its site, catchment area and community.

Such concerns as what proportion of space should be cut off and what open, how wide openings should be, how high the partition walls, the best siting and relationship of the different spaces, the overall shape of the school – linear, square, or wrapped around a central courtyard – all have repercussions in architectural and educational terms. For example, the shape of the building will determine the roof structure and supports, which in turn will then determine the size and location of the teaching areas.

In several countries – USA, Sweden, Australia and New Zealand – the view has been that the provision of large undifferentiated barn-like spaces offered the greatest freedom of movement and use. Theoretically this is attractive, but educationally it proved to be barren. The physical environment is too uniform, bland and characterless and often has poor acoustics to confound the problems of use. These designs are the results of new technology which ignored completely the purpose of the building. In this country the view has generally been the opposite: the provision of a variety of different types of space, each with its own identity or built-in character. The influence of technology here has been geared towards the development of building components that have, in the hands of good designers, been utilized to give greater scope and freedom of use to the educator. The danger still exists though, that the standardized components can lead to the standardized building. With the provision of a variety of space, the architect, whether he is aware of it or not, is 'deliberately inhibiting limitless freedom of manoeuvre in the interest of security and order' (Medd, 1973).

### Architect's Brief

The architect's brief is the local education authority's definition of what it wants the architect to design. In theory the object of the brief is to accurately define the problem without imposing a solution, but in practice the content of briefs varies widely, reflecting in part the different ways the design process is conceived, implemented and coordinated in LEAs. A summary of the contents of a sample of briefs is presented in Table 1, Appendix D. Some briefs are purely philosophical in nature, e.g. 'facilities appropriate to modern teaching and learning methods should be provided' containing no specifications of the number or preferred size of areas. Others carefully detail the size of specific areas and their relationship to other parts of the building and the numbers of children likely to be using them, but provide little information on the purpose or use of the areas defined. A few are detailed in all aspects, linking the aims of education to the possible organization, and grouping of children to the type of activities and the need for particular spaces.

The DES building bulletins are referred to in some briefs and some cite specific publications to illustrate particular points, and one LEA even includes them on a reading list attached to the brief for further reading. There is, however, some disagreement about their usefulness. The Pilkington Report felt that 'the forms are copied, though the educational reasons for them may not be understood very adequately and the basic data on building function and its use is neither published nor re-created'. And research into the briefing process (Bristol, 1979) found that 'In no case was there strong evidence of the use of outside published guidance such as that produced by the Department'. Some architects feel that the building bulletins represent one-off designs and that what is shown is the solution that the DES devised for a particular problem. Others feel that they play an important role in influencing their design work. Perhaps what is needed is a different kind of information from the DES which would make architects more aware of educational aims and practices in a way that could be utilized in school design.

The quality of the final product rests heavily on the relationship between the architect and the LEA, usually represented by an adviser who generally lacks any architectural expertise. The document already referred to on the briefing process (Bristol, 1979) has argued that 'there is little doubt that the most important over-riding principle is that good design is the outcome of full and effective collaboration between administrative, educational and architectural services operating as equal partners'. In practice, however, there appear to be severe problems of communication. Since neither party has an adequate understanding of the other's discipline there is a great danger of both talking past each other and this was freely admitted in interviews. This is not helped by the architect's lack of time and encouragement to evaluate the building on completion. In interviews with architects in 27 local education authorities they agreed that little assessment of their work occurred whilst also agreeing that more visits should be made to schools. One architect felt very strongly about this, saying, 'frequently a school is built and no one goes and tells the head and staff how the building is intended to be used in its design. This sort of involvement would see it being used with more understanding. It doesn't mean it's the only way it can be used, but how it was designed.' He further commented on the value of school visits – 'I only wish the whole of my department could go out and sit in a school that's really working and see for themselves, as I did. It had a lot of effect on my design' (Bennett *et al.*, 1976).

Lack of systematic evaluation has robbed architects of invaluable feedback from teachers which could benefit future design.

When crucial information is not collected over a period of time costly mistakes, both technical and educational, are bound to occur. To improve school design, careful, continuous evaluation of new schools is critical, and must involve the viewpoints of all the different groups of people concerned with the building. Particular reference should be made to the views of the staff of the school, the 'users', who are the only group of people to have the first-hand experience of using the building. Their contribution is rarely sought and acknowledged, the argument being that they are only using the building in one way. From early discussions it was found that a number of headteachers and teachers and advisers were sceptical about the kinds of involvement tried, such as 'consultative committees', 'design groups' or 'building panels', feeling that 'consultation is seen as an exercise in diplomacy rather than in the expectation of plans being radically altered' or 'the fact of consultation itself is the key thing, not the design modifications that may result' (Bennett *et al.*, 1976). However, their evaluation, however limited, should say something to the designer about the constraints or freedom of his design. Is it not justifiable that educational buildings be appraised against educational criteria, i.e. the effectiveness of the building educationally?

Acoustics

Problems in the siting and shape of specific spaces within the school have already been considered, but before leaving the question of design, acoustics should be considered, given that noise is a source of discontent in open plan designs. When schools were designed to comprise self-contained classrooms they needed to be acoustically isolated from each other, but with school design changing to a concept of inter-connected spaces, the acoustic needs are different. Recommendations for acoustics in school buildings from the DES (Great Britain, 1974) say that 'Acoustic conditions should be appropriate to the range of activities within the various spaces and should take into account their relation to adjacent spaces and external conditions.' The noise factor is frequently associated with open plan schools and in many cases is justified. It is however difficult to diagnose because individual reaction and tolerance to noise varies. A noise level of 65 decibels has been suggested as being generally acceptable. At this level, the maximum distance between teachers and children at which intelliglbe speech communications can occur is approximately 2.1 m (7 ft). When this is exceeded, there could be a number of effects particularly for young children's language development. As Walsh (1975) points out 'high noise levels can cause distraction and annoyance, prevent concentration and can reduce the ability to communicate'. Clearly, there is the possibility that the frequency and quality of communication could suffer in large spaces with high background noise levels.

In half the case study schools, noise was mentioned as a factor of poor design, and was given as the reason for timetabling constraints, as well as for the way that different spaces were able to be used or not used. But good listening conditions and the control of noise interference can be achieved by planning, adopting measures for control of the noise, and by making sure that the spaces have reasonable sound ambience appropriate to the activities of teachers and pupils in the space.

It is therefore important for the designer to be aware of the ways in which arrangement of spaces can help to make designs acoustically good.

The best attenuator is distance, and linear designs can often offer quieter working conditions since sound spreads over an increased distance, and there is then a proportional reduction in intensity. A squarish plan, with minimal space even if it has partial enclosure, having close juxtaposition of quiet/noisy spaces, can be more disruptive than a more open but linear arrangement. The separation by distance, the introduction of bigger zones between very quiet activities and those spaces generating noise, can often be achieved at the initial design stage. Certain activities require acoustic privacy to insulate either the pupils inside or outside the spaces. For example, concentrating on an intensive piece of work needs protection from distraction. In the case of a group producing music, those surrounding the space may find the music-making interfering with their activity. The introduction of suitable sound-resisting walls, doors and in some cases perhaps glazed partitions can also provide in the planning stage for the necessary freedom from distraction.

The control of noise can generally be manipulated by the use of reflecting and absorbent materials. It is necessary, however, to ascertain the group size and use of the spaces, the height of the ceiling and the correct reverberation time. From these calculations the number of absorption units and speech interference levels can be established. With this information the amount of absorption required to either control the noise within a space or to control the flow of sound to outside the space can be found. The use of carpets, acoustic tiled ceilings, curtains and in some cases wall surfaces can all contribute to the necessary absorption levels. To preserve speech intelligibility, the correct balance of reflection and absorption has to be achieved. The provision of over-absorption can lead to attenuation and lack of clarity of the spoken word.

There are many publications available on acoustics, but the fact remains that many schools are poor in acoustical terms. Whether this is mainly due to economic reasons or whether there is a misunderstanding or ignorance of the general principles of acoustic design among architects is not known.

Fire Regulations

Although they cannot be dealt with extensively here, fire regulations can influence the design and therefore the use of buildings. The latest guidelines are provided in Building Bulletin No. 7 (Great Britain, DES, 1975) and seem to limit the extensive use of pin-up areas, and the introduction of fire compartments which can result in the division of spaces in unexpected ways. In some designs this results in an interruption in the flow of space and may affect the definition of territorial areas in the schools in relation to the sub-division of teaching spaces.

These factors are mentioned here simply because in some schools visited, design solutions circumventing the fire regulations have been incompatible with educational considerations.

*Teaching Organization*

Although it might seem obvious that the design of spaces would have an influence on the teaching organization adopted and evolved, teachers were not totally convinced. Some felt that the design had a great deal of influence because it prevented the implementation of certain methods of organization and teaching. Others felt that the design had little if any influence on the way that they were working because they would have worked that way wherever they were. There is no building that does not have some inherent constraints. An enclosed classroom of adequate size can be constraining to some teachers, but ideal for others. The aims that teachers have play a large part in how they are organized, and the implementation of these aims is either promoted or thwarted by the design of the teaching space available.

All the units where teachers felt that the space was satisfactory were under-pupilled and also had a higher than average teaching space per child, varying from 2.9 to 4.4 $m^2$ (31.22–47.36 $ft^2$). Where teachers expressed feelings of lack of space the space available ranged from 1.9 to 2.3 $m^2$ (20.45–24.76 $ft^2$).

If practice meshes with the design and space provision is adequate, few problems exist. The unit illustrated in Figure 7 is one example.

This is a Type 1 three teacher unit which was designed for 115 children and used by only 87. Total teaching space is 250 $m^2$ (2,691 $ft^2$), giving 2.2 $m^2$ (23.67 $ft^2$) per child as designed and

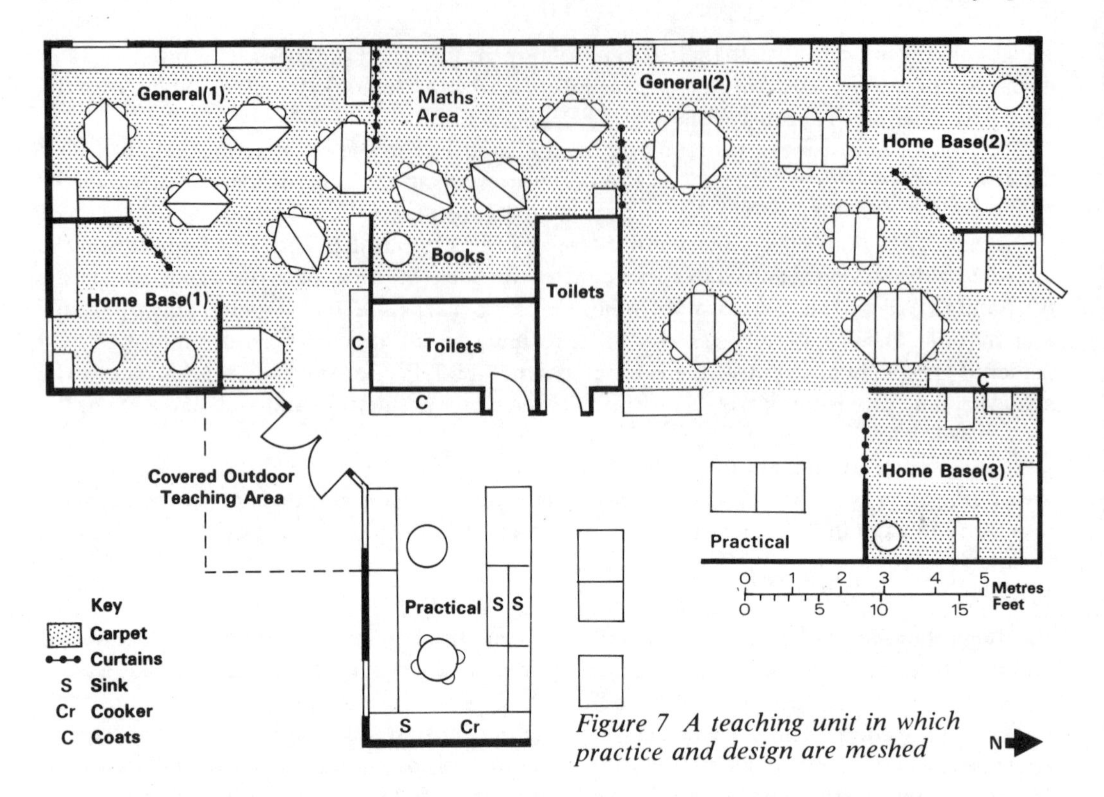


*Figure 7 A teaching unit in which practice and design are meshed*

2.9 m² (31.22 ft²) per child actual. The space is divided into three small home base areas, 14.8 per cent of the total, three general teaching spaces of different sizes (62 per cent), and a shared practical area (23 per cent). Each teacher is responsible for her own class and all the space is shared, each teacher having her own home base area. The children are in four ability groups and are given a choice of assignments. The teachers spend the rest of their time working with individual children and with the class as a whole. The teachers feel that the design is flexible and works well, that there is enough space to work quietly away from distraction, and that it enables the children to use the wet and dry areas effectively. They feel that the placement of the practical area is good for supervision, and that both the teaching and practical areas are away from the main circulation space, and so movement and distraction are minimized.

If, on the other hand, organizational practice clashes with the design, and space is limited, many problems result. A multi Type 1 unit designed for 320 children and housing 311 illustrates this (see Case Study 2, Chapter 10, Figure 3 for school plan).

Total teaching space is 645.4 m² (6,947.3 ft²) giving a designed 2.02 m² (21.74 ft²) per child and an actual 2.1 m² (22.6 ft²) per child. The space is one large carpeted rectangle which is divided by low portable screens into three teaching areas of different sizes (52.1 per cent of the total), a three-sided shared practical area also used as dining space (33.5 per cent), and three quiet rooms of different sizes (14.4 per cent). The teachers are in notional teams of two or three but each works only with her own class. Each teacher has her particular space in the area clearly delineated in her own mind and defined by furniture, and her children stay within those confines. The children are grouped by ability within each class, and the mornings are devoted to 3R work, the afternoons to other activities. Teachers work directly with individuals or the whole class. The teachers feel that the design imposes to a large extent their oganization and style of teaching. They have tried working as teams of 4, 3 and 2 within each space, where each teacher was responsible for an area and the children all moved round, but they felt the children lost a lot by moving around and so reverted back to each teacher keeping her own class all the time. Problems of noise and movement are a constant distraction, space already felt to be at a premium is eroded still further by the need to have furniture for each class to use. The teachers feel that the design is too open and does not allow children or adults any privacy. The three quiet rooms are used as classrooms throughout the day by three classes. The limiting effect of the design goes further by restricting where different kinds of activities can take place: the general teaching space is carpeted and so no messy activities can take place there, and use of the practical area, which goes round the toilet block and alongside the three quiet rooms and hall, has to be timetabled so that all classes get a fair share of using it. The practical area, due to its shape and position, has to be constantly supervised and is not usable for a period before dinner each day when it is being prepared for the meal. Because of the organization, the teachers feel they have had to adapt to fit the design. The practical area is the only circulation route to all other parts of the school, which means there is constant disturbance through the area, and this increases the noise level. As space is at such a premium, the hall is also scheduled throughout the day for activities. As storage is poor, all materials needed in the practical area and hall have been carried from the general teaching area and cannot be left out. This in turn causes problems to the classes in the quiet rooms near the practical area to such an extent that they have been forced to adopt an organization that is governed by whatever everyone else is doing nearby. The degree of the clash between the design and the organization implemented determines the way compromises are sought and found, but as Seaborne (1971b) points out, 'It has to be recognised that some schools are basically of such bad design that no amount of improvisation will enable the staff to teach the children in the best possible way.'

*Furniture*

The interaction of the building and teaching organization determines what possibilities are seen as feasible, and how the space is used and divided with furniture and equipment. Furniture, like school design, has undergone immense changes. Through the work of different consortia, there is now available a variety of lightweight loose furniture, such as colourful tables and chairs, cupboards of assorted shapes and sizes, as well as versatile screens and storage units that can combine and relate to each other in different ways. Model school furniture is available to 1/20 scale which can be used as a designer's tool, so that space can be designed and built around furniture, and teachers can use them to get a better appreciation of the space they are furnishing.

The selection of furniture varies from LEA to LEA. In some, the selection is done by the educator, in others it is the architect, and in others the supplies department. Each will have different priorities when making the selection. The first will tend to be influenced by what has been used before, the second will be mainly concerned with the appearance within the building, and the third with the cheapest buy. The provision of loose as opposed to built-in furniture offers the teachers increased possibilities to adapt the space, rather than the building, to their particular style of working. Some LEAs have a policy of only providing 70 per cent seating instead of 100 per cent, on the basis that not all children will be required to sit at the same time;

a policy that is ideal for some teaching methods that require a more open use of space, but presents problems for methods that require all children to be seated at the same time. In a situation where the latter is the case and the school is a replacement for an older building, teachers have brought their old heavy furniture from their previous school and incorporated it into the smaller spaces of the new school, thus causing a darkened and cluttered teaching space with congested circulation space. One such school had done this because they felt that the storage and provision of furniture was inadequate. Folding screens planned by the architect never materialized and the teachers felt the need to divide their space off in order to cut down on visibility and distraction, and to have their chalkboards to teach from. The effect of this additional furniture plus the the furniture already provided in the unit, meant a radical reduction in the floor space, as can be seen from the figures below.

| | |
|---|---|
| Total teaching area provided | 237.5 $m^2$ |
| Provision of furniture on plan | |
| – 82 chairs | 41.0 $m^2$ approx |
| – 24 tables | 12.0 $m^2$ approx |
| Floor space taken on the plan | 53.0 $m^2$, leaving 1.5 $m^2$ (16.15 $ft^2$) per child actual |
| Approx. floor space taken by furniture in unit – 167 chairs | 83.6 $m^2$ |
| 4 teachers' desks + 49 tables | 26.5 $m^2$ |
| Furniture from old school | 14.75 $m^2$ |
| Other furniture (bookcases, etc.) | 15.0 $m^2$ |
| | 139.75 $m^2$ leaving 0.8 $m^2$ (8.61 $ft^2$) per child actual |

From these calculations it can be seen that the planned furniture took 22.3 per cent of the total teaching area, but that the extra furniture brought in by teachers increased this to 52.5 per cent of the area. The obvious effect is that the space per child is drastically reduced from a designed 2.02 $m^2$ (23.68 $ft^2$) to 0.8 $m^2$ (8.61 $ft^2$) per child.

*Density*

A further factor that complicates the problem of space is the number of children and adults using a given amount of space, here called the space density. The repercussions of overcrowding, whether it is recognized on paper or seen in reality, are made evident in the kinds of organizations adopted, and affected by the amount of furniture and equipment needed. The problems that emerge from overcrowding in the day-to-day operation are a constant source of pressure to those working within them. Schools which are overcrowded and were designed during the lean period of space provision (1973–5) suffer most, but the problems are not just confined to that period. It is of interest that only children are counted in density figures, adults presumably taking up no room!

There are, as mentioned earlier, units that are under-pupilled on paper but are crowded in reality. An example of this is a unit built in 1975/6 which won an architectural design award (Figure 8). The unit was designed for 70 children and 2 teachers (1.8 $m^2$ (19.36 $ft^2$) per child), and was being used by only 43 children and 2 teachers (2.9 $m^2$ (31.22 $ft^2$) per child). The total teaching space amounts to 124.5 $m^2$ (1,340 $ft^2$) (9.8 per cent), leaving 31.5 per cent for the general teaching area. Both teachers work as a team and the children work on a system of

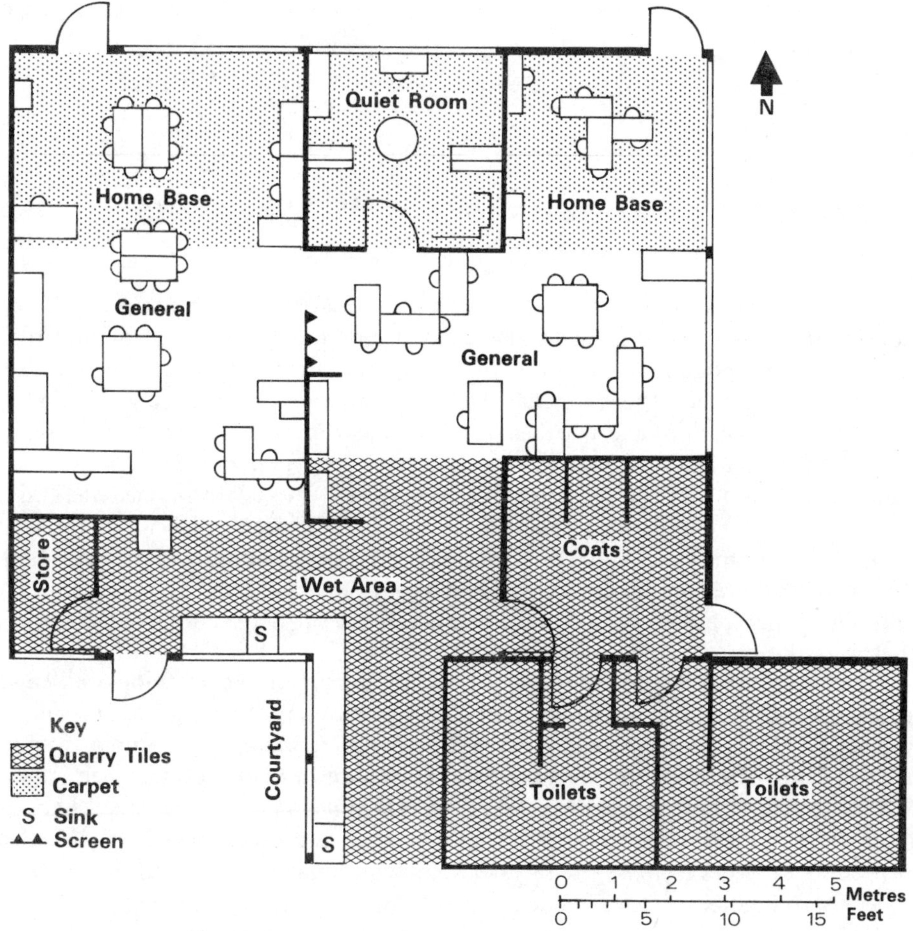


*Figure 8 An example of poor provision of space*

rotating assignments covering language and maths in the mornings, and topic in the afternoon. The teachers feel that the unit is only adequate for 50 children, not 70, and feel that it is impossible to get all 43 children in the larger general teaching space for work organization or teaching. Nor can they see all the children working from any point in the unit. They feel that the quiet room is wasted space because they cannot see into it to supervise, and so use it mostly for storing materials and equipment. The practical area is a narrow strip which in a conventionally built school would not even have sufficed for a corridor, and which functions as one throughout the day, preventing the intended use of the area. Considering all these points the breakdown of available space is as follows and bears out the teachers' feelings of lack of space:

| | |
|---|---|
| Total teaching area | 124 m$^2$ (1,340 ft$^2$)<br>1.8 m$^2$ (19.39 ft$^2$)<br>per child as designed |
| Approx. space taken by furniture | 34.0 m$^2$ (365.97 ft$^2$) leaving 1.3 m$^2$<br>(13.99 ft$^2$) per child actual |

| | |
|---|---|
| Built-in furniture + circulation space in practical area | 27.0 $m^2$ (280.63 $ft^2$) |
| | 63.6 $m^2$ leaving 0.9 $m^2$ (9.69 $ft^2$) per child actual |
| Available space for 43 children per child | 1.5 $m^2$ (16.15 $ft^2$) |
| Available space for 70 children per child | 0.9 $m^2$ (9.69 $ft^2$) |

*Circulation Space*

In 1967 the Pilkington Report pointed out that 'In the examination and re-examination of school design that has been dictated by the nation's continuing need for economy, a main emphasis has been to minimise circulation area while obtaining the maximum area usable for teaching purposes'. The report recommends the 'examination of the dual use of certain spaces (e.g. teaching and circulation) and whether it is convenient or not'; and 'consideration of the problems of circulation and supervision'. Ten years later the problems have been exacerbated by the continuing decline in the provision of teaching space. The lack of any clear definition of what constitutes circulation space on a plan has meant, and still means, that circulation space is often counted as teaching space in order to meet the MTA regulations. It seems reasonable to argue that areas that are continually crisscrossed by movement should not be counted as 100 per cent teaching space, but as was mentioned earlier 20 out of 30 units observed had practical areas that were the main circulation route for all children.

The design of the unit is perhaps the biggest contributing factor to circulation problems and this is taken up in Case Study 7 in Chapter 10. But in addition to the design, the organization employed can add to the problems of lack of proper circulation space. For example, in one four teacher Type 1 unit observed the teachers had evolved an organization that necessitated a continual movement of both teachers and children four times a day, so that all of them could have a fair share of the one classroom size enclosed room and other spaces available (which teachers preferred to work in). The general area is thus continually crisscrossed with movement to the hall, AV room, library, lower junior unit and administration offices, as well as to other areas within the unit. Yet it was in an attempt to cope with the problems of constant distraction that this organization was implemented.

A further spanner in the circulation works is the placement of furniture. As seen earlier, the amount of furniture in a unit has a profound effect on the amount of available space, but *where* it is placed becomes even more important when space is at a premium. In some units observed all the circulation routes were confounded by furniture, so whichever way one moved from one space to another meant negotiating a hazardous route through tables, chairs and equipment. The consequent constant distraction and noise were inevitable.

**Summary**

The main influences on the use of space were shown in Figure 6. The design of the unit itself sets parameters of what is or is not possible unless the space is physically changed by the teachers, i.e. by building or knocking down walls. The design interacts with the type of organization used by the teachers, and depending on their aims either meshes or clashes with it. The type of organization adopted in turn influences circulation routes by the placement of furniture, and what spaces are used for. The design of the unit also determines the circulation routes and these can be complicated by organization and furniture. It is clear that there is no one factor which could be said to influence how the building is used, but a complicated interaction of several different factors. In different designs one or other of these will be stronger, and these could be either architecturally or educationally dictated, depending on what the architect conceived and what the teachers perceived. There is a strong feeling from both architects and educators that the architect should have the opportunity to go and explain to the teachers using the new building what were envisaged as the uses of the different spaces. Perhaps this would clarify some of the enigmas that exist in teachers' minds about what the architect could possibly have been thinking of in the design process. The very least it would do would be to start a much needed dialogue between designer and user, a dialogue which is still sadly lacking within the educational system.

*Chapter 10*

# *Case Studies*

---

Examples from the units observed have been used through the text to illustrate aspects of the study. However, none of the units have been considered as a whole. Seven case studies are presented in this chapter to highlight interesting or important facets of open plan schooling. The first six are in three groups of two units to enable comparison. Thus the first two contrast differing approaches to the education of young inner city children and show that although overall aims might be similar, practice may vary widely.

The second pair was chosen since, on paper at least, they appear to have adopted a very similar system of team teaching. Observation soon dispelled this notion, however, illustrating the simple point that there is no necessary relationship between structural organization and teaching style.

The third pair provides a contrast of organization in identically designed units. Many teachers would claim that design dictates method. This may be true in a very general sense but the units described here illustrate that many alternatives to organization are possible within the same design.

The final case study is included to highlight typical design weaknesses in open plan schools. This school was visited in the familiarization stage of the study and included in an earlier report as an example of poor design. It is by no means the worst example but has been chosen, firstly because the weaknesses in this school appear to be fairly typical, and secondly because, following the visit, the LEA advisory staff continued their interest in school design and invited a DES architect to provide another evaluation. This study is therefore a joint project/adviser contribution.

**Differing Approaches to the Education of Inner City Children: Case Studies 1 and 2**

**Case Study 1 – An Inner City School (Unit W)**

This infant school is not very prepossessing in appearance and is dominated by surrounding dwellings. Its stark exterior is accentuated by a high wire fence and by the total lack of trees or

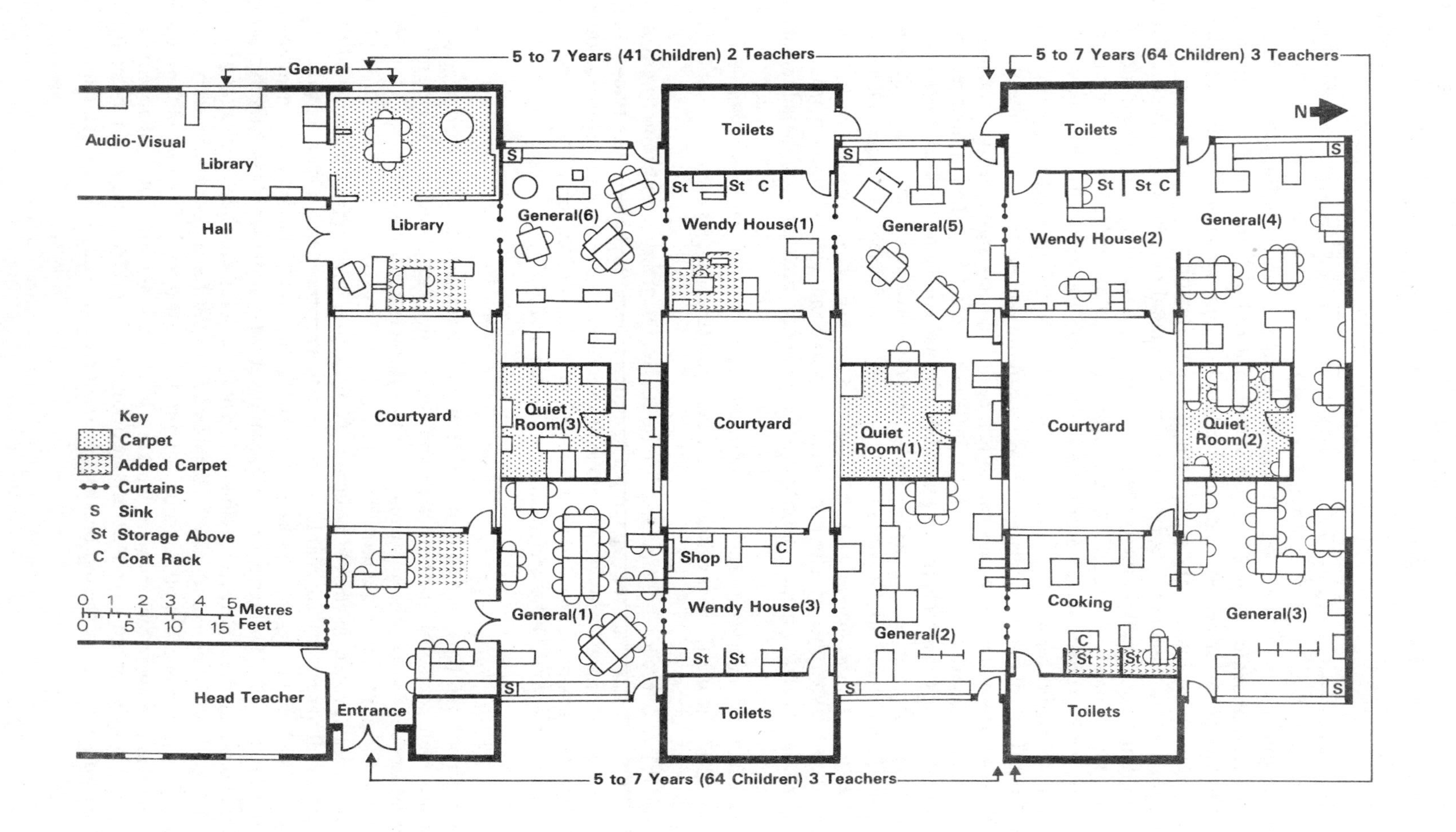


*Figure 1 Unit W design of the unit*

grass. The school was opened in 1971 as part of an urban renewal programme and is situated adjacent to the old building which it was intended to replace. The upper parts of the building still houses the junior section but the lower part is used as an extension to the new school.

Built to accommodate 240 children, there were 234 on roll when the school was visited during the autumn term. A further 60 children were listed to join the school during the spring and summer term. Most lived in the concrete houses and flats in the immediate vicinity of the school. An appreciable number came from immigrant families, largely West Indian in origin.

In addition to a nursery in the old building, and a community room across the hall, the school comprises one very large teaching area which is sub-divided into a series of interlinked spaces surrounding three courtyards (Figure 1). There are three carpeted quiet rooms, but there is no clear delineation of practical area, since most of the floor is covered in vinyl tiles and sinks are provided in all of the larger spaces. At the time of the visit many of these sinks could not be used because the wooden surrounds had rotted. Staff had been consulted when the school was at the design stage but it was reported that little notice had been taken of their recommendations. Apart from curtaining, the only modification made to the school has been the provision of double doors to separate the hall from the teaching area and to act as a noise barrier.

The headteacher already had considerable experience of teaching in open plan buildings when he came to the school two years after it opened. His views on open plan were predominantly favourable since he considered that an open building helped to promote unification among the staff, independence and self confidence in children, and made it easier to involve parents and volunteers without disrupting activities. Noise was the major problem, together with visual distraction and, with reference to this particular building, poor ventilation. For several afternoons in the previous term the temperature had exceeded 100° F and children had been sent home.

Of the 13 infant teachers only four had been at the school for any considerable length of time. Most of the new staff had been appointed as probationers, the headteacher being given the right of refusal. The main problem mentioned by these teachers related to circulation through teaching areas, lack of storage and poor cloakroom facilities. They considered the building to be too small and would have preferred a more open design.

*Teaching Organization*

Several forms of teaching organization had been tried. For two years prior to the appointment of the present headteacher, staff had been working in pairs, one of each pair taking maths and the other language work. The following year the staff reverted to class teaching. An increase in the number of pupils meant that the old building had to be used, so for the next year all seven year olds were housed in the old building. To overcome problems of isolation in the old building a wall was removed to enable two teachers to work together, and to cope with a further increase in roll, vertical grouping was introduced. A corporate decision was then taken by the staff to work in teams. This system was in operation at the time of the visit with the exception of the very young children. On an experimental basis a reception area had been created in the old school. Young children could stay in the reception area for a year if necessary but most were expected to move into other groups within their first term. Two teams of three teachers and one team of two teachers were working in the new building. A further team of two teachers and one team of two teachers were working in the new building. A further team of two teachers were working in the old building. A resource area had also been created in the old building. In the mornings this was used by a small group of children and one teacher, who was replaced by the deputy head. In the afternoons two children from each team were sent to the resource area to work with the deputy.

Within each team one teacher was entitled the 'Ask Me Person' and was responsible for the overall supervision of the area leaving the other teachers free to attend to the individual needs of children. Each teacher was responsible for assessing and monitoring the progress and development of a group of 20 or more children. There were no team leaders but discussions were held regularly between team members, usually at lunch time and at the end of the day. Every two to three weeks all the teams met together to report and discuss current issues.

*Curriculum Organization*

The curriculum was based on the needs of the children as perceived by the headteacher and staff. All the children came from working-class homes, many of them came from one parent families and some of them were in care. The staff estimated that about half the children had speech defects – 'A lot of them don't talk at all'. The children were also described as needing a great deal of security and affection. Accordingly the curriculum was geared to the promotion of independence and security in the child and a language-based approach had been adopted. The child's ability to be self directing, to plan, formulate hypotheses and predict outcomes was considered an important prerequisite to the development of basic skills. The staff stressed the need to strike an even balance between cognitive and affective aims by providing a stimulating atmosphere in which each child could develop in every way.

The headteacher was opposed to any overall standardized form of testing or measurement of standards, but thought it reasonable that each school should be expected to provide a statement of what it was trying to do and should be open to some sort of external assessment. The language policy of the school was formulated and outlined in a document which listed the skills required for listening, speaking, reading and writing, the assessment of reading readiness, the use of 'Breakthrough to Literacy' materials, the banded reading scheme used in the school and examples of activities in which the child's development of sub-skills might be observed.

In his dealings with members of staff the headteacher aimed to establish an atmosphere of mutual trust and confidence. For instance, decisions taken in the staff room were decisions made by the majority. In the same way he considered that if children were involved in decisions about what they wanted to do, then they would be more motivated in their activities. He saw the role of his staff as one of planned knowledgeable intervention based on detailed knowledge of children's interests and needs. In turn the staff considered the provision of guidance and practical help as part of the function of the headteacher.

The curriculum was integrated in the sense that the only timetabling that had been introduced was that in relation to the use of the hall and the resource area. Technically all the children had free choice but limitations were placed on the number of children who could engage in a particular activity. Teachers were left sufficiently free to observe what the children were doing, and to reach decisions as to whether it was appropriate to intervene, to leave the child at that level or to redirect. Written records were kept which included lists of children's activities, samples of work, reading progress and notes on social development.

Teachers provided for a variety of activities, some of which were changed from day to day. Permanent features included the shop, Wendy House, sand and water, painting and collage. A variety of reading material was always available.

Observations were undertaken of one team. The curriculum allocation and pupil involvement were as follows:

| *Curriculum Area* | *Time* | *Curriculum Involvement* | *Time All Infants* |
|---|---|---|---|
| Maths | 14.1 | 81.6 | 15.8 |
| Language | 42.5 | 83.5 | 36.7 |
| Environmental studies | – | – | 3.5 |
| Aesthetics | 8.6 | 81.4 | 9.6 |
| PE | 1.2 | 91.7 | 3.9 |
| Social and moral education | 7.1 | 88.7 | 8.1 |
| Administration/Transition | 26.6 | – | 22.2 |

*Table 1 Allocation and involvement (%)*

| *Task Activity* | *Overall Involvement* | *Non-involvement* |
|---|---|---|
| Administration | – | 0.6 |
| Transition | – | 26.0 |
| Teacher class group discussion | 3.7 | – |
| Teacher small group discussion | 2.9 | – |
| Practical maths | 0.5 | 0.1 |
| Constructing toys | 1.0 | – |
| Maths games | 1.6 | 0.6 |
| Sand activity | 3.1 | 0.1 |
| Water activity | 2.7 | 0.7 |
| Cooking | 0.4 | 0.7 |
| Reading to teacher | 0.9 | 0.2 |
| Reading – free | 3.2 | 1.6 |
| Audio reading | 0.1 | 0.3 |
| Language games | 6.3 | 0.9 |
| Writing – free | 1.9 | 0.7 |
| Story | 5.7 | 0.2 |
| Painting | 1.0 | 0.3 |
| Draw/crayon | 4.9 | 1.4 |
| Making music | 7.3 | 2.1 |
| Singing | 1.8 | 0.3 |
| PE large apparatus | 0.9 | 0.1 |
| Social play | 11.5 | 1.7 |

*Table 2 Time spent in task activities (PBS) (%)*

The effect of the language policy is shown in the observed emphasis on language work, one of the highest in the infant sample. As a result less time is afforded maths, environmental studies, PE and social/moral education. The involvement of pupils within time available for curriculum activities is high but administration/transition time is also very high, taking up more than a quarter of the school day.

The stated aims of activities such as painting or making included the fostering of visual discrimination, fine motor control and skills of interpretation. Children were continually questioned about what they were doing, what their next move might be and what they hoped or thought they might achieve. Such activities tended therefore to be more readily classified under the heading of language rather than aesthetics. More specific information on the activities of children is given in Table 2.

The activities listed in Table 2 reveal the heavily practical approach to the curriculum. Instead of being involved in computation children were to be observed playing snakes and ladders, using cardboard money in the shop, cooking or playing with sand or water. A great deal of art work was observed, most of which was accompanied by personalized writings. Games requiring the use of language were common and a considerable amount of time was spent in social and imaginative play. Few activities of a passive nature were observed. This is further illustrated in the breakdown of the teaching/learning situation given in Table 3, which shows that less than 20 per cent of curriculum time was given to direct teaching. The dominant approach was one of individual and small group work.

| *Teaching/Learning Situation* | *Time* | *All Infants* |
|---|---|---|
| Individual work | 42.9 | 24.0 |
| direct teaching | 2.6 | 1.6 |
| Small group work | 37.3 | 24.7 |
| direct teaching | 7.1 | 4.9 |
| Whole class work | – | 9.6 |
| direct teaching | 3.2 | 22.7 |
| 2+ class work | – | 0.2 |
| direct teaching | 6.9 | 12.2 |

*Table 3 Teaching/learning situation (%)*

The unit was unusual not only in the amount of time spent in individual and small group work but also in the frequency of pupil–pupil and pupil–adult interaction which accounted for approximately one third of the time in either social or work-related discussion. Much of the discussion was instigated by teachers as they intervened in the course of pupil activities to redirect, question, reassure or dissipate arguments.

The attitude of the headteacher and staff towards parents and aides was a most interesting feature of the school. Extensive use was made of ancillary help who, once appointed, were regarded as part of the team. 'She is very much like us except that she is not qualified, she does the same sort of things, she is the 'Ask Me Person' twice a week, she takes groups for sewing, does group activities and hears children read.' According to the headteacher helpers responded very well to this: 'They much prefer to be involved than simply washing paint pots.'

When the headteacher came to the school he made it a matter of priority to establish links with the newly established community through liaison with playgroup committees, the local tenants association and the adventure playground.

> It is not just a question of saying that parents can come into the school, you have also to show that individually in the school you value the things that are going on in the local

> community. We have found that if you get the teacher with their husband or their boyfriend at a local dance behaving as people this is beneficial to relationship with parents. We are a school that is committed as a matter of policy to being open to parents and encouraging parents. The school belongs to them. They can come into the school whenever they want to, not necessarily to help in the classrooms. I think we would regard it as one of our unspoken principles – to do away with as much of the artificial nature of a school as possible, to have an open school in every sense of the word.

Involvement of parents in classroom activities was left to the discretion of staff: 'They take groups for cooking, sewing, play a number game or just talk to the children.'

On the question of in-service training, it was the headteacher's view that training should continue throughout a teacher's whole career. Although he had worried about putting probationers into a team teaching situation these fears had proved groundless. Most of the probationers who had come to the school felt that it had been an advantage to work as a member of a team: 'We are still very much aware that there are some problems in working in an open plan building but I think our attitude towards it now is a positive one and we also look at the advantages and how we can capitalise on them.'

*Use of Space*

Use was made of all available space. The designed space amounted to 2.2 m$^2$ (23.68 ft$^2$) per pupil but this was increased in practice because of the use of the old building.

The use of space by one of the three teams in the new building is illustrated in Figure 2. The area available to this team is indicated by the thick black line. Percentage pupil posture is also shown. On average 14.2 per cent of a pupil's day was spent outside the teaching area, 6.9 per cent of this was spent in the hall and 6.7 per cent outside the building or in the resource area provided in the old building. On average 2.8 per cent of a pupil's day was spent in the internal courtyard which was used for water activities. Even though children were not easily visible in the quiet room, 14.7 per cent of a pupil's day was spent in this space, where children gathered together in their pastoral group for milk in the morning and for story. The entrance to the school (marked A on the plan) was used by the team as a reading area and accounted for 12.2 per cent of observations. The shop and Wendy House were situated in the area marked C on the plan. Since these activities were limited to a few children at any one time only 8.3 per cent of observations were made in this space. The two areas marked B and D show the greatest use by children. Area B was equipped with tables and chairs and was used by the children for writing activities, language or maths, games and collage. An average of 21 per cent of observations were made in this area. Area D was equipped with a play corner, table and chairs, sand trays and easels. 22.4 per cent of observations were made in this space. A further 2 per cent of observations were made in Area A where the cooker was situated. This area belonged to another team.

The impression gained by observers was that of a fairly crowded unit. No doubt the greater degree of movement entailed by an active curriculum contributed to this impression, but there were other factors involved. The individual linked spaces were rather small and the design was such that circulation from one area to another often necessitated passing through other spaces. The figures showing percentage movement are very high but they refer only to those children belonging to the observed team and did not include the through traffic of children occupying other parts of the unit. It seems likely that the provision of several small areas rather than fewer larger spaces serves to exacerbate circulation problems so that the amount of space per child is effectively reduced.

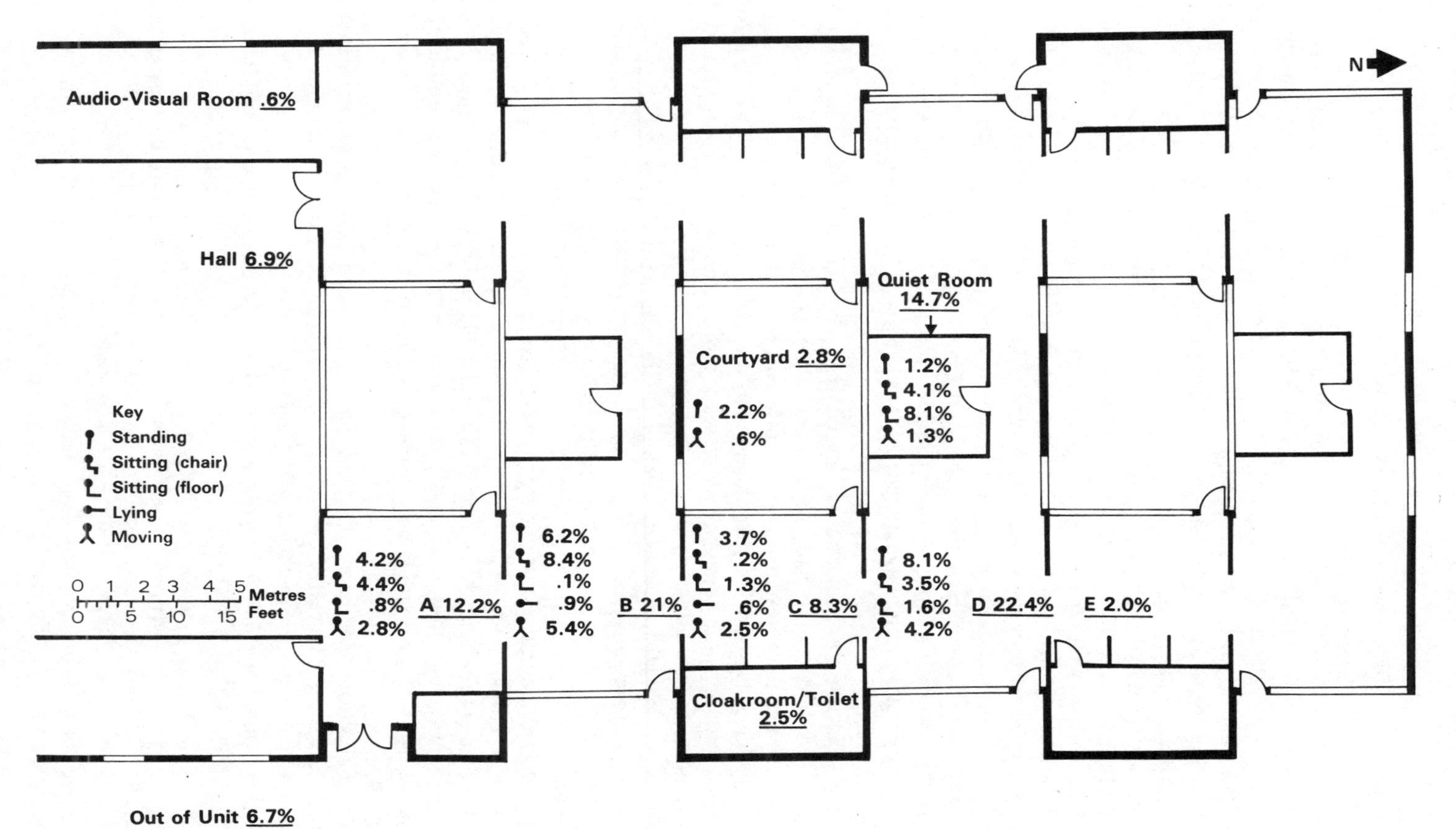


*Figure 2 Use of space in Unit W*

**Case Study 2 – An Inner City School (Unit U)**

Unit U is situated in a first school located in a densely populated urban area. The school was built in 1973 to replace an old building on another site.

Built to accommodate 320 children from nursery to 9 years of age, there were 311 children on roll when the school was visited in the spring term. The catchment area of the school covered a large area with many types of housing including new municipal flats, high density town housing and older Victorian property some of which had been converted into flats. The majority of children attending the school were children born to immigrants, mainly West Indian in origin but including some Asians.

The unit is very open in design (Figure 3) with one large carpeted teaching area. Adjacent to this is a vinyl-tiled practical/dining area which is partly divided by a large toilet block. In addition there are two smaller enclosed rooms and one of classroom size.

Staff had not been consulted about the design of the school. Consultation had not been thought necessary because the building was modelled on a previous design which was deemed to be successful. Unfortunately costs rose and the eventual building bore little relation to the prototype. The response to the escalating costs had been to reduce considerably the general teaching area and the hall leaving an administration block of generous proportions. Modifications to the original building have included the extension of one cloakroom and the partial enclosure of another to provide extra teaching space.

Neither the head nor the staff had any previous experience of teaching in an open plan school. Senior members of staff had visited other schools prior to transfer but these were felt not to be useful since their design was quite different, being much more open. Transfer was made gradually. Two classes of six year olds were moved first and when they were accustomed to their new surroundings the younger children were moved, followed by the top infant classes and lower juniors.

The headteacher held strong views on open plan. She was adamant that buildings should be flexible in design to accommodate different or changing methods of teaching and that more space should be provided to allow for traffic through working areas. She would have preferred a less open design with separate classrooms and shared practical areas. She thought that very open designs placed too much strain on teachers, especially when they were constricted by lack of space. Open designs might be of benefit to probationary teachers but lack of discipline in one class could spread throughout the school. Noise was a big problem. For example, in a classroom situation when children were all making the same mistake a teacher could stop the whole class to explain, but in an open situation teachers had to repeat the same explanation to different groups.

There were 11 full-time members of staff, one part-time teacher and two nursery nurses at the time of the observation. The staff were unanimous in stating that the building was too small, overcrowded and that noise constituted the biggest problem.

> Whatever you want to do it is governed by what everybody else is doing. Personally I would rather be in a classroom.

> I've always chosen to have an integrated day and I have never before had all the children sitting writing. I've always had a certain number of children painting or using clay. I've always been able to stop, have a story, a few quiet minutes, have a couple of songs, move the chairs and tables back and do a few physical jerks.

One member of staff complained that the heating system contributed to the noise level, another complained about the need for artificial light at all times. Visual distraction was also

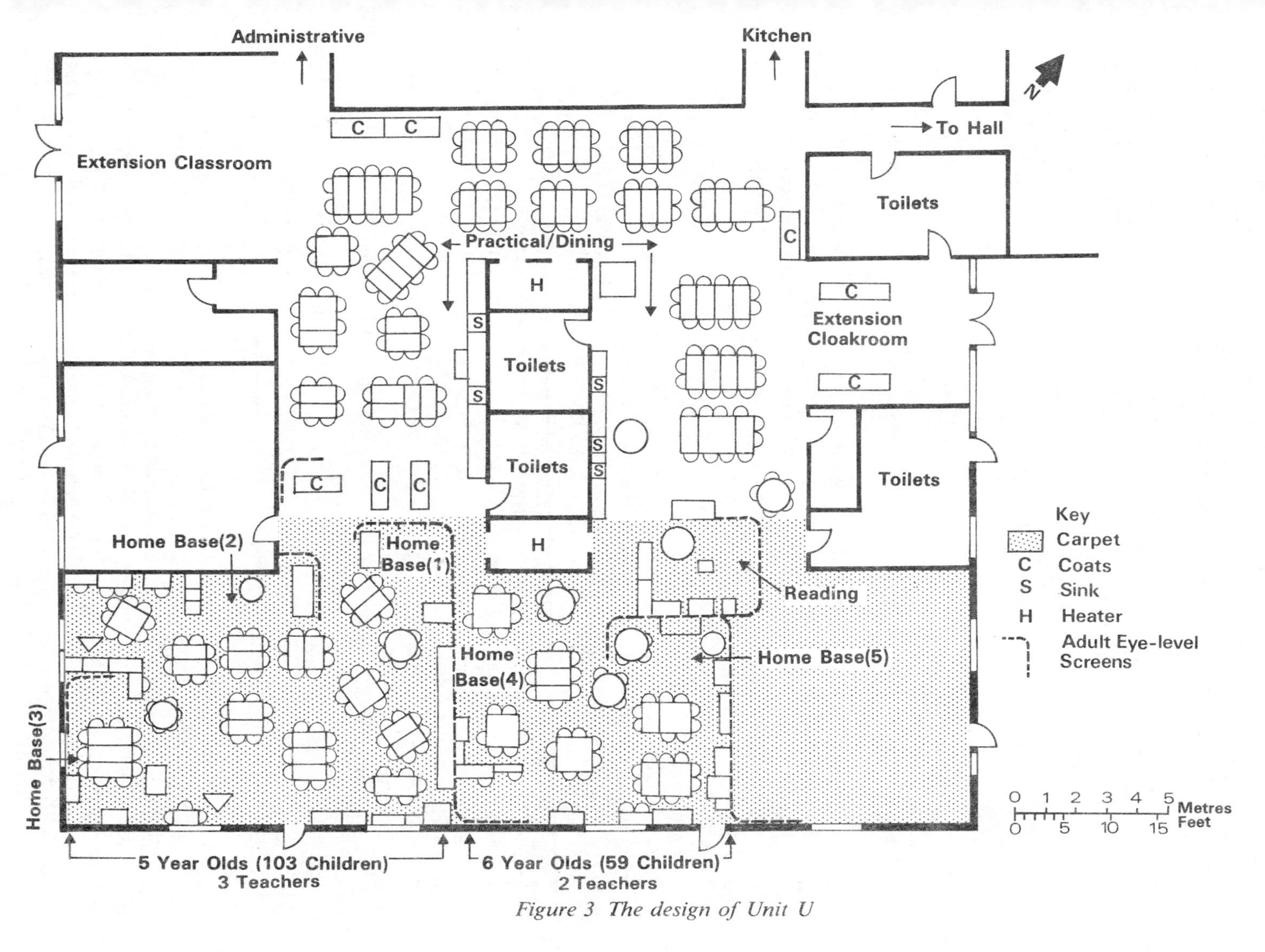


*Figure 3 The design of Unit U*

mentioned by several teachers, but others thought that it was good for children to see what others were doing and that in open plan children learned to respect other people.

Although teachers appreciated the extensive carpeting and the dampening effect it had on noise it appeared to constrain activities, since no glue or paint could be used in the general teaching area. Milk had to be taken in the practical area and even water was liable to produce a stain if it was spilt.

> Carpets are bound to limit the noise but on the carpeted area we can't use paint or glue, if we have a blackboard we have to make sure that there is a mat underneath so that the carpets don't get dusty. The children have to change their shoes everytime they come into school.

In fact the time taken in changing shoes had led to the policy that the children only went out for breaks in summer.

Several teachers mentioned the advantages of having access to all facilities and being able to see what others were doing and pool ideas. One teacher likened the open situation to being 'on a beach' and appreciated the gregarious nature of the design, but qualified this by asserting the need for a constrast of quiet places. This was reiterated by another member of staff: 'There are no nooks and crannies. Children can't get away from us and we can't get away from them.' Most of the teachers stated that they would have preferred more enclosed home bays which opened onto a communal area.

*Teaching Organization*

Each teacher had her own class group. A mixture of single year grouping and two year vertical grouping was in operation. The older seven–eight year olds occupied the classroom, a smaller group of brighter children occupied what was designed as a medical room and the slower children ocupied the extra space made available by the extension. The large general teaching area was divided into three sections by movable screens. Three groups of four- and five-year-old children filled one space, two groups of six-year-old children occupied the centre space and two groups of six- and seven-year-old children used the remaining space. A slightly smaller group of six- and seven-year-old children used the quiet room for a home base and the tiled area for working. Use of the practical area and the hall was timetabled. There were two floating teachers, one who was part-time and another who divided her time between the nursery and the five-year-old children.

A form of team teaching had been tried between four teachers in charge of the youngest age group during the year prior to the visit. The children had been split into four ability groups for reading, writing, number and creative work. In the beginning each teacher had taught one subject area for one week and the children moved from teacher to teacher, but this had given rise to organizational problems: 'I could not work out who I was supposed to be teaching next week.'

A different system was then tried whereby teachers supervised reading for one week, number for another, writing for a third and creative activities for a fourth week. This was followed by an experimental system in which each teacher specialized in one area of the curriculum. When the fourth teacher was made responsible for the introduction of a 'Breakthrough to Literacy' programme the remaining teachers found their groups rather too large to manage and, in order to meet the needs of students coming in for teaching practice, reverted to separate class teaching. These three teachers still held regular discussions in which the nursery nurse and floating teacher also took part. One of these teachers expressed a wish for more discussion between themselves and the teachers in the other bays.

*Curriculum Organization*

According to the headteacher 70 per cent of the children were very limited in their use of vocabulary, and unable to express themselves fluently. Teachers also referred to the language difficulties of many of the children. English was a second language for the small percentage of Asian children but much of the difficulty encountered by West Indian children stemmed from differences in sentence construction. 'They have their own sentence construction and we don't know what they are so we assume they are speaking our sentences inadequately and in fact they are not.' These children were also described as boisterous.

The overall aims of the school according to the headteacher were that 'children must learn certain basic skills, reading, writing, and number skills, and we give each child as much time as we can to develop him academically, physically, mentally and creatively'. The role of language development was emphasized. One teacher stated her expectation clearly:

> I would be very happy if after one year they could write their names, give me a reasonable sentence and relate to me their experiences. I know that this might sound silly but in this school to be able to tidy up . . . I make a record of who can and who can't . . . I think that's really important because they have got to live here for four or five years. In written work, I would like to think that they can build up their own sentences with the words that are on the board. I would like them to have read their introductory book, to be able to make and match sets, to be able to make comparisons such as long and short, count up to ten and add up to five.

The curriculum was organized so that basic skills were covered in the morning and the afternoon was reserved for more creative work. The headteacher reasoned that more time was available and that the children could cope more easily with things that take a lot of mental or physical effort in the morning. However, timetabling of the hall and practical area meant that some children, usually the younger ones, had to have creative activities in the morning. Most of the class groups were timetabled to have use of the practical area on two occasions each week: 'If it's my turn for creative then we go and create.' The constraints imposed by the need to keep the carpet clean imposed considerably on the way that the curriculum was organized, 'It's very sad, if you were doing number work for example they could go and paint but you can't do that. We do a lot of cutting and tearing, that can be hoovered up.'

At 11.30 the practical area had to be vacated in preparation for dining which created other problems: 'The dinner ladies come across and take all our chairs out.'

The period between 11.30 and 12 was used for quiet work in the carpeted area.

> We stick to a timetable. I like to make sure that everyday I've got some time for letter signs, some time for reading, flash cards in groups or with the class, I like to hear the readers every day even if it means staying in at lunch time, and I stick to the timetable for things like poetry and nature, RE and number work.

> Really you work your timetable around hall time, PE time, television time and quiet times and apart from that you've just got to work in basic subjects plus creative activities.

Almost all the teachers interviewed stated that they did a lot of phonic work and used 'Breakthrough'. Both the part-time teacher and the floating teacher took withdrawal groups in the use of 'Breakthrough' materials. Two of the reception teachers had attended a course on

Fletcher mathematics, and although they would have liked to use Fletcher mathematics in their curriculum they explained that it was too expensive and that there would be no continuity since teachers of the older year groups tended to concentrate on a more traditional approach. Instead these teachers had a meeting in the holidays to discuss the progression outlined in Fletcher and had adapted their own number work accordingly.

Children within each class were grouped by ability level although these grouping arrangements were not quite so clear-cut in the reception classes where children who had attended the nursery tended to be ahead of the others in social development and could concentrate for longer periods.

The emphasis placed on language development is demonstrated in Table 4, which shows the mean percentage curriculum allocation for one group of teachers over a four day period. It can be seen that language work accounts for nearly half of all curriculum time. The extra time devoted to this area is at the expense of maths and aesthetics, the latter due in part perhaps to the concern about the carpeted areas.

| *Curriculum Area* | *Time* | *Curriculum involvement* | *Time (all infants)* |
|---|---|---|---|
| Maths | 9.7 | 70.1 | 15.8 |
| Language | 47.9 | 77.5 | 36.7 |
| Environmental studies | 2.5 | 88.0 | 3.5 |
| Aesthetics | 6.8 | 72.1 | 9.6 |
| PE | 2.3 | 87.0 | 3.9 |
| Social/moral education | 7.6 | 90.8 | 8.1 |
| Administration/transition | 23.1 | – | 22.2 |

*Table 4 Allocation and involvement (%)*

Involvement tends to be near the infant norm with the exception of aesthetics, which is ten per cent lower. Transition time accounted for 13.5 per cent of the school day. When children were due to change location, either to go to the hall for PE or to go to the far end of the practical area for morning milk all the children were required to tidy away and form a queue adjacent to the practical area, where they waited until everyone was ready. 9.1 per cent of the school day was spent by children waiting in such queues. Specific activities are shown in Table 5.

These show a dearth of messy activities such as the use of sand, water, glue, paint or clay. Instead there is more emphasis on class open discussion, TV, story and drawing with crayons.

Table 6 shows the frequency of different teaching/learning situations.

Direct teaching accounts for nearly half of the curriculum time, 16.4 per cent of it in combination with other class groups, as in assembly or singing practice. 25.2 per cent of time was spent in whole class direct teaching, as in story or discussion. 5.8 per cent of time was taken up with direct teaching to small groups which was due largely to the practice of withdrawing small groups of children for instruction in the use of 'Breakthrough' materials. The dominant mode of working was that of small groups with 12.8 per cent of curriculum time being devoted to work in which all children were given similar tasks. Individual work accounted for only 8.1 per cent of curriculum time.

Although the amount of observed pupil interaction was near the average for the whole sample pupils were as in Unit W more frequently seen arguing, pushing or otherwise behaving

| *Task Activity* | *Overall Involvement* | *Non-involvement* |
|---|---|---|
| Administration | – | 4.6 |
| Transition | – | 18.5 |
| Teacher class group discussion | 9.3 | – |
| Teacher small group discussion | 3.7 | – |
| Computation | 0.4 | 0.1 |
| Practical maths | 3.3 | 2.5 |
| Constructing toys | 1.5 | 0.2 |
| Reading to teacher | 0.7 | 0.2 |
| Reading scheme | 1.5 | 1.1 |
| Reading – free | 1.1 | 0.5 |
| Spelling | 2.0 | 1.4 |
| Writing copy | 1.2 | 0.6 |
| Writing – free | 4.6 | 4.0 |
| Story | 10.5 | 1.1 |
| Recitation | 0.8 | – |
| Draw/crayon | 4.2 | 3.7 |
| Singing | 3.5 | 0.1 |
| Making music | 0.3 | 0.1 |
| PE small apparatus | 1.6 | – |
| Games | 0.3 | 0.3 |
| Social play | 2.4 | 0.2 |
| TV | 7.0 | 0.3 |
| Helping teacher | 0.1 | 0.5 |

*Table 5 Time spent in task activities (PBS)*

| *Teaching/learning situation* | *Time* | *All Infants* |
|---|---|---|
| Individual work | 8.1 | 24.0 |
| Individual direct teaching | 1.4 | 1.6 |
| Small group work | 30.3 | 24.7 |
| Small group direct teaching | 5.8 | 4.9 |
| Whole class work | 12.8 | 9.6 |
| Whole class direct teaching | 25.2 | 22.7 |
| 2+ class work | – | 0.2 |
| 2+ class direct teaching | 16.4 | 12.2 |

*Table 6 The frequency of different teaching/learning situations (%)*

in a negative manner. Teacher exhortations to good behaviour were also common. The average percentage of pupil–teacher interaction was slightly less than the average across all infant units.

In the absence of school records teachers were meticulous about record keeping but no one method predominated.

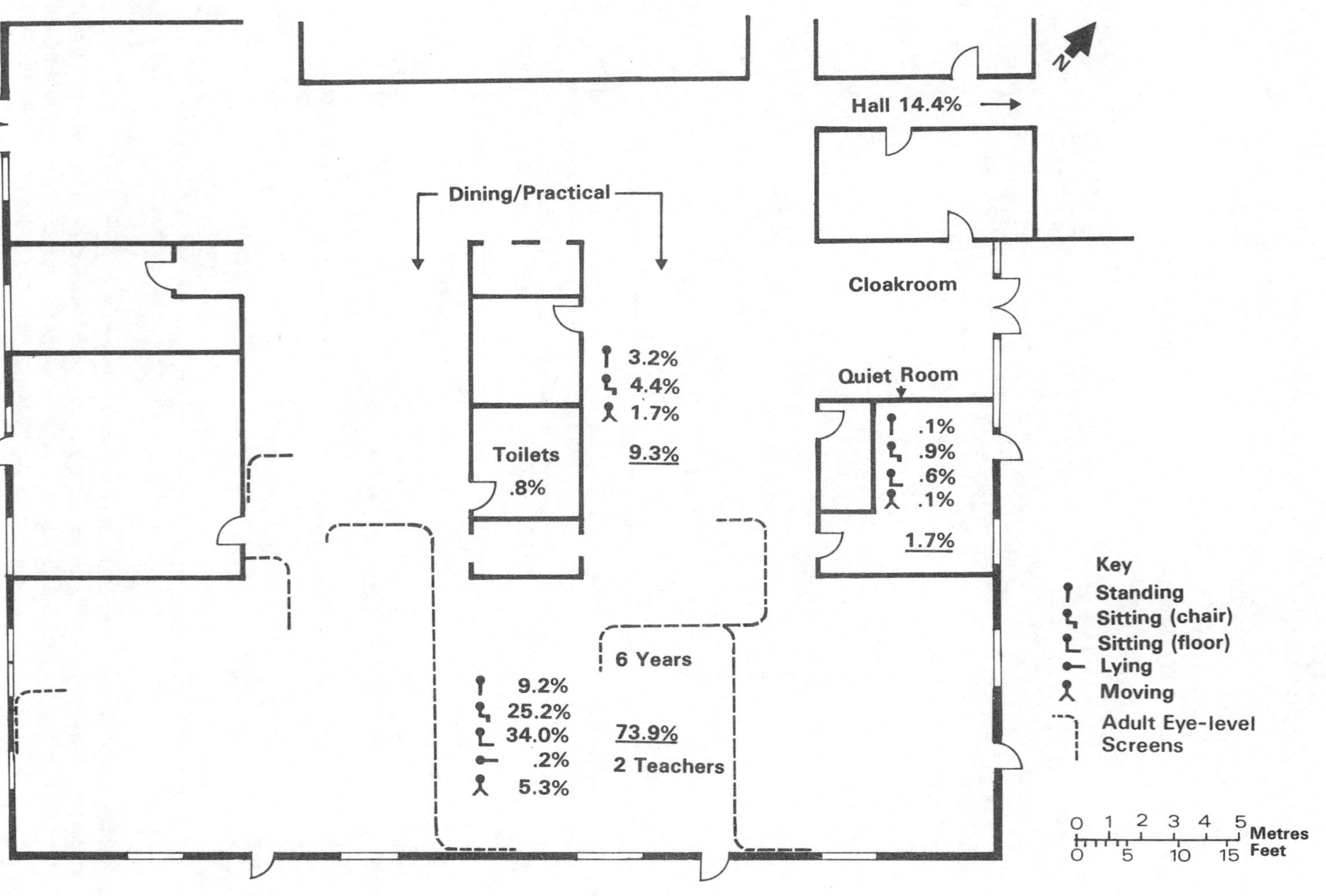


*Figure 4 The use of space in Unit U*

> 'We've been given freedom to keep any sort of records we can in order to establish what sort of records work most efficiently.'

All the teachers interviewed kept records on progress in reading, writing and number, and many were quite detailed.

*Use of Space*

Calculated in relation to the number of children on roll at the time of the visit the amount of space available per child was 2.1 $m^2$ (22.6 $ft^2$). This compares with an average of 2.8 $m^2$ (30.14 $ft^2$) across the other infant units. Observed use of space with posture for 24 six year old children over a four day period is shown in Figure 4. On average 26.6 per cent of the pupil day was spent outside the shared general teaching area. 14.4 per cent of this was spent in the hall for PE, singing, assembly or games; 9.3 per cent was spent in the practical area; 1.7 per cent in the quiet room and 0.8 per cent in the toilets. 73.9 per cent of the pupil day was spent in the screened teaching bay on the carpeted area. Of this 25.2 per cent was spent sitting at tables, 34 per cent was spent sitting on the floor, 9.2 per cent standing and 5.2 per cent moving.

For most afternoons one or another class group would be working in the practical area, leaving more space for the other children, but in the mornings most of the children were in the teaching bay and there was little room for children to work. On the other hand the practical area was almost empty: 'It's timetabled for them all to sit and have their books in front of them – you find that the books are overlapping.'

*Parents*

The headteacher said that she thought that relationships with parents had improved since the school had moved into the new building but that was probably because the school was now physically less removed from the community it served. Open evenings were held twice a year and there were fund-raising events in which parents helped. Parents were welcome to come into school to discuss matters concerning their children with the teachers but it was not the policy of the headteacher to involve parents in school activities. There were two reasons for this – firstly not all parents were suitable and secondly they might displace the NNEB assistants. These views were shared by some members of staff but they were not unanimously held.

> I learn a lot about their children and their way of life. I'd like to be able to meet the parents on their own terms but I don't know how to do this. I'd like to be able to go visiting but it's not the sort of thing that's done, is it?
> What I'm thrilled about was the fact that last term we had the parents in every Wednesday for a tea-party for fund-raising. For us it was an advantage, we saw our children's parents.

Quite a lot of in-service training was available at the teachers' centre and some of the staff had been on courses, but the headteacher said that she thought the most useful form of in-service training would be something held in the school itself. This would enable teachers to talk out their ideas in front of someone who was impartial, an advisor for instance.

> Teachers have to work together much more closely, there's no time for any reservation between teachers whether their personalities aren't quite sympathetic or otherwise, you want patience and consideration for others, possibly more patience in open plan. We've got to keep an open mind and if someone came along with a bright idea we'd be willing to listen. To keep up the standard the teachers have had to work twice as hard.

Members of staff were in agreement on this last point:

> You have to organize every minute, I've always done a lot of preparation but I'm more aware of its benefits now.
>
> Nerve-racking for teachers . . . I don't feel it so much during the day . . . sometimes I get headaches . . . but when I get home I just want to collapse.

*Discussion*

Two case studies of inner city schools have been presented. They serve to illustrate a contrast of approach by teachers in response to similar problems. Both of these schools had a large immigrant population. In both cases the teaching units were very large although one was very open in design and one consisted of a series of interlinked smaller spaces. In neither case was the building felt to be ideal by the teaching staff.

The main curriculum emphasis in both schools was the development of language. Little difference was observed in the average level of overall involvement of pupils (percentage of the school day in which pupils were observed on task). Having said this, there is little else that is similar between the two cases.

In one unit teachers worked together in teams, whereas in the other each teacher had his or her own class group. In the former, children were vertically grouped spanning a three year age range, and in the latter by virtue of the numbers of children in each age group, class groupings spanned a 1 to $1^1/_2$ year age range.

A child-centred curriculum was in operation in one unit. Children had almost total free choice of activity and teachers were left free to guide, structure and intervene when and how they thought necessary. A great variety of materials was provided to stimulate the children's interest. The active approach to curriculum organization described in Chapter 7 is amply demonstrated.

The curriculum in the other unit centred around the use of space and the idea that basic skills are better tackled in the morning than in the afternoon. Strict timetabling was enforced. Since no messy activities were allowed in the carpeted area and classes were limited to two sessions per week in the practical area, such activities were either very rare or non-existent. Despite the enthusiasm, dedication and hard work of teachers, the children were provided with a much more passive curriculum.

In one unit every inch of available space was used, including the staffroom, the entrance hall and the lower floor of the old school building. Provision of space in relation to the numbers of children was lower in the other unit where the practical area was underused in relation to its size.

Attitudes to parents and the involvement of parents in activities also differed between the two schools. One unit was situated in a community school and both the headteacher and staff had done their best to establish links between the school and community. Parents were welcome to come into schools at any time either to talk about their children or to help with activities. The level of pupil–adult interaction was very high. Although there was a very positive attitude towards parents in the other case study, teacher–parent contact was limited by comparison and the level of pupil–adult contact was much lower.

There were also differences between the two schools with regard to in-service training. Teachers' centre courses were available to the staff of both schools but in one, staff also had access to centrally organized courses and benefited from on-the-spot training devised by local headteachers.

The major problems cited by staff in both units were those relating to noise and circulation. Staff in one unit would have preferred a more open design which would have facilitated both circulation and supervision, whereas staff in the other would have preferred a building more conducive to their preferred method of separate teaching. In both schools there was thus a conflict between design and teaching approach.

## Contrasts in Team Teaching Organizations: Case Studies 3 and 4

### Case Study 3 (Unit H)

The subject of this case study is an open plan unit in a first (5 – 9) school situated in a suburban area. The unit is built as an extension to a cellular 1960s school, and houses 120 children in the 7 – 9 age range. Another 218 children are housed in the original building.

The school's catchment area is clustered around the school and consists mainly of owner-occupied houses on a fairly new estate. The parents are described by the headteacher as 'mainly youngish people on their way up'. There is a considerable degree of movement, families moving into and away from the area. Children entering the school at 5 are described as 'linguistically good'; there are no socially deprived children in the usual sense of the term. Where children do have special needs, the head reports, it is usually due to one or other of two things; the surprisingly high incidence of broken homes and excessive pressure stemming from the aspirations of the parents.

The open plan unit is classified as a quad Type 2, having four large home bases, each with its own small quiet room, and a central wet area. However, it should be stressed that the central area is unusually large and that the configuration of space which this particular unit enjoys is crucial to the teaching and curriculum organization employed (Figure 5). The unit gives the impression of spaciousness, though this is in part due to being designed for 160 children rather than the 120 who actually occupy it. The amount of space available per pupil was 2.9 $m^2$ (31.21 $ft^2$). The quality of finish is high, circulation presents no problems because of the size of the central area, sound-absorbent finishes to floors in the home bays and ceilings throughout help to make the unit an extremely quiet one, and the provision of storage and other facilities is adequate. The home bases have the apparent luxury of being enclosable, Marley screens being fitted between each home base and the central area, though the screens have never, in fact, been used. The availability of a small enclosed quiet room off each home base probably renders the screens unnecessary. No modifications have been made since the building was completed, and none are contemplated.

At the design stage the headteacher was consulted by the advisers and architects involved. The modifications he requested were that the quiet room doors should be part glass, and that seating in the quiet rooms should not be fixed – the latter, he felt, would make these spaces rather inflexible. Both modifications were accepted. The headteacher was satisfied with the general lay-out suggested by the architect, but reports that he found it very difficult to imagine what the building would be like. On the involvement of heads and teachers in design he questions the wisdom of giving practitioners too much say in the matter. The 'right mix' of expertise in design terms was, he felt, very difficult to define.

The headteacher's own background included a period during which, as a member of a group of headteachers, he was invited to report on school designs for the benefit of local authority architects. He had therefore thought a great deal about open plan design, had seen a large number of such schools in operation, and thus when he came to the task of organizing this unit, had a very clear mental model to work to.

A detailed description of the unit's teaching and curriculum organization are included later in this case study. However, it is perhaps appropriate at this point to report the headteacher's approach to his role, his leadership style, and the manner he chooses to turn his mental model into classroom practice.

> I have very strong views about this. I know that some people think that the teachers and the head should plan together how it will work, but I've seen this fail because it was a new venture and no-one really knew how to go about it. A group of people sitting down to share their common ignorance is hardly a recipe for success. You place people, unfairly, in an insecure position if you expect them to prepare plans for something of which they have little or no knowledge or experience. I think that the headteacher, who is paid to exercise a leadership role, should have a very clear idea of how the thing will work from the beginning, and be able to prepare the teachers for what may be a situation not of their choice. That was certainly so for the members of my staff.
>
> First, then, the head must have a very clear educational philosophy and know what the policies will be, then I think his or her role is to be with the teachers as often as possible, to talk with them, and by exposition, explanation and discussion weld them into a team having a common purpose within the framework of an explicit educational philosophy. That does not mean that the teachers have no autonomy, it does not mean that they can exercise no choice. The sort of analogy I use is this:
>
> If you get four people on a patch of grass with a net stretched across, give them rackets and balls and let them start hitting the balls across the net, they are not necessarily playing the game of tennis. Indeed, if they are each free to make up their own rules all may find their attempts to play a game at all totally frustrated by conflicting rules invented by the others. Only when a framework of rules is laid down within which they all play can they be said to be playing a game, and only then is each person free to develop his own style of play, his own particular skills and playing strategies. Similarly, with a teaching team, someone must first draw up a framework within which people will work together, and then they can be free to develop their skills, their ideas, and make their own special contribution, knowing that they will not be in conflict with their colleagues, but rather that they are strengthening the ability of the team to achieve its objectives.
>
> I believe that the person responsible for drawing up that framework is the headteacher.

In general the headteacher is very much in favour of *his* kind of open plan unit, but rightly sees the term as too wide, to all-embracing, to make a response to the question 'do you favour open plan designs?' possible. To summarize, then, this headteacher's attitude to his school's open plan unit is entirely positive, although he does add the proviso that in his case he is able to place staff who dislike the open plan unit in the original part of the school which is of conventional design. No teacher is forced to work in the open plan setting, although the same teaching philosophy is applied throughout the school.

Views of teachers who work in the open plan unit are similar to those expressed by the head, though none of the teachers who were placed in the unit originally wished to move from their classrooms. Now, none of them would wish to revert to a more conventional setting. It should be added, however, that the teachers did stress the importance of the team working well together, there being no 'personality clashes'. The tension between the similarity of approach and attitude, and the variety of expertise and specialisms required seems to be crucial. As one teacher said, it is important that no one teacher should 'stand out beyond the rest, character-wise . . . ability-wise . . .'

The positive attitudes expressed by the teachers are no doubt to some extent a function of the clarity and cohesiveness of the relationship between aims and practices in the unit. Underlying the whole organization of the unit is the belief that children learn best when their activities are

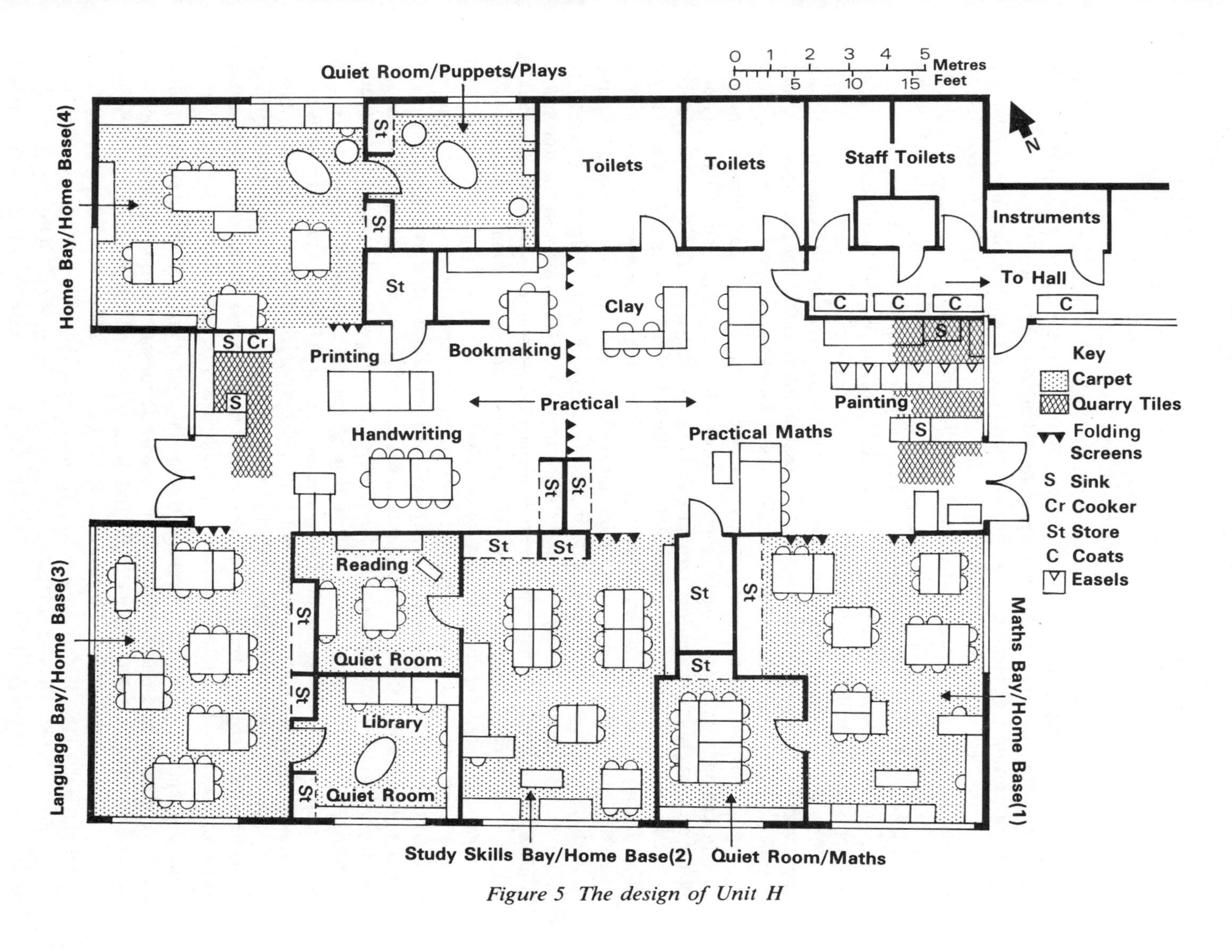


*Figure 5 The design of Unit H*

informed by experience. The variety of experiences which would have to be provided for the children led to the conceptualizing of the unit as a learning workshop, which would provide for as wide a range of activities as possible in use-specific areas. Space in the unit is identified by its use, and its use is clearly defined by the kinds of provision made within it. The four home bases are known as the 'maths' area, the 'home' area, the 'study skills' area and the 'language' area, while the large central wet area is broken down into smaller spaces for painting, pottery, textile activities and so on, the precise use varying according to current need.

The organization of teaching in the unit is classified as team teaching, involving a large element of subject specialism. However, it should be stressed that there are many differences between this example of team teaching and that illustrated in the following case study. The allocation of duties and responsibilities to teachers is only one dimension of the definition of the teachers' roles. As crucial, it seems, to the learning experiences of the children is that dimension of the teachers' role which is concerned with the relative dominance of teacher-directed and pupil self-directed activities. In this unit the children are attached to one teacher for purposes of registration, pastoral care and overall record-keeping. Reading progress is also monitored by the registration teacher. For maths, the children in the unit are allocated to small groups by ability, each teacher having responsibility for two small groups. Each small group has two intensive direct teaching sessions each week in one of the small quiet rooms, each session leading to practical or other follow-up work which has to be completed by each child before the next group session. Apart from PE and music sessions the rest of the curriculum time is less structured by the teachers, the children being largely self directing as to when they do what. During these times, which account for most of each day, the roles of the teachers are essentially consultative. Each teacher mans one of the use-specific spaces – maths bay, study skills bay, language bay, 'home' bay and central activity area – children going to the appropriate space for the activity they choose to follow. Thus, for instance, the teacher responsible for the maths bay is present in that space for the whole of these periods, available for children to consult her and supervising the various activities taking place there. Maths practical work requiring the use of water or other 'messy' materials takes place in the part of the central activity area adjacent to the maths bay under the supervision of the same teacher.

Apart from mathematics, which is seen largely as a separate and distinct programme, curriculum activities are centred on a theme, typically lasting for half a term, which serves as a starting point rather than a straitjacket. Children are encouraged to follow their own particular interests within the theme, and most of their curriculum activities – reading, writing, illustrating, making etc., are centred on the topics they select. One of the stated aims of the headteacher is that children should not distinguish between those activities traditionally regarded as 'skills' and 'frills'. Thus, activities such as painting, pottery and collage which are sometimes regarded as play are as highly valued here as more 'basic' activities. Teachers demonstrate expectations of high standards in all curriculum activities.

For the children, a typical day begins with a brief period of registration and administrative activities followed by discussions with 'their' teacher about the opportunities available to the children that day, reminders about maths follow-up work, and suggestions for the development of work already done. Because the pupil–teacher ratio is favourable, this is done thoroughly and all the children are involved in the process. The children then move off to their various activities which may continue with or without change throughout the day. There may be structured periods during the day – a maths group session, assembly, a PE lesson, phonics (word-building, spelling), reading for slower learners, a handwriting session, but otherwise pupils direct their own activities in the sense that they choose what they will do and when, but not where – within the broad parameters set by the teachers.

This organization of teaching and curriculum demands detailed planning and preparation, and the organization of the learning environment, both in terms of display and availability of materials, is crucial to the success of this approach. Constant evaluation and planning by the team was an aspect of the job which all the teachers stressed.

The observation data in the school case study is drawn principally from that collected through the PBI, based on the observations of 24 children over a period of four days. Pupil case study data from the LES instrument, based on intensive whole day observation of individual pupils will be referred to where appropriate.

One of the features of Unit H is the pupils' high level of task involvement, averaging 87 per cent curriculum involvement and 75.4 per cent overall involvement, the highest in the whole sample. Table 7 shows the levels of curriculum involvement in different curriculum contexts.

| | *Unit H* | | *All Junior Units* |
|---|---|---|---|
| Curriculum Area | Time | Curriculum involvement | Time |
| Maths | 13.8 | 89.9 | 17.1 |
| Language | 27.5 | 84.4 | 30.7 |
| Environmental studies | 17.5 | 76.6 | 13.2 |
| Aesthetics | 23.3 | 94.8 | 10.3 |
| PE | – | – | 9.4 |
| Social and moral education | 4.2 | 100.0 | 6.3 |
| Administration/transition | 13.7 | – | 13.0 |
| Curriculum involvement | – | 87.0 | 76.2 |

*Table 7 Time allocated to curriculum contexts (PBS) (%)*

Clearly, as in all the units studied, language is the dominant curriculum context. In general, this unit is not distinguished from the rest of the sample by its curriculum allocations, although the involvement figures are higher, particularly in mathematics. The absence of PE from this table and the inflated aesthetics score is accounted for by the use of PE time for music concert practice.

The actual activities subsumed by these curriculum contexts are shown in Table 8.

The high incidence of teacher class group discussion is largely accounted for by the sessions described earlier, in which teachers discuss with children the opportunities available to them and any particular requirements there may be.

It should be clearly stated that in this unit the fact of a thematic form of curriculum organization makes the differentiation between curriculum contexts somewhat problematic, and that reference to the actual activities table gives the reader a more reliable guide to the curriculum activities experienced by the children.

| *Task activity* | *Overall involvement* | *Non-involved* |
| --- | --- | --- |
| Administration | – | 1.7 |
| Transition | – | 11.9 |
| Teacher class discussion group | 17.0 | – |
| Teacher small group discussion | 5.9 | – |
| Computation | 5.2 | 1.0 |
| Practical maths | 1.4 | 0.5 |
| Read to teacher | 0.3 | – |
| Read – free | 3.0 | 1.6 |
| Audio-reading | 0.5 | – |
| Writing – copy | 1.6 | 0.3 |
| Handwriting | 1.7 | 0.5 |
| Writing – composition | 0.9 | 0.3 |
| Writing – free | 5.3 | 3.4 |
| Story – listen | 1.6 | – |
| Recitation | 0.7 | – |
| Draw/crayon | 4.1 | 0.6 |
| Making | 4.1 | 0.4 |
| Clay-work | 4.7 | 0.8 |
| Sewing | 4.7 | 1.5 |
| Singing | 1.9 | 0.1 |
| Making music | 0.7 | – |
| Music – listening | 0.2 | – |
| Concert/show | 9.9 | – |
|  | 75.4 | 24.6 |

*Table 8 Time spent in task activities (PBS) (%)*

The distribution of time between teaching/learning situations has been discussed in Chapter 7 where the relationship with degree of pupil choice is discussed. Unit H can be described as one in which pupils are required to be self directing to a very large extent, and, as might be expected, the distribution of time between teaching/learning situations in Table 9 reflects this feature of organization. (NB The LES data was collected in a separate week.)

| *Teaching/Learning Situations* | *Time* |
| --- | --- |
| Individual work | 61.9 |
| Individual direct teaching | 1.4 |
| Small group work | 3.4 |
| Small group direct teaching | 2.3 |
| Whole class work | 4.9 |
| Whole class direct teaching | 16.6 |
| 2+ class work | 0.0 |
| 2+ class direct teaching | 3.5 |
| Administration/transition | 6.1 |

*Table 9 Teaching/learning situations: Unit H (%)*

Having discussed the relevant observation data it is perhaps appropriate to record that the subjective impressions of the research team were not at variance with the excellence suggested by the data. The children's level of interest and motivation was unusually high, and their work – in all areas of the curriculum – quite outstanding. The concern for quality in the environment stressed by the teachers in interview was certainly reflected in the children's work and attitudes. Further, the unit ran smoothly. Disruptive or other negative behaviour was virtually non-existent and the unit had in abundance that much sought after but elusive quality of primary schools, a happy purposeful atmosphere.

The reasons advanced by the head and staff for this happy state of affairs are fairly predictable. All stressed the vital importance of the teachers functioning as a team in the sense that there was agreement on aims and how to meet them. Although the broad organizational structure is laid down by the headteacher, the process of evaluation and planning is always done by the team. Other features stressed by the staff are stability of organization, the careful training of children new to the unit and the highly advantageous adult–pupil ratio (achieved through the use of parents). Finally, the design and quality of the building is seen as important and is appreciated by the head and teachers.

**Case Study 4 (Unit K)**

The subject of this case study is a Multi Type 2 organized as two three teacher units, one of which was observed. Built in 1973, it was located in a large junior school serving a small town, a neighbouring village and the surrounding rural area. The children come from what the headteacher describes as the 'full range of home backgrounds'. The proportion of children with learning difficulties or other special needs is described as very small.

The school is new, purpose-built, and was provided to replace the old and dispersed buildings of an existing Church of England school. However, as this school is a County school and as a smaller Church of England school remains in the town, this school is best seen as a mixture of 'replacement' and 'new'.

The building is an unusual one in that it is flexible. The configuration of space can be changed radically by means of erecting or moving large, floor-to-ceiling pinewood screens. Thus, space can be arranged to meet the wishes of the teachers working in each unit, enabling units to be as open or closed as desired. However, the moving of screens is a fairly major operation – a weekend's work on the part of the teachers. The unit on which this case study focusses was arranged as a three teacher Type 2 unit, being divided into three distinct classroom size teaching bases linked by curtained openings. The building seemed to be of a high standard, giving an impression of spaciousness even though each pupil enjoyed only 2.1 $m^2$ (22.60 $ft^2$). The quality of finish is excellent.

Consultation between the local authority and the headteacher over the design of the building was not possible as the latter was appointed only 3 months before the school opened. No modifications have been made by the head, other than those made possible by the pinewood screens. The only modification planned is for the provision of a sound-proofed music room to serve the whole school.

The headteacher's background does include experience as deputy head of a semi-open plan school, though this seems not to have provided definite notions about the organization of teaching in this kind of building: 'I realized from my own experiences that it wasn't possible to do the same thing with everybody at the same time and each member of staff approached the situation and approached the environment in a completely different way . . . '

The headteacher's views on open plan are generally positive. In particular, the advantage of being able to have parents in school 'to see what is going on' is stressed. The educational advantages in terms of teaching and curriculum organization are seen as wholly dependent on the particular teacher's reaction to the open plan environment. The head does not see involvement in the organization or day-to-day running of units or classes as part of his role. In his own words, his role is to 'keep out of the teachers' way as much as possible so they can get on with the job in hand.'

The teachers' attitudes to the open plan situation are fairly favourable, though none stated a clear preference for either a conventional or open plan building. The advantages claimed for the open situation were the facilitation of teamwork, the presence and availability of other adults, the community atmosphere. The major worry was that perhaps some children needed the greater security of a classroom, working with one teacher.

The organization of teaching in the unit under discussion is a highly structured form of cooperative teaching based on the allocation of children, by ability, to sets for the teaching of basics. Each of the 108 children in the unit is a member of one set for English and of another set for mathematics, and, for organizational convenience, PE. There are three sets for each of these basics, teachers having responsibility for one English set and one maths/PE set for a half term. The sets then 'move around', so that all the children are taught by all the teachers for both basic subject areas during a half year. The rationale given for this rotation is that the children should be taught by all the unit teachers at different times, and that all three teachers should have equal time with each of the three ability levels.

The sets operate in the mornings, apart from the first half hour, when children are in mixed ability registration groups – a period of registration and other administration during which children read and are heard reading by their registration teacher. Children spend the rest of the morning in their maths and English sets. In the afternoons children are typically in their registration groups for topic work, art and craft and other curriculum activities.

Within both the sets and the mixed ability registration groups, the activities of the children are highly teacher-directed, all the members of a set or registration group (both class sized) carrying out the same tasks at the same time. Choice is not available to the children in any of the three dimensions of choice – what, where and when – observed in primary schools. This traditional and formal approach to teaching is recognized as such by the teachers, and has not been adopted without consideration of other forms of teaching organization. Other less formal approaches had been tried and rejected because the teachers felt that standards in the basics were slipping.

Although the teaching organization is clearly influenced by cognitive aims, these are not stressed by the teachers, who express greater concern for the children's social development. The headteacher stressed the importance of a 'happy pleasant atmosphere' in 'providing the best education that we can for the children who come here every day'. Taking the organization of the school alongside the statements made by the staff it does seem that concern for the 'basics' as the major business of schooling is implicit in this case.

A clear distinction is made by the head and teachers between the 'basics' and other subjects. This leads to an interesting point of comparison between this unit and Unit H. In fact the 'less formal' form of organization tried and rejected by the teachers in this unit after half a term was very similar to that now carried on successfully in Unit H. The crucial point of difference seems

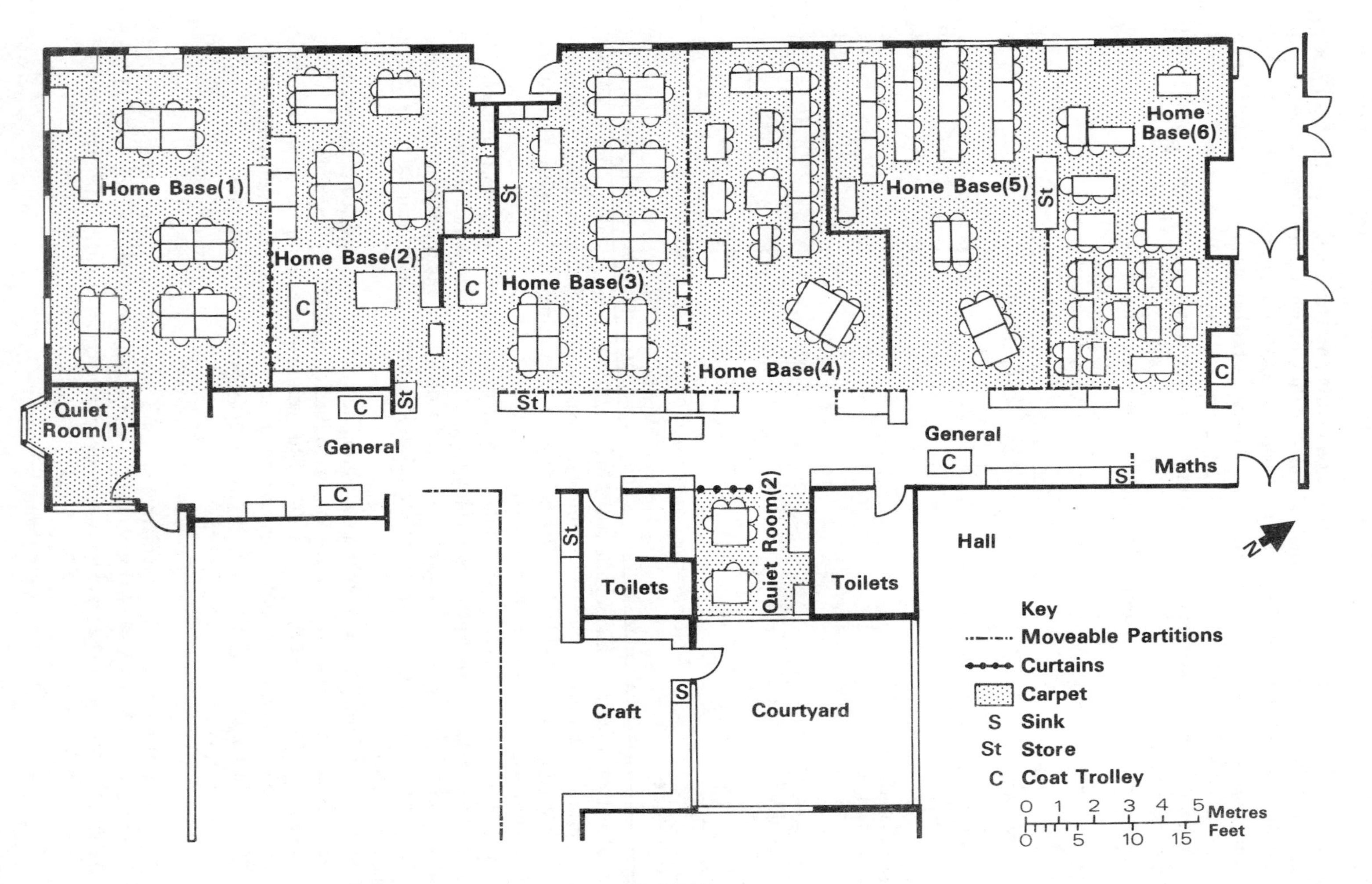


*Figure 6 The design of Unit K*

to be in the attitude of the teachers to aesthetics and other practical activities. In Unit H these are highly valued activities seen as crucial informers of the children's work in the basics. In Unit K, however, clear boundaries are maintained between curriculum areas, and there is a clear differentiation of values between the basics and the rest. A further reason for the very different experiences of the two units is the difference in the type and configuration of space provided. While in Unit H there is excellent provision for practical activities, in Unit K such provision is virtually non-existent.

The actual balance of curriculum activities in this unit is shown in Table 10.

| | *Unit K* | | *All Junior Units* |
|---|---|---|---|
| Curriculum Area | Time | Curriculum involvement | Time |
| Maths | 20.3 | 75.4 | 17.1 |
| Language | 42.4 | 74.5 | 30.7 |
| Environmental studies | 9.9 | 85.9 | 13.2 |
| Aesthetics | 6.8 | 92.6 | 10.3 |
| PE | 2.7 | 1.9 | 9.4 |
| Social/moral education | 5.1 | 100.0 | 6.3 |
| Administration/transition | 12.8 | – | 13.0 |
| Curriculum involvement | | 78.8 | 76.2 |

*Table 10 Time allocated to curriculum contexts (PBS) (%)*

These figures for time allocated to various areas of the curriculum clearly illustrate the dominance of mathematical and language activities in this unit. Maths is allocated rather more time than is typical in the units studied, while language is nearly 12 per cent above the norm. As one would expect, this is balanced by less time being given to 'non-basic' areas of the curriculum. Involvement is less than in Unit H but still above average.

The actual task activities subsumed under the curriculum contexts are shown in Table 11.

The relative frequency of teaching/learning situations is a reflection of the high level of teacher direction in Unit K. The virtual absence of individual work and the dominance of whole class work and whole class direct teaching are a clear indication of the traditional nature of the teaching in this unit.

Children's learning experiences are almost wholly determined and directed by the teacher. Children work in class size groups (ability groups for basics) in which all the children carry out similar tasks. This form of teaching applies to all curriculum contexts – to needlework no less than to computation, and is probably the most striking illustration encountered during the Project of the fact that open settings do not necessarily house open education.

**Conclusion**

The organizational differences between the two units are essentially the manifestation of differences between an open or active approach and a closed or passive approach to the organization of teaching and curriculum. It should be stressed that, in the subjective opinions

| *Task activity* | *On task* | *Non-task* |
|---|---|---|
| Administration | – | 0.9 |
| Transition | – | 12.1 |
| Teacher class group discussion | 16.2 | – |
| Computation | 10.2 | 3.9 |
| Practical maths | 0.5 | 0.1 |
| Maths games | 0.2 | – |
| Cooking | 0.4 | 0.1 |
| Reading to teacher | 0.8 | – |
| Reading scheme activities | 2.2 | 0.9 |
| Reading – free | 8.1 | 4.0 |
| Spelling | 0.9 | – |
| Writing – copy | 0.1 | 0.3 |
| Handwriting | 2.3 | 0.5 |
| Writing – composition | 3.8 | 3.8 |
| Writing – free | 4.1 | 1.0 |
| Story – listen | 5.0 | 0.5 |
| Recitation | 0.2 | 0.3 |
| Draw/crayon | 3.6 | 1.3 |
| Making | 0.4 | 0.9 |
| Clay work | 0.5 | – |
| Seiving | 1.9 | 0.2 |
| Drama | 0.1 | – |
| Music/movement | 2.2 | – |
| Singing | 1.1 | – |
| PE – small apparatus | 0.7 | 0.1 |
| Games | 0.9 | 0.7 |
| TV/film | 2.3 | – |
| | 68.7 | 31.3 |

*Table 11 Time spent in task activities: Unit K (PBS) (%)*

| *Teaching/Learning Situations* | *% Time* |
|---|---|
| Individual work | 2.6 |
| Individual direct teaching | 0.9 |
| Small group work | 13.6 |
| Small group direct teaching | 0.4 |
| Whole class work | 43.5 |
| Whole class direct teaching | 16.9 |
| 2+ class work | 0.2 |
| 2+ class direct teaching | 5.7 |
| Administration/transition | 16.1 |

*Table 12 Time spent in teaching/learning situations: Unit K (LES) (%)*

of the Project team, both schools were good examples of their kinds, and that both were successful in terms of the outcomes illustrated by the observational data and the standards of work produced by the children.

The differences in teaching and curriculum organization have been described in some detail. Other differences are perhaps worth a mention, especially differences in the roles played by the headteachers. Surprisingly, perhaps, the head of Unit H is very much more directive than the head of Unit K. Whereas the former has a clear and detailed vision of how the school's aims should be operationalized and has directed the organization of the unit through personal involvement, the latter has adopted a much more *laissez-faire* attitude, encouraging his staff to arrive at their own ideal form of organization, not involving himself in the day-to-day activities of the unit.

Differences in the organization of space and furniture are also marked. In Unit H furnishing varies enormously between spaces, reflecting the range of activities which children are expected to experience, while in Unit K the spaces are furnished almost identically, reflecting the expectation that children will spend most of their time sitting at tables.

The similarities between the two units are that both are open plan junior units and that both operate their own versions of team teaching. There the similarities end. The definitions of schooling and the beliefs of teachers about how children learn embodied in their organizations could hardly be further apart.

## Differing Organizations in Identical Space: Case Studies 5 and 6

### Case Study 5 (Unit P)

The subject of this case study is a three teacher infant unit in a one form entry primary school. The school is situated on the outskirts of a depressed industrial town; grim reminders of the industrial revolution on the one hand, rugged open countryside on the other. The 278 pupils are drawn from a mixed catchment area. In the school's immediate vicinity are modern owner-occupier estates; a little further away are rows of older terraced houses. Children are drawn mainly from lower-middle- and middle-class backgrounds.

The school was purpose-built as an open plan primary school for 280 pupils and opened in 1973. The infant unit which is the subject of this case study consists of three home bases, a shared 'wet' area, a large enclosed room and a small room originally intended as the deputy headteacher's study (Figure 7). The only major modification to the original design was the conversion of the 'study' to a semi-enclosed space which is used as a Wendy House. No other modifications were requested and none is planned.

The headteacher's background includes experience as deputy head of a new open plan school. That experience was, he says, crucial to his thinking about the organization of this school. He holds clear aims, stressing the importance of basic skills and especially skills of communication. He places special emphasis on the importance of good social relationships within the school and on the quality of the learning environment. Children are encouraged to be self directing and to develop their skills of inquiry.

The headteacher's attitudes to his open plan building are decidedly positive. He does not believe that the aims of open plan schools should be seen as different from those of schools housed in traditional buildings – the building simply helps the realization of those aims, by providing a physical environment which helps to foster socialization and the development of good attitudes to work.

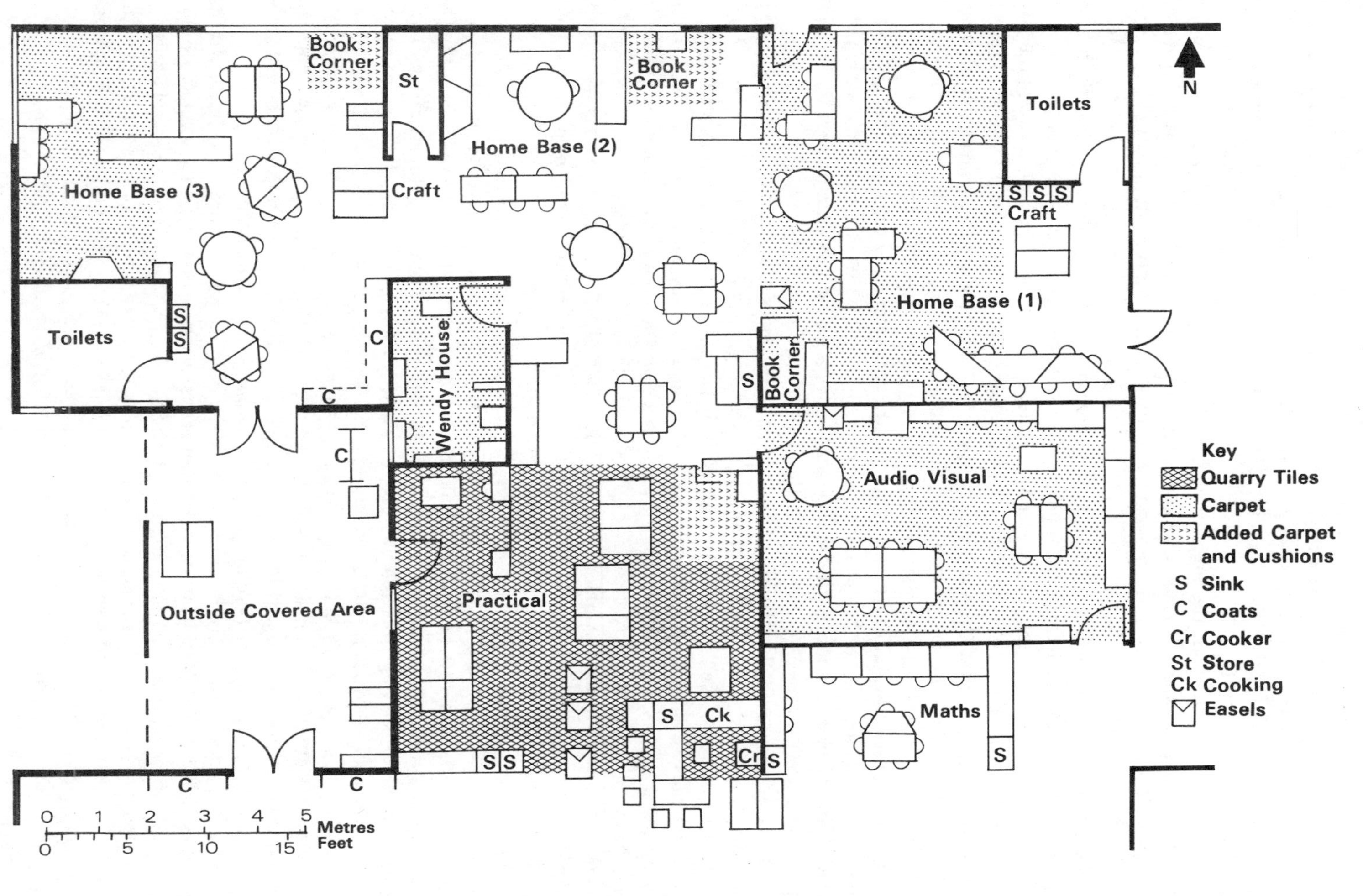


*Figure 7 The design of Unit P*

However, the headteacher believes that the quality of relationships in his school owes much to the fact that he was given a major say in the selection of staff. As this was a new school he was able to select staff, four of whom were probationers, whose attitudes to education were congruent with his aims.

The one complaint about the building which is voiced – by head and teachers – is not an unusual one: lack of space. In fact all the space in the school is regarded as learning space, the staff room and headteacher's room being frequently used as activity areas. Even so, space is very limited.

The attitudes of the staff towards their open plan building are positive, although there are aspects of the design which they find unhelpful. The one stressed by the teachers is the difficulty of supervising children in the shared wet area. This space is not visible from two of the home bases, which means that the teacher in the central home base is the only one who can supervise both her home base and the wet area at the same time. Overall, teachers did express a preference for the open plan environment, quoting the sharing of resources and the range of activities possible in the large wet area as particular advantages.

The unit houses 120 children and is staffed by the equivalent of 4 full-time teachers. In fact, three of the teachers are full-time, each having responsibility for a class of 40 children. Two other teachers, one of whom is the deputy head, have a part-time committment to the infant unit, working with groups of children withdrawn from the three classes.

The classes operate independently in that each of the three class teachers is responsible for the work of her own class. Team or cooperative teaching is not a feature of the organization in this unit. However, teachers do plan cooperatively as the need arises and operate a common policy on the use of shared spaces. In fact, a common policy on teaching and curriculum organization applies, with only minor differences. Team and cooperative teaching approaches have been tried, and were rejected by both headteacher and teachers because of the organizational restraints which became apparent – the needs of the system were dominant, rather than the needs of the children. The head also expressed a belief that it may be better for young children to have the security of his or her own teacher.

Children are vertically grouped into the three classes, allocated so that each class has a similar mix of 'reception', 'middle' and 'top' infants. This is the only criterion used in the allocation of children to teachers. The children spend much of their time in their own classes where all aspects of the curriculum are covered. In addition each child is allocated to one of five groups on the basis of age and reading ability. Each of these groups spend one morning each week in the enclosed room with the deputy head. A variety of activities takes place in these groups – topic, science work, maths – but usually aimed at developing children's basic skills in language and number. The headteacher also involved himself in the work of the unit, both formally and informally, taking the oldest group for handwriting once a week and much more frequently working with individuals in small groups on an ad hoc basis.

The adult–child ratio is further improved by the involvement of parents in the day-to-day activities of the school. The headteacher believes that parents are a much neglected resource, and that the benefits in the area of home/school relations can be immense. Parents are welcomed into school and are encouraged to go along regularly and work under the guidance of the staff. Parents can be seen teaching cookery, pottery, sewing, woodwork, telling stories and hearing competent readers. The purposes and key teaching points in the parents' work – e.g. the measuring processes in cookery – are clearly identified by the teacher in prior discussions with the parents.

In-service training of the staff is regarded as very important by the headteacher. However, although LEA courses are valued, he sees the school itself as the real focus of in-service training, and the teachers themselves as the real agent of that work. Teachers meet regularly, often in one of the units rather than the staffroom, so that they can discuss the work going on in that area. The aims and purposes of activities are thus not 'taken for granted', but examined and discussed by the whole staff.

Within each of the three classes the children are grouped by ability. These groups exist as much for the allocation of tasks as for direct teaching purposes. Children are given a number of assignments and can choose the order in which they carry them out. The period of time for which assignments are given increases as the children mature, so that some of the older children may have a set of assignments to cover a two day period. Younger children are more closely directed, the teacher specifying their activities throughout the day and more often in groups until they are ready for a greater measure of self direction.

Space is fairly use-specific, and children are trained to use the appropriate area for their chosen activity. Language and number activities take place mainly in the home bases, creative activities in the wet area, reading in the staffroom and so on. Numbers in certain spaces are subject to limits and children know that if space for their chosen activity is full they have to choose something else until space is available. In fact, although numbers are high for the space available and the building does seem cramped, this system apparently works well.

The aim of developing pupils' ability to direct their own work is operationalized in the teaching organization described above. The degree of choice which pupils have is gradually increased as their ability to cope with choice improves. Table 13 shows the balance of teaching/learning situations experienced by the children in the LES sample in this unit. The most

| *Teaching/Learning Situations* | *Time* |
|---|---|
| Individual work | 17.0 |
| Individual direct teaching | 2.8 |
| Small group work | 27.1 |
| Small group direct teaching | 3.9 |
| Whole class work | 3.7 |
| Whole class direct teaching | 19.9 |
| 2+ class work | 1.5 |
| 2+ class direct teaching | 7.8 |
| Administration/transition | 16.3 |

*Table 13 Teaching/learning situations: Unit P (%)*

frequently occurring situation is small group work, followed by whole class direct teaching and individual work. The balance here reflects the range of situations experienced by middle infants in this unit. The incidence of individual work (self-directed) is higher than it would be for a sample of younger children and lower than it would be for a sample of older children.

The curriculum schemes used are common to all the classes. The maths scheme is one that the head and staff have developed for themselves. The head feels that the adoption of any one commercially produced scheme could lead to a 'routine', rather than a child-centred, approach to mathematics. A range of maths schemes is available for teachers to consult, but they produce their own materials and work cards to suit the needs of their pupils. A range of reading schemes is also available.

| | Unit P | | All Infant Units |
|---|---|---|---|
| Curriculum Area | Time | Curriculum involvement | Time |
| Maths | 15.7 | 59.2 | 15.8 |
| Language | 39.2 | 70.4 | 36.7 |
| Environmental studies | 4.5 | 93.3 | 3.5 |
| Aesthetics | 8.1 | 80.2 | 9.6 |
| PE | 3.0 | 83.3 | 3.9 |
| Social and moral education | 6.9 | 94.2 | 8.1 |
| Administration/transition | 22.6 | – | 22.2 |
| Curriculum involvement | | 73.2 | |

*Table 14 Time allocated to curriculum contexts (PBS) (%)*

Teachers were asked about the balance of curriculum activities, whether there was an emphasis on one curriculum area or another. They felt that, although they hoped that all curriculum areas were equally valued, language activities were probably dominant. One teacher said 'I get the impression from the children that they think writing is obviously very important, and they must have got this from us.'

In fact the figures for curriculum allocation based on the PBS sample do indicate a dominance of language activities. As Table 14 shows, the balance of curriculum activities is close to the mean for all the infant units observed.

Language is slightly higher than the mean. As in all the infant units it is by far the most frequently occurring curriculum context.

The actual task activities subsumed under the context headings are shown in Table 15.

The task involvement score based on the PBS sample is below the mean for all infant units, at 56.8 per cent.

The casual visitor would recognize the school as 'different'. The configuration of space, of course makes the strongest immediate impression. But the real differences lie in the area of relationships and attitudes. These are dimensions of schooling which are difficult to quantify and no 'hard' data are offered here. However, the impressions, not of casual visitors, but of the research team, are that the quality of relationships in this unit is exceptional. Children always seem to be cooperative and friendly, the atmosphere relaxed and free of tension and an air of purposeful and pleasurable endeavour pervades. The headteacher stressed the importance of relationships when discussing his aims. The respect and care which he and the teachers show to the children is reciprocated. The other point stressed by the headteacher when stating his aims is that these should not be different from those of any school. In terms of the range of curriculum activities there is nothing unusual or different from what one would expect to find in any infant classroom. What is different is the social context in which the activities take place.

| *Task activity* | *On task* | *Non-task* |
|---|---|---|
| Administration | – | 5.4 |
| Transition | – | 16.8 |
| Teacher class group discussion | 9.1 | – |
| Teacher small group discussion | 3.5 | – |
| Computation | 2.1 | 4.2 |
| Practical maths | 3.8 | 1.5 |
| Constructing toys | 0.5 | 0.1 |
| Sand activity | 0.9 | 0.4 |
| Cooking | 0.4 | 0.1 |
| Reading to teacher | 2.3 | 0.7 |
| Reading scheme activities | 3.4 | 1.2 |
| Reading – free | 0.7 | 0.6 |
| Writing – copy | 0.5 | 0.1 |
| Writing – composition | 0.5 | 0.7 |
| Writing – free | 5.2 | 6.4 |
| Story – listen | 10.4 | 0.8 |
| Recitation | 0.3 | – |
| Painting | 2.8 | 1.5 |
| Draw/crayon | 1.7 | 2.0 |
| Making model | 0.5 | 0.1 |
| Experiments | 0.2 | – |
| Singing | 2.2 | 0.1 |
| Making music | 1.2 | – |
| Listen music | 0.4 | – |
| PE small apparatus | 0.7 | – |
| PE large apparatus | 1.8 | 0.5 |
| Social play | 1.6 | – |
| TV film | 0.1 | – |
| *Total* | 56.8 | 43.2 |

*Table 15 Time spent in task activities (PBS) (%)*

**Case Study 6 (Unit 0)**

The subject of this case study is an open plan infant unit of identical design to that described in the previous case study (P). It is clear from this pair of case studies that design need not influence organization since two very different organizational forms are represented by these two units.

Unit 0 is the infant department of an IFE primary school. The catchment area includes council housing, old but well-maintained terraced housing and three private estates. The social class background of the school's 256 children is described by the head as predominantly 'upper working and middle class'.

The school was purpose-built as a replacement for an old Victorian building. The school transferred as a whole in 1973. The infant unit with which this case study is concerned consists of three home bases, a shared 'wet' area, a large enclosed room and a small room known as the 'study' (Figure 8).

No modifications to the original plan have been carried out and at present none is anticipated. The major complaint against the building is the same as that voiced by teachers in Unit P – lack of space. However, the strategy adopted for coping with this differs here. It was decided that there should be four classes rather than three, and that the 'wet' area would be used as the extra class home base. The large room had been tried as a home base, but its lack of windows made it too claustrophobic.

Unit 0 houses 120 infant children and is staffed by four full-time teachers. In addition the deputy head spends approximately half her time in the unit. There is also a part-time ancillary helper. There is one reception class, as the head feels that the youngest children are best catered for in a separate class. The rest of the infants, over a $2^1/_2$ year span, are vertically grouped into three classes of equal size and mix with 30 children in each class. These classes exist for the purposes of registration, language work and some of the PE and storytimes. Each child is also allocated by age to one of the three colour groups in which children do maths, handwork, topic work, music and some PE. Each teacher has responsibility for one class and one colour group. Thus, all teachers operate in all curriculum areas – there is no teacher specialism other than that of the deputy head, who withdraws 24 children a day for individual reading.

Teachers work independently with their own classes and colour groups, but common curriculum schemes are operated in maths and reading. Topics are often planned cooperatively. The maths scheme is based on a series of work cards developed by the teachers themselves, with one teacher (the infant team leader) responsible for coordinating the maths work throughout the unit. The common reading scheme is 'Kathy and Mark'. Overall, although teachers work independently, there is a substantial measure of cooperative planning.

Within the classes and colour groups, children's work is highly teacher directed, much of the work being done on a whole class basis – all the children in a given class or colour group carrying out the same tasks at the same time. Throughout the units, basics tend to be taught in the morning and the other areas of the curriculum in the afternoon.

The head's attitudes to his open plan building indicate no strong preferences. His own experience has been mainly in small schools with no previous experience of open plan schools. However, as this school was transferred from other premises, the head and staff were able to carry out a series of 'trial runs' in the old building.

The head says that the aims of the school and its ethos have not been changed as a result of the move. There is a major concern with the 3Rs and the structure and direction of children's learning – 'We tend to teach', the head says.

The attitudes of the teachers to their unit have changed over time. Initially there was a feeling of lost privacy – 'We put the blackboards between (the home bases) . . . we were too insecure'. Gradually, teachers adjusted to working in an open situation. Attitudes to the building now are fairly positive, but all teachers complain that space is very limited. Typical of the comments made is, 'it ought to have been twice as big . . . I don't think you'll find anything wrong with it except that' and 'It's light, bright, open . . . the biggest difficulty is space; it isn't big enough'. Related to the simple size problem is the difficulty of circulation and the disruption it causes. In part, the teaching organization is a response to this perceived problem; children tend to move in large numbers at set times – there is little movement between areas except at these times. Teachers operating in the carpeted areas feel restricted: '. . . just that very tiny amount of floor

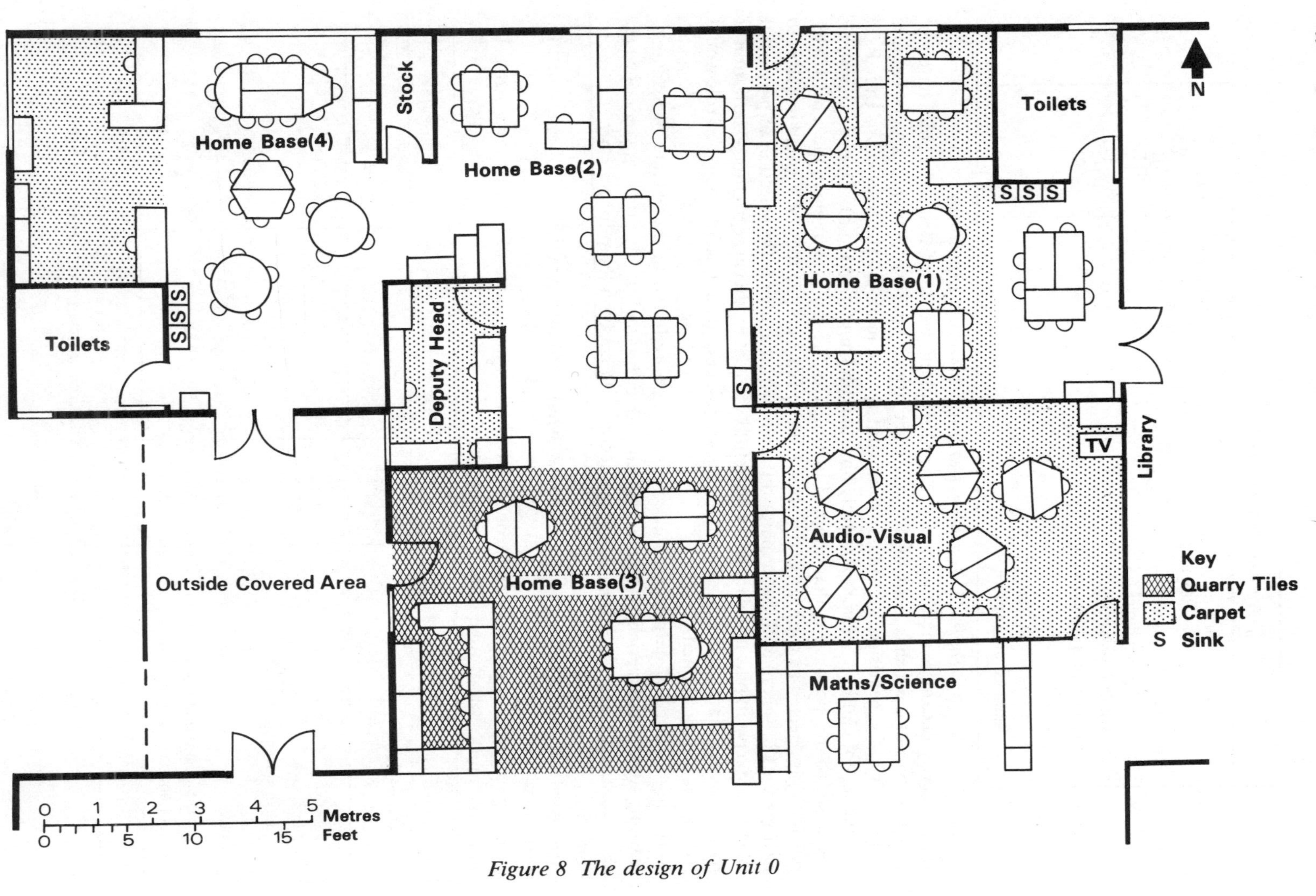


*Figure 8 The design of Unit 0*

| *Teaching/Learning Situations* | *% Time* |
|---|---|
| Individual work | 0.9 |
| Individual direct teaching | 0.7 |
| Small group work | 10.8 |
| Small group direct teaching | 1.0 |
| Whole class work | 33.4 |
| Whole class direct teaching | 21.3 |
| 2+ class work | 0.0 |
| 2+ class direct teaching | 7.0 |
| Administration/transition | 24.7 |

*Table 16 Teaching/learning situations: Unit 0 (%)*

space where you can use anything messy . . . '. Most of the 'wet' area is used as a home base, but even that part of it which is available for messy activities is little used, say the teachers, because of difficulty of supervision – a similar complaint to one made by the teachers in Unit P.

Numbers of children are comparatively high in both Unit 0 and Unit P. One of the possible responses to this problem is that adopted in Unit P – the use of parents in the school. This possibility is rejected by the head and staff in Unit 0. Teachers say that they would not want to have parents in school and that a major difficulty with the idea is the selection of parents. 'I think you'd have to pick and choose very carefully . . . that might cause friction'. The notion of parent-assisted learning in school is totally rejected. If parents were allowed in their role would have to be strictly limited.

The highly directed nature of children's learning is reflected in the balance of teaching/learning situations experienced by the children. Table 16 shows clearly the dominance of whole class work and whole class direct teaching, accounting between them for 54.7 per cent of the total time.

Children's learning experiences are almost wholly teacher directed, in all areas of the curriculum.

The stated aims of the head and teachers stress the importance of the 3Rs, and Table 17 shows the allocation of time to curriculum areas.

| | *Unit 0* | | *All Infant units* |
|---|---|---|---|
| Curriculum Area | Time | Curriculum Involvement | Time |
| Maths | 18.5 | 61.6 | 15.8 |
| Language | 29.1 | 77.3 | 36.7 |
| Environmental studies | 6.9 | 82.6 | 3.5 |
| Aesthetics | 12.3 | 64.6 | 9.6 |
| PE | 3.9 | 79.5 | 3.9 |
| Social and moral education | 7.7 | 94.8 | 8.1 |
| Administration/transition | 21.8 | – | 22.3 |
| Curriculum involvement | | 77.4 | |

*Table 17 Time allocated to curriculum contexts (PBS) (%)*

In fact the time allocated to maths and language in Unit 0 represents 47.6 per cent, rather less than the mean across all the infant units (52.5 per cent) even though maths is slightly higher. However, closer examination of pupils' actual curriculum activities in Table 18 reveals a greater emphasis on computation and writing activities than is usual in infant units.

The level of task involvement based on PBS observations is 60.3 per cent, very similar to the average for all infant units.

**Conclusion**

Observations in identical units were undertaken to assess the degree of similarity in organization. There was in fact very little. The decisions made by head and staff had resulted in a

| *Task activity* | *Overall involvement* | *Non-involved* |
|---|---|---|
| Administration | – | 3.9 |
| Transition | – | 17.9 |
| Teacher class group discussion | 10.1 | – |
| Teacher small group discussion | .6 | – |
| Computation | 4.9 | 4.2 |
| Practical maths | 2.7 | 2.2 |
| Constructing toys | 1.0 | .1 |
| Maths games | 1.1 | .5 |
| Reading to teacher | 1.1 | .2 |
| Reading – free | 1.7 | 1.3 |
| Spelling | .6 | .3 |
| Writing – copy | 2.2 | .4 |
| Writing – composition | 1.4 | .3 |
| Writing – free | 5.5 | 4.1 |
| Story – listen | 7.8 | .5 |
| Recitation | 1.6 | .1 |
| Painting | .4 | .5 |
| Draw/crayons | 3.9 | 1.8 |
| Making | 4.1 | .6 |
| Singing | 4.3 | – |
| PE small apparatus | 2.3 | .2 |
| PE large apparatus | .8 | .5 |
| Social play | 1.2 | .1 |
| TV/film | .6 | .1 |
| Helping teacher | .4 | – |
| | 60.3 | 39.8 |

*Table 18 Time spent in task activities (PBS) (%)*

highly directed and structured organization in Unit 0 and a more open or informal one in Unit P. This is shown in the teaching/learning situation where whole class work and direct teaching dominate in one, and individual and small group work predominate in the other. The curriculum balance achieved is also different. More time is devoted to language in Unit P but less to maths, and more surprisingly, aesthetics. An examination of actual curriculum activities also indicates a greater emphasis on computation and writing in Unit 0 but less time on practical maths. Administration/transition time is very similar on PBI observations. However, involvement is somewhat lower in Unit P and shows particularly in language and aesthetics.

The concern here is not to argue that one organization is better than the other but to make the simple point that identical designs house very different organizations and underlying philosophies. Many teachers argue that design dictates method. This might be true in a general sense – it is more difficult to operate a one teacher, one class system in open plan schools just as it is more difficult to teach cooperatively in conventional buildings. But within any building, organizational alternatives are possible and it would seem that the expertise and philosophy of the staff are the central determinants, not the design of the building.

**A Case Study in Design Problems: Case Study 7**

The final case study relates to problems in school design. The school chosen to highlight these was by no means the worst designed school visited but was chosen because the problems here are fairly typical in kind to those found generally, and secondly because the interest of the project team prompted an interest among LEA advisory staff. What follows is therefore a joint contribution.

This school, which opened in 1975, is in an authority which was newly formed in 1974 as a result of a merger of parts of two former authorities. It was visited in the first few months of the Project's work and included in *Journeys into Open Space* as an example of poor architectural design (see Figures 9 and 10). This is what was written at that time.

1. The building is sited such that the infant unit (classes 1–4) is in almost permanent shadow, rarely receiving any sun.
2. Large spaces under toilet doors allow, according to the head, maximum opportunity for peeping Toms and Marys and leads to constipation among the timid.
3. Soap dispensers in the infant toilets delighted the children, who poured all the soap down the sink.
4. The practical areas in both infant and junior units are very badly sited. They are both major thoroughfares since all pupils must pass through them to gain access to their class base from the school entrance; to gain access to the hall and library from their class base, and in the case of the junior unit, to gain access to class 5 (the only quiet room in the school) from their class base. Incredibly, there is only one sink provided in each practical area and at the time of building there was no provision for an electric socket.
   Part of the junior practical area has to be used as a cloakroom since no cloak facilities were provided. In the infant practical area this cannot be done because of extra space taken up by sand and water. The infant cloaks have therefore had to be kept in the hall.
5. There is a large opening between the infant classes 1 and 2 and the hall. Between the two stores in this unit is a carpeted area which is utilized a great deal by the infants. All the noise from activities in the hall – PE, music, drama, is received directly by the infants. There is also a reverse flow of noise, infant singing swamping lessons in the hall.
6. A similar problem here. The wide access to the library is directly on to the hall. Pupils working in this area are also inflicted with noise from the hall. Since this is the major access, pupils entering the library can distract pupils working in the hall. A separate

entrance to the library from the junior unit was demanded and provided.

7. There was no provision for quiet areas in the design; however, the headteacher requested a door to be placed on the entrance to class 5 and this was done. This room is now totally enclosable and is used for class teaching. Lack of soundproofing means that noise is discernible from infant class 4 on the other side of the partition.
8. All movement from classes 7 and 8 to class 5, the practical area, the hall, and the main entrance, necessitates walking through classes 6 and 9. Teachers of classes 7 and 8 cannot see their pupils in the practical area.

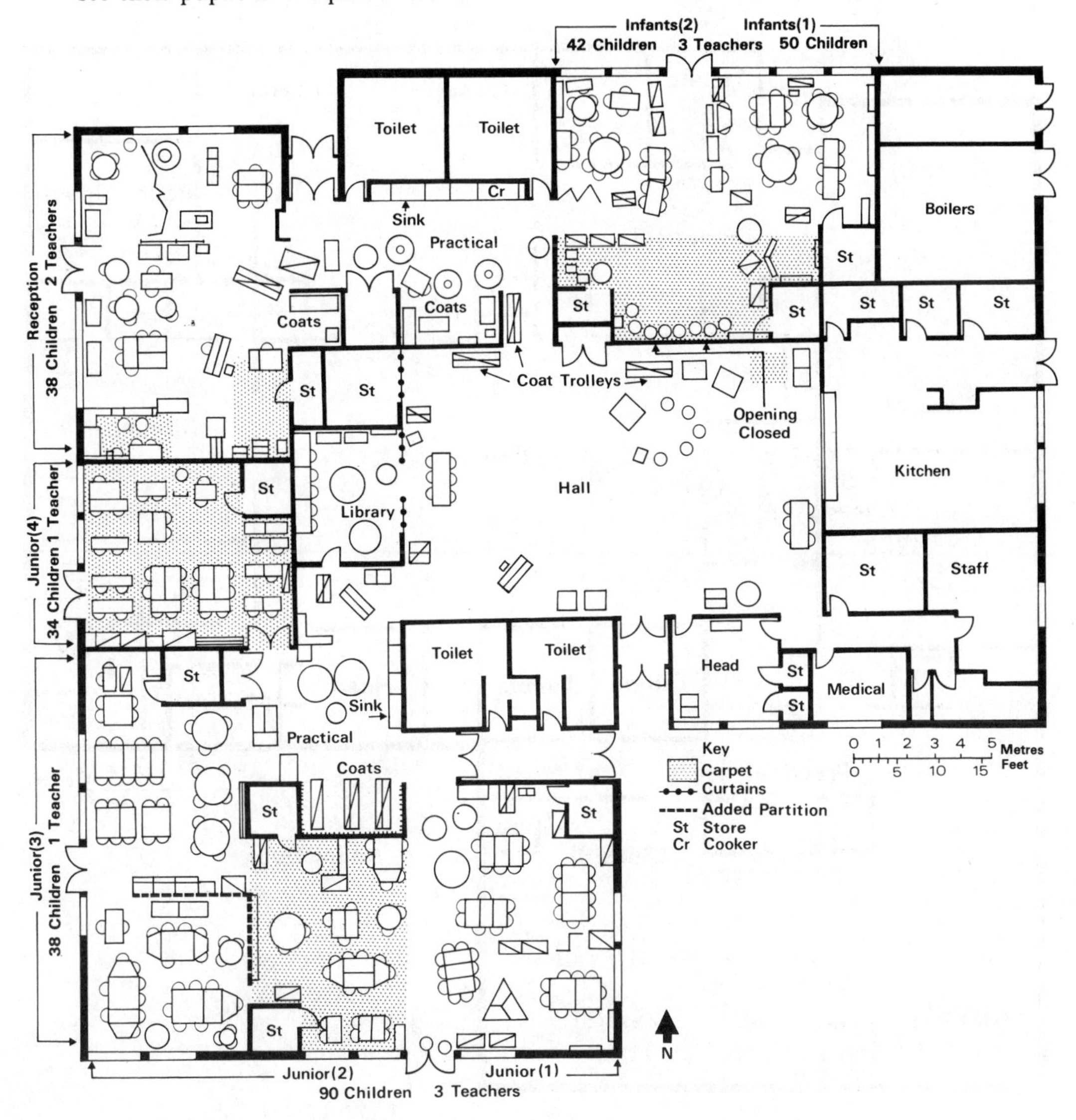


*Figure 9 A Poorly Designed Unit in Detail*

9. Space is very tight in the junior unit. This cramps versatility of approach, obviating the flexibility claimed for open plan schools. Although the school is not particularly overcrowded (built for 280 and now housing 292) there are no space working areas where groups of children can be sent, or a spare seat when all children are present.
Acoustics are poor. The teacher of class 8, for example, cannot read her class a story if class 9 is engaged on a noisier activity. Some teaching staff complained of noise although the subjective impression of the visitor was that it was quiet. Nevertheless, this design could make teaching impossible with noisy and/or disruptive pupils.

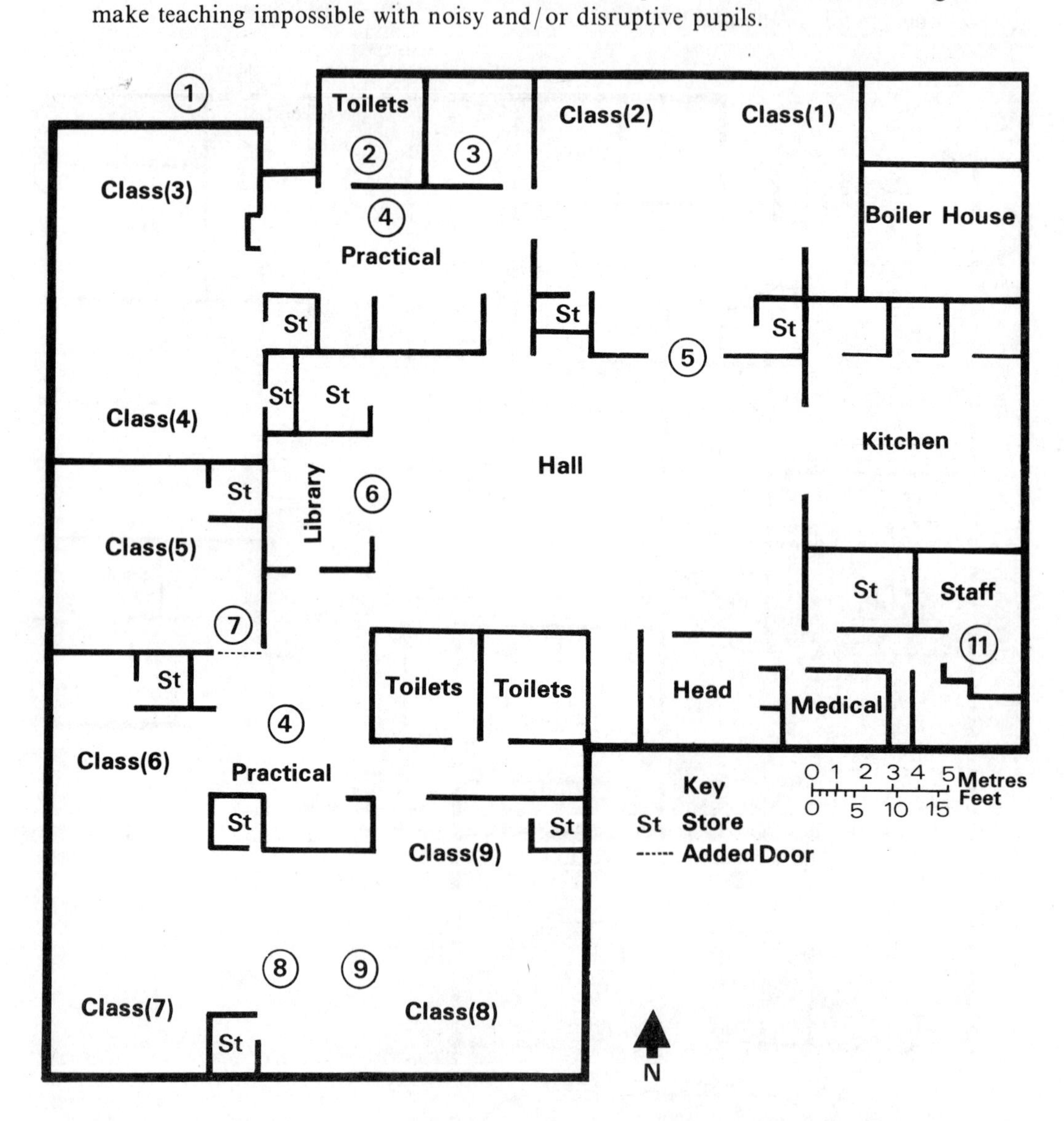


*Figure 10 An Outline Example of a Poorly Designed Unit*

Only one blackboard is supplied between two classes, necessitating swopping of class space to enable its use.

10. Internal wall finishes are very poor. If dirty marks are wiped off the wall the bare plaster shows through. The school is built by a type of unit construction which, in the words of one teacher 'go soggy and fall down after five years'! The exterior wall finish is also poor.
11. The staff room is too small.
12. There is insufficient car parking space.

At the same time the authority's primary advisers were looking at the various designs recently built within the authority in an attempt to analyse the use being made of these schools, and to record what teachers saw to be the good and bad features of the designs. There was also considerable concern expressed about the sizes of teaching areas being provided, and the bases on which decisions about space were being made. It was felt that to design the minimum teaching area imposed intolerable limitations upon any attempt to provide adequate working conditions in schools, and that the minimum teaching area (MTA) appeared to be something of a historical accident lacking any justifications or support from research. Answers to questions, such as 'How much space do we need to develop a complete range of primary activities?' or 'How does one analyse the use being made of a building?' or 'If we feel that a building is overcrowded, how do we decide what we mean by overcrowding?' etc. will only be found by careful observation in and assessment of the buildings already built. Against this background the comments of the Project created particular interest in this school. David Medd, who was, at that time, the head of the building development section at DES, and his wife, Mary, who is also an architect, were invited to join with the primary advisers concerned in looking at a number of new and remodelled buildings, and this school was included. After some discussion the Medds produced the following comments:

1. Staff: Head + 10 teachers.
2. NOR: 292.
3. Designed as 1 FE JMI, i.e. 20 pupils.
4. *Present Organization:*

| | |
|---|---|
| Reception – | 38 pupils with 2 teachers |
| Infants – | |
| 1st year 50 pupils<br>2nd year 42 pupils | 92 pupils with 3 teachers |
| Juniors – | |
| 1st year<br>2nd year | 90 pupils with 3 teachers |
| 3rd year | 38 pupils with 1 teacher |
| 4th year | 34 pupils with 1 teacher |
| Total | 292 pupils with 10 teachers. |

5. *Working Areas:*
   (a) Reception and infants, years 1 and 2 – 209.38 sq.m (2253.75 sq. ft) i.e. 1.610 sq.m/pupil (17.3 sq.ft/pupil) at 130 pupils.
   (b) Juniors, years 1 – 4 – 268.945 sq.m (2894.9 sq.ft) i.e. 1.66 sq.m/pupil (17.86 sq.ft/pupil) at 162 pupils.
   (c) Hall (shared by all) – 162.45 sq.m (1748.6 sq.ft)

6. *Total Working Areas:*
   640.775 sq.m (6897.24 sq.ft) i.e. 2.288 sq.m/pupil (24.6 sq.ft/pupil) at 280 pupils
   2.194 sq.m/pupil (23.6 sq.ft/pupil) at 292 pupils.

7. *Minimum Teaching Area (MTA)*
   for 280 pupils at 2.01 sq.m (21.64 sq.ft)/pupil = 564 sq.m·(6,070.85 sq.ft)
   for 292 pupils at 2.08 sq.m (22.39 sq.ft)/pupil = 582 sq.m (6,264.6 sq.ft)

8. *Net Area:* to centre lines of grid of 1.90 m (6.23 ft)
   271 grids x 3.61 sq.m (38.86 sq.ft) = 978.31 sq.m (10,530.44 sq.ft)
   i.e. 3.494 sq.m/pupil (37.6 sq.ft) at 280 pupils
   3.35 sq.m/pupil (36 sq.ft) at 292 pupils

9. *Dining:* 2 sittings at 105 pupils (210 total) in the hall.

   *Reasons for Discomfort in the School*
   The school provides very uncomfortable working conditions, partly because of overcrowding and partly because of unsatisfactory planning. The school only offers 76 sq. m (818.06 sq. ft) over the minimum for the actual enrolment. The regulations MTA has never been defended as a minimum educationally acceptable figure; it is regarded as a figure well below that. However, this alone is not a measure of the unsatisfactory nature of the plan. There are two other factors – the definition of MTA and the quality of the planning.

10. *Definition of MTA*
    The figure of 640.77 sq. m (6897.19 sq. ft) total working area is probably that defined by the LEA. However, much of this area is compromised by circulation both in the local working areas and in the hall. Figure 11 shows diagramatically the inevitable cross circulation between entrances, coats, lavatories, bases and hall which severely compromise the two 'practical activity areas' for the infants and the juniors. Figure 11 also shows the nine openings into the hall which are continuously in use for circulation (originally there were ten but one has since been closed). The hall is also compromised by dining. A fairer assessment of the MTA would take account of these compromising influences, and the shaded area indicates this.
    Thus the total working area would be reduced from 640.77 sq. m (6897.19 sq. ft) to 538.79 sq. m (5799.49 sq. ft) (from 65.5 per cent to 55 per cent respectively of the net area), and to a figure well below the MTA for 280 pupils and 292 pupils. This figure of 538.79 sq. m (5799.49 sq. ft) gives a clearer measure of the discomfort experienced in the school.

11. *An Acceptable Working Area* (indicated diagrammatically in Figure 11)
    (a) If area alone is to be the measure of the quality of a primary school, the figures derived

from the development projects in the 1954-63 period, and the national figures in that period, offer a better yardstick in educational terms. During this period the national average net area for primary schools was between 40 and 42 sq. ft (3.72 – 3.9 sq. m) per pupil, and the working area not less than 60 per cent of this. In Imperial terms, this gave 20 sq. ft (1.86 sq. m)/pupil in local working areas (i.e. 800 sq. ft (74.32 sq. m) classrooms for 40 pupils and 1600 sq. ft (148.64 sq. m) hall – although there was some evidence that the halls should be larger in junior schools). This division of 'local' and 'shared' (hall) working areas is reasonable in primary schools, provided it is remembered that the proportion of 'shared' areas might well increase and the 'local areas' decrease at the upper end of junior schools, as it does in middle schools.

(b) Local Working Areas
If these were planned at 1.9 sq. m (20.45 sq. ft)/pupil:
For 130 infants the present 209.38 sq. m (2253.75 sq. ft) would be increased to 247 sq m (2658.69 sq. ft)
For 162 juniors the present 268.94 sq. m (2894.9 sq. ft) would be increased to 307.8 sq. m (3313.13 sq. ft)
Therefore an extra 'local' working area 76.475 sq. m (823.17 sq. ft) is required for 292 pupils and of 53.675 sq. m (577.75 sq. ft) for 280 pupils.
(These areas are extra to the working areas as assessed, not the effective working areas which are smaller).

Figure 11 indicates that the 42.71 sq. m (459.73 sq. ft) has been taken off the area of the hall as a measure of compromise by circulation, reducing its effective area to 119.74 sq. m (1288.87 sq. ft). This is a nominal rather than a real measure. The capacity of the existing local working area of 478.32 sq. m (5148.59 sq. ft) at 1.9 sq. m (20.45 sq. ft)/pupil would be 251 pupils.

Therefore in quantitative working area terms alone there should not be more than 250 pupils in the school. At the design stage (for 280 pupils) there should have been an additional 155.65 sq. m (1675.4 sq. ft) of working area provided, 101-98 sq. m (1097.7 sq. ft) for under assessment and 53.67 sq. m (577.7 sq. ft) to bring the area up to the 1.95 sq. m (20.99 sq ft)/pupil standard). It therefore appears that the under-assessment of the MTA is more serious than the failure to achieve 1.9 sq. m (20.45 sq. ft)/pupil.

12. *An Acceptable Total Net Area*
978.31 sq. m (10830.44 sq. ft) provided.
If this were planned at 3.8 sq. m/pupil (40-42 sq. ft/pupil), the area would be 1109.6 sq. m (11943.64 sq. ft) for 292 pupils (add 131.29 sq. m (1413.19 sq. ft)
or
1064 sq. m (11452.8 sq. ft) for 280 pupils (add 85.69 sq. m (922.36 sq. ft))
The existing plan at 3.8 sq. m (40.9 sq. ft)/pupil would take 257 pupils. This relates to the assessment of 251 pupils for the working area, and confirms that the present school should not have more than 250-55 pupils in it. However, all these figures do not include the qualitative aspects which are harder to define.

13. *Some Qualitative Aspects*

(a) Circulation within hall. The ten openings into the hall mean that interruption (physical or acoustic) is almost continuous.

(b) Coats. These were designed to be stored on trolleys in bays. Because the trolleys fully occupy the bays, access is only possible when the trolleys are moved out into adjacent working areas, which is, in fact what happens (see infants area Figure 9). It would be better to have pegs on the walls of the bays and correspondingly fewer trolleys making access to them possible. This has been done in the juniors' areas.

(c) Orientation. The infants face exclusively north, the reception north and west, Juniors 4 and 3 exclusively west, Juniors 2 exclusively south, and Juniors 1 south and east. Therefore only 2 of our 8 groups can be considered to have a reasonable orientation and a share of the available sun.

(d) No outdoor working areas.

(e) No enclosed teaching room of any size provided originally. This has been subsequently achieved to a degree by the provision of doors to Junior 4, and a hardboard faced screen to two sides of the area between Junior 2 and Junior 3, but even this has two permanent openings.

(f) 'Activity' areas. These are, to a very large degree, compromised by circulation as Figure 11 indicates. For example, they are crossed transversely by movement from lavs to coats, from entrance to coats, and longitudinally by movement from the entrance to the bases and to the hall. Each activity area has one small sink, i.e. two sinks for 280 pupils. The yardstick that used to be assumed for sinks was one per teacher group, and is still relevant. It will be noticed that the main worktops in which the sinks are placed are not in any way recessed so that pupils circulating inevitably brush past those working at the benches.

(g) The library was planned as the central bay off the west end of the hall, which is unsuitable for acoustic, access and lighting reasons.

(h) The carpeted areas were not planned or furnished in a way that could be used as shared quiet study areas, and are not used as such.

(i) It does not seem that the original plan was designed to serve or support an identifiable organization, being very open and with only vestigial practical and quiet areas. It is not surprising that the school, as can clearly be seen from the furniture layouts and the modifications to doors and screens, has, with the exception of the reception group, attempted to work itself into eight independent table and chair teaching groups. Only the more obvious shortcomings have been noted from this brief visit but, as is common in these circumstances, the atmosphere of the school lacks serenity and security, and the character is dense and disorderly. Were the enrolment reduced to 250, or area added to reduce the density as suggested above, the school would be more comfortable, but the quality shortcomings noted above would remain.

Subsequently the authority has altered the catchment area that the school serves, in order to reduce the numbers in the school. To do this while protecting the best interests of the children concerned means that such changes will inevitably be gradual, and to date the

roll has been reduced by about 20 children. The other thing the authority has done is to increase the amount of available space at the school by providing a demountable. This has added a further 77.76 sq. m (837 sq. ft) of teaching area, making considerable improvements to the ratios shown above. For example:
Total working area becomes 718.535 sq. m (7734.25 sq. ft) i.e. 2.66 sq m (28.63 sq. ft)/pupil at 270 pupils.
Or reducing this total by the amount of space allowed for circulation (see Figure 11) we get a new total of 616.55 sq. m (6636.49 sq. ft) i.e. 2.28 sq. m (24.54 sq. ft)/pupil at 270 pupils.
Again, planned at 1.9 sq. m/pupil the capacity of the new local working areas (allowing for circulation) is 292 pupils.

Lastly, the staffing ratios of teaching and ancillary staff have been considerably improved in the school.

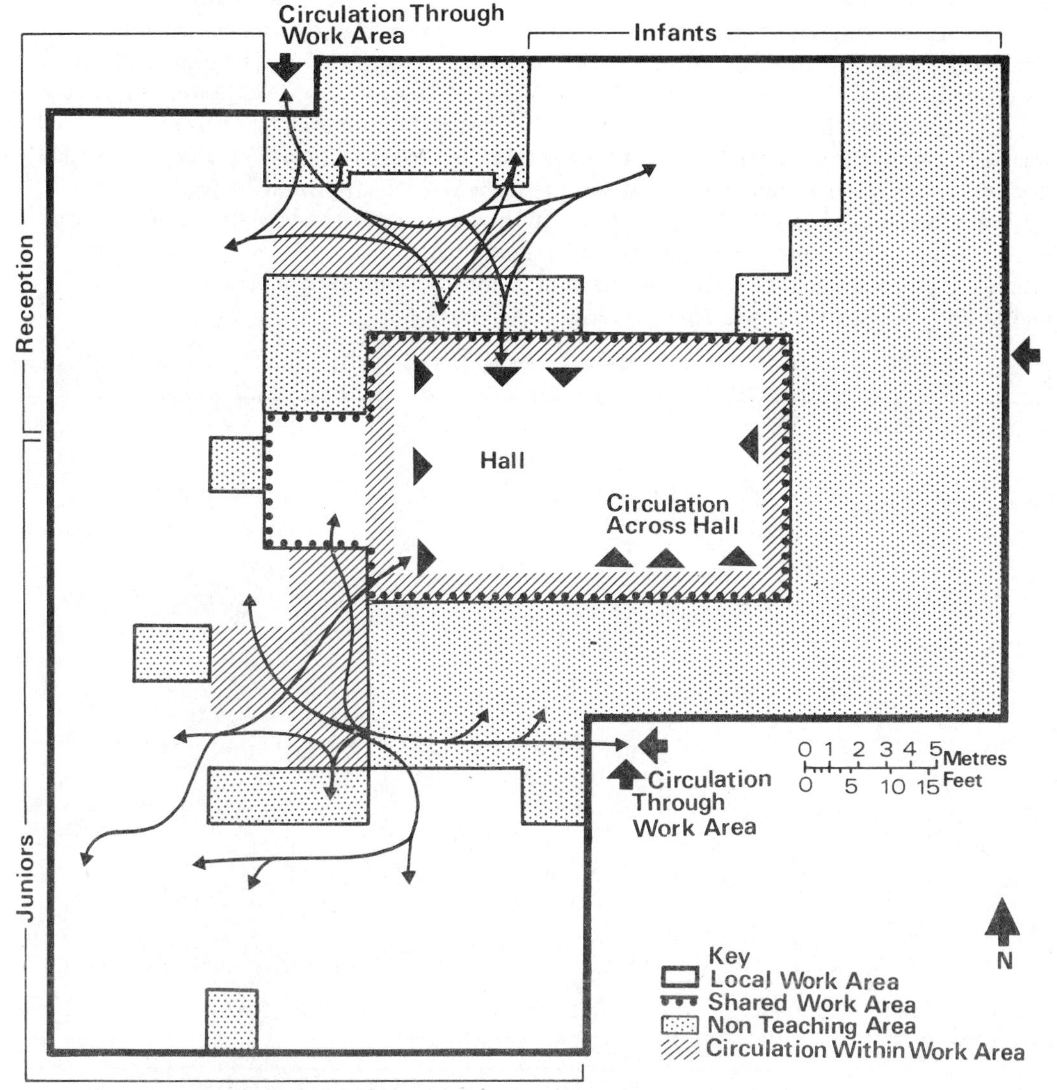


*Figure 11 Circulation flow between various areas*

In spite of the attempts on the part of the authority to decrease the number of pupils, increase the available working area, and improve the staffing in this school, so many of the design faults mentioned above will remain, and one of the purposes of this case study is to draw attention to these and similar faults for future reference. It is also hoped that it will suggest other ways of looking at buildings so as to compare more easily one with another. However, nothing has been said in this case study of the in-service training and preparation offered to teachers moving into open plan schools, nor of the many other features of a school that, in fairness, and given time, should be recorded. Whatever else goes unreported, it must be said that the staff in this particular school care greatly for the children in the school, and do their utmost to provide the very best for them.

Whatever the shortcomings of a case study such as this, it must leave in question the competence of the design process at the local authority level, and doubt the adequacy of the preparation given to teachers, advisers, administrators and architects for participating in this process. The questions relating to the contribution made by central government usually remain unanswered: but in this case the submission that was made in 1972 to central government proposed a school with teaching area of 776 sq. m (8352.79 sq. ft). However, it was pointed out to the authority in March 1972 by central government that the minimum teaching area required was 564 sq. m (6,070.85 sq. ft). No objection was taken to the provision of a greater than normal area where this could be obtained within permitted costs, but clearly, in this case, such an excess was not possible. The cost limit basis reflected in this account has changed since 1972 but there is still, within the current arrangements, the same tendency to cut down on space in new schools. If this case study helps to make us think again about the time scale in which we design and build schools, then it will have served a useful purpose.

*Chapter 11*

# *Conclusion*

## The Design Process

The number of open plan schools has increased markedly since the middle of the 1960s and since the early 1970s a new school of conventional design has been a rarity. Thus by 1976 some ten per cent of all primary schools were open plan. This development has not been without its critics, a common feeling being that it was simply a response to economic pressures – that schools without walls have been foisted on the teaching profession purely to save money. Costs cannot be discounted entirely but in tracing the *origins* of open planning there appears to have been a clear educational rationale. Such schools were designed to mirror the flexibility perceived in contemporary teaching practice, i.e. to provide a match between the built environment and what educators and architects perceived as a significant shift in primary school teaching. However, it is probably true to say that the basis for their continued development has been an economic one. A number of architects are clearly of the view that they cannot now design a conventional building within current cost limits, although this is not a view shared by all. Rattenbury (1978), a staff inspector in the DES Architects and Buildings Branch has recently argued that 'despite the mythology of the staffroom there is no truth in the belief that more open planning has been developed by architects as a means to save money. Any money saved by reducing the number of interior walls has been deliberately ploughed back into an increase in area or an improvement of fittings and finishes.' However, this argument that economies have been used to increase teaching area does not square with DES figures on space standards which show that these have been steadily falling over the last decade. Indeed, in the last DES study of school building a minimum standard of 3.72 $m^2$ (40 $ft^2$) per pupil is proposed, a standard which has not been met since 1968.

Extensive visits to open plan schools, together with an analysis of school plans, indicates clearly that they do not form a homogenous group, a finding which supports those of Gran (1971) and Traub *et al.* (1973). Nevertheless, the assumption that they are has led to basic weaknesses in previous research and underlines erroneous stereotypes generally. In practice, there are large variations in design reflected in the size, area, purpose and configuration of spaces, and they are far from being the large barn-like structures commonly conceived. The majority of teaching units are designed for two or three teachers and over half provide no shared teaching spaces (i.e. Type 2 designs). Paradoxically the most prevalent design types are those which teachers least prefer, just one indicator of the mismatch between design and practice.

One of the most disquieting findings of the study has been the lack of evidence of coherent design policy in most LEAs. This has led to a pattern of school design which is generally fragmented and individualistic instead of a carefully controlled progression whereby new schools are based on the most successful features of earlier buildings.

The reasons for this are not difficult to find. A recent DES report argued that the most important overriding principle is that good design is the outcome of full and effective collaboration between administrative, educational and architectural services operating as equal partners. Such collaboration rarely occurs. Lack of common knowledge and a common vocabulary has led to communication problems and as a result many LEAs find it difficult to provide the right kind of design brief. This is particularly noticeable when there is no adviser in the LEA with special responsibilities in this area. The fact that advisers and architects seldom systematically observe the practice they are supposed to be designing for does not improve the situation. In this context Rattenbury (1978) has argued that this has meant that 'the vast majority of school designs have stemmed solely from instructions to, rather than observations by, architects'.

Not surprisingly, lack of observation, inadequate design briefs and poor communication between educators and architects often leads to poor design, as is shown in the case study in Chapter 10 which highlights typical design problems. In a great many schools complaints were rightly made against practical areas or teaching areas being necessarily used as major thoroughfares, causing additional noise and distraction as well as resulting in loss of teaching space. Circulation space is a critical problem which has not attracted critical concern or policy, although the latest DES design, that of Guillemont school in Hampshire, has spaces which look like short corridors in an attempt to circumvent circulation problems.

The size and siting of spaces are of paramount importance. Restricted space, as in a small quiet room, often results in restricted use, a situation which is exacerbated if the facility is not easily seen from the teaching areas. Many quiet and practical areas are not visible and therefore cannot be adequately supervised. Chapter 9 elaborates the links between poor design and poor usage, a combination which is critical when the amount of space itself is at a premium.

It would be wrong to saddle architects with all the blame for ineffective use of space, but many teachers felt it would have been helpful had the architect visited the school after completion to inform them of the rationale behind the design and the way they had envisaged the use of the spaces provided. Unfortunately most do not, reflecting a wider indisposition to evaluate their buildings. Lee (1976) condemns the lack of evaluation which, he claims, leaves them open to the jibe that they have a cuckoo mentality whereby buildings are laid like the eggs of that irresponsible bird and then hopefully abandoned. Evaluations should be an integral part of the brief and include consultations with the teachers using the building. Teachers clearly desire such a dialogue which could serve to incorporate teacher experiences into future designs.

The gloomy picture described above is, of course, not true of all LEAs or all architects. Some have made determined efforts to seek improvements in practice and have been successful. But for others the process is choked with blocked or unused communication channels. In addition to those already mentioned there is little attempt by LEA staff or architects to communicate with colleagues in other authorities to exchange problems, expertise or experience.

**The Teaching Process**

The erroneous stereotype of open plan schools as large barn-like structures is matched by the equally erroneous stereotype that such schools house a particular kind of teaching – because the building is open so too must be the teaching. This incorrect assumption underlies many previous research efforts but descriptive studies have since dispelled this illusion. An open plan school is no guarantee of open or informal teaching whether it be located in the United States, Canada, Australia, New Zealand, Sweden or Great Britain.

The questionnaire responses in this study indicate that many more teachers claim to be working independently, as they would in conventional classrooms, than cooperatively, irrespective of the age of their pupils. However, this may not hold for ever, since teachers view more cooperation as an ideal. Of interest was the clear relationship between teaching organization and unit design, particularly at the infant level, where there was more cooperation occurring in the more open designs which incorporated shared teaching spaces.

Descriptions of teaching organization emanating from the questionnaire were inevitably fairly broad and should be set against the description of the units observed. The comparisons made in Chapter 6 provide indications of common features but every organization was in reality unique. Not only were they unique but they were also constantly changing. The case studies of organizational history demonstrate this, as do the informal contacts made with the schools subsequent to the observations. Organizations are thus not static but continuously evolving as alternatives are tried, evaluated and modified.

Nevertheless the amount of timetabling of curriculum and space and the frequency of ability grouping within teaching units may surprise some. This is also reflected in smaller case study research such as that of Evans (1979) who found 'the move to an open plan building produced the introduction of a timetable, subject specialisation at the top of the school and a considerable amount of streaming. Thus the very barriers which the educational architects claimed were dissolving . . . were in fact reinforced and in some cases instigated in response to the new forms.'

The questionnaire responses relating to curriculum organization show that it is dominated, particularly at junior level, by the split day approach whereby basics are covered in the mornings and other activities in the afternoons. Nearly 70 per cent of junior teachers claimed that they followed such an approach, a pattern which mirrors that found in Scotland where 'regardless of type of building, there still exists a basic one teacher one class organisation, with generally the basic skills being taught in the morning with environmental studies, projects, centres of interest, choice activities etc. in the afternoons' (Strathclyde, 1976).

Assignment systems, whereby work is assigned for the day or the week with or without pupil choice in order of activity, were used by many teachers, but thematic approaches were rare. About one in eight infant teachers and one in ten junior teachers stated that they formed the basis of the curriculum.

The observational studies were guided by the increasing empirical and theoretical interest in aspects of time (cf. Bennett, 1978a). Focus was therefore placed on curriculum allocation – the amount of time devoted to different areas of the curriculum, and pupil involvement – the amount of time pupils spend on legitimate activities. For curriculum allocation, a coarse and fine grain classification was adopted. The coarse classification broke down the curriculum into areas of experience in much the same manner as the HMI 11–16 curriculum report. The fine classification comprised the actual curriculum activity or task.

In both infant and junior units approximately half the time available was devoted to maths and language activities. As expected, more time was spent on language at infant level but slightly less on maths. The heavy emphasis in these areas meant that there was proportionately less time for others, and in infant units environmental studies and PE both suffered, accounting for less than 4 per cent of the week on average. In junior units time allocated to these areas was higher, at 13 per cent and 9 per cent respectively.

The most surprising finding was the large amount of transition time. Administration took up only a small proportion of the week but transition, which included time spent in changing activities or changing location, took up about a fifth of the school week in infant units. Some researchers have expressed considerable disquiet at the amount of such time, calling it 'non-substance' or 'wasted' time and have used it as an index for operating efficiency (Gump, 1974). This is probably too naive a view. For example, a secondary teacher would not expect to have to tie pupils' shoelaces and would probably consider such a task to be unconnected with teaching. An infant teacher on the other hand might regard this as a legitimate teaching activity. This latter view is accepted, although it is still maintained that such time is non-curricular. As such the distinction made here is between curricular and non-curricular time, which recognizes that non-curricular time could be devoted to useful means. Tying shoe-laces, for example, may well be deemed manipulative or social skill training even though some would argue that it is not the school's responsibility.

The amount of time spent in transitional activities in schools has attracted little research. No study on transition in conventional primary schools in Britain has been located and only one in the United States. There it was found to be less in conventional than open plan schools, but this study was small and the findings not generalizable.

Given the high level of teacher autonomy in Britain it is the class or unit teacher who is usually responsible for the curriculum balance achieved. This balance is important since the evidence would indicate that, other things being equal, one curriculum is intrinsically neither better nor worse than another, but that different curricula result in different patterns of knowledge (Berliner and Rosenshine, 1976). In other words there is a link between curriculum balance and pupil attainment. Concern must therefore be expressed at the large variations found in allocations of time. Some pupils are given the opportunity to study maths for only two hours a week, others for seven hours. Some experience four hours a week of language activities, others twelve hours. Some children get little or no opportunity to work on environmental studies whilst others get seven hours. These figures are based on the observation of only 23 units and the range is therefore probably restricted. A larger sample would probably show greater discrepancies and a perusal of the actual curriculum activities shows even wider discrepancies in the sub-areas of the curriculum.

Gross varieties of this kind are not restricted to open plan primary schools. In an earlier questionnaire study of 871 conventional schools teachers were requested to give details of the amount of time spent on curriculum activities in the previous week. English and maths showed variations from less than two to eight hours per week (Bennett, 1976). Similarly Ashton *et al.* (1975) in the *Aims of Primary Education* study questioned 68 junior headteachers and found that the time spent on language, for example, varied from 3¾ to 13¾ hours per week. In the most recent survey by Bassey (1978) of 893 teachers in Nottinghamshire it was found that time devoted to maths in junior classes varied from less than one hour to eight hours a week, and in language from less than one to ten hours a week.

Large discrepancies in time allocation are therefore widespread, as might be expected in an educational system where there is little central or local control of curriculum. This is not a veiled suggestion that allocation should be standardized. To do so would imply that there is one best balance. Nevertheless, teachers should be aware of the likely outcomes of differing balances and keep in mind that 'the pattern of time allocation to various subject areas and sub-areas is an important consideration when planning and implementing instruction' (Fisher *et al.*, 1977). This is particularly necessary in an organization allowing high pupil choice where some of the responsibility for balance is shared by the pupil.

Curriculum allocation relates to the opportunity teachers provide pupils to study a given curriculum content, whereas pupil involvement represents what pupils make of that opportunity. The first question asked in this latter context was 'what proportion of the school day, discounting breaks and lunch, are pupils involved on curriculum activities?' The average in the junior schools studies was 66.4 per cent, the remainder being made up of 21 per cent non-involvement and 13 per cent administration/transition time. Involvement varied in the different units ranging from 58 per cent to 75 per cent. These averages are based on 24 pupils in each unit, but if individual pupils are considered then the range is far wider. Average involvement in infant units was 61.3 per cent, in part due to the very high levels of administration and transition. The range here was 53 per cent to 70 per cent.

These findings can of course be interpreted in different ways. Some might wish to argue that pupils are involved for nearly two thirds of the week whereas others might complain that on the basis of these figures 9 of the 25 hours a week spent at school are devoted to non-curricular activities. It is of interest that some teachers manage to keep their pupils involved for 19 hours a week and others only 13, a gain of over one day per week. But equally there is likely to be an optimal level, since nobody can maintain 100 per cent involvement. Rosenshine and Berliner (1977), for example, concluded: 'The primary goal of a teacher should be to obtain sufficient academic engaged time (pupil involvement). Unfortunately at this time we do not know how much engaged time is possible or reasonable in a given area, for example, reading, nor do we know the optimal distribution of direct instruction, discussion and individual work.'

In the only published study carried out in Britain available for comparative purposes, Boydell (1975) found that average involvement in six informal junior classrooms was 67 per cent but these observations were carried out in maths lessons only and thus included no transition time. In the light of the limited evidence available it would seem reasonable to suggest that open plan schools are little different in this respect.

The second question posed was 'What proportion of time available for curriculum activities are pupils involved?' For this index, administration and transition time was left out and as a result the figures are substantially higher at 76 per cent for juniors and 79 per cent for infants. Analyses were also undertaken to assess whether involvement varied in the different areas of the curriculum. Of interest here was the fact that the curriculum areas on which most time was spent, i.e. mathematics and language, showed the lowest involvement levels.

Curriculum balance has thus far only been considered in terms of curriculum allocation, but pupil involvement also needs to be considered, since, for example, a very high time allocation to language is no guarantee that pupils will be highly involved, as the illustrations in Chapters 7 and 8 show. Perhaps a better indicator of balance is to be gained from what pupils do rather than what teachers allocate.

It is worth reiterating a point made by Rosenshine and Berliner (1977) that there are problems and discrepancies in the way that researchers have defined and conceptualized pupil involvement, in addition to the usual problems of inference in observational studies. Nevertheless, the importance of pupil involvement levels is less open to dispute. A number of investigations have demonstrated the positive relationships between involvement and achievement (Bennett, 1978). In fact Bloom (1976) goes so far as to argue that pupil involvement is the clearest indicator of the effectiveness of instruction, and a number assert that the secret of successful management is in keeping pupils actively engaged on productive activities (Good, *et al.*, 1975). In fact Westbury (1977) actually defines teaching as 'the management of the attention and time of pupils vis-à-vis the primary educational ends of the classroom'. However, as Gage (1978) points out, time is an empty vessel. There is little point in keeping pupils involved on tasks or activities unless they are comprehensible and worthwhile. The quality of pupil activities in terms of the appropriateness of structure, sequence, level and feedback has attracted little classroom based research but must be a priority for the future.

**Teacher Attitudes**

The design and teaching processes have been considered, but what of teachers themselves – their attitudes to, and preference for, working in an open plan environment? From their responses to the fairly limited list of aims in the questionnaire these do not appear to be different from those in conventional schools, but working in open plan would appear to be different. Teachers stated that the demands made on them are very high, quoting the necessity for careful organization of methods and assessment, for curriculum planning and cooperation, together with the physical exertion brought on by demands on their attention.

These factors, together with the problems of noise and distraction, lead to considerable strain and a concern with keeping their pupils quiet. On the other hand the curriculum is seen as wider and allows for better continuity. Teachers also believe that open plan schools engender a wider involvement with parents and the wider community. Certainly many schools make good use of parents to the benefit of teacher, parent and pupils. Teachers also believe that pupils benefit socially from an open plan setting and are better able to develop independence and initiative. They also believe that certain kinds of children, notably the timid, insecure and difficult would be better placed in a conventional school. More surprising perhaps is the majority's view that standards of work are higher in conventional schools.

Teaching is seen as more stimulating in open plan schools and job satisfaction appears reasonably high. But paradoxically preference for working in such schools is fairly low. Only one in three teachers, compared with over half of headteachers, expressed an actual preference. Perhaps some teachers would be prepared to exchange some of the stimulation and satisfaction found in open plan schools for lower demands made on them in conventional schools. The mediating factors in preference have been outlined in previous research – excessive work loads, the constitution and size of teams, noise and distraction and so on. An additional factor can now be added, the design of the teaching unit. The teachers indicating highest preference worked in the more open Type 1 units. Most approval came from teachers working in two teacher Type 1 units and least approval from those in two teacher Type 2 units. This latter type of design has sometimes been erroneously referred to as semi-open and would seem to deprive the teacher of the autonomy of a conventional classroom without providing the necessary configuration of space for easy cooperation. As mentioned earlier, the two teacher Type 2 design is the most prevalent in schools. That which teachers like the least is provided the most.

Unlike teachers, a majority of headteachers prefer to work in open plan schools since they feel it allows them easier access to the teaching situation and provides the opportunity for them to become more involved in the organization of teaching. Both heads and teachers feel that the role of the head is different, particularly essential being the provision of leadership and support in the teaching units. Heads thus have to walk a tight line – providing overt support without trespassing on the desire for teacher autonomy. Many styles of leadership or abdication of leadership were perceived in schools. This is illustrated to some extent by Case Studies 3 and 4 in Chapter 10 where one head had clear and definite views of the teaching and learning environment he wished to create and converted his staff to his way of thinking and working, whereas the other head adopted a non-leadership role, rationalizing his actions on the grounds of teacher autonomy.

A consensus of adviser opinion is that the school is as good as the head and its staff (Bennett *et al.*, 1976). Comments illustrating this included: 'the head is the key', 'the main factor is the head', 'success depends on the willingness and capability of teachers to consider new approaches and methods', and 'success depends on the relationships of staff working in it'. Given such views and the evidence provided by the questionnaire and interview studies, staffing becomes a vital factor.

**Staffing and Training**

Many LEAs recognize staffing as a very important issue in open plan schools yet conclude that it remains a most intractable problem because of the general lack of expertise in this area. Some have therefore adopted a policy of grooming deputy heads in other open plan schools for headships of new schools, but this does not overcome the problem of training assistant staff. The solution to this must surely lie in pre- and in-service training.

But the majority of headteachers were very unhappy about teacher training, arguing that the products of teacher training simply do not have the skills and competencies necessary for working in open plan settings. In particular they isolated organizational and interpersonal skills necessary for cooperative teaching, expertise in a wide range of teaching methods involving individuals, small and class groups, the ability to make detailed plans of work and appropriate record keeping, specific skills in the teaching of basics, and the capacity to maintain a structured curriculum and share ideas, materials and space. They believe that these can be achieved by the provision of more knowledge on the theory of open plan schooling provided by tutors with actual experience of such schools allied with more active participation in teaching situations on a cooperative basis. Selection should be stricter, to ensure that the students themselves are expert in the basic skills areas.

From their replies it would seem that few colleges have made any specific provision for teachers intending to seek employment in open plan schools, even though there is a one in ten chance that they will do so, a proportion which is likely to increase given current cost limits. The inadequacy of teacher training in this respect is not just a British problem, as can be gauged from Chapter 2, but clearly there is room for more critical thinking and planning in this sector.

It might be thought that in-service training could counteract some of the felt deficiencies in initial training, but this would not appear to be so. Some LEAs have made progress, but they suffer from a problem in common with training colleges: there are few lecturers or advisers with actual experience of teaching in such schools. Visits to other open plan schools form the basic in-service diet, but many teachers feel this to be of limited usefulness since the design is often different to that of their own school and organization. An organization which might be suitable in one design may be impossible in another. The quality of the remaining courses varies, in the words of one teacher, from 'good to hopeless'. Interviews with headteachers and staff brought out the fact that what they ideally require is school based in-service training so that they can make the best of the building they work in. A few LEAs do employ advisory teachers to work in this way, but this practice does not seem to be widespread and its growth is hampered by lack of actual experience in the advisory service. It is hoped that this report may provide ideas or information appropriate for such training.

The staffing policies of LEAs frequently do not help. In staffing new schools 40 per cent of heads are appointed immediately prior to opening, as are all assistant staff. This appears to be an unsatisfactory arrangement given the general lack of experience. It provides no opportunity for common planning or for the development of interpersonal relationships which are so crucial for successful cooperative teaching. The freedom given to the head in selecting staff also varies widely. In considering staffing it is appropriate to consider the findings of earlier research described in Chapter 2. This indicated that ideally only those teachers whose philosophies of education match the proposed organization should be employed, i.e. they should be committed volunteers. It should also be accepted that not all teachers are suited to the open environment.

**Epilogue**

A multi-method approach incorporating a large number of informal visits to schools and LEAs, a national questionnaire survey, extensive observation and in-depth interviews with teachers and those involved with the development of open plan schools was undertaken to investigate the many facets of open plan schooling. This has enabled the presentation of descriptions at differing levels of generality from national statistics to accounts of individual teaching units and pupils. All were directed towards the same purpose – to provide as comprehensive a picture as possible, given the usual constraints, and to highlight problems and perceived successes. However, the purpose was not to pronounce a judgement but to feed back relevant information to interested parties as a genuine diagnostic tool so that they may become aware of the issues in general, and hopefully become stimulated to reflect upon their own practice in particular. There are many implications embedded in the information provided and it is for each of the interested parties – architects, advisers, teachers, teacher trainers and administrators – to consider their relevance and applicability to their own situation. What is needed is a coordinated effort to achieve the common objective of creating an organizational and structural framework which will support optimal learning environments for children.

# *Glossary*

(terms used in this book)

**1. Curriculum terms**

| | |
|---|---|
| Mathematics | Activities designed to develop mathematical concepts and skills including computation, measurement, maths games and sand/water play and cooking dependent on teachers' objectives. |
| Language | Activities which aim to develop language skills – reading, writing, spelling, listening to stories, recitation, etc. |
| Environmental Studies | Activities designed to promote knowledge of the environment comprising the traditional subject areas of history, geography, science and nature study. |
| Aesthetics | Activities linked with the promotion of imaginative self expression; includes painting, drawing, modelling, drama, dance and music. |
| Physical Education | Activities designed to lead to the acquisition of motor skills and coordination and physical well-being; PE, music and movements, swimming, games. |
| Social Education | Activities associated with learning to live together. These include social play (as in Wendy House) and activities with an emphasis on cooperation rather than content. |
| Moral Education | Activities with a religious or moral theme. Includes assembly, certain kinds of singing and story and recitation (as in prayers). |
| Administration | Such activities as taking the register, dinner money, and general directions not directly related to matters of curriculum. |
| Transition | Usually instigated by the teacher in beginning or terminating an activity involving clearing materials, moving groups to a new location, preparation for PE, etc. |
| Curriculum Allocation | The amount of the school day or week allocated to different areas of the curriculum. This is usually determined by the teacher but can to some extent be pupil determined in organizations allowing a degree of pupil choice. |
| Curriculum Balance | Used here to refer to the profiles of curriculum allocations across all curriculum areas. |

Involvement

| | |
|---|---|
| i) Overall | The proportion of the time pupils actually spend working on legitimate curriculum activities in relation to the whole school day (minus breaks and lunch) or school week. |
| ii) Curriculum | As above but with administration and transition time deducted from length of school day or week. |
| Active Curriculum | A term derived from the work of Bussis and Chittenden. Used here to denote an organization which allows a degree of pupil choice in both content and process. |
| Passive Curriculum | Used here to denote an organization which is teacher centred. Pupils have little choice in content and process. |
| Assignment | Organization whereby the teacher assigns work (tasks/activities) to pupils for the whole day or sometimes the whole week. The teacher may or may not allow pupils choice in the order in which these tasks are undertaken. |
| Rolling Timetable | An organization in which pupils are assigned work (tasks/activities) in relation to a given number of curriculum elements which are repeated, e.g. maths, language, creative activities, PE; then, maths, language, creative activities, PE . . . Sometimes called a workwheel. |
| Split Day | An organization where basics are covered in the morning and other work such as art and craft and environmental studies, topic work and so on in the afternoon. |
| Thematic Approach | An organization whereby the curriculum is derived from a series of topics or projects. Pupils may or may not have a degree of choice in the topic chosen. |

**2. Physical/Design Terms**

| | |
|---|---|
| Type I | A design of teaching unit which incorporates shared teaching space in addition to shared practical and/or quiet room facilities. |
| Type II | A design of teaching unit which does not incorporate shared teaching space although shared practical and/or quiet rooms are usually available. |
| Quiet Room | Also known as withdrawal room, group room, kiva or den. Here defined as a room varying in size but not larger than $32m^2$ (344.44 sq. ft), having four walls and a door and located in the teaching unit. Designed for small group work, noisy or quiet activities. |

| | |
|---|---|
| Practical Area | Also known as wet or messy areas. These are defined as those areas which have sinks and a floor finish which is suitable for wet activities e.g. quarry or tiles of non-slip finish, and situated in the teaching unit. Occasionally this area contains cooking facilities, kiln, etc. Designed for work in the aesthetics area. |
| Shared Teaching Space | Found in Type I designs and includes all space other than practical areas or quiet rooms which are designed for shared teaching and working. |
| Home Base | Dependent on unit design this could be a classroom size space (in Type 2 units) or a small semi-enclosed occasionally carpeted space in the shared teaching space. Often used for registration, story time, administration, etc. |
| Space Density | |
| i) Designed | The area per pupil as in the design brief. |
| ii) Actual | The area per pupil in relation to the actual number of pupils in the unit. |
| Over-pupilled | Indicates a unit which houses more pupils than it was designed for. |
| Under-pupilled | Indicates a unit which houses fewer pupils than it was designed for. |
| Circulation Spaces | What are called corridors in conventional schools but ill-defined in open plan schools. Circulation space is here defined as the space required for teachers and pupils to move from one location within the unit to another. This is not usually specified on school plans and is counted as teaching space. |
| MTA | Recommended minimum teaching area defined in terms of space per pupil. |
| Design or Architect's Brief | A document provided for the architect by the LEA defining what it wants the architect to design. The scope and contents of such briefs vary widely. |

# APPENDIX A
## Questionnaire Survey

| | *Actual Teaching Organization* | | | | *Ideal Teaching Organization* | | | |
|---|---|---|---|---|---|---|---|---|
| | Infant | First | Junior | Primary | Infant | First | Junior | Primary |
| (a) Teachers operating independently | 18.7 | 14.7 | 20.1 | 20.3 | 7.6 | 4.3 | 6.2 | 5.5 |
| (b) Teachers mainly operating independently but cooperating a little with other teacher(s) e.g. reading story to two groups | 52.6 | 42.3 | 33.7 | 46.1 | 26.8 | 19.0 | 12.5 | 17.8 |
| (c) Teachers mainly operating independently but planning cooperatively, e.g. who teaches what, where and at what time | 37.6 | 49.7 | 41.8 | 42.5 | 28.7 | 38.7 | 26.7 | 31.1 |
| (d) Teachers operating independently for basic subjects but cooperating on project/topic work | 36.1 | 39.3 | 34.1 | 39.8 | 32.1 | 27.6 | 28.9 | 39.1 |
| (e) Teachers cooperating for basic subjects but operating independently for project/topic work | 8.4 | 8.6 | 14.3 | 8.7 | 7.6 | 8.0 | 9.2 | 7.7 |
| (f) Cooperative/team teaching planned on a day-to-day basis | 11.8 | 17.8 | 12.8 | 8.6 | 12.4 | 15.3 | 11.7 | 8.6 |
| (g) Cooperative/team teaching with each teacher specializing in certain areas of the curriculum | 12.4 | 12.9 | 22.0 | 14.9 | 16.1 | 23.9 | 26.4 | 18.0 |
| (h) Cooperative/team teaching with no teacher specialism | 14.7 | 14.7 | 17.2 | 11.1 | 17.6 | 8.6 | 15.0 | 13.2 |
| (i) Other | | | | | 4.7 | 6.7 | 4.0 | 3.6 |
| N = | 380 | 163 | 273 | 713 | 380 | 163 | 273 | 713 |

*Table A1 Actual and ideal teaching organization by type of school (headteachers) (%)*

| | Actual Teaching Organization | | | | Ideal Teaching Organization | | | |
|---|---|---|---|---|---|---|---|---|
| | Infant | First | Junior | Primary | Infant | First | Junior | Primary |
| (a) Usually operate as an independent teacher | 26.4 | 28.1 | 28.6 | 32.5 | 15.2 | 11.4 | 14.4 | 14.8 |
| (b) Mainly independent but cooperate a little with other teacher(s) e.g. reading a story to two groups | 45.8 | 46.3 | 22.7 | 38.5 | 27.2 | 28.4 | 11.7 | 23.8 |
| (c) Mainly independent in teaching but plan cooperatively e.g. who teaches what, where and at what time | 16.2 | 23.0 | 24.0 | 21.0 | 11.2 | 13.2 | 15.5 | 15.0 |
| (d) Independent for basic subjects but cooperate on project/topic work | 18.7 | 21.0 | 21.7 | 18.9 | 17.8 | 22.3 | 21.5 | 20.0 |
| (e) Cooperate for basic subjects but independent for project/topic work | 2.2 | 4.3 | 8.2 | 3.2 | 2.9 | 2.8 | 6.2 | 2.9 |
| (f) Usually cooperate/team teaching but without a lot of prior planning, i.e. plan on a day-to-day basis | 3.2 | 2.3 | 2.0 | 2.1 | 2.0 | 1.8 | 1.1 | 1.1 |
| (g) Usually cooperative/team teaching but with each teacher specializing in certain areas of the curriculum | 7.0 | 10.4 | 14.9 | 9.7 | 9.4 | 11.1 | 16.5 | 12.8 |
| (h) Usually cooperative/team teaching with no teacher specialism | 12.6 | 7.8 | 9.0 | 7.8 | 12.2 | 8.1 | 9.6 | 7.2 |
| (i) Other/undecided | | | | | 9.4 | 11.7 | 10.6 | 10.8 |
| N = | 712 | 395 | 759 | 1497 | 712 | 395 | 759 | 1497 |

*Table A2 Actual and ideal teaching organization by type of school (teachers) (%)*

| Teaching Organization | Pairs | | Triples | | Quads | | Multis | | Type 1 | Type 2 |
|---|---|---|---|---|---|---|---|---|---|---|
| Type | 1 | 2 | 1 | 2 | 1 | 2 | 1 | 2 | | |
| (a) Usually operate as an independent teacher | 15.8 | 34.1 | 21.9 | 33.8 | 15.0 | 25.7 | 16.2 | 28.2 | 17.2 | 30.5 |
| (b) Mainly independent but cooperate a little with other teacher(s) e.g. reading story to two groups | 37.0 | 45.7 | 43.3 | 51.9 | 43.9 | 46.3 | 37.8 | 52.4 | 40.5 | 49.1 |
| (c) Mainly independent in teaching but plan cooperatively e.g. who teaches what, where and at what time | 18.5 | 17.8 | 24.5 | 18.8 | 33.6 | 26.3 | 18.0 | 12.6 | 23.7 | 18.9 |
| (d) Independent for basic subjects but cooperate on project/topic work | 25.3 | 18.2 | 24.5 | 14.4 | 24.3 | 25.1 | 18.0 | 22.3 | 23.0 | 20.0 |
| (e) Cooperate for basic subjects but independent for project/topic work | 3.7 | 3.5 | 0.4 | 3.8 | 8.4 | 2.9 | 7.2 | 1.9 | 4.9 | 3.0 |
| (f) Usually cooperative/team teaching but without a lot of prior planning, i.e. plan on a day-to-day basis | 4.0 | 2.4 | 3.4 | 0.0 | 5.6 | 4.6 | 2.7 | 0.0 | 3.9 | 1.8 |
| (g) Usually cooperative/team teaching with each teacher specializing in certain areas of the curriculum | 17.2 | 7.3 | 10.3 | 7.2 | 15.0 | 3.4 | 8.1 | 7.8 | 12.7 | 6.4 |
| (h) Usually cooperative/team teaching with no teacher specialism | 12.5 | 8.1 | 14.2 | 6.6 | 15.0 | 5.7 | 18.9 | 6.8 | 15.2 | 6.8 |
| N = | 297 | 455 | 233 | 320 | 107 | 175 | 111 | 108 | 748 | 1053 |

*Table A3 Teaching organization of infant teachers by design of unit (%)*

| | Pairs | | Triples | | Quads | | Multis | | Type 1 | Type 2 |
|---|---|---|---|---|---|---|---|---|---|---|
| Type | 1 | 2 | 1 | 2 | 1 | 2 | 1 | 2 | | |
| (a) Usually operate as an independent teacher | 14.4 | 34.2 | 14.3 | 24.6 | 16.8 | 36.9 | 20.3 | 31.2 | 16.5 | 31.7 |
| (b) Mainly independent but cooperate a little with other teacher(s) e.g. reading story to two groups | 13.8 | 28.4 | 22.9 | 21.5 | 20.0 | 27.7 | 20.3 | 19.5 | 19.3 | 24.3 |
| (c) Mainly independent in teaching but plan cooperatively e.g. who teaches what, where and at what time | 26.9 | 21.4 | 29.5 | 33.8 | 28.4 | 27.2 | 23.0 | 35.1 | 27.0 | 29.4 |
| (d) Independent for basic subjects but cooperate on project/topic work | 24.0 | 19.7 | 41.0 | 32.3 | 37.9 | 18.0 | 23.0 | 20.8 | 31.5 | 22.7 |
| (e) Cooperate for basic subjects but independent for project/topic work | 2.4 | 8.4 | 5.7 | 10.0 | 1.1 | 3.9 | 5.4 | 9.1 | 3.7 | 7.9 |
| (f) Usually cooperative/team teaching but without a lot of prior planning i.e. plan on a day-to-day basis | 1.8 | 1.4 | 1.9 | 0.0 | 7.4 | 2.4 | 1.4 | 0.0 | 3.1 | 1.0 |
| (g) Usually cooperative/team teaching with each teacher specializing in certain areas of the curriculum | 30.5 | 11.0 | 14.3 | 14.6 | 8.4 | 10.2 | 14.9 | 10.4 | 17.0 | 11.6 |
| (h) Usually cooperative/team teaching with no teacher specialism | 10.2 | 7.2 | 13.3 | 5.4 | 18.9 | 3.9 | 10.8 | 3.9 | 13.3 | 5.1 |
| N = | 167 | 345 | 105 | 130 | 95 | 206 | 74 | 77 | 441 | 758 |

*Table A4 Teaching organization of junior teachers by design of unit (%)*

| | Actual Curriculum Organization | | | | Ideal Curriculum Organization | | | |
|---|---|---|---|---|---|---|---|---|
| | Infant | First | Junior | Primary | Infant | First | Junior | Primary |
| (a) Pupils being given assignments at the beginning of the day or week to be carried out in the order given by the teacher | 21.3 | 25.8 | 27.8 | 24.5 | 15.0 | 17.2 | 19.4 | 17.5 |
| (b) As (a) but pupils given free choice as to the order in in which they carry out assignments | 22.1 | 26.4 | 25.3 | 24.7 | 22.9 | 23.9 | 22.3 | 22.3 |
| (c) Pupils being assigned a basic curriculum consisting of a given number of activities which are repeated. Teachers sometimes call this a 'rolling timetable' e.g. maths, creative work, English, leading to maths, creative work, English, etc. | 25.5 | 15.3 | 15.4 | 17.5 | 22.4 | 14.7 | 13.2 | 16.5 |
| (d) Curriculum mainly taught by the teacher but varying from day to day | 28.7 | 29.4 | 25.6 | 27.9 | 16.8 | 12.9 | 17.2 | 17.1 |
| (f) Major emphasis on project/topic work (incorporating basics) mainly chosen by the teacher | 16.6 | 17.8 | 14.3 | 13.5 | 14.7 | 11.7 | 15.4 | 13.0 |
| (g) Major emphasis on project/topic work (incorporating basics) mainly chosen by the pupils | 8.2 | 8.0 | 3.7 | 2.7 | 9.7 | 8.6 | 5.1 | 5.8 |
| (h) Other | | | | | 4.5 | 8.0 | 3.7 | 4.3 |
| N = | 380 | 163 | 273 | 713 | 380 | 163 | 273 | 713 |

*Table A5 Actual and ideal curriculum organization by type of school (headteachers) (%)*

| | Infant | First | Junior | Primary |
|---|---|---|---|---|
| (a) Pupils are given assignments at the beginning of the day or week and pupils carry out these assignments in the order given by the teacher | 14.5 | 20.3 | 12.8 | 17.1 |
| (b) As (a) but pupils are given free choice as to the order in which they are carried out | 15.0 | 16.5 | 15.4 | 18.2 |
| (c) Groups of pupils are assigned a basic curriculum consisting of a given number of activities which are repeated. Teachers sometimes call this a 'rolling timetable' e.g. maths, creative work, English, leading to maths, creative work, English etc. | 26.1 | 17.0 | 10.8 | 15.0 |
| (d) Basics usually covered in the morning and creative activities/topic work in the afternoon | 36.4 | 48.9 | 63.2 | 51.9 |
| (e) Curriculum mainly taught by the teacher but varied from day to day | 22.6 | 20.8 | 20.8 | 22.1 |
| (f) Major emphasis on project/topic work (incorporating basics) mainly chosen by the teacher | 10.0 | 10.8 | 8.6 | 6.3 |
| (g) Major emphasis on project/topic work (incorporating basics) mainly chosen by the pupils | 3.7 | 4.1 | 0.9 | 1.2 |
| N = | 712 | 395 | 759 | 1497 |

*Table A6 Actual curriculum organization by type of school (teachers) (%)*

| | *Infant* | *First* | *Junior* | *Primary* | *Rank Order* | | | |
|---|---|---|---|---|---|---|---|---|
| N = | 380 | 163 | 273 | 713 | I | F | J | P |
| 1. To enable the child to develop as a happy, cheerful and well-balanced individual | 4.6 | 4.6 | 4.5 | 4.5 | 1 | 1 | 1 | 1 |
| 2. To equip the child with basic skills in reading, writing and number | 4.5 | 4.6 | 4.5 | 4.5 | 2 | 1 | 1 | 1 |
| 3. To encourage the child to be tolerant, respecting and appreciating the feelings and views of others | 4.4 | 4.4 | 4.4 | 4.3 | 3 | 3 | 3 | 3 |
| 4. To develop in the child good attitudes to work | 4.3 | 4.4 | 4.3 | 4.2 | 4 | 3 | 4 | 4 |
| 5. To encourage the child to learn how to learn | 4.3 | 4.4 | 4.3 | 4.2 | 4 | 3 | 4 | 4 |
| 6. To inculcate good standards of behaviour | 4.1 | 4.1 | 4.1 | 4.0 | 8 | 8 | 6 | 6 |
| 7. To help children to learn to cooperate with each other | 4.2 | 4.3 | 4.1 | 4.0 | 6 | 6 | 6 | 6 |
| 8. To enable the child as an individual to come to terms with and live in our society | 4.2 | 4.2 | 4.1 | 4.0 | 6 | 7 | 6 | 6 |
| 9. To help the child to find enjoyment in all aspects of school life | 4.0 | 3.9 | 3.9 | 3.9 | 9 | 11 | 10 | 9 |
| 10. To develop the child's creative abilities to the full | 3.9 | 4.0 | 4.0 | 3.9 | 11 | 9 | 9 | 9 |
| 11. To develop in the child a high level of oracy | 4.0 | 4.0 | 3.9 | 3.8 | 9 | 9 | 10 | 11 |
| 12. To encourage the child to conform to the accepted morals and values of our society | 3.8 | 3.7 | 3.8 | 3.7 | 12 | 12 | 12 | 12 |
| 13. To encourage self-expression | 3.7 | 3.6 | 3.7 | 3.6 | 13 | 13 | 13 | 13 |
| 14. To promote a high level of academic attainment | 3.3 | 3.2 | 3.4 | 3.3 | 14 | 14 | 14 | 14 |
| 15. To prepare the child for academic work in the secondary school | 2.8 | 2.8 | 3.1 | 3.1 | 15 | 15 | 15 | 15 |

*Table A7 Aims of Education: headteachers by type of school (mean scores)*

| | Infant | First | Junior | Primary | Rank Order | | | |
|---|---|---|---|---|---|---|---|---|
| N = | 712 | 395 | 759 | 1497 | I | F | J | P |
| 1. To equip the child with basic skills in reading, writing and number | 4.6 | 4.5 | 4.6 | 4.6 | 1 | 2 | 1 | 1 |
| 2. To enable the child to develop as a happy, cheerful and well-balanced individual | 4.6 | 4.6 | 4.4 | 4.5 | 1 | 1 | 2 | 2 |
| 3. To encourage the child to be tolerant, respecting and appreciating the feelings and views of others | 4.3 | 4.3 | 4.3 | 4.2 | 3 | 3 | 3 | 3 |
| 4. To encourage the child to learn how to learn | 4.2 | 4.2 | 4.1 | 4.2 | 4 | 4 | 4 | 3 |
| 5. To help children to learn to cooperate with each other | 4.1 | 4.1 | 4.0 | 4.1 | 5 | 5 | 5 | 5 |
| 6. To develop in the child good attitudes to work | 4.1 | 4.1 | 4.0 | 4.0 | 5 | 5 | 5 | 6 |
| 7. To enable the child as an individual to come to terms with and live in our society | 4.1 | 4.0 | 4.0 | 4.0 | 5 | 7 | 5 | 6 |
| 8. To help the child to find enjoyment in all aspects of school life | 4.1 | 3.8 | 3.7 | 3.9 | 5 | 8 | 9 | 8 |
| 9. To inculcate good stands of behaviour | 4.0 | 3.8 | 3.9 | 3.9 | 9 | 8 | 8 | 8 |
| 10. To develop the child's creative abilities to the full | 3.8 | 3.7 | 3.7 | 3.8 | 10 | 10 | 9 | 10 |
| 11. To encourage self-expression | 3.8 | 3.7 | 3.7 | 3.7 | 10 | 10 | 9 | 11 |
| 12. To develop in the child a high level of oracy | 3.8 | 3.7 | 3.6 | 3.7 | 10 | 10 | 13 | 11 |
| 13. To encourage the child to conform to the accepted morals and values of our society | 3.8 | 3.6 | 3.7 | 3.6 | 10 | 13 | 9 | 13 |
| 14. To promote a high level of academic attainment | 3.1 | 3.1 | 3.1 | 3.1 | 14 | 14 | 15 | 14 |
| 15. To prepare the child for academic work in the secondary school | 2.9 | 3.0 | 3.2 | 3.1 | 15 | 15 | 14 | 14 |

*Table A8 Aims of Education: teachers by type of school (mean scores)*

| | *Infant* | *First* | *Junior* | *Primary* |
|---|---|---|---|---|
| *Teaching and Curriculum Organization* | | | | |
| It is hard to maintain standards | 3.2 | 3.2 | 3.0 | 3.3 |
| Use can be made of teacher specialism | 2.5 | 2.5 | 2.5 | 2.5 |
| Teachers agree on methods and standards | 2.4 | 2.5 | 2.7 | 2.3 |
| A lot of organization is required | 1.6 | 1.7 | 1.7 | 1.7 |
| It is easier to organize the curriculum | 3.1 | 3.1 | 3.2 | 3.2 |
| It is easy for a teacher to work with small groups | 2.8 | 2.8 | 2.9 | 2.8 |
| Teachers have to cooperate | 1.9 | 2.0 | 2.0 | 1.9 |
| It is easier to cover for teacher absence | 3.0 | 3.2 | 2.9 | 2.9 |
| A smaller teacher — pupil ratio is essential | 1.7 | 1.8 | 1.8 | 1.8 |
| Teachers share materials | 2.0 | 2.0 | 2.2 | 2.0 |
| Teachers share their problems | 2.0 | 2.0 | 2.2 | 2.1 |
| There are excessive demands on teachers' attention | 2.3 | 2.3 | 2.3 | 2.3 |
| Job satisfaction is high | 2.4 | 2.5 | 2.7 | 2.4 |
| Teachers feel exposed | 3.3 | 3.2 | 3.2 | 3.2 |
| Teachers are very tired at the end of the day | 1.9 | 1.9 | 1.9 | 1.9 |
| Tempers tend to get frayed as the day goes on | 3.2 | 3.0 | 2.9 | 3.2 |
| Teachers worry about keeping their own group quiet | 2.6 | 2.4 | 2.5 | 2.5 |
| There is a family atmosphere | 2.4 | 2.6 | 2.7 | 2.5 |
| Supervision is difficult | 3.1 | 3.0 | 3.1 | 3.1 |
| Getting to know all the children is difficult | 3.7 | 3.6 | 3.6 | 3.8 |
| I would prefer to teach in a room of my own | 3.0 | 2.9 | 2.7 | 2.8 |
| There are no personality clashes bet'.een teachers | 3.0 | 3.0 | 3.2 | 2.9 |
| There is insufficient privacy | 3.1 | 3.0 | 2.9 | 2.9 |
| Teaching opportunities are lost | 3.2 | 3.1 | 3.0 | 3.2 |
| Teachers have to be more adaptable | 1.8 | 1.8 | 1.8 | 1.8 |
| Teachers learn a great deal from each other | 2.0 | 2.0 | 2.2 | 2.1 |
| There are too many visitors | 3.3 | 3.1 | 3.2 | 3.2 |
| *Design of Unit* | | | | |
| The design enables teachers to work together | 2.4 | 2.4 | 2.5 | 2.4 |
| There is great freedom of movement | 2.3 | 2.4 | 2.7 | 2.5 |
| There is plenty of space to do things | 3.1 | 3.1 | 3.4 | 3.3 |
| Noise spreads from one group to another | 2.1 | 2.1 | 2.0 | 2.1 |
| There is easy access to equipment | 2.1 | 2.2 | 2.4 | 2.3 |
| There are interruptions from people passing through | 2.9 | 2.6 | 2.6 | 2.7 |
| The design is conducive to team teaching | 2.6 | 2.6 | 2.8 | 2.7 |
| It is possible to close off | 3.1 | 3.0 | 3.3 | 3.1 |
| The design dictates teaching style | 2.9 | 2.8 | 2.9 | 3.0 |
| Space is well utilized | 2.4 | 2.4 | 2.8 | 2.6 |
| There are too many pupils for the space provided | 2.4 | 2.3 | 2.3 | 2.2 |
| *Pupils* | | | | |
| Children have a lot of contact with other teachers | 2.5 | 2.5 | 2.6 | 2.5 |
| Children are distracted by noise | 2.6 | 2.5 | 2.4 | 2.5 |
| Children tend to rush around | 3.1 | 3.0 | 3.1 | 3.2 |
| It is easy to cater for the insecure child | 3.3 | 3.3 | 3.5 | 3.3 |
| It is easy to cater for the difficult child | 3.4 | 3.5 | 3.5 | 3.4 |
| Children tend to wander about | 3.0 | 2.8 | 2.9 | 2.9 |

NB A score of 1 indicates strong agreement, 5 strong disagreement

*Table A9 Attitudes to open plan: teachers in infant, first, junior and primary schools (mean scores)*

| | Infant | | First | | Junior | | Primary | |
|---|---|---|---|---|---|---|---|---|
| | Conv. | OP | Conv. | OP | Conv. | OP | Conv. | OP |
| 1. Children are more independent and responsible | 3.6 | 2.2 | 3.7 | 2.2 | 3.6 | 2.2 | 3.6 | 2.3 |
| 2. Teachers have more preparation to do | 3.8 | 2.0 | 3.8 | 1.9 | 3.8 | 1.9 | 3.9 | 1.9 |
| 3. Bright children progress more | 3.3 | 2.9 | 3.1 | 2.9 | 3.1 | 2.9 | 3.0 | 3.0 |
| 4. Teaching is more stimulating | 3.7 | 2.1 | 3.7 | 2.2 | 3.5 | 2.2 | 3.5 | 2.3 |
| 5. Probationers benefit more | 3.4 | 2.4 | 3.4 | 2.3 | 3.2 | 2.3 | 3.3 | 2.6 |
| 6. The average child escapes notice more | 3.5 | 3.5 | 3.6 | 3.2 | 3.5 | 3.1 | 3.5 | 3.2 |
| 7. Standards of work tend to be higher | 3.2 | 3.1 | 3.1 | 3.2 | 3.0 | 3.1 | 3.0 | 3.2 |
| 8. Children are more easily distracted | 3.7 | 2.7 | 3.6 | 2.7 | 3.8 | 2.6 | 3.7 | 2.5 |
| 9. Children benefit more socially | 3.8 | 1.9 | 3.8 | 1.9 | 3.8 | 2.0 | 3.8 | 2.0 |
| 10. Teaching is more of a strain | 3.8 | 2.2 | 3.9 | 2.1 | 3.9 | 2.1 | 3.9 | 2.0 |
| 11. The dull child benefits less | 3.1 | 3.7 | 3.1 | 3.6 | 3.2 | 3.5 | 3.0 | 3.5 |
| 12. There are more discipline problems | 3.5 | 3.2 | 3.4 | 3.3 | 3.5 | 3.2 | 3.5 | 3.1 |
| 13. Parental involvement is easier | 3.7 | 2.3 | 3.7 | 2.3 | 3.6 | 2.4 | 3.6 | 2.3 |
| 14. There is greater continuity for children | 3.4 | 2.3 | 3.5 | 2.4 | 3.3 | 2.6 | 3.3 | 2.5 |
| 15. The curriculum is wider | 3.5 | 2.6 | 3.7 | 2.5 | 3.6 | 2.5 | 3.5 | 2.6 |
| 16. Community involvement is easier | 3.6 | 2.3 | 3.7 | 2.3 | 3.5 | 2.4 | 3.5 | 2.5 |
| 17. Teachers feel more confident | 2.7 | 3.1 | 2.7 | 3.0 | 2.7 | 3.0 | 2.6 | 3.2 |
| 18. More curriculum planning is required | 3.8 | 1.9 | 3.8 | 1.8 | 3.7 | 1.9 | 3.7 | 2.0 |
| 19. The timid/insecure child is better off | 2.9 | 3.1 | 2.8 | 3.0 | 2.8 | 3.1 | 2.8 | 3.1 |
| 20. The design dictates teaching method | 3.2 | 2.7 | 3.1 | 2.6 | 3.0 | 2.5 | 2.9 | 2.6 |
| 21. Keeping areas orderly and tidy is difficult | 3.7 | 2.5 | 3.6 | 2.5 | 3.7 | 2.5 | 3.7 | 2.4 |
| 22. It is possible to provide a wider variety of equipment | 3.8 | 2.0 | 3.9 | 1.9 | 3.7 | 2.1 | 3.7 | 2.2 |
| N = | 380 | | 163 | | 273 | | 713 | |

NB A score of 1 indicates strong agreement, 5 strong disagreement.

*Table A10 Opinions about open plan and conventional schools: headteachers (mean scores)*

| | Infant | | First | | Junior | | Primary | |
|---|---|---|---|---|---|---|---|---|
| | Conv. | OP | Conv. | OP | Conv. | OP | Conv. | OP |
| 1. Children are more independent and responsible | 3.5 | 2.5 | 3.3 | 2.6 | 3.2 | 2.7 | 3.3 | 2.6 |
| 2. Teachers have more preparation to do | 3.6 | 2.3 | 3.4 | 2.3 | 3.4 | 2.3 | 3.5 | 2.3 |
| 3. Bright children progress more | 3.0 | 3.1 | 2.8 | 3.1 | 2.7 | 3.2 | 2.8 | 3.3 |
| 4. Teaching is more stimulating | 3.4 | 2.5 | 3.2 | 2.6 | 3.1 | 2.8 | 3.3 | 2.6 |
| 5. Probationers benefit more | 3.1 | 2.7 | 2.9 | 2.9 | 3.0 | 2.8 | 3.0 | 2.8 |
| 6. The average child escapes notice more | 3.7 | 3.0 | 3.6 | 3.1 | 3.6 | 3.0 | 3.7 | 3.1 |
| 7. Standards of work tend to be higher | 2.9 | 3.3 | 2.7 | 3.3 | 2.6 | 3.4 | 2.8 | 3.5 |
| 8. Children are more easily distracted | 3.8 | 2.4 | 3.8 | 2.2 | 3.7 | 2.4 | 3.8 | 2.3 |
| 9. Children benefit more socially | 3.6 | 2.1 | 3.4 | 2.2 | 3.4 | 2.4 | 3.5 | 2.2 |
| 10. Teaching is more of a strain | 3.8 | 2.3 | 3.7 | 2.2 | 3.7 | 2.3 | 3.8 | 2.3 |
| 11. The dull child benefits less | 3.2 | 3.4 | 3.3 | 3.4 | 3.4 | 3.2 | 3.3 | 3.3 |
| 12. There are more discipline problems | 3.7 | 2.9 | 3.7 | 2.8 | 3.7 | 2.7 | 3.8 | 2.8 |
| 13. Parental involvement is easier | 3.4 | 2.4 | 3.4 | 2.6 | 3.3 | 2.7 | 3.5 | 2.6 |
| 14. There is greater continuity for children | 3.2 | 2.6 | 3.1 | 2.7 | 2.9 | 2.9 | 3.2 | 2.7 |
| 15. The curriculum is wider | 3.5 | 2.6 | 3.4 | 2.9 | 3.2 | 2.8 | 3.4 | 2.8 |
| 16. Community involvement is easier | 3.5 | 2.5 | 3.4 | 2.6 | 3.3 | 2.7 | 3.4 | 2.6 |
| 17. Teachers feel more confident | 2.7 | 3.2 | 2.7 | 3.2 | 2.7 | 3.3 | 2.7 | 3.2 |
| 18. More curriculum planning is required | 3.5 | 2.2 | 3.4 | 2.1 | 3.4 | 2.3 | 3.5 | 2.2 |
| 19. The timid/insecure child is better off | 2.5 | 3.4 | 2.5 | 3.4 | 2.6 | 3.4 | 2.6 | 3.4 |
| 20. The design dictates teaching method | 3.0 | 2.7 | 2.9 | 2.7 | 3.0 | 2.7 | 3.1 | 2.7 |
| 21. Keeping areas orderly and tidy is difficult | 3.8 | 2.7 | 3.7 | 2.6 | 3.7 | 2.5 | 3.8 | 2.4 |
| 22. It is possible to provide a wider variety of equipment | 3.7 | 2.1 | 3.6 | 2.2 | 3.4 | 2.5 | 3.6 | 2.4 |
| N = | 712 | | 395 | | 759 | | 1497 | |

NB A score of 1 indicates strong agreement, 5 strong disagreement.

*Table A11 Opinions about open plan and conventional schools: teachers (mean scores)*

| | Infant/ Junior | Quiet Rooms | Teaching Area | Practical/ Wet Area | Storage | Display | Cloaks/ Toilets | Furniture | Hall |
|---|---|---|---|---|---|---|---|---|---|
| Noisy—quiet | I | 2.5 | 2.6 | 2.3 | N/A | N/A | 1.7 | 1.0 | 2.6 |
| | J | 2.3 | 2.7 | 2.1 | | | 1.6 | 0.9 | 2.5 |
| Restricting—not restricting | I | 1.8 | 2.9 | 2.6 | 2.0 | 2.7 | 1.9 | 2.6 | 3.2 |
| | J | 1.5 | 2.4 | 2.0 | 1.6 | 2.4 | 1.5 | 2.3 | 2.8 |
| Light—dark | I | 1.8 | 2.0 | 2.1 | 1.6 | 1.3 | 2.3 | N/A | 1.6 |
| | J | 1.5 | 2.2 | 2.1 | 1.4 | 1.2 | 2.4 | | 1.7 |
| Small—large | I | 1.6 | 2.7 | 2.2 | 2.0 | 3.0 | 2.0 | 1.3 | 3.5 |
| | J | 1.3 | 2.4 | 1.8 | 1.8 | 2.6 | 1.8 | 1.4 | 3.0 |
| Adequate—inadequate | I | 2.2 | 2.7 | 3.0 | 3.2 | 2.4 | 3.2 | 2.0 | 1.8 |
| | J | 2.2 | 2.9 | 3.1 | 3.3 | 2.6 | 3.2 | 2.3 | 2.4 |
| Badly sited—well sited | I | 2.3 | 3.2 | 2.9 | 2.8 | 3.0 | 2.9 | 1.1 | 3.5 |
| | J | 2.0 | 2.9 | 2.5 | 2.4 | 2.9 | 2.5 | 1.1 | 3.1 |
| Visible—not visible | I | 1.7 | 1.3 | 1.9 | 1.7 | 1.5 | 2.5 | N/A | 1.6 |
| | J | 1.4 | 1.1 | 1.8 | 1.4 | 1.6 | 2.2 | | 1.6 |
| Well designed—badly designed | I | 2.1 | 2.7 | 3.0 | 3.0 | 2.5 | 3.2 | 2.0 | 2.0 |
| | J | 2.1 | 3.1 | 3.2 | 3.1 | 2.5 | 3.3 | 2.4 | 2.6 |

*Table A12 Perceptions of teaching spaces: infant and junior teachers (mean scores)*

# APPENDIX B
Observational Study

| | *Type 1* | | | | | | | *Type 2* | | | |
|---|---|---|---|---|---|---|---|---|---|---|---|
| *Unit* | M | O | P | R | S | U | V | N | Q | T | W |
| Administration and transition | 21.7 | 21.8 | 22.2 | 25.5 | 26.9 | 23.1 | 23.1 | 21.1 | 20.8 | 12.4 | 26.6 |
| Mathematics allocation | 11.0 | 18.5 | 15.7 | 23.6 | 9.6 | 9.7 | 16.7 | 14.6 | 24.6 | 15.7 | 14.1 |
| Mathematics involvement | 8.7 | 11.4 | 9.3 | 13.9 | 7.2 | 6.8 | 10.6 | 7.4 | 17.6 | 9.4 | 11.5 |
| Language allocation | 37.9 | 29.1 | 39.2 | 33.3 | 37.0 | 47.9 | 36.1 | 34.0 | 39.3 | 28.0 | 42.5 |
| Language involvement | 33.3 | 22.5 | 27.6 | 23.5 | 29.7 | 37.1 | 29.4 | 28.8 | 31.4 | 17.9 | 35.5 |
| Environmental studies allocation | - | 6.9 | 4.5 | 1.3 | 1.8 | 2.5 | 5.6 | 7.5 | - | 8.3 | - |
| Environmental studies involvement | - | 5.7 | 4.2 | 1.2 | 1.5 | 2.2 | 3.8 | 6.4 | - | 7.4 | - |
| Aesthetic allocation | 13.8 | 12.3 | 8.1 | 9.1 | 15.8 | 6.8 | 8.4 | 6.4 | 9.5 | 6.9 | 8.6 |
| Aesthetic involvement | 12.8 | 10.4 | 6.5 | 7.0 | 14.2 | 4.9 | 6.7 | 5.5 | 7.6 | 4.8 | 7.0 |
| PE allocation | - | 3.9 | 3.0 | 1.1 | 4.7 | 2.3 | 3.6 | 1.8 | 1.3 | 20.3 | 1.2 |
| PE involvement | - | 3.1 | 2.5 | 1.0 | 4.2 | 2.0 | 3.4 | 1.6 | 1.1 | 19.6 | 1.1 |
| Social education allocation | 2.3 | 1.7 | 1.6 | 4.4 | 3.2 | 3.7 | 2.8 | 4.8 | - | 0.1 | 5.4 |
| Social education involvement | 2.3 | 1.6 | 1.6 | 4.2 | 3.2 | 3.1 | 2.2 | 3.9 | - | 0.1 | 4.9 |
| Moral education allocation | 13.3 | 6.0 | 5.3 | 2.1 | 1.3 | 3.9 | 4.3 | 9.8 | 3.9 | 8.2 | 1.7 |
| Moral education involvement | 13.0 | 5.7 | 4.9 | 2.1 | 1.3 | 3.8 | 4.3 | 9.5 | 3.8 | 8.0 | 1.4 |
| Overall Involvement | 70.1 | 60.3 | 56.8 | 52.8 | 61.1 | 60.0 | 60.4 | 63.0 | 61.7 | 67.1 | 61.4 |

*Table B1 Individual unit profiles of curriculum allocation and observed involvement: infants*

| *Unit* | *Type 1* | | | | | | | *Type 2* | | | | | | |
|---|---|---|---|---|---|---|---|---|---|---|---|---|---|---|
| | M | O | P | R | S | U | V | N | Q | T | W | Type 1 | Type 2 | All |
| Mathematics | 79.1 | 61.6 | 59.2 | 58.9 | 76.0 | 70.1 | 63.4 | 50.7 | 71.5 | 59.9 | 81.6 | 66.9 | 65.9 | 66.5 |
| Language | 87.9 | 77.3 | 70.4 | 70.6 | 80.3 | 77.5 | 81.4 | 84.7 | 79.9 | 63.9 | 83.5 | 77.9 | 78.0 | 77.9 |
| Environmental studies | - | 82.6 | 93.3 | 100.0 | 83.3 | 88.0 | 67.9 | 85.3 | - | 89.2 | - | 85.9 | 87.3 | 86.2 |
| Aesthetics | 92.8 | 84.6 | 80.2 | 76.9 | 89.9 | 72.1 | 79.8 | 85.9 | 80.0 | 69.6 | 81.4 | 82.3 | 79.2 | 81.2 |
| Physical education | - | 79.5 | 83.3 | 90.1 | 89.4 | 87.0 | 94.4 | 88.9 | 84.6 | 96.6 | 91.7 | 87.3 | 90.5 | 88.6 |
| Social and moral education | 98.1 | 94.8 | 94.2 | 98.5 | 100.0 | 90.8 | 91.5 | 91.8 | 97.4 | 97.6 | 88.7 | 95.4 | 93.9 | 94.9 |
| Total curriculum | 89.5 | 77.4 | 73.2 | 71.1 | 83.5 | 78.2 | 78.5 | 80.0 | 78.0 | 77.0 | 83.3 | 78.8 | 79.6 | 79.1 |

*Table B2 Individual unit profiles: percentage involvement* within curriculum area: infants*

* % involvement $= \frac{\text{on task x 100}}{\text{allocated time}}$

| | *Type 1 (7 units)* | | *Type 2 (4 units)* | | *Active (5 units)* | | *Passive (6 units)* | | *All (11 units)* | |
|---|---|---|---|---|---|---|---|---|---|---|
| | Inv. | Non-inv. | Inv. | Non-inv. | Inv. | Non-inv. | Inv. | Non-inv. | Inv. | Non-inv. |
| Administration and transition | - | 23.4 | - | 20.3 | - | 24.9 | - | 20.2 | - | 22.3 |
| Teacher — class group discussion | 11.6 | - | 16.5 | - | 9.6 | - | 16.5 | - | 13.4 | - |
| Teacher — small group discussion | 2.1 | - | 2.8 | - | 2.3 | - | 2.5 | - | 2.4 | - |
| Computation | 2.3 | 2.3 | 1.7 | 2.5 | 1.8 | 2.3 | 2.3 | 2.5 | 2.1 | 2.4 |
| Practical maths | 3.4 | 2.2 | 2.6 | 1.5 | 3.4 | 2.0 | 2.8 | 1.9 | 3.1 | 1.9 |
| Construction toys | 1.6 | .3 | 1.0 | .1 | 1.3 | .2 | 1.4 | .2 | 1.4 | .2 |
| Maths games | .2 | .1 | .3 | .2 | .3 | .1 | .2 | .1 | .2 | .1 |
| Sand | .5 | .1 | 1.0 | .1 | 1.0 | .1 | .4 | .1 | .7 | .1 |
| Water | - | - | .7 | .2 | .6 | .1 | - | - | .3 | .1 |
| Cooking | .1 | - | .3 | .6 | .2 | .2 | .2 | .3 | .2 | .3 |
| Reading to teacher | 1.1 | .3 | .7 | .1 | .9 | .3 | 1.0 | .2 | 1.0 | .2 |
| Reading scheme | 1.4 | .6 | .9 | .6 | 1.0 | .4 | 1.4 | .8 | 1.2 | .6 |
| Reading – free | 1.3 | .8 | 1.6 | 1.2 | 1.8 | .9 | 1.1 | .9 | 1.4 | .9 |
| Audio-reading | .1 | - | .1 | .1 | .1 | .1 | .1 | - | .1 | - |
| Spelling/phonics | .9 | .4 | .4 | .3 | .6 | .2 | .7 | .5 | .7 | .4 |
| Language/games | - | - | 1.7 | .4 | 1.3 | .2 | .1 | .1 | .6 | .1 |
| Writing – copy | .9 | .5 | .7 | .8 | .5 | .3 | 1.1 | .9 | .8 | .6 |
| Handwriting | .1 | - | - | - | .1 | - | - | - | .1 | - |
| Writing – comprehension | .8 | .4 | .4 | .2 | .7 | .5 | .6 | .2 | .6 | .3 |
| Writing – free | 4.1 | 3.9 | 2.5 | 2.2 | 4.0 | 3.9 | 3.1 | 2.7 | 3.5 | 3.3 |
| Story | 8.6 | .4 | 5.3 | .3 | 6.6 | .2 | 8.0 | .5 | 7.4 | .4 |
| Recitation | .8 | - | .9 | - | .5 | - | 1.1 | - | .8 | - |
| Painting | .9 | .4 | .9 | .6 | 1.3 | .6 | .5 | .5 | .9 | .5 |
| Drawing/crayon | 3.5 | 2.0 | 3.3 | 1.7 | 3.8 | 1.9 | 3.1 | 1.9 | 3.4 | 1.9 |
| Making | 3.0 | .6 | 4.6 | 1.3 | 2.9 | 1.0 | 4.1 | .8 | 3.6 | .9 |
| Sewing | - | - | .1 | - | - | - | - | - | - | - |
| Drama | - | - | .4 | .1 | - | - | .4 | - | .2 | - |
| Music/movement | .5 | - | - | - | .7 | - | - | - | .3 | - |
| Singing | 3.8 | .2 | 2.8 | .4 | 2.9 | .2 | 3.9 | .3 | 3.4 | .3 |
| Making music | .3 | - | - | - | .3 | - | .1 | - | .2 | - |
| Listening to music | .4 | - | .1 | - | .5 | - | .1 | - | .3 | - |
| PE small apparatus | 1.1 | .1 | .8 | .2 | .7 | - | 1.2 | .2 | 1.0 | .1 |
| PE large apparatus | .8 | .2 | .5 | .1 | 1.2 | .2 | .3 | .1 | .7 | .2 |
| Games/sports | - | - | 4.2 | - | - | - | 2.8 | .1 | 1.5 | .1 |
| Social play | 1.5 | .2 | 3.5 | .6 | 3.6 | .5 | 1.1 | .2 | 2.2 | .3 |
| Helping teacher | .1 | .1 | - | - | - | - | .1 | .1 | .1 | .1 |
| TV/film/radio | 2.1 | .1 | - | - | 1.4 | .1 | 1.3 | .1 | 1.3 | .1 |
| Concert/show | .4 | .1 | - | - | .5 | .1 | .1 | .1 | .2 | .1 |
| | 60.3 | 39.7 | 63.3 | 36.7 | 58.4 | 41.5 | 63.7 | 36.5 | 61.3 | 38.7 |
| | 100.0% | | 100.0% | | 99.9% | | 100.2% | | 100.0% | |

NB Due to rounding off these figures do not always summate to 100.0%

*Table B3 Specific curriculum activities: mean percentage involvement in relation to pupil choice and type of unit: infants*

Percentage Occurrence
Within Curriculum Area (LES)

| | Type 1 | | | | | | | Type 2 | | | | | | | Mean Percentage Occurrence | |
|---|---|---|---|---|---|---|---|---|---|---|---|---|---|---|---|---|
| | Maths. | Lang. | Env.st. | Aes. | PE | Soc. | Mor. | Maths. | Lang. | Env.st. | Aes. | PE | Soc. | Mor. | Type 1 | Type 2 |
| Direct teaching — individual | 2.3 | 2.6 | 0.4 | - | - | - | - | 0.5 | 4.0 | - | - | - | 5.3 | - | 1.6 | 1.7 |
| Direct teaching — small group | 7.4 | 4.9 | 3.5 | 1.0 | - | - | - | 13.2 | 7.4 | 0.8 | 6.2 | - | - | - | 3.8 | 6.9 |
| Direct teaching — whole class | 7.1 | 30.6 | 21.5 | 24.4 | 38.3 | 31.7 | 21.5 | 5.9 | 32.9 | 24.8 | 4.9 | 38.6 | 23.4 | 33.0 | 23.7 | 20.8 |
| Direct teaching — 2 or more classes | 1.2 | 6.6 | 20.5 | 19.7 | - | 4.3 | 77.9 | - | - | - | - | 50.6 | 6.4 | 65.6 | 13.8 | 9.5 |
| Work — individual | 40.8 | 27.7 | 24.1 | 18.1 | 2.9 | 17.3 | - | 14.7 | 17.2 | 8.3 | 63.4 | - | 6.4 | - | 25.3 | 21.8 |
| Work — small group | 33.7 | 17.3 | 12.9 | 29.8 | 10.3 | 35.3 | - | 51.3 | 27.0 | 66.1 | 25.5 | 3.6 | 58.5 | - | 20.8 | 31.6 |
| Work — whole class | 7.4 | 9.6 | 17.2 | 7.1 | 48.6 | 11.5 | - | 14.4 | 11.5 | - | - | 7.2 | - | 1.4 | 10.6 | 7.8 |
| Work — 2 or more classes | - | 0.7 | - | - | - | - | 0.7 | - | - | - | - | - | - | - | 0.3 | - |
| | 99.9 | 100.0 | 100.1 | 100.1 | 100.1 | 100.1 | 100.1 | 100.0 | 100.0 | 100.0 | 100.0 | 100.0 | 100.0 | 100.0 | 99.9 | 100.1 |

NB Due to rounding off these figures do not always summate to 100%

*Table B4 The teaching/learning situation by gross curriculum context and type of unit: infants (%)*

*Percentage Occurrence Within Curriculum Area (LES)*

| | *Choice* | | | | | | | *No Choice* | | | | | | | *Mean Percentage Occurrence* | | |
|---|---|---|---|---|---|---|---|---|---|---|---|---|---|---|---|---|---|
| | Maths. | Lang. | Env.st. | Aes. | PE | Soc. | Mor. | Maths. | Lang. | Env.st. | Aes. | PE | Soc. | Mor. | Choice | No Choice | All |
| Direct teaching — individual | 2.5 | 3.9 | .3 | - | - | 3.4 | - | .5 | 2.5 | .3 | - | - | - | - | 2.0 | 1.2 | 1.6 |
| Direct teaching — small group | 4.4 | 4.3 | 5.2 | 3.0 | - | - | - | 16.4 | 6.8 | .3 | 3.0 | - | - | - | 3.5 | 6.2 | 4.9 |
| Direct teaching — whole class | 5.6 | 25.9 | 17.6 | 21.4 | 32.6 | 36.5 | 14.6 | 7.8 | 35.2 | 27.6 | 11.7 | 41.3 | 14.8 | 33.5 | 18.9 | 25.8 | 22.4 |
| Direct teaching — 2 or more classes | 1.3 | 5.0 | 12.7 | 14.1 | 1.1 | 2.8 | 84.4 | - | 4.0 | 21.8 | 9.6 | 25.2 | 9.1 | 65.5 | 11.0 | 13.2 | 12.1 |
| Work — individual | 37.6 | 42.0 | 36.4 | 35.3 | - | 14.5 | - | 20.4 | 11.9 | 2.4 | 36.3 | 3.0 | 10.2 | - | 35.1 | 14.7 | 24.9 |
| Work — small group | 48.2 | 16.1 | 19.0 | 26.3 | 19.6 | 42.8 | - | 32.6 | 23.6 | 27.2 | 30.3 | 1.8 | 47.7 | - | 26.1 | 23.5 | 24.8 |
| Work — whole class | .5 | 1.7 | 8.8 | - | 46.7 | - | - | 22.3 | 16.1 | 20.4 | 9.2 | 28.7 | 18.2 | 1.0 | 2.9 | 15.5 | 9.2 |
| Work — 2 or more classes | - | 1.1 | - | - | - | - | 1.0 | - | - | - | - | - | - | - | .4 | - | .2 |
| | 100.1 | 100.0 | 100.0 | 100.1 | 100.0 | 100.0 | 100.0 | 100.0 | 100.1 | 100.0 | 100.1 | 100.0 | 100.0 | 100.0 | 99.9 | 100.1 | 100.1 |

NB Due to rounding off these figures do not always summate to 100%

*Table B5 The teaching/learning situation by gross curriculum context and degree of choice: infants*

| Unit | Type 1 A | C | E | F | G | I | J | Type 2 B | D | H | K | L |
|---|---|---|---|---|---|---|---|---|---|---|---|---|
| Administration and transition | 16.2 | 11.1 | 13.8 | 9.7 | 15.0 | 13.8 | 16.9 | 9.0 | 11.4 | 13.6 | 13.0 | 13.0 |
| Mathematics allocation | 17.1 | 9.2 | 14.3 | 25.0 | 22.9 | 15.5 | 18.0 | 26.5 | 12.1 | 13.8 | 20.3 | 10.9 |
| Mathematics involvement | 10.7 | 5.6 | 10.0 | 14.6 | 14.6 | 11.3 | 10.9 | 16.8 | 8.2 | 12.4 | 15.3 | 7.6 |
| Language allocation | 25.5 | 37.3 | 16.6 | 46.4 | 19.5 | 28.6 | 25.9 | 29.2 | 37.7 | 27.5 | 42.4 | 31.9 |
| Language involvement | 18.9 | 29.9 | 10.0 | 31.7 | 12.4 | 22.8 | 12.8 | 18.7 | 25.1 | 23.2 | 31.6 | 22.8 |
| Environmental studies allocation | 17.7 | 10.1 | 29.2 | - | 11.5 | 11.5 | - | 12.6 | 10.3 | 17.5 | 9.9 | 28.1 |
| Environmental studies involvement | 13.2 | 8.2 | 19.4 | - | 10.3 | 9.1 | - | 11.4 | 7.3 | 13.4 | 8.5 | 21.9 |
| Aesthetic allocation | 11.3 | 10.3 | 2.3 | 5.3 | 6.7 | 12.7 | 11.7 | 11.9 | 17.7 | 23.3 | 6.8 | 3.3 |
| Aesthetic involvement | 9.9 | 8.3 | 1.9 | 3.6 | 5.0 | 10.1 | 9.9 | 8.0 | 12.4 | 22.1 | 6.3 | 1.9 |
| Physical education allocation | 6.2 | 18.1 | 12.0 | 6.7 | 13.7 | 10.7 | 19.8 | 7.3 | 8.8 | - | 2.7 | 6.4 |
| Physical education involvement | 6.2 | 18.1 | 10.6 | 5.7 | 12.9 | 8.8 | 19.8 | 7.1 | 8.7 | - | 1.9 | 5.8 |
| Social education allocation | 2.7 | .9 | .3 | - | 8.9 | 5.8 | 3.1 | - | - | 2.7 | - | 1.4 |
| Social education involvement | 2.1 | .9 | .3 | - | 8.9 | 5.8 | 2.8 | - | - | 2.7 | - | 1.2 |
| Moral education allocation | 3.4 | 3.7 | 11.5 | 6.6 | 2.0 | 2.1 | 2.5 | 4.4 | 1.9 | 1.5 | 5.1 | 5.0 |
| Moral education involvement | 3.3 | 3.3 | 10.9 | 6.1 | 2.0 | 2.1 | 1.7 | 4.2 | 1.9 | 1.5 | 5.1 | 4.9 |
| Overall involvement | 64.3 | 74.3 | 63.1 | 61.7 | 66.1 | 70.0 | 57.9 | 66.2 | 63.6 | 75.3 | 68.7 | 66.1 |

*Table B6 Individual unit profiles of curriculum allocation and observed involvement (%)*

Percentage Occurrence

| Curriculum Area | Type 1 Maths. | Type 1 Lang. | Type 1 Env.st. | Type 1 Aes. | Type 1 PE | Type 1 Soc. | Type 1 Mor. | Type 2 Maths. | Type 2 Lang. | Type 2 Env.st. | Type 2 Aes. | Type 2 PE | Type 2 Soc. | Type 2 Mor. | Mean Percentage Type 1 | Mean Percentage Type 2 | Mean Percentage All |
|---|---|---|---|---|---|---|---|---|---|---|---|---|---|---|---|---|---|
| Direct teaching — individual | 1.5 | 2.0 | .2 | .3 | - | - | - | 1.1 | 1.5 | - | 1.1 | .6 | - | - | 1.1 | 1.0 | 1.1 |
| Direct teaching — small group | 2.7 | 1.6 | 4.5 | 7.9 | 10.9 | - | - | - | 3.1 | - | 1.7 | 1.7 | - | - | 4.0 | 1.5 | 2.8 |
| Direct teaching — whole class | 1.7 | 10.2 | 6.6 | 27.0 | 35.6 | 29.6 | 3.9 | 9.3 | 24.5 | 17.0 | 13.3 | 37.2 | - | - | 12.3 | 18.2 | 15.3 |
| Direct teaching — 2 or more classes | - | 4.1 | 5.0 | 14.3 | 3.8 | 44.4 | 62.6 | - | .6 | 3.2 | 5.7 | - | 100 | 90.9 | 8.0 | 5.4 | 6.7 |
| Work — individual | 47.7 | 36.2 | 31.5 | 34.2 | 2.8 | - | - | 32.0 | 26.9 | 66.7 | 39.8 | - | - | 9.1 | 32.5 | 34.6 | 33.6 |
| Work — small group | 37.6 | 23.5 | 40.7 | 16.3 | 20.5 | 25.9 | 6.2 | 5.2 | 5.6 | 4.1 | 18.5 | 34.3 | - | - | 26.8 | 8.8 | 17.8 |
| Work — whole class | 8.8 | 22.2 | 11.6 | - | 26.4 | - | 24.1 | 52.2 | 37.9 | 8.9 | 20.0 | 26.2 | - | - | 15.1 | 30.5 | 22.8 |
| Work — 2 or more classes | - | .1 | - | - | - | - | 3.1 | .3 | - | - | - | - | - | - | .2 | - | .1 |
| | | | | | | | | | | | | | | | 100 | 100 | 100.2 |

NB Due to rounding off these figures do not always summate to 100%

*Table B7 The teaching/learning situation by gross curriculum context and type of unit: juniors (%)*

| Unit | Type 1 | | | | | | | Type 2 | | | | | Mean % Involvement | | |
|---|---|---|---|---|---|---|---|---|---|---|---|---|---|---|---|
| | A | C | E | F | G | I | J | B | D | H | K | L | Type 1 | Type 2 | All |
| Mathematics | 62.6 | 60.9 | 69.9 | 58.4 | 63.8 | 72.9 | 60.6 | 63.4 | 67.8 | 89.9 | 75.4 | 69.7 | 64.2 | 73.2 | 67.9 |
| Language | 74.1 | 80.2 | 60.2 | 68.3 | 63.6 | 79.7 | 49.4 | 64.0 | 66.6 | 84.4 | 74.5 | 71.5 | 67.9 | 72.2 | 69.7 |
| Environmental studies | 74.6 | 81.2 | 66.4 | - | 89.6 | 79.1 | - | 90.5 | 70.9 | 76.6 | 85.9 | 77.9 | 78.2 | 80.4 | 79.3 |
| Aesthetics | 87.6 | 80.6 | 82.6 | 67.9 | 74.6 | 79.5 | 84.6 | 67.2 | 70.1 | 94.8 | 92.6 | 57.6 | 79.6 | 76.5 | 78.3 |
| Physical education | 100.0 | 100.0 | 88.3 | 85.1 | 94.2 | 82.2 | 100.0 | 97.3 | 98.9 | - | 70.4 | 90.6 | 92.8 | 89.3 | 91.5 |
| Social and moral education | 88.5 | 91.3 | 94.9 | 92.4 | 100.0 | 100.0 | 80.4 | 95.5 | 100.0 | 100.0 | 100.0 | 95.4 | 92.5 | 98.2 | 94.9 |
| Total curriculum | 76.3 | 83.7 | 73.2 | 67.7 | 77.2 | 80.8 | 69.5 | 72.9 | 71.5 | 87.0 | 78.8 | 76.1 | 75.5 | 77.2 | 76.2 |

*Table B8 Individual unit profiles: percentage involvement* within curriculum areas: juniors*

* % involvement = $\frac{\text{on task x 100}}{\text{allocated 'time'}}$

| | *Mean Percentage* | | | | | | | | |
|---|---|---|---|---|---|---|---|---|---|
| | *Type 1* | | | *Type 2* | | | *All* | | |
| | Alloc. | Inv. | Non-inv. | Alloc. | Inv. | Non-inv. | Alloc. | Inv. | Non-inv. |
| Administration and transition | 13.7 | - | 13.7 | 12.0 | - | 12.0 | 13.0 | - | 13.0 |
| Teacher/class group discussion | 11.8 | 11.8 | - | 12.3 | 12.3 | - | 12.0 | 12.0 | - |
| Teacher/small group discussion | 2.1 | 2.1 | - | 1.8 | 1.8 | - | 2.0 | 2.0 | - |
| Computation | 13.2 | 7.8 | 5.4 | 10.3 | 7.0 | 3.3 | 12.0 | 7.5 | 4.5 |
| Practical maths | 2.1 | 1.6 | .5 | 2.1 | 1.5 | .6 | 1.6 | 1.5 | .5 |
| Construction toys | .3 | .2 | .1 | - | - | - | .2 | .1 | .1 |
| Maths games | .6 | .5 | .1 | .1 | .1 | - | .4 | .3 | .1 |
| Cooking | - | - | - | .4 | .2 | .2 | .2 | .1 | .1 |
| Reading to teacher | .2 | .1 | .1 | .6 | .6 | - | .4 | .3 | .1 |
| Reading scheme | 4.3 | 2.7 | 1.6 | 1.6 | 1.1 | .5 | 3.1 | 2.0 | 1.1 |
| Reading — free | 3.8 | 2.0 | 1.8 | 8.0 | 4.9 | 3.1 | 5.5 | 3.2 | 2.3 |
| Audio-reading | .1 | .1 | - | .3 | .3 | - | .2 | .2 | - |
| Spelling activities | .6 | .5 | .1 | .9 | .6 | .3 | .7 | .5 | .2 |
| Language games | .1 | .1 | - | - | - | - | .1 | .1 | - |
| Writing — copy | .4 | .2 | .2 | .8 | .6 | .2 | .6 | .4 | .2 |
| Handwriting | 1.0 | .6 | .4 | 1.3 | 1.0 | .3 | 1.2 | .8 | .4 |
| Writing — comprehension | 5.5 | 2.6 | 2.9 | 5.2 | 3.0 | 2.2 | 5.4 | 2.8 | 2.6 |
| Writing — free | 6.8 | 4.4 | 2.4 | 10.3 | 6.2 | 4.1 | 8.2 | 5.1 | 3.1 |
| Story | 3.2 | 3.1 | .1 | 3.6 | 3.4 | .2 | 3.3 | 3.2 | .1 |
| Recitation | .2 | .2 | - | .5 | .5 | - | .3 | .3 | - |
| Painting | .7 | .5 | .2 | 2.5 | 1.4 | 1.1 | 1.5 | .9 | .6 |
| Drawing/crayon | 7.8 | 5.1 | 2.7 | 3.3 | 2.6 | .7 | 5.9 | 4.0 | 1.9 |
| Making | 3.5 | 2.7 | .8 | 4.1 | 2.6 | 1.5 | 3.8 | 2.7 | 1.1 |
| Clay work | - | - | - | 1.2 | 1.0 | .2 | .5 | .4 | .1 |
| Sewing | .3 | .2 | .1 | 2.3 | 1.8 | .5 | 1.2 | .9 | .3 |
| Dance | .3 | .2 | .1 | - | - | - | .2 | .1 | .1 |
| Drama | 1.1 | .8 | .3 | .1 | .1 | - | .7 | .5 | .2 |
| Music/movement | .2 | .2 | - | .4 | .4 | - | .3 | .3 | - |
| Singing | 1.7 | 1.5 | .2 | 2.2 | 2.1 | .1 | 1.9 | 1.7 | .2 |
| Making music | .3 | .2 | .1 | 1.4 | 1.1 | .3 | .8 | .6 | .2 |
| Listening to music | .4 | .4 | - | .1 | .1 | - | .3 | .3 | - |
| Experiments | .1 | .1 | - | 1.4 | 1.1 | .3 | .6 | .5 | .1 |
| Nature walk | .1 | .1 | - | 1.1 | 1.1 | - | .5 | .5 | - |
| Pets | - | - | - | .3 | .3 | - | .1 | .1 | - |
| PE small apparatus | 3.1 | 2.5 | .6 | .6 | .4 | .2 | 2.0 | 1.6 | .4 |
| PE large apparatus | .3 | .1 | .2 | .3 | .3 | - | .3 | .2 | .1 |
| Games | 5.4 | 5.4 | - | 2.7 | 2.7 | - | 4.3 | 4.3 | - |
| Swimming | 2.4 | 2.4 | - | 1.1 | 1.1 | - | 1.9 | 1.9 | - |
| TV/film/radio | .3 | .3 | - | .7 | .7 | - | .5 | .5 | - |
| Concert | 1.6 | 1.6 | - | 2.0 | 2.0 | - | 1.8 | 1.8 | - |
| Helping teacher | .4 | .3 | .1 | .7 | .7 | - | .5 | .5 | - |
| | 100.0 | 65.2 | 34.8 | 99.9 | 68.0 | 31.9 | 99.8 | 66.4 | 33.4 |
| | N = 168 | | | N = 120 | | | N = 288 | | |

*Table B9 Mean percentage allocation of specific curriculum activities with involvement and non-involvement by type of unit (PBS)*

# APPENDIX C
## Use of Space

| Unit Letter | Type of Unit | Size $m^2$ | Children Day | Children am | Children pm | Adults Day | Adults am | Adults pm | Main Activities: Children | Main Activities: Adults | Materials and Equipment | Additional Information |
|---|---|---|---|---|---|---|---|---|---|---|---|---|
| M[1]* | PT1 | 7.5 | 1.1 | 8.0 | 1.3 | 0 | 0 | 0 | Wendy House play 0.9 | None observed | Wendy House equipment | called the 'den' and for whole school. Set up and used as Wendy House by 4 youngest classes. |
| M[2] | PT1 | 7.5 | 0.9 | 0.5 | 1.4 | 0 | 0 | 0 | Wendy House play 1.6 | None observed | " | " " |
| N | PT2 | No enclosed quiet room | | | | | | | | | | |
| O | TT1 | 8.75 | 0.6 | 0.7 | 0.4 | 9.5 | 12.5 | 6.3 | Reading 0.2 | Direct teaching individual 8.3<br>Work organization and materials 0.6 | Storage of art paper | Deputy head's room used by her for remedial readers |
| P | TT1 | 8.75 | 1.8 | 2.4 | 1.1 | 0.5 | 1.0 | 0 | Wendy House play 1.8 | Organization of materials 0.5 | Wendy House equipment | Deputy head's room set up and used as Wendy House for 3 classes. |
| R[1]a** | TT1 | 20.5 | 7.6 | 29.6 | 4.1 | 13.8 | 15.6 | 12.4 | Waiting for teacher 2.4<br>Listening to teacher 1.2<br>Writing 1.1 | Direct teaching group 5.7<br>Individual discussion 2.9 | Woodwork bench and tools and reading books | Called writing room. Used by 3 classes |
| b | | 20.5 | 10.4 | 6.7 | 14.1 | 5.2 | 1.1 | 7.2 | Listening to teacher 6.2<br>Writing 2.1<br>Maths book 1.6 | Direct teaching class 1.7<br>Administration 1.7 | Library books, balance scale, teacher-made word cards | Called maths room. Used by 3 classes. |
| R[2]a | TT1 | 20.5 | 6.8 | 11.0 | 3.1 | 9.6 | 11.6 | 7.8 | Listening to teacher 3.2<br>Writing 1.8 | Direct teaching individual 5.1<br>General supervision 1.0 | Maths equipment, Teacher-made maths cards | Both a and b used by 3 classes |

* Raised numerals are used where more than one unit was observed in a single school

** Lower case letters indicate number of quiet rooms

*Table C1 Percentage use of quiet rooms (infant) in relation to size and activity based on three day observation*

Table C1 (Continued)

| Unit Letter | Type of Unit | Size m² | Children Day | Children am | Children pm | Adults Day | Adults am | Adults pm | Main Activities: Children | Main Activities: Adults | Materials and Equipment | Additional Information |
|---|---|---|---|---|---|---|---|---|---|---|---|---|
| b | | 20.5 | 6.6 | 11.1 | 2.7 | 6.6 | 9.5 | 3.9 | Listening to teacher 2.9<br>Writing 1.1 | Direct teaching individual 3.0<br>Discussion class 1.5 | Teacher-made word cards, phonic books | Both a and b used by 3 classes |
| S | TT1 | | | | | | | | | | | AV room for total school use. |
| Q¹ | TT2 | 8.0 | 1.8 | 0.9 | 2.8 | 3.0 | 1.1 | 5.1 | Making music 1.0 | Direct group teaching 3.0 | TV, library books, Drum | Called a 'kiva' and shared by whole school — 6 classes. |
| Q² | TT2 | 8.0 | 0 | 0 | 0 | 0 | 0 | 0 | None observed | None observed | " " | " " |
| T | QT2 | | | | | | | | | | | AV room for total school use. |
| U | MT1 | | | | | | | | | | | Quiet room used only by junior class. |
| V | MT1 | No enclosed quiet room | | | | | | | | | | |
| Wa | MT2 | 16.0 | 8.1 | 7.7 | 8.6 | 4.4 | 3.0 | 5.7 | Listening to teacher 6.4<br>Drinking milk 1.4 | Direct teaching individual 1.7<br>General supervision and Direct teaching class 0.7 | Reading books and materials | Used by three teachers |
| b | | 16.0 | 10.5 | 5.9 | 15.0 | 8.3 | 6.1 | 10.4 | Listening to teacher 6.4<br>Drinking milk 1.4 | Cooperative teaching 2.4<br>Class discussion )<br>work organization )0.7<br>Watching TV )<br>Direct teaching )<br>Ind/class ) | Matching games | Used by three teachers |
| c | | 16.0 | 2.0 | 1.5 | 2.4 | 1.0 | 0 | 1.9 | Moving 0.6<br>Reading 0.5 | Group discussion 0.5 | Dressing-up clothes and Wendy House equipment. | Used by two teachers |

| Unit Letter | Type of Unit | Size m² | Children Day | Children am | Children pm | Adults Day | Adults am | Adults pm | Main Activities: Children | Main Activities: Adults | Materials and Equipment | Additional Information |
|---|---|---|---|---|---|---|---|---|---|---|---|---|
| A[1] | PT1 | 12.25 | 2.9 | 3.2 | 2.6 | 8.5 | 15.8 | 0 | Writing 0.9<br>Getting materials 0.7 | Direct teaching individual 7.0<br>Discussion individual 1.4 | Library books, teacher-made topic cards, reading books | Shared by 2 classes. |
| A[2] | PT1 | 12.25 | 0.3 | 0.6 | 0 | 0 | 0 | 0 | Writing 0.2 | None observed | Reading materials and books | Shared by 2 classes. |
| B[1] | PT2 | 24.75 | 2.2 | 2.6 | 1.6 | 8.8 | 1.9 | 15.8 | Writing 0.7<br>Getting materials 0.5 | Organizing materials 3.5<br>Direct teaching individual 2.7 | Library books, reading books, reference books | Shared by 3 classes. |
| B[2] | PT2 | 24.75 | 1.4 | 1.7 | 1.1 | 10.9 | 16.9 | 3.9 | With teacher interacting 0.6<br>Getting materials 0.4 | Discussion individual 10.0<br>Work organization 0.9 | Library books, teacher-made language cards, word games, record player | Shared by 2 classes. |
| C | TT1 | 23.50 | 16.6 | 14.0 | 19.4 | 17.7 | 13.3 | 22.6 | Listening to teacher 11.3<br>Writing 2.7 | Direct teaching class 5.3<br>Checking work 4.4 | Games, a globe | Used exclusively by one class as home base |
| D[1] | TT1 | 26.0 | 7.0 | 5.6 | 8.4 | 7.3 | 3.6 | 10.6 | Writing 3.9<br>Listening to teacher 3.6<br>Reading 2.0 | Direct teaching individual 5.1<br>Direct teaching group/class 2.6 | Maths books, teacher-made maths cards and maths equipment | Shared by 3 classes and set up as a maths area |
| D[2] | TT1 | 17.50 | 2.8 | 1.4 | 4.0 | 3.8 | 3.6 | 4.1 | Listening to teacher 4.2<br>Watching TV 1.2 | Administration 2.6<br>Direct teaching group/class 1.7 | TV, percussion instruments, word games, RE story books. | Shared by 3 classes. Used as a home base. |
| E | QT1 | 18.0 | 4.6 | 4.7 | 4.4 | 6.2 | 7.4 | 4.8 | Maths book and card 1.8<br>Listening to teacher 1.5 | Checking work 1.7<br>Talking to adults 1.7 | Teachers' own books and papers | Shared by 4 classes Used as home base. |

*Table C2 Percentage use of quiet rooms (junior) in relation to size and activity based on three day observation*

*Table C2 (Continued)*

| Unit Letter | Type of Unit | Size $m^2$ | Children Day | Children am | Children pm | Adults Day | Adults am | Adults pm | Main Activities: Children | Main Activities: Adults | Materials and Equipment | Additional Information |
|---|---|---|---|---|---|---|---|---|---|---|---|---|
| F | QT1 | 11.0 | 1.0 | 1.4 | 0.5 | 4.1 | 5.4 | 2.7 | Writing 0.4 | Organizing materials )<br>General supervision )0.9<br>Direct teaching individual ) | Reading books and materials, Resource books | Deputy head's room used for individual children to work in. |
| G¹a | QT1 | 16.75 | 5.7 | 2.0 | 10.4 | 4.2 | 1.4 | 7.0 | Listening to teacher 3.5<br>Waiting for teacher 0.8 | Direct teaching class 1.4<br>Work organization )<br>Individual and class discussion )0.7 | Belling cooker, maths books, typewriter | Shared by 4 classes. |
| b | | 16.75 | 4.4 | 1.7 | 8.0 | 4.2 | 2.9 | 5.6 | Listening to teacher 2.5<br>Writing 1.2 | Direct teaching class 1.4<br>Discussion individual )<br>Direct teaching individual )0.7 | None | Used exclusively by one class as home base. |
| G²a | QT1 | 16.5 | 5.5 | 6.5 | 4.3 | 4.7 | 5.3 | 4.1 | Listening to teacher 4.6<br>Writing 0.4 | Discussion class 3.3<br>Work organization/ Group discussion 0.7 | None | Used by 4 classes and as home base. |
| b | | 16.5 | 6.4 | 6.0 | 6.9 | 8.7 | 5.3 | 12.2 | Listening to teacher 3.5<br>Writing 1.6 | Direct teaching individual and class 3.3<br>Work organization/ Direct teaching group 0.7 | Art supplies | Used by 4 classes and as a home base. |
| Ha | QT2 | 16.0 | 5.2 | 8.4 | 2.1 | 1.4 | 2.6 | 0 | Listening to teacher 4.3 | Work organization/ Individual discussion 0.5 | Maths equipment | Used by 4 classes and for maths |

*Table C2 (Continued)*

| Unit Letter | Type of Unit | Size m² | Children Day | Children am | Children pm | Adults Day | Adults am | Adults pm | Main Activities: Children | Main Activities: Adults | Materials and Equipment | Additional Information |
|---|---|---|---|---|---|---|---|---|---|---|---|---|
| b | | 16.0 | 2.3 | 1.9 | 2.6 | 6.5 | 0.9 | 13.1 | Reading 0.8<br>Listening to teacher 0.7 | Direct teaching individual 4.6 | TV and AV equipment | Used by four classes for remedial reading and maths |
| c | | 16.0 | 5.0 | 3.2 | 6.8 | 2.8 | 0.9 | 5.1 | Listening to teacher 2.7<br>Reading 2.0 | Direct teaching class 1.9 | Reference and library books | Used as library for four classes |
| d | | 16.0 | 2.2 | 1.5 | 2.9 | 0.9 | 0 | 2.0 | Listening to teacher 2.2 | Class discussion 0.5<br>Direct teaching class 0.5 | Puppets, dressing up clothes, dolls and bed | Used as home area by four classes |
| I | MT1 | 21.0 | 1.1 | 1.5 | 0.7 | 0.4 | 0.8 | 0 | Listening to teacher 2.6<br>Writing 0.9 | Direct teaching group/class 1.2<br>Work organization/ Direct teaching individual 0.8<br>Talking to teachers 0.8 | Tape recorders and tapes, reading books, reference books | Used by six classes for writing and reading or quiet work and tapes |
| J | MT1 | | | | | | | | | | AV room for whole school | |
| K | MT2 | 10.0 | 2.5 | 3.0 | 1.9 | 4.2 | 7.6 | 0.8 | With teacher interacting 1.0<br>Listening to teacher 0.8 | Direct teaching individual 2.8<br>Direct teaching group 2.3<br>Direct teaching class 1.9 | Scrap materials | Used by three lower junior classes |
| La | MT2 | 32.0 | 1.1 | 0.8 | 1.5 | 0.5 | 0 | 1.0 | Writing 0.3<br>Music 0.3 | Individual discussion 1.0 | Reference books, radio equipment | Used by six classes |
| b | | 32.0 | 2.9 | 1.5 | 4.3 | 1.4 | 0.9 | 1.9 | Listening to teacher 2.0<br>Watching TV 0.8 | Direct teaching class 0.9<br>Class discussion 0.5 | TV and video equipment, percussion instruments | Used by six classes and story in afternoon |

*Table C2 (Continued)*

| Unit Letter | Type of Unit | Size m² | Children Day | Children am | Children pm | Adults Day | Adults am | Adults pm | Main Activities: Children | | Main Activities: Adults | | Materials and Equipment | Additional Information |
|---|---|---|---|---|---|---|---|---|---|---|---|---|---|---|
| c | | 32.0 | 3.2 | 2.5 | 3.9 | 1.4 | 1.8 | 1.0 | Listening to teacher | 2.6 | Direct teaching class | 0.9 | Display of work | Used by six classes and story in afternoon |
| | | | | | | | | | With teacher interacting | 0.5 | Organizing materials | 0.5 | | |
| d | | 32.0 | 1.1 | 1.1 | 1.0 | 5.1 | 5.4 | 4.8 | With teacher interacting | 0.6 | Direct teaching individual | 2.8 | Reading books | Used by six classes and remedial reading teacher |
| | | | | | | | | | Reading | 0.4 | Direct teaching | | | |

| Unit Letter | Type of Unit | Size m² | Children Day | Children am | Children pm | Adults Day | Adults am | Adults pm | Main Activities: Children | | Main Activities: Adults | | Materials and Equipment | Additional Information |
|---|---|---|---|---|---|---|---|---|---|---|---|---|---|---|
| M[1] | PT1 | 43.75 | 12.3 | 15.8 | 9.0 | 19.1 | 22.4 | 15.6 | Drinking milk | 2.2 | Individual discussion | 6.4 | | Used by two classes |
| | | | | | | | | | Clearing up | 1.6 | Clearing up | 4.3 | | |
| | | | | | | | | | Drawing | 1.2 | Individual direct teaching | 3.2 | | |
| M[2] | PT1 | 46.25 | 14.8 | 15.9 | 13.7 | 24.0 | 24.1 | 23.9 | Building | 3.2 | Organizing materials | 3.5 | | Used by two classes |
| | | | | | | | | | Constructing | 2.0 | Clearing up | 0.9 | | |
| | | | | | | | | | Moving | 1.9 | | | | |
| | | | | | | | | | Maths book | 1.7 | | | | |
| N | PT1 | 15.0 | 1.6 | 2.1 | 0.2 | 4.3 | 5.4 | 3.4 | Clearing up | 0.8 | Organizing materials | 3.5 | | Used by three classes. |
| | | | | | | | | | Sand play | 0.5 | Clearing up | 0.9 | | |
| O | TT1 | 56.25 | 15.9 | 14.8 | 17.1 | 16.1 | 14.8 | 17.5 | Writing | 4.1 | Individual direct teaching | 4.8 | | Used as a home base and teaching space throughout the day |
| | | | | | | | | | Listening to teacher | 1.8 | Checking work | 2.4 | | |
| | | | | | | | | | Transition | 1.8 | Direct teaching group | 1.8 | | |
| | | | | | | | | | With teacher/maths | 1.6 | | | | |
| P | TT1 | 56.25 | 6.5 | 7.1 | 5.8 | 18.4 | 15.7 | 20.9 | Painting | 2.4 | General supervision | 5.2 | | Used by three classes |
| | | | | | | | | | Sand | 1.2 | Organizing materials | 3.8 | | |
| | | | | | | | | | Cooking | 0.9 | Group discussion | 2.8 | | |
| R[1]a | TT1 | 50.00 | 15.0 | 11.7 | 18.3 | 15.0 | 11.5 | 16.5 | Maths book | 3.6 | Direct teaching individual | 12.7 | | Used by three classes for maths work, cooking, and general use |
| | | | | | | | | | Writing | 2.9 | Discussion individual | 2.3 | | |
| | | | | | | | | | Waiting for teacher | 2.8 | Organizing materials | 1.7 | | |
| b | | 24.00 | 3.5 | 3.8 | 3.2 | 17.8 | 22.2 | 14.4 | Painting | 1.7 | Organizing materials | 10.7 | | Called art/craft area; used by three classes for this |
| | | | | | | | | | Constructing | 0.6 | Talking to teacher | 3.6 | | |
| | | | | | | | | | Getting materials | 0.4 | Clearing up | 2.0 | | |

*Table C3 Percentage use of practical/wet areas (infant) in relation to size and activity based on three day observation*

Table C3 (Continued)

| Unit Letter | Type of Unit | Size $m^2$ | Children Day | Children am | Children pm | Adults Day | Adults am | Adults pm | Main Activities: Children | | Main Activities: Adults | | Materials and Equipment | Additional Information |
|---|---|---|---|---|---|---|---|---|---|---|---|---|---|---|
| $R^2$a | TT1 | 52.00 | 11.2 | 15.8 | 7.1 | 21.3 | 22.1 | 20.6 | Drinking milk<br>Painting<br>Constructing | 2.6<br>2.5<br>1.5 | Organizing materials<br>Talking to teacher<br>Clearing up | 10.7<br>3.6<br>2.0 | | Used by three classes for cooking and art and craft activities |
| b | TT1 | 22.00 | 7.0 | 8.8 | 5.5 | 13.2 | 11.6 | 14.7 | Wendy House play<br>Constructing<br>Clearing up | 2.0<br>1.2<br>1.0 | Organizing materials<br>Individual discussion<br>Clearing up )<br>Direct teaching )<br>individual ) | 7.1<br>2.0<br>1.5 | | Divided into art and Wendy House areas. Used by three classes |
| S | TT1 | 58.00 | 7.5 | 6.7 | 8.1 | 10.5 | 9.0 | 12.1 | Painting<br>Constructing<br>Drawing | 1.7<br>1.1<br>1.0 | Direct teaching group<br>Discussion group | 3.0<br>2.3 | | Used by three classes |
| $Q^1$ | TT2 | 83.00 | 5.4 | 5.7 | 5.1 | 9.5 | 8.9 | 10.3 | Painting<br>Clearing up<br>Sand | 1.6<br>0.6<br>0.6 | Direct teaching group<br>Organizing materials<br>General supervision | 3.6<br>2.4<br>1.8 | | Used by three classes |
| $Q^2$ | TT2 | 83.00 | 9.5 | 10.4 | 8.5 | 10.0 | 7.4 | 12.9 | Constructing<br>Painting<br>Clearing up | 2.2<br>2.1<br>1.3 | Organizing materials<br>Individual discussion<br>Direct teaching group | 2.3<br>2.3<br>2.3 | | Used by three classes |
| T | QT1 | 51.75 | 20.2 | 11.3 | 13.5 | 22.4 | 20.6 | 30.6 | Constructing<br>Painting<br>Drawing | 5.9<br>2.5<br>0.9 | Organizing materials<br>Individual discussion<br>General supervision | 9.2<br>5.4<br>3.8 | | Used by three classes. Staffed by full-time ancillary |

*Table C3 (Continued)*

| Unit Letter | Type of Unit | Size $m^2$ | Children Day | Children am | Children pm | Adults Day | Adults am | Adults pm | Main Activities: Children | | Main Activities: Adults | | Materials and Equipment | Additional Information |
|---|---|---|---|---|---|---|---|---|---|---|---|---|---|---|
| Ua | MT1 | 67.00 | 11.1 | 13.6 | 8.5 | 13.7 | 14.7 | 12.6 | Constructing<br>Drawing<br>Building | 1.7<br>1.5<br>1.4 | General supervision<br>Individual discussion<br>Clearing up<br>Organizing materials | 3.6<br>3.6<br>2.9<br>1.4 | | Used by eleven classes on timetable basis. Also for dinners — only way to hall, toilets, etc. |
| b | | 60.00 | 2.6 | 2.2 | 3.1 | 2.5 | 2.1 | 3.0 | Drawing<br>Listening to teacher<br>Drinking milk | 0.8<br>0.6<br>0.4 | General supervision | 1.1 | | Used by eleven classes on timetable basis. Also for dinners. Only wall to hall, toilets, etc. |
| c | | 63.00 | 3.8 | 4.3 | 3.1 | 9.0 | 11.2 | 6.7 | Reading<br>Writing<br>With teacher interacting | 1.3<br>1.0<br>0.5 | Individual direct teaching<br>Discussion<br>Individual<br>Organizing materials | 7.2<br><br>0.7<br>0.7 | | Used for Break-through reading groups and dinners and circulation |
| Va | MT1 | 21.00 | 1.8 | 1.1 | 2.5 | 7.9 | 4.9 | 10.2 | Painting<br>Clearing up<br>Constructing | 0.5<br>0.4<br>0.3 | Clearing up<br>Organizing materials<br>General supervision<br>Individual discussion | 4.1<br>2.1<br>0.9<br>0.9 | | Used by three classes 5–6 years |
| b | | 24.00 | 0.8 | 0.8 | 0.8 | 2.1 | 0 | 3.6 | Constructing<br>Transition<br>Getting materials | 0.2<br>0.2<br>0.1 | Talking to teacher<br>Individual discussion )<br>General supervision )<br>Clearing up ) | 0.6<br><br>)0.3 | | Used by three classes, 6–7 years |
| W | MTI | 10.00 x 6 | No accurate figures as counted within general teaching areas during observation | | | | | | | | | | | Designated general teaching space by teachers, practical activities taking place throughout areas. |

| Unit Letter | Type of Unit | Size $m^2$ | Children Day | Children am | Children pm | Adults Day | Adults am | Adults pm | Main Activities: Children | % | Main Activities: Adults | % | Materials and Equipment | Additional Information |
|---|---|---|---|---|---|---|---|---|---|---|---|---|---|---|
| A[1] | PT1 | 13.5 | 7.4 | 8.0 | 6.8 | 4.2 | 2.6 | 6.1 | Transition<br>Painting<br>Constructing | 2.3<br>2.0<br>2.0 | General supervision<br>Individual discussion | 1.4<br>1.4 | Art and craft supplies, clay, woodwork tools and bench | Used by two classes. Circulation to other units and hall and administration |
| A[2] | PT1 | 13.5 | 4.3 | 8.4 | - | 4.4 | 9.3 | - | Transition | 4.3 | General supervision | 4.4 | Art and craft supplies, woodwork bench and tools, Plasticene | Used by two classes. Circulation to other units and hall and administration |
| B[1] | PT2 | 46.75 | 25.7 | 26.1 | 25.3 | 20.4 | 22.2 | 18.6 | Listening to teacher<br>Reading<br>Writing | 8.5<br>3.5<br>3.4 | Direct teaching class<br>Work organization<br>Administration | 3.5<br>3.5<br>3.5 | Maths equipment and books, art and craft supplies, science equipment, projector | Used by three classes, one all the time as a home base and time-tabled for other two. Circulation to rest of school |
| B[2] | PT2 | 46.75 | 13.1 | 14.4 | 11.9 | 18.2 | 18.6 | 17.6 | Writing<br>Maths book<br>Drawing | 4.2<br>2.2<br>2.0 | Individual discussion<br>Direct teaching individual<br>General supervision | 6.4<br>4.5<br>2.7 | Cooker and equipment, sewing machine, games and maths equipment, dolls house, art materials | Used by two classes. Circulation to rest of school |
| Ca | TT1 | 32.00 | 8.0 | 10.0 | 5.9 | 1.8 | - | 3.8 | Writing<br>Maths book<br>Constructing | 2.9<br>1.8<br>1.2 | General supervision<br>Organizing materials | 0.9<br>0.9 | Art and craft supplies, maths equipment and books | Used by three classes |
| b | | 23.0 | 10.3 | 14.5 | 5.9 | 10.6 | 16.7 | 3.8 | Writing<br>Getting materials<br>Listening to teacher | 4.5<br>2.3<br>1.1 | Individual discussion<br>Administration<br>Group discussion | 1.8<br>1.8<br>1.8 | Art materials | Used by one class most of time as general work-in area |

*Table C4 Percentage use of practical.wet areas (junior) in relation to size and activity based on three day observation (%)*

*Table C4 (Continued)*

| Unit Letter | Type of Unit | Size m² | Children Day | Children am | Children pm | Adults Day | Adults am | Adults pm | Main Activities: Children | | Main Activities: Adults | | Materials and Equipment | Additional Information |
|---|---|---|---|---|---|---|---|---|---|---|---|---|---|---|
| D[1] | TT1 | 38.0 | 4.2 | 5.6 | 2.9 | 4.7 | 7.2 | 2.5 | Painting<br>Constructing<br>Drawing<br>Listening to teacher | 2.4<br>1.4<br>1.3<br>1.3 | Organizing materials<br>Direct teaching individual<br>Talking to teacher | 2.6<br>1.7<br>0.9 | Art and craft supplies, kiln and clay, easels | Used by three classes. Very badly designed space |
| E | QT1 | 44.0 | 11.0 | 7.2 | 15.2 | 18.6 | 16.0 | 21.7 | Listening to teacher<br>Maths book<br>Writing<br>Constructing | 2.1<br>1.3<br>1.3<br>1.2 | Checking work<br>Organizing materials<br>General supervision<br>Discussion group<br>Direct teaching group | 13.4<br>2.8<br>2.8<br>2.3<br>2.3 | Three paper cutters, guinea pig, clay supplies, cooker and equipment, needle-work supplies, science supplies, woodwork | Used on timetabled basis by four classes |
| F | QT1 | 23.0 | 1.9 | 1.1 | 2.8 | 0.9 | - | 1.8 | Getting materials<br>Constructing<br>Painting | 0.6<br>0.5<br>0.4 | General supervision<br>Discussion individual | 0.5<br>0.5 | Kiln and clay, art supplies, paper cutter | Used by five classes. Very small shut-off area |
| G[1] | QT1 | 15.0 | 6.5 | 4.4 | 9.2 | 10.6 | 10.0 | 11.1 | Painting<br>Getting materials<br>Writing | 2.1<br>1.3<br>1.1 | General supervision<br>Organizing materials<br>Checking | 3.5<br>2.1<br>2.1 | Kiln and clay, art supplies | Used by four classes |
| G[2] | QT1 | 25.0 | 11.5 | 10.7 | 12.4 | 15.3 | 15.8 | 14.9 | Painting<br>Getting materials<br>Writing | 2.1<br>1.3<br>1.1 | General supervision<br>Organising materials<br>Checking | 3.5<br>2.1<br>2.1 | Art and craft supplies | Used by four classes |
| H | QT2 | 115.5 | 16.9 | 28.0 | 6.4 | 25.9 | 34.2 | 16.1 | Painting<br>Getting materials<br>Constructing | 5.9<br>1.7<br>1.6 | Organizing materials<br>Discussion individual<br>Discussion group | 8.8<br>4.2<br>3.7 | Easels, art and craft supplies, woodwork equip-ment, sand and water trays and equipment, maths equipment, cooker and equip-ment, printing equipment | Used by four classes. Long, large area |

*Table C4 (Continued)*

| Unit Letter | Type of Unit | Size $m^2$ | Children | | | Adults | | | Main Activities | | | | Materials and Equipment | Additional Information |
|---|---|---|---|---|---|---|---|---|---|---|---|---|---|---|
| | | | Day | am | pm | Day | am | pm | Children | | Adults | | | |
| Ia | MT1 | 47.0 | 2.3 | 1.9 | 2.7 | 5.0 | 4.1 | 6.6 | Painting<br>Getting materials | 0.7<br>0.4 | Individual discussion<br>Clearing up | 1.6<br>1.2 | Cooker and equipment, easels, art and craft supplies, | Used by two classes and circulation |
| b | | 31.0 | 1.1 | 1.0 | 1.2 | 0.4 | 0.8 | - | Constructing<br>Getting materials | 0.6<br>0.2 | Work organization | 0.4 | maths equipment, art and craft supplies | Used by two classes and circulation |
| c | | 36.0 | 7.9 | 9.3 | 6.5 | 0.4 | 0.8 | - | Constructing<br>Writing<br>Maths book<br>Sand | 1.8<br>1.8<br>1.2<br>0.8 | Discussion individual<br>Direct teaching individual<br>Work organization | 1.2<br>1.2<br>0.8 | Sand tray and equipment, art and craft supplies, reference books, maths equipment, paper cutter | Used by two classes and circulation |
| Ja | MT1 | 62.0 | 5.3 | 6.3 | 4.4 | 5.6 | 5.5 | 5.6 | Constructing<br>Painting<br>Writing | 1.9<br>0.7<br>0.5 | Organizing materials<br>General supervision<br>Individual discussion | 3.4<br>0.9<br>0.9 | Kiln, potter's wheel, clay equipment, art and craft supplies | Used by six classes and circulation space to school |
| b | | 49.0 | 0.6 | 0.5 | 0.6 | 0.4 | 0.9 | - | Getting materials | 0.4 | Individual discussion | 0.4 | Fridge, dryer, cooker and equipment, ironing board and iron, washing machine, art materials | Used by six classes, mostly cooking |
| Ka | MT2 | 45.0 | 1.8 | 0.5 | 3.2 | 3.4 | 1.5 | 5.3 | Cooking<br>Clearing up | 0.7<br>0.4 | Group discussion<br>Individual discussion | 2.3<br>0.8 | Two mobile coat racks, three cupboards, 1 screen, 1 globe | Used by three classes |
| b | | 48.0 | 0.9 | 0.3 | 1.6 | - | - | - | Transition<br>Getting materials | 0.5<br>0.2 | | | Two mobile coat racks, 1 screen, art materials, book trolley and books | Used by three classes |

*Table C4 (Continued)*

| Unit Letter | Type of Unit | Size $m^2$ | Children Day | Children am | Children pm | Adults Day | Adults am | Adults pm | Main Activities: Children | | Main Activities: Adults | | Materials and Equipment | Additional Information |
|---|---|---|---|---|---|---|---|---|---|---|---|---|---|---|
| La | MT2 | 32.0 | 2.3 | 4.0 | 0.5 | 1.4 | 0.9 | 1.9 | Writing<br>Listening to teacher | 0.9<br>0.4 | Individual discussion | 0.9 | Art supplies, display of work | Used by two classes and circulation |
| b | | 32.0 | 0.3 | 0.3 | 0.2 | - | - | - | Clearing up | 0.1 | | | Water tray, art supplies, animals | Used by two classes and circulation |
| c | | 32.0 | 1.3 | 0.7 | 2.0 | 1.4 | - | 2.9 | Drawing | 1.0 | Organizing materials<br>Clearing up<br>Direct teaching individual | 0.5<br>0.5<br>0.5 | Art supplies | Used by one class and circulation |
| d | | 32.0 | 0.6 | 0.8 | 0.4 | - | - | - | Getting materials<br>Painting and<br>Clearing up | 0.1<br>0.1<br>0.1 | | | Two woodwork benches and equipment, art supplies | Used by one class and circulation |

| School | Children | | | | | | | | | | | | | | | | | | | | | | | | | | | | |
|---|---|---|---|---|---|---|---|---|---|---|---|---|---|---|---|---|---|---|---|---|---|---|---|---|---|---|---|---|---|
| | Reading | Writing | Practical maths | Maths book | Cooking | Drawing | Painting | Construction building | Construction modelling | Sand | Water | Wendy House | Dolls House | Sewing | Singing | Music | Interacting with teachers | Waiting for teacher | Listening to teacher | Getting materials | Looking | Clearing up | Moving | Milk | Chat | Transition | TV | Listening record/tape | Large apparatus |
| PT1 $M^1$ | .9 | 7.5 | 1.3 | 5.3 | 0 | 2.8 | .2 | 0 | 0 | 0 | 0 | .1 | 0 | 0 | 0 | 0 | 2.1 | 4.3 | 7.2 | 3.3 | 1.3 | 4.8 | .2 | 0 | .1 | 0 | 0 | 0 | 0 |
| PT1 $M^2$ | .1 | 15.2 | 2.4 | 6.7 | 0 | .1 | 0 | 0 | 0 | 0 | 0 | 0 | 0 | 0 | 0 | 0 | 1.9 | 5.1 | 3.5 | 2.1 | 1.4 | .9 | 0 | 0 | 0 | 1.7 | 0 | 0 | 0 |
| TT1 0 | .6 | 6.9 | 3.4 | 6.7 | 0 | 2.5 | .5 | 3.1 | .6 | 0 | 0 | .2 | 0 | 0 | 0 | 0 | 1.2 | 5.2 | 19.9 | 1.0 | .3 | 1.0 | 1.0 | .5 | .3 | 1.4 | .7 | 0 | 0 |
| TT1 P | 1.8 | 12.4 | 1.3 | 4.2 | 0 | .4 | 0 | 0 | 1.0 | 0 | 0 | .1 | 0 | 0 | 0 | 1.3 | 1.2 | 6.8 | 19.0 | 2.6 | .3 | .5 | 0 | 0 | 0 | 4.7 | 0 | 0 | 0 |
| TT1 $Q^1$ | 1.6 | 5.9 | 4.0 | 4.7 | 0 | 3.0 | 0 | 3.9 | 4.0 | 0 | 0 | 2.2 | 0 | 1.5 | 1.0 | .3 | 2.4 | 3.3 | 30.9 | 2.9 | 1.1 | 3.3 | 1.8 | 1.0 | 0 | .9 | 3.9 | 0 | 0 |
| TT1 $Q^2$ | 2.5 | 6.7 | 4.2 | 4.8 | 0 | 2.7 | .1 | 3.6 | .6 | 0 | 0 | 1.1 | 0 | 0 | 0 | 0 | 2.1 | 2.7 | 35.1 | 1.5 | .8 | 6.7 | 3.1 | 3.1 | 1.0 | 2.5 | 0 | 1.0 | .3 |
| TT1 $R^1$ | 4.8 | 8.1 | .8 | 4.8 | .2 | .7 | .2 | 2.0 | 1.7 | 0 | 0 | .3 | 0 | 0 | .6 | 0 | .9 | 6.6 | 14.2 | 1.1 | .7 | 1.0 | 1.3 | .2 | 0 | 0 | 0 | 0 | 0 |
| TT1 $R^2$ | 1.9 | .6 | 1.1 | .5 | .4 | 3.0 | 2.5 | 1.5 | 4.3 | 0 | .2 | 0 | 0 | 0 | 1.9 | 0 | 1.5 | 6.9 | 32.3 | .7 | 2.0 | 1.5 | 3.7 | 2.7 | 0 | .3 | 4.7 | 0 | 0 |
| TT1 S | 1.2 | 10.9 | .5 | 2.1 | 0 | 1.2 | 0 | .8 | 0 | 0 | 0 | 0 | 0 | 0 | 0 | 0 | 2.7 | 1.8 | .4 | 1.3 | .1 | 1.9 | 0 | 0 | 0 | 1.9 | 7.0 | 0 | 0 |
| MT1 U | 1.8 | 8.0 | 3.9 | 2.3 | .1 | 3.3 | .9 | .7 | .9 | 0 | 0 | 2.1 | 0 | .1 | 0 | 0 | 2.3 | 4.0 | 24.7 | 1.0 | .1 | .6 | .8 | 0 | 0 | .4 | 6.5 | 0 | .1 |
| MT1 V | 1.7 | 8.4 | 3.8 | 2.2 | 0 | 1.3 | 0 | .9 | 2.3 | 0 | 0 | .1 | 0 | 0 | 0 | 0 | 1.5 | 2.8 | 1.4 | 5.0 | .1 | .9 | .2 | 0 | 0 | .5 | 0 | 0 | 0 |
| Average | 1.6 | 8.2 | 2.4 | 4.0 | .1 | 1.9 | .4 | 1.5 | 1.4 | 0 | 0 | .6 | 0 | .1 | .3 | .1 | 1.9 | 4.5 | 17.1 | 2.0 | .8 | 2.1 | 1.1 | .7 | .1 | 1.3 | 2.1 | .1 | 0 |

*Table C5 Activities over three days in shared teaching areas: infant units (%)*

| School | Adults | | | | | | | | | | | | | | | | | | | | |
|---|---|---|---|---|---|---|---|---|---|---|---|---|---|---|---|---|---|---|---|---|---|
| | Administration | Work organization | Organizing material | Clearing up | General supervision | Discussion – individual | Discussion – group | Discussion – class | Checking work | Direct teaching – individual | Direct teaching – group | Direct teaching – class | Discipline | Talk to teachers | Talk to ancillary | Talk to other adults | Out | TV/record | Cooperative teaching | PE/drama | Assembly |
| PTI M[1] | 0 | 4.3 | 3.2 | 4.3 | 3.2 | 4.3 | 1.1 | 0 | 6.4 | 9.6 | 5.3 | 0 | 0 | 2.1 | 0 | 0 | 0 | 0 | 3.2 | 0 | 0 |
| PTI M[2] | 3.0 | 5.0 | 7.0 | 3.0 | 2.0 | 2.0 | 2.0 | 0 | 7.0 | 17.0 | 2.0 | 0 | 0 | 0 | 0 | 0 | 0 | 0 | 2.0 | 0 | 0 |
| TTI O | 1.2 | 5.4 | 3.6 | .6 | 3.6 | 4.2 | 0 | 1.2 | 10.7 | 7.1 | 2.4 | 10.1 | .6 | 1.2 | 0 | 0 | 0 | 0 | 2.4 | 0 | 0 |
| TTI P | .9 | 4.2 | 3.8 | 1.9 | 1.9 | 3.3 | 0 | 1.4 | 3.3 | 10.4 | 3.8 | 6.6 | .9 | 2.4 | 0 | .5 | 0 | 0 | 0 | 0 | 0 |
| TTI Q[1] | 3.0 | 1.8 | 3.6 | 1.8 | 7.1 | 11.3 | 4.2 | 5.4 | 1.8 | 11.9 | 3.0 | 12.5 | 0 | 0 | 0 | .6 | 0 | 0 | 3.6 | 0 | 0 |
| TTI Q[2] | 3.1 | 2.3 | 3.8 | 2.3 | 10.8 | 15.4 | 3.1 | 5.4 | 4.6 | 15.4 | 3.1 | 13.8 | 0 | 0 | 0 | .8 | 0 | .8 | .8 | 0 | 0 |
| TTI R[1] | 3.4 | 2.9 | 6.9 | 1.7 | 0 | 5.2 | 3.4 | .6 | 1.7 | 13.2 | 1.1 | 5.2 | .6 | .6 | 0 | .6 | 0 | 0 | 0 | 0 | 0 |
| TTI R[2] | 4.6 | 1.0 | 7.6 | 1.0 | 1.0 | 0 | 2.5 | 1.0 | .5 | 5.6 | 4.1 | 12.2 | 0 | 3.0 | 0 | .5 | 0 | 2.5 | 1.5 | 0 | 0 |
| TTI S | 0 | 3.0 | 1.5 | 2.6 | 1.5 | 4.5 | 0 | 0 | 3.0 | 12.8 | 3.0 | 0 | 0 | 0 | 0 | 0 | 0 | 6.0 | 1.5 | 0 | 0 |
| MTI U | 4.3 | 2.5 | 3.2 | .7 | 4.7 | 1.8 | 1.4 | 1.8 | 2.2 | 9.6 | 3.6 | 10.1 | 1.1 | 1.8 | 0 | 0 | 0 | 3.2 | 3.6 | 0 | 0 |
| MTI V | .9 | .9 | 5.0 | 1.8 | 5.6 | 4.1 | 0 | .3 | 6.8 | 8.5 | 0 | 1.2 | 1.5 | 2.1 | .9 | 0 | 0 | 0 | 0 | 0 | 0 |
| Average | 2.2 | 3.0 | 4.4 | 3.4 | 3.8 | 5.1 | 1.6 | 1.6 | 4.4 | 11.0 | 2.9 | 6.5 | .4 | 1.2 | .1 | .3 | 0 | 1.1 | 1.7 | 0 | 0 |

*Table C6 Activities over three days in shared teaching areas: infant units (%)*

| School | Children | | | | | | | | | | | | | | | | | | | | | | | | | | | |
|---|---|---|---|---|---|---|---|---|---|---|---|---|---|---|---|---|---|---|---|---|---|---|---|---|---|---|---|---|
| | Reading | Writing | Practical maths | Maths book | Cooking | Drawing | Painting | Construction building | Construction modelling | Sand | Water | Wendy House | Dolls house | Sewing | Singing | Music | Interacting with teachers | Waiting for teacher | Listening to teacher | Getting materials | Looking | Clearing up | Moving | Milk | Chat | Transition | TV | Listening to record / tape |
| PT1 A[1] | 3.0 | 19.4 | 1.2 | 6.8 | 0 | 2.0 | 1.1 | 0 | 1.7 | 0 | 0 | 0 | 0 | 3.9 | 0 | 0 | 3.0 | 3.5 | 19.1 | 5.1 | 0 | 0 | 0 | 0 | .3 | 0 | 0 | 0 |
| PT1 A[2] | 2.4 | 15.3 | 0 | 13.2 | 0 | 4.5 | 1.3 | 0 | .2 | 0 | 0 | 0 | 0 | .2 | 0 | 0 | 8.7 | 4.9 | 25.2 | 2.9 | 0 | 1.4 | 0 | 0 | 0 | 0 | 0 | 0 |
| PT1 C | .6 | 6.6 | 0 | 1.6 | 0 | .7 | 0 | 0 | .3 | 0 | 0 | 0 | 0 | 0 | 0 | 0 | .5 | .3 | 1.1 | 3.3 | 0 | .1 | 0 | 0 | 0 | 0 | 0 | 0 |
| QT1 F | .4 | 13.0 | .2 | 18.4 | .2 | 1.4 | 0 | 0 | .8 | 0 | 0 | 0 | 0 | 0 | 0 | 0 | .9 | 1.9 | 0 | 3.3 | 0 | .3 | 0 | 0 | 0 | 0 | 0 | 0 |
| QT1 E | .4 | 5.3 | .3 | 6.1 | .9 | .6 | .1 | 0 | .9 | 0 | 0 | 0 | 0 | .5 | 0 | 0 | 1.1 | 1.9 | 7.0 | 2.0 | .1 | .1 | 0 | 0 | 0 | 0 | 0 | 0 |
| QT1 G[1] | 1.5 | 17.4 | 2.8 | 15.6 | 0 | 1.1 | 0 | 0 | 0 | 0 | 0 | 0 | 0 | 0 | 0 | 0 | 1.5 | 6.8 | 9.6 | 6.3 | .9 | .9 | 2.3 | 0 | .5 | 0 | 3.1 | 1.5 |
| QT1 G[2] | 2.3 | 15.9 | .9 | 10.2 | 0 | .1 | 0 | 0 | 0 | 0 | 0 | 0 | 0 | .2 | 0 | 0 | .8 | 1.5 | 11.1 | 4.4 | 1.3 | .3 | .6 | .2 | .1 | 0 | 0 | .2 |
| MT1 I | .4 | 16.1 | .5 | 8.2 | 0 | .2 | 0 | 0 | 0 | 0 | 0 | 0 | 0 | .4 | 0 | 0 | 1.4 | .8 | 2.2 | 2.9 | .5 | .7 | 0 | 0 | 0 | 0 | .6 | 0 |
| MT1 J | 1.8 | 15.5 | .9 | 7.9 | 0 | 5.6 | .2 | 0 | .1 | 0 | 0 | 0 | 0 | .7 | 0 | 0 | 1.4 | 4.2 | 4.8 | 2.0 | .1 | 0 | 0 | 0 | 0 | 0 | 1.1 | 0 |
| Average | 1.4 | 13.8 | .8 | 9.8 | .1 | 1.8 | .3 | 0 | .4 | 0 | 0 | 0 | 0 | .7 | 0 | 0 | 2.0 | 2.9 | 8.9 | 3.6 | .3 | .4 | .3 | 0 | .1 | 0 | .5 | .2 |

*Table C7 Activities over three days in shared teaching areas: junior units*

| School | Adults | | | | | | | | | | | | | | | | | | | | |
|---|---|---|---|---|---|---|---|---|---|---|---|---|---|---|---|---|---|---|---|---|---|
| | Administration | Work organization | Organizing material | Clearing up | General supervision | Discussion - individual | Discussion - group | Discussion - class | Checking work | Direct teaching - individual | Direct teaching - group | Direct teaching - class | Discipline | Talk to teachers | Talk to ancillary | Talk to other adults | Out | TV/record | PE/drama | Assembly | Cooperative teaching |
| PTI $A^1$ | 2.8 | 9.9 | 5.6 | 0 | 2.8 | 2.8 | 2.8 | 0 | 11.3 | 16.9 | 1.4 | 9.9 | 2.8 | 0 | 0 | 0 | 0 | 0 | 0 | 0 | 2.8 |
| PTI $A^2$ | 0 | 5.9 | 4.4 | 0 | 4.4 | 0 | 0 | 0 | 14.7 | 30.9 | 5.9 | 2.9 | 0 | 2.9 | 0 | 0 | 0 | 0 | 2.9 | 0 | 8.8 |
| TTI C | 3.5 | 1.8 | .9 | 0 | .9 | 2.7 | 2.7 | 0 | 1.8 | 4.4 | 0 | .9 | 0 | 1.8 | 0 | 0 | 0 | 0 | 0 | 0 | 0 |
| QTI F | .9 | .5 | 4.1 | 0 | .9 | 6.4 | 0 | 0 | 6.4 | 11.8 | 0 | .5 | 0 | 0 | 0 | 0 | .5 | 0 | 0 | 0 | 0 |
| QTI E | .6 | 1.1 | 5.6 | 1.7 | 4.0 | 2.3 | 0 | 2.3 | 2.3 | 2.3 | 0 | 1.7 | 0 | 0 | 0 | 0 | 0 | 0 | 0 | 0 | 3.4 |
| QTI $G^1$ | 2.8 | 1.4 | 10.6 | .7 | 3.5 | 9.9 | .7 | 1.4 | 3.5 | 11.8 | 6.3 | 4.2 | 1.4 | 2.8 | 0 | 0 | 0 | 4.5 | 0 | 0 | 0 |
| QTI $G^2$ | 0 | .7 | 2.7 | .7 | 0 | 7.3 | 0 | 0 | 6.0 | 14.7 | 4.7 | 3.3 | 6.7 | 0 | 0 | 0 | 0 | 0 | 0 | 0 | 0 |
| MTI I | 0 | 2.9 | .6 | 1.6 | 3.3 | 9.0 | .8 | 0 | 7.4 | 9.4 | 4.1 | 0 | 0 | 1.6 | 0 | 0 | 0 | 0 | 0 | 0 | 0 |
| MTI J | 3.0 | 4.3 | 8.2 | 0 | 5.2 | 6.0 | 4.3 | .4 | 3.0 | 3.9 | .9 | 1.3 | 0 | 0 | 0 | 0 | 0 | 0 | 0 | 0 | 0 |
| Average | 1.5 | 3.2 | 4.7 | .5 | 3.6 | 5.2 | 1.3 | .5 | 6.3 | 11.8 | 2.6 | 2.7 | 1.2 | 1.0 | 0 | 0 | .1 | .5 | .3 | 0 | 1.7 |

*Table C8 Activities over three days in shared teaching areas: junior units*

# APPENDIX D
## Comparison of LEA Briefs

| *Teaching Space Suggested* | *Organization or Grouping* | *Size of Space specified* | *m²* | *sq. ft* | *Other design points mentioned* |
|---|---|---|---|---|---|
| MTA + 6% | 3 units | 1) Open area – | 110 | 1184 | The building seen as a |
| circulation | 1) 80 – 2) 80– | Quiet/noisy | 25 | 269 | square shape, with hall |
| = 597.8m² | 3) 120 children | 2) Open area | 111 | 1195 | near centre. The practical |
| (6,405 sq. ft) | | Small quiet/noisy | 11 | 118 | area also seen as square |
| | | Large quiet/noisy | 22 | 237 | rather than rectangular. |
| | | Studio | 25 | 269 | |
| | | 3) Practical | 120 | 1292 | |
| | | Large quiet/noisy | 29 | 312 | |
| | | Hall | 130 | 1399 | |
| | | ½ group room | 9 | 97 | |
| MTA + 10% | Teachers in | General – | NS | | The general area should |
| = 620.4m² | twos or in | Kiva | 15 | 161 | not be long and narrow. |
| (6,680 sq. ft) | threes | Library | 20-30 | 215-323 | The hall should be |
| | | Home base infant | 12 | 129 | square. |
| | | Cooking junior | 15 | 161 | |
| | | Practical | 3¼ | 35 | |
| | | Maths/science | 20-25 | 215-269 | |
| | | AV room | 30 | 323 | |
| MTA + 10% | Teachers in | 2 Project each | 37 | 398 | The infant project area |
| = 620.4m | twos or more | Home base | 14 | 151 | should be adjacent to |
| (6,680 sq. ft) | | 4 Home base | 37 | 398 | home base. |
| | | 4 Quiet | 14 | 151 | |
| | | Library | 4.7 | 51 | |
| | | Project | 37 | 398 | |
| 620m² | A. two group 70 | each unit to have | | | Covered outdoor |
| (includes MTA) | two groups 70 | general area | | | related to practical area. |
| (6,675 sq. ft) | 3 groups | 2 home bays | 20 | 215 | |
| | 105 children | (215 sq. ft) (at least) | | | |
| | | and practical area. | | | |
| | | 2 enclosed rooms | | | |
| | | for the school each | | | |
| | | of classroom size, | | | |
| | | total teaching space | 470 | 5059 | |
| | | Library | 20 | 215 | |
| | | Hall | 130 | 1399 | |
| 680m² | 7 classes with | Home bases | 13-14 | 140-151 | The arrangement of |
| (includes MTA) | provision for | (per 40 children) | | | some teaching areas |
| (7,320 sq. ft) | individual, | AV | 20-25 | 215-269 | to be as workshops. |
| | small group | Practical – ⅓ of | | | Design of the immediate |
| | and class work | teaching areas | | | environment to provide |
| | | Hall | 144 | 1550 | visual impact. |
| | | General area | 33-36 | 355-388 | |
| | | (per 40 children) | | | |
| 707.5m² | 4 groups of 70 | AV | 29.16 | 314 | The building should be a |
| (includes MTA) | children each | Hall | 124.74 | 1342 | stimulus in its appear- |
| (7,615.47 sq. ft) | sub-divided into | 8 Quiet | 103.68 | 1106 | ance. Key focal points |
| | 2 of 35 | 4 Practical | 99.63 | 1066 | around the building very |
| | | 8 General | 284.31 | 3060 | important. |
| | | 8 Book areas | 21.06 | 227 | |

*Table D1 Comparison of schedules for a one-form entry primary school from LEA briefs*

# References


ADAMS, J. (1922). *Modern Developments in Educational Practice.* University of London Press.

ADELMAN, C. and WALKER, R. (1974). 'Open Space – Open Classroom', *Education 3-13,* **2,** 2, 103–7.

ALDERSON, A. and HIRD, B. (1973). Prior Weston – an observation study of a new primary school. Inner London Education Authority Education Research and Statistics Group Report no.RS 578/73.

ALLEN, D.I. (1972). *Open Areas in British Columbia.* Barnaby, British Columbia, Canada: Simon Fraser University.

ALLEN, D.I. (1974). 'Student Performance, Attitude and Self esteem in Open Area and Self Contained Classrooms', *Alberta Journal of Educational Research,* **20,** 1, 1–7.

ALLEN, D.I. (1976). Research on Open Area Classrooms. Paper presented at annual conference of Australian Association for Research in Education, Brisbane.

ALLEN, D.I., HAMELIN, R. and NIXON, G. (1976). 'Need for Structure, Programme Openness and Job Satisfaction among Teachers in Open Area and Self Contained Classrooms', *Alberta Journal of Educational Research,* **22,** 2, 149–53.

ANGUS, M.J., EVANS, K.W., and PARKIN, B. (1975). *An Observation Study of selected Pupil and Teacher Behaviour in Open Plan and Conventional designed Classrooms.* Technical Report 4, Australian Open Area Schools Project. Perth, Australia.

ANGUS, M.J., BECK, T.M., HILL, P.W. and McATEE, W.A. (1979). *Open Plan Schools – An Evaluative Study of Teaching and Learning in Primary Schools of Conventional and Open Area Design in Australia.* Canberra: Australian Government Publishing Service (ERDC Report no.21).

ANNIFANT, D.C. (1972). Risk taking Behaviour in Children experienced in Open Space and Traditional School Environments. Unpublished PhD dissertation, University of Maryland, USA.

ARIKADO, M.S. and MUSELLA, D.F. (1973). Status Variables related to Team teacher Satisfaction in the Open Plan School. Paper presented at the American Educational Research Association, New Orleans, USA. ERIC, ED 076 562.

ARKWRIGHT, D., HEWITT, M.C., THORNE, K. and WEBB, W. (1975). Survey of Open Plan Primary Schools in Derbyshire. Derbyshire Education Authority.

ARLIN, M. and PALM, L. (1974). 'The Interaction of Open Education Procedures, Student Characteristics, and Attitudes Towards Learning'. Paper presented on the annual meeting of APA, New Orleans, USA.

ARMSTRONG, D.G. (1975). 'Open Space versus Self-Contained', *Eductional Leadership,* **32,** 4, 291–5.

ASHTON, P., KNEEN, P., DAVIES, F. and HOLLEY, B.J. (1975). *The Aims of Primary Education: A study in Teachers' opinions (Schools Council Research Studies).* Macmillan Education.

AUSTRALIA. *Education Department of South Australia* (1976). A Report of the National In-service Conference convened by the Education Department of South Australia.

BAINES, G. (1971). 'Learning in a Flexible School'. In: WALTON J. (Ed) *The Integrated Day in Theory and Practice.* Ward Lock Educational.
BALLARD, P.B. (1925). *The Changing School.* University of London Press, 1934 edition.
BASSEY, M. (1978). *Nine hundred Primary School Teachers.* Windsor: NFER Publishing Company.
BEALS, J.P. (1972). An Investigation of Emotive Perception among Students in Open-Space and Conventional Learning Environments. Unpublished EdD thesis, University of Tennessee, USA.
BEARDSLEY, B., BRICKER, K. and MURRAY, J. (1973). 'Hints for Survival in Open Plan Schools', *Curriculum Theory Network,* 11, 47–64.
BECKLEY, L.L. (1972). Comparative study of elementary School Student Attitudes Toward School and Self in Open Concept and Self-Containing Environments. Unpublished PhD thesis, Purdue University, Indiana, USA.
BELL, A.E., SWITZER, F. and ZIPURSKY, M.A. (1974). 'Open-Area Education: an Advantage or Disadvantage for beginners', *Perceptual and Motor Skills,* **39,** 1, 407–16.
BELL, A.E., ZIPURSKY, M.A. and SWITZER, F. (1976). 'Informal or Open-Area Education in relation to Achievement and Personality', *Brit. J. Educ. Psychol.,* **46,** 3, 235–43.
BELL, A.E., ABRAHAMSON, D.S. and GROWSE, R. (1977). 'Achievement and Self-reports of Responsibility for Achievement in Informal and Traditional Classrooms', *Brit. J. Educ. Psychol.,* **47,** Part 3, 258–67.
BENNETT, S.N., BOOTH, J., DOCHERTY, A., MORGAN, E., SCOTT, J., TURNER, M. and WALLS, E. (1975). 'An enquiry into Cumbria's Open Plan Schools'. Lancaster: University of Lancaster.
BENNETT, S.N. *et al.* (1976). *Teaching Styles and Pupil Progress.* Open Books.
BENNETT, S.N., ANDREAE, J., HEGARTY, D. and WADE, B. (1976). *Journeys into Open Space.* Lancaster: University of Lancaster.
BENNETT, S.N. and BATLEY, D. (1977). 'Pupils' reactions to Open-Plan', *Education 3–13,* **5,** 20–3.
BENNETT, S.N. (1978a). 'Recent Research on Teaching: a Dream, a Belief and a Model', *Brit. J. Educ. Psychol.,* **48,** Part 2, 127–47.
BENNETT, S.N. (1978b). 'The Organisation of Teaching and Curriculum in Open Plan Schools', *Aspects of Education,* **21,** 35–49.
BERLINER, D.C. and ROSENSHINE, B. (1976). The Acquisition of Knowledge in the Classroom. Technical Report IV-I of Beginning Teacher Evaluation Study, San Francisco, Far West Laboratory, USA.
BLACK, M.S. (1974). Academic Achievement and Self-Concept of fourth-Grade Pupils in Open Area and Traditional Learning Environments. Unpublished Phd thesis, University of Michigan, USA.
BLISHEN, E. (Ed) (1969). *Blond's Encyclopaedia of Education.* Blond Educational.
BLOOM, B.S. (1976). *Human Characteristics and School Learning.* New York: McGraw Hill.
BLUMENTHAL, D. and REISS, S. (1975). 'Do Open Space Environments encourage Children to seek immediate Gratification?', *Journal of School Psychology,* **13,** 2, 91–6.
BOWER, J. (1968). 'Primary School Design'. In: THOMPSON, R.H. (Ed) 'The Primary School in Transition' (University of Hull), *Aspects of Education,* 8, December, 85–92.
BOYDELL, D. (1975). 'Pupil Behaviour in Junior Classrooms', *Brit. J. Educ. Psychol.,* **45,** Part 2, 122–9.

BROPHY, J.E. and EVERTSON, C.M. (1976). *Learning from Teaching: a developmental perspective.* McGraw-Hill.
BRISTOL UNIVERSITY. School of Advanced Urban Studies (1979). *The Briefing Process in School Design.* HMSO.
BROWARD COUNTY SCHOOL BOARD (1972a). 'Evaluation of Innovative Schools: CCDQ results for fifth year teachers'. Report no.53. Florida.
BROWARD COUNTY SCHOOL BOARD (1972b). 'Evaluation of Innovative Schools: research Questionnaire Tabulations for Fifth Year Pupils and Teachers. 1970-1971'. Report no.54. Florida.
BROWARD COUNTY SCHOOL BOARD (1972c). 'Evaluation of Innovative Schools: Student Achievement. 1970-1971'. Report no.55. Florida.
BRUNETTI, F.A. (1971). 'Open Space: a Status Report'. Memo No. 1, School Environment Study. Stanford, California: Stanford University.
BRUNETTI, F.A., COHEN, E.G., MAYER, J.W. and HOLNAR, F.R.F. (1972). 'Studies of Team Teaching in the Open-Space School', *Interchange,* **3,** 2-3, 85–101.
BURNHAM, B. (1971). 'Achievement of Grade I pupils in Open Plan and Architecturally Conventional Schools', Aurora, Ontario: York County Board of Education.
BURNHAM, B. (1973c). 'Reading, Spelling and Mathematics Achievement of Grade 2 Pupils in Open Plan and Architecturally Conventional Schools', *Studies in Open Education,* No.6. Aurora, Ontario: York County Board of Education.
BURNHAM, B. (1973a). 'Reading, Spelling and Maths Achievement of Grade two pupils in Open Plan and Architecturally Conventional Schools', *Studies in Open Education,* No. 6. Aurora, Ontario: York County Board of Education.
BURNHAM, B. (1973b). 'Reading and Mathematics Achievement of Grade Three Pupils in Open Plan and Architecturally Conventional Schools – the Third Year of a longitudinal Study', *Studies in Open Education,* No. 10. Aurora, Ontario: York County Board of Education.
BUSSELLE, S.M. (1972). 'Training Teachers to Work in Open Space', *National Elementary Principal,* **52,** 1, 87–90.
BUSSIS, A.M. and CHITTENDEN, E.A. (1970). *Analysis of an Approach to Open Education.* Princeton, New Jersey, USA: Educational Testing Service.
BUSSIS, A.M., CHITTENDEN, E.A. and AMAREL, M. (1976). *Beyond Surface Curriculum: an interview study of teachers' understandings.* Boulder, Colorado, USA: Westview Press.
BUTSON, T.T. (1975). A study of the Effects of an Alternative School Program on Selected Cognitive and Affective Areas of Growth of non-Urban Students. Unpublished PhD thesis, University of Minnesota.
CANTER, D. (1973). 'Evaluating Buildings: Emerging Scales and the Salience of Building elements over Constructs'. In: KULLER, R. (Ed) *Architectural Psychology.* Stroudsburg, Pa, USA: Dowden, Hutchinson & Ross.
CARBONARI, J.P. (1971). 'Report of an Evaluation Study of an Open Concept School'. *Educators' Report and Fact Sheet,* 8, 1–2.
CARROLL, J.B. (1963). 'A model of School Learning', *Teachers College Record,* 64, 723–33.
CARSON, R.B., JOHNSON, F.T. and OLIVA, F.D. (1973). 'The Open Area School: Facilitator for or Obstacle to Instructional Objectives', *Journal of Education,* 155, 18–30.

CHARTERS, W.W. (1978). The Effects of the Team Organisation of Elementary Schools on Teacher Influence and Work attitudes. Paper presented at the annual conference of the American Educational Research Association, Toronto.
CHEEK, R.E. (1970). Opinions of Teachers Teaching in Selected Open-Space Elementary Schools. Unpublished PhD thesis, Wayne State University, Michigan, USA.
COLLINS, K.T. *et al.* (Eds) (1973). *Key Words in Education.* Longman.
COOK, G. (1973) 'Problems of Teacher-Student Organisation in Open Rooms'. Studies in Open Education No. 8. Aurora, Ontario: York County Board of Education.
CORRIE, M. (1974). *Space for Learning: teaching and learning in some Scottish open plan primary schools.* Edinburgh: Scottish Council for Research in Education.
COX, C.B. and BOYSON, R. (Eds) (1975). *Black Paper, 1975.* Dent.
CRAMER, H.L. and BARNES, J.P. (1973). 'Orientating New Users and New Spaces'. *Canadian Educational Facility Planners' Journal,* 11, 9–11.
CULVERWELL, E.P. (1913). *The Montessori Principles and Practice.* Bell.
CURTIS, S.J. (1948). *History of Education in Great Britain.* University Tutorial Press (1965 edition).
DANIELS, J.G. (1974). A Comparison of the Achievement and Attitudes of students attending Open Space Schools with Students attending Traditional Schools. Unpublished EdD thesis, University of Florida.
DAY, H.I. (1973). 'Curiosity, Creativity among Pupils in Open Plan and Architecturally Conventional Schools'. *Studies in Open Education* No. 7. Aurora, Ontario: York County Board of Education.
DAY, H.I. (1974). 'Curiosity, Creativity and Attitude to Schooling in Open Plan and Traditional Schools', *Studies in Open Education* No. 12. Aurora, Ontario: York County Board of Education.
DENNISON, P.F. (1976). An Observational Study of a Classroom in an Open Plan School. Unpublished MA dissertation, University of Lancaster.
DILLING, H.J. and TRAN, C.T. (1973). 'A comparison of Teacher-Pupil Verbal Interaction in Open Plan and Closed Classrooms'. Scarborough: Board of Education Research Department.
DIXON, A. (1978). 'How unstreamed are infant schools?', *Forum,* **28,** 2, 43–5.
DREW, P. (1970). 'Open Plan', *Canadian Architect,* 15, 46–57.
DURLAK, J.T. and LEHMAN, J. (1974). 'User Awareness and Sensitivity to Open Space: A Study of Traditional and Open Plan Schools'. In: CANTER, D.V. and LEE, T. (Eds) *Psychology and the Built Environment.* Architectural Press.
ELLISON, M., GILBERT, L.L. and RATSOY, E.W. (1969). 'Teacher behaviour in Open Area Classrooms', *Canadian Administrator,* **8,** 5, 17–21.
EVANECHKO, P.O. McCULLOUGH, K.R. and AYERS, J.D. (1973). 'Elementary Students look at the Open Area and Team Teaching', *Principals and Vice-Principals Newsletter,* 14, 119—28.
EVANS, K. (1974). 'The Spatial Organization of Infants' Schools', *Journal of Architectural Research,* **3,** 1, 26–32.
EVANS, K. (1979). 'The physical form of the school', British Journal of Educational Studies, **27,** 1,29–42.
FISHER, C.W. (1974). 'Education and Environments in elementary Schools differing in

Architecture and Programme Openness'. Paper presented at the annual conference of the American Educational Research Association (AERA), Chicago.

FISHER, C.W., FILBY, N.N. and MARLIAVE, R.S. (1977). Instructional Time and Student Achievement in Second Grade Reading and Mathematics. Paper presented at the annual conference of the American Educational Research Association (AERA), New York.

FITZPATRICK, G.S. and ANGUS, M.J. (1974). Through Teachers' eyes: Teaching in an Open Space Primary School. Technical Report No. 1, Australian Open Area Schools Project.

FITZPATRICK, G.S. and ZANI, T.L. (1974). Teachers' comments on Open Area and Conventional School Design. Technical Report No. 2, Australian Open Area Schools Project.

FOWLER, G.W. (1970). An evaluation of Open Area Schools in the Calgary Public School District. Calgary, USA, School Board.

FRENCH, R. (1972). Quoted in: GEORGE, P.S. 'Ten Years of Open Space Schools'. Gainsville, Fla: Florida Educational Research and Developmental Council.

GAGE, N.L. (1978). *The Scientific Basis of the Art of Teaching.* New York: Teachers College Press, Columbia University.

GARDNER, D.E.M. (1966). *Experiment and Tradition in Primary Schools.* Methuen.

GARTNER, A. *et al.* (1971). *Children Teach Children: learning by teaching.* New York: Harper & Row.

GATHERCOLE, F.J. (1970). Evaluation of Open Space Schools. A report to the Director of Education from the Saskatoon Public Schools Open Space Sub-Committee.

GILL, W.M. (1977). 'Classroom Architecture and Classroom Behaviours: A Look at the Change to Open-Plan Schools in New Zealand', *New Zealand Journal of Educational Studies,* **12,** 1, 3–16.

GOOD, T.L., BIDDLE, B.J. and BROPHY, J.E. (1975). *Teachers Make a Difference.* New York: Holt, Rhinehart & Winston.

GRAN, B. (1971). The Open Plan Schools in the Malmo Region: a Study of Problems and an interdisciplinary Method Development. Malmo: School of Education.

GRAPKO, M.F. (1972). A comparison of Open Space and Traditional Classroom Structures according to Independence Measures in Children, Teachers' Awareness of Children's Personality Variables and Children's Academic Progress. Ontario: Ministry of Education.

GRAY, W.A. (1976). Open Areas and Open Education Examined: a Research Study. Paper presented at the annual conference of Australian Association for Research in Education, Brisbane.

GRAY, W.A. (1977). 'Innovations and Practice: preparing Teachers for Open Space Schools', *South Pacific Journal of Teacher Education,* **2,** 1, 64–70.

GREAT BRITAIN. *Department of Education and Science* (1977a). *Building Survey.* HMSO.

GREAT BRITAIN. *Department of Education and Science* (1972a). *Eveline Lowe School, Appraisal.* HMSO (Building Bulletin No. 47).

GREAT BRITAIN. *Department of Education and Science* (1975). *Fire and the Design of Schools.* HMSO (Building Bulletin No. 7).

GREAT BRITAIN. *Department of Education and Science* (1974). *Guidelines on Environmental Design in Educational Buildings.* HMSO.

GREAT BRITAIN. *Department of Education and Science* (1973). 'Open Plan and Younger Children', *Trends in Education,* 31, 31–4.

GREAT BRITAIN. *Department of Education and Science* (1972b). *Open Plan Primary Schools.* HMSO (Education Survey 16).

GREAT BRITAIN. *Department of Education and Science and Welsh Office* (1977b). *A Study of School Building: Report.* HMSO.

GREAT BRITAIN. *Department of Education and Science HM Inspectorate* (1977c). *Curriculum, 11—16,* London: Department of Education and Science.

GREAT BRITAIN. *Ministry of Education* (1957). *The Story of Post-War School Building.* HMSO.

GREAT BRITAIN. *Ministry of Education* (1959). *Primary Education.* HMSO.

GUMP, P.V. (1974). 'Operating Environments in Schools of Open and Traditional Design', *School Review,* **82,** 4, 575–93.

HADOW REPORT. GREAT BRITAIN. *Board of Education* (1931). *Report of the Consultative Committee on the Primary School.* HMSO.

HALLINAN, M.T. (1976). 'Friendship Patterns in Open and Traditional Classrooms', *Sociology of Education,* **49,** 4, 254–65.

HALTON COUNTY BOARD OF EDUCATION (1969). Final Report: Evaluation. Oakville, Ontario: Committee of the Innovation Centre.

HAMILTON, D. (1977). *In search of Structure, a Case Study of a New Scottish Open Plan Primary School.* Hodder & Stoughton, for the Scottish Council for Research in Education.

HARNISCHFEGER, A. and WILEY, D.E. (1975). 'Teaching-Learning processes in Elementary School: A Synoptic View', *Studies of Education Processes,* No. 9. University of Chicago, USA.

HARNISCHFEGER, A. and WILEY, D.E. (1978). 'Conceptual Issues in Models of School Learning', *Journal of Curriculum Studies,* **10,** 3.

HEIMGARTNER, N.L. (1972). 'The Comparative Study of Self Concept: Open Space versus Self Contained Classrooms'. Study No. 4. Greeley, Colorado: University of Northern Colorado.

HERSOM, N.L. and MACKAY, D.A. (1971). A Study of Open Area Schools. University of Alberta, Edmonton, USA.

HOLMES, E.G.A. (1911). *What Is and What Might Be: A Study of Education in General and Elementary Education in Particular.* Constable.

HOLMQUIST, A.L. (1972). A Study of the Organizational Climate of Twelve Elementary Schools in the Albuquerque Public School System: each having Architecturally-Open and Architecturally-closed Classrooms. Unpublished EdD thesis, University of New Mexico, USA.

HORWITZ, R.A. (1976). *Psychological Effects of Open Classroom Teaching on Primary School Children: a Review of the Research.* North Dakota Study Group on Evaluation. Dakota: University of North Dakota.

HURLIN, A. (1975). 'Open Plan Schools and Inquiry/Discovery Learning', *Cambridge Journal of Education,* **5,** 2, 98–103.

HYLAND, J.T. (1978). *Open Plan Schools and Open Education.* Unpublished PhD thesis, University of Lancaster.

JARMAN, C. (1977). 'The Organization of Open Plan Primary Schools. The Oxfordshire Experience'. In: BELL, S. *The Organization of Open Plan Primary Schools: Report of a National Course on Organization of Open Plan Primary Schools.* Glasgow: Jordanhill College of Education.

JAWORWICZ, E.M. (1972). 'Open-Space School Design as a Situational Determinant of Organizational Climate and Principal Leader Behavior'. Unpublished PhD thesis, Wayne State University, Michigan, USA.

JEFFREYS, J.S. (1970). An Investigation of the Effects of Innovative Educational Practices on Pupil-Centeredness of Observed Behaviors and on Learner Outcome Variables. Unpublished PhD thesis, University of Maryland, USA.

JUDD, D.E. (1974). The Relationship of Locus-of-Control as a Personality Variable to Student Attitude in the Open School Environment. Unpublished PhD thesis, University of Maryland, USA.

JUSTUS, J.E. (1971). 'An Educator Views Open Space and the Planning Process', *CEFP Journal,* **9,** 5, 12–4. Special Report No. 6, *Space: Catalyst for Education.*

KAELIN, W.C. (1970). Open Space Schools: Advantages and Disadvantages perceived by Teachers and Principals in Selected Open Space Schools. Unpublished PhD thesis, Florida State University, USA.

KENNEDY, V.J. and SAY, M.W. (1971). 'Comparison of the Effects of Open Area versus Closed Area Schools on the Cognitive Gains of Students', *Educators Report and Fact Sheet,* 4, 1–4.

KILLOUGH, C.K. (1971). 'An Analysis of the Longitudinal Effects that a non Graded Elementary Program conducted in an Open Space School had on the Cognitive Achievement of Pupils'. Houston, USA: Bureau of Educational Research and Services, University of Houston.

KLEPARCHUK, H. (1970). 'Supervisory Services Considered desirable by Teachers and Principals in Open Space Elementary Schools'. Oregon, USA: Oregon School Study Council (Bulletin 2).

KRUCHTEN, P.M. (1971). Survey of Teachers' Perceptions in Open Area Schools, MEd thesis, University of Calgary, USA.

KYZAR, B.L. (1971). 'Comparison of Instructional Practices in Classrooms of differing design *Final Report*'. Natchitoches, La, USA: Northwestern State University.

LA FORGE, H.E. (1972). The Effects of the Open Space Design of an Elementary School on Personality Characteristics of Students. Unpublished PhD thesis, University of Houston, USA.

LEDBETTER, T.A. (1969). A Study of Open Spaces for Teaching. Unpublished PhD thesis, University of Tennessee, USA.

LEE, S.A. (1973). 'Environmental Perception Preference and the Designer'. In: KULLER, R. (Ed) *Architectural Psychology.* Stroudsburg, Pa, USA: Dowden, Hutchinson & Ross.

LEE, T. (1976). *Psychology and the Environment.* Methuen.

LUKASEVITCH, A. (1976). A Study of Relationships among Instructional Style (Open versus Non Open), Architectural Design (Open Space versus Non Open Space) and Measures of Self Concept in reading and Mathematics Achievement of third grade Children. Unpublished PhD thesis, University of British Columbia, Canada.

LYNCH, A.J. (1924). *Individual Work and the Dalton Plan: the Working of the Dalton Plan in an Elementary School.* Philip.

McCALLUM, C.J. (1971). Children's Problems as perceived by Children and Teachers in Open-Space team Teaching and Traditional Elementary Schools. Unpublished PhD thesis, University of Colorado, USA.

McDANIEL, N.H. (1970). Factors relating to Personal–Social Adjustments of First- and Second-Grade Children in Self-Contained and Team Teaching Classrooms. Unpublished PhD thesis, North Texas State University, USA.

McPHERSON, M. (1972). 'Open Space Schools in Saskatoon'. Regina, Canada: Regina Research Centre.

McRAE, B.C. (1970). 'The Effect of Open Area Instruction on Reading Achievement'. Vancouver, Canada: Department of Research and Special Services.

MANNING, P. (1967). The Primary School: an environment for education. Liverpool: Pilkington Research Unit, University of Liverpool.

MARRAM, G.D. (1972). The Impact of Learning and the Visibility of Teaching on the Professionalism of Elementary School Teachers. Stanford, California, USA: Stanford University.

MARTIN, L.S. and PAVAN, B.N. (1976). 'Current research on Open Space, Nongrading, Vertical Grouping, and Team Teaching', *Phi Delta Kappa,* **57,** 5, 310–5.

MEDD, D. (1968). 'People in Schools: an Attitude to design', *Royal Institute of British Architects (RIBA) Journal,* June.

MEDD, D. (1973). 'School Design: Responding to Change', *Trends in Education,* **31,** July, 26—30.

MEYER, J., COHEN, E. *et al.* (1971). The impact of the Open Space School upon Teacher Influence and Autonomy. The effects of an Organisational Innovation. Stanford, California, USA: Stanford University.

MILLER, J.D. (1974). 'Effects of noise on people', *Journal of the Acoustical Society of America,* **56,** 3, 729–64.

MISTER, D. and McCANN, L. (1971). Survey of Teachers Assessments of Open Area Schools. Toronto: Ontario Teachers Federation.

MONTESSORI, M. (1912). *The Montessori Method.* Heinemann.

MONTESSORI, M. (1949). *The Absorbent Mind.* India: Kalakshetra Pubs. (1973 edition).

MOODIE, A.G. (1971). A Survey of Reading Achievement in a Secondary School Population, Research Report 71–03. Vancouver, Canada: Board of School Trustees.

MURRAY, N.E. (1971). The Opinions of Teachers teaching in Open Space Elementary Schools in the Windsor Separate School Board. MEd thesis, Wayne State University, Michigan, USA.

MYERS, R.E. (1971). 'A comparison of the Perceptions of Elementary School Children in Open Area and Self-Contained Classrooms in British Columbia', *Journal of Research and Development in Education,* **4,** 3, 100–6.

NASH, B.C. and CHRISTIE, T.G. (1972). *Open Schools Project.* Sudbury, Ontario: Institute for Studies in Education, Mid-Northern Centre.

NATIONAL UNION OF TEACHERS. *Primary Advisory Committee* (1974). *Open Planning: A Report with Special Reference to Primary Schools.* NUT Publications.

NEW ZEALAND (1977). *Report on Open Education in New Zealand Primary Schools.* Wellington: Government printer.

NUNN, T.P. (1920). *Education: Its Data and First Principles.* Edward Arnold (3rd edition, revised and in part rewritten, 1945).

O'BRIEN, M. and FEENEY, J.D. (1973). A Comparison of Open Space and Closed Space Schools on some aspects of Openness. Toronto, Canada: Metropolitan Toronto Separate School Board.

O'NIELL, P. (1974). 'Creative Children in an Open Space and Self Contained Classrooms'. In: *Educational and Psychological Effects of Open Space Education in Oak Park, Illinois.* University of Illinois, Chicago Circle, USA.

PALMER, R. (1971). *Space, Time and Grouping.* Macmillan.

PARKHURST, H. (1922). *Education on the Dalton Plan.* Bell.

PEARSON, E. (1972). *Trends in School Design.* Macmillan (for the Anglo-American Primary Education Project).

PLOWDEN REPORT. GREAT BRITAIN. *Department of Education and Science Central Advisory Council for Education* (England) (1967). *Children and their Primary Schools.* Volume 1. HMSO.

PLUCKROSE, H.A. (1975). *Open School, Open Society.* Evans.

PRITCHARD, D. and MOODIE, A.G. (1971). 'A survey of Teachers' Opinions regarding Open Areas' (ED 157 102). Vancouver, Canada: School Board of School Trustees.

PROSHANSKY, E. and WOLFE, M. (1974). 'The Physical Setting and Open Education', *School Review,* **82,** 4, 556–74.

RATTENBURY, P. (1978). 'More or less Open. The present day design of Primary Schools', *Aspects of Education,* 21, 28–34.

READ, F.L. (1973). Initial Evaluation of the Development and Effectiveness of Open-Space Elementary Schools. Unpublished PhD thesis, United States International University, California, USA.

REISS, S. and DYHDALO, N. (1975). 'Persistence, Achievement and Open-Space Environments', *Journal of Educational Psychology,* **67,** 4, 506–14.

RIDGWAY, L. (1976). *Task of the Teacher in the Primary School.* Ward Lock.

RINTOUL, K.A.P. and THORNE, K.P.C. (1975). *Open Plan Organization in the Primary School.* Ward Lock Educational.

ROBSON, E.R. (1972 facsimile of 1874 edition). *School Architecture.* Leicester: Leicester University Press.

ROECKS, A.L. (1978). 'Instructional cost and utilisation of classroom time for fifth grade students'. Paper presented at annual conference of the American Educational Research Association (AERA), Toronto.

ROMANS, G.R. (1974). 'Open Plan and the Teacher', *Trends in Education,* 34, 19–22.

ROSENSHINE, B. (1976). 'Classroom Instruction'. In: GAGE, N.B. (Ed) *The Psychology of Teaching Methods.* Seventy-fifth Yearbook of the National Society for the Study of Education (NSSE). Chicago: University of Chicago Press.

ROSENSHINE, B. and BERLINER, D.C. (1977). 'Academic Engaged Time'. Paper presented at the annual meeting of the American Educational Research Association (AERA).

RUDAWSKI, J. (1974). The Comparative Effect of Open Space versus Self-Contained Classroom on Pupil Self-Concept development. Unpublished PhD thesis, Saint Louis University, USA.

RUDVALL, G. (1973). Research and Development in the Malmo Region. Malmo, Sweden: Department of Education and Psychology Research.

RUEDI, J. and WEST, C.K. (1973). 'Pupil Self Concept in an "Open" School and in a "Traditional" School', *Psychology in the Schools,* **10,** 1, 48–53.

SACKETT, J.W. (1971). A Comparison of Self-Concept and Achievement of Sixth Grade Students in an Open Space School, self-contained School and Departmentalized School. Unpublished PhD thesis, University of Iowa, USA.

SADLER, J.E. (1975). *Concepts in Primary Education*. Allen & Unwin.

SALMON, E.A.M. (1972). Team Teaching and the 'Active' Classroom: a comparative Study of the Impact of Self-Contained Classrooms and Open-Space Team Teaching Schools on Classroom 'Activity'. Unpublished PhD thesis, Stanford University, USA.

SCHILLER, L.C. (1969). 'The Progressive Ideas in State Schools'. In: ASH, M. (Ed) *Who are the Progressives Now?*. Routledge & Kegan Paul.

SEABORNE, M. (1971a). *The English School: its Architecture and Organisation, Vol I, 1370-1870*. Routledge & Kegan Paul.

SEABORNE, M. (1971b). *Primary School Design*. Routledge & Kegan Paul.

SEABORNE, M. and LOWE, R. (1977). *The English School: Its Architecture and Organization, Vol. II, 1870-1970*. Routledge & Kegan Paul.

SEEFELDT, C. (1973). 'Open Spaces, Closed Learning?', *Educational Leadership*, **30**, 4, 355–7.

SEF (Study of Educational Facilities) (1971). E5: Academic Evaluation – an Interim Report. Toronto, Canada: Metropolitan Toronto School Board.

SEF (1975). E6: Academic Evaluation. Toronto, Canada: Metropolitan Toronto School Board.

SEIDMAN, M.R. (1975). 'Comparing physical openness and Climate Openness of Elementary Schools', *Education*, **95**, 4, 345–50.

SELLECK, R.J.W. (1972). *English Primary Education and the Progressives 1914–1939*. Routledge & Kegan Paul.

SIGNATURE, D.J. and REISS, S. (1974). 'Friendship Patterns'. In: *Educational and Psychological Effects of Open Space Education, Oak Park, Illinois*. University of Illinois, Chicago Circle.

SMITH, W.O. (1957). *Education: an Introductory Survey*. Penguin (1969 edition).

SOAR, R.S. (1973). Follow Through Classroom Process Measurement and Pupil Growth, Final Report. Gainesville, Fla, USA: University of Florida.

SPIGEL, J. (1974). Open Area Study. Final Report. Mississagi, Ontario: Peel Board of Education.

STEWART, W.A.C. (1968). *The Educational Innovators. Volume 2, Progressive Schools 1881–1967*. Macmillan.

STOWERS, M.H. (1974). Student Attitudes and Achievement in Open Plan versus Architecturally Conventional Elementary Schools. Unpublished EdD thesis, University of California, Los Angeles, USA.

STRATHCLYDE REGIONAL COUNCIL (1976). *Primary School Building Report*.

TEDRICK, G.D. (1973). Pupil Perceptions of Open Area School Facilities. MA thesis, University of Calgary, USA.

THOMPSON, P. (1963). *Architecture: Art or Social Service?* The Fabian Society.

TOBIER, A.J. (1972). 'The Open Classroom: Humanizing the Coldness of Public Places.' In: SOBEL, H.W. and SALZ, A.E. (Eds) *The Radical Papers, Readings in Education*. New York: Harper & Row.

TOWNSEND, J.W. (1971). A Comparison of Teacher Style and Pupil Attitude and Achievement in Contrasting Schools – Open Space, Departmentalized and Self Contained. Unpublished EdB thesis, University of Kansas, USA.

TRAUB, R., WEISS, J., FISHER, C., MUSELLA, D. and KAHN, S. (1973). An Evaluation Study of the Wentworth County R.C. Separate School Board Schools. Educational Evaluation Centre, Ontario Institute for Studies in Education.

WALSH, D.P. (1975). 'Noise Levels and Annoyance in Open Plan Educational Facilities', *Journal of Architectural Research,* **4,** 2, 5–16.

WARNER, J.B. (1970). A Comparison of Students' and Teachers' performances in an Open Area Facility and in Self Contained Classrooms. Unpublished EdB thesis, University of Houston, USA.

WELLS, B.W.P. (1965). 'The Psycho-social Influence on Building Environment: Sociometric Findings in a Large and Small Office Space', *Building Science,* 1, 47–63.

WESTBURY, I. (1977). The Curriculum and the Frames of the Classroom. Paper presented at the annual conference of the American Educational Research Association (AERA), New York.

WHITBREAD, N. (1972). *The Evolution of the Nursery–Infant School.* Routledge & Kegan Paul.

WILKINSON, B. (1973). Open Plan Primary Schools and their Effects upon Teaching. Unpublished MEd thesis, University of Newcastle Upon Tyne.

WILSON REPORT. GREAT BRITAIN. (1963). *Parliament House of Commons Committee on the Problem of Noise. Final Report.* HMSO.

WILSON, F.S., LANGEVIN, R. and STUCKEY, T. (1969). Are pupils in the Open Plan School Different? Paper presented to the Seventh Canadian Conference of Educational Research, Victoria, British Columbia.

WREN, J.P. (1972). A Comparison of Affective Factors between Contained Classrooms and Open Area Classrooms. EdB thesis, University of Houston, USA.

ZEIGLER, S. (1973). 'Open Plan Schools, Open Area Schools and Open Education Attitudes and Practices in the Borough of York'. Toronto: York Board of Education.

# Index